Italian Cultural Studies

Italian
Cultural Studies

An Introduction

Edited by David Forgacs
and Robert Lumley

OXFORD
UNIVERSITY PRESS

OXFORD
UNIVERSITY PRESS

Great Clarendon Street, Oxford OX2 6DP

Oxford University Press is a department of the University of Oxford.
It furthers the University's objective of excellence in research, scholarship,
and education by publishing worldwide in

Oxford New York

Athens Auckland Bangkok Bogotá Buenos Aires Calcutta
Cape Town Chennai Dar es Salaam Delhi Florence Hong Kong Istanbul
Karachi Kuala Lumpur Madrid Melbourne Mexico City Mumbai
Nairobi Paris São Paulo Singapore Taipei Tokyo Toronto Warsaw

with associated companies in Berlin Ibadan

Oxford is a registered trade mark of Oxford University Press
in the UK and in certain other countries

Published in the United States
by Oxford University Press Inc., New York

©David Forgacs and Robert Lumley 1996

First published 1996

British Library Cataloguing in Publication Data

Data available

Library of Congress Cataloging in Publication Data

Italian cultural studies: an introduction / edited by David Forgacs
and Robert Lumley.
Includes bibliographical references and index.
1. Italy—Civilization—20th century. 2. Italy—Politics and
government—20th century. 3. Popular culture—Italy—History—20th
century. I. Forgacs, David. II. Lumley, Robert, 1951- .
DG450.I795 1996 945.09—dc20 96-6464

ISBN 0-19-871508-0
ISBN 0-19-871509-9 (pbk)

10 9 8 7 6 5

Printed in Great Britain
on acid-free paper by
Biddles Ltd,
Guildford and King's Lynn

Acknowledgements

TULLIO DE MAURO's chapter is a condensed and updated version of an article which first appeared, with the title 'Minoranze linguistiche: questioni teoriche e storiche', in 1974 and has since been reproduced in his book *L'Italia delle Italie* (Rome 1987), 19–46. It is published here in this form with the author's permission. Christopher Wagstaff's shot analysis of *Ladri di biciclette* is an abridged version of an article which first appeared in *Sight and Sound*, 2/7 (November 1992), 25–7; we are grateful to the editor of the magazine for permission to print these extracts.

The translations of contributions originally in Italian are by Allan Cameron (Chapters 4 and 13), Jenny Condi (Chapter 10), Judith Landry (Chapter 18), Martin Ryle (Chapter 8), and Emma Sansone (Chapter 5). We should like to thank the following for their generous help towards translation costs: the Italian Cultural Institute, London; the Departments of Italian at the University of Cambridge and University College London.

Franco Bianchini, Massimo Torrigiani, and Rinella Cere would like to thank Carla Bodo, Antonio Chiarenza, Pierre Lanfranchi, Paolo Leon, Everardo Minardi, and Mario Rotta for help in researching their chapter; they also benefited from contributions by Giorgio Bersano, Jude Bloomfield, Mauro Felicori, and Charles Landry in their capacity as visiting lecturers within the MA in European Arts and Cultural Policy at De Montfort University, Leicester, during the academic year 1992/3.

The chapters by David Forgacs and Stephen Gundle draw in part on work for an ESRC-sponsored research project on 'Cultural Industries, Governments and the Public in Italy, 1938–1954' which they conducted between 1991 and 1994 with the collaboration of Marcella Filippa. Stephen Gundle wishes to thank Katia Pizzi for her comments on a draft version of his chapter. Marcella Filippa wishes to thank Pier Milanese and Paolo Ferrari for partly unpublished information concerning the latest musical developments among young people.

The editors wish to thank for helping track down illustrations and obtain reproductions Sergio Borsi, Vittoria Di Palma, Hippolytus M. Eze, Goffredo Fofi, Giovanni Giovanetti, Marco Zaccarelli, Diego Zancani, and, among the authors, John Dickie, Jeff Pratt, Marcella Filippa, Paola Filippucci, Luisa Passerini, and Christopher Wagstaff.

The news of the death of our colleague and friend Mauro Wolf on 14 July 1996, at the age of 48, reached us just as this book was going to press. We would like, therefore, to dedicate this book to him, and to remember his humour, humanity, and major contribution to media and cultural studies.

Contents

List of Contributors

Franco Bianchini is Reader in Cultural Planning and Policy at De Montfort University, Leicester. He is co-editor of *Cultural Policy and Urban Regeneration: The West European Experience* (Manchester, 1993).

Ann Hallamore Caesar is Lecturer in the Department of Italian at the University of Cambridge and a Fellow of Corpus Christi College. She is co-editor of *The Quality of Light: Modern Italian Short Stories* (London, 1993).

Rinella Cere is Lecturer in Media Studies at Sheffield Hallam University. She is author of 'Dangerous Television: the tv *a luci rosse* phenomenon', *Media, Culture and Society*, 17/3 (1995).

Elena Dagrada teaches in the Sciences of Information, Communication and Arts programme at the University of Bordeaux III. She is author of *A parer nostro. La critica televisiva nella stampa quotidiana in Italia* (Rome, 1992).

Tullio De Mauro is Professor of Philosophy of Language at the University of Rome 'La Sapienza'. He is author of *Capire le parole* (Rome and Bari, 1994).

John Dickie is Lecturer in Italian Studies at University College, London. He is author of 'La "sicilianità" di Francesco Crispi', *Meridiana*, 23 (1996).

Michael Eve teaches in the Languages Department of the University of Turin. He is author of *Dentro l'Inghilterra. Miti e ragioni di un'identità* (Venice, 1990), which looks at aspects of Britain in a comparative perspective.

Marcella Filippa lives in Turin, where she researches in social history, using oral and popular written sources. She is author of 'La voglia di vivere', in L. Boccalatte, G. De Luna, and B. Maida (eds.), *Torino in guerra, 1940–1945* (Turin, 1995).

Paola Filippucci is a Research Fellow in Social Anthropology at New Hall, Cambridge. She is author of 'Tradition in Action: The Carnevale of Bassano, 1824–1989', *Journal of Mediterranean Studies*, 2/1 (1992).

David Forgacs is Lecturer in the Department of Italian at the University of Cambridge and a Fellow of Gonville and Caius College. He is author of *Italian Culture in the Industrial Era: Cultural Industries, Politics and the Public 1880–1980* (Manchester, 1990).

Gabriella Gribaudi is Associate Professor of Contemporary History in the Faculty of Sociology at the Frederick II University of Naples. She is author of *A Eboli. Il mondo meridionale in cent'anni di trasformazioni* (Venice, 1990).

Stephen Gundle teaches Italian history at Royal Holloway College, University of London. He is author of *I comunisti italiani tra Hollywood e Mosca. La sfida della cultura di massa (1943–1991)* (Florence, 1995).

Robert Lumley is Lecturer in Italian Studies and Director of the Centre for Italian Studies at University College London. He is author of *States of Emergency: Cultures of Revolt in Italy from 1968 to 1978* (London, 1990).

Vanessa Maher is Lecturer in Cultural Anthropology, Faculty of Political Sciences, University of Turin. She is co-author of *Uguali e diversi. Il mondo culturale, le reti di rapporti, i lavori degli immigrati non europei a Torino* (Turin, 1991).

Peppino Ortoleva teaches mass media at the University of Turin and is a professional media and history consultant. He is author of *Un ventennio a colori. Televisione privata e società in Italia, 1975–1995* (Florence, 1995).

Simon Parker is Lecturer in Politics as the University of York. He is co-editor of *The New Italian Republic: From the Fall of the Berlin Wall to Berlusconi* (London, 1996).

Luisa Passerini is Professor of Contemporary European History in the Department of History and Civilisation at the European University Institute, Florence. She is author of 'La costruzione del femminile e del maschile: dicotomia sociale e androginia simbolica', in A. Del Boca, M. Legnani, and M. G. Rossi (eds.), *Il regime fascista. Storia e storiografia* (Rome and Bari, 1995).

Jeff Pratt is Senior Lecturer in Social Anthropology in the School of European Studies, University of Sussex. He is author of *The Rationality of Rural Life* (Chur, Switzerland, 1984).

Massimo Torrigiani is Research Fellow in the Cultural Planning Research Unit at De Montfort University, Leicester. He has recently contributed to the Council of Europe's *Concepts and References*, i. *Culture and Neighbourhoods* (Strasbourg, 1995).

Christopher Wagstaff is Senior Lecturer in Italian Studies at the University of Reading. He is co-editor of *Italy in the Cold War: Politics, Society and Culture 1948–1958* (Oxford, 1995).

List of Figures

List of Maps

List of Tables

Abbreviations

AD	Alleanza Democratica
AICRET	Associazione Italiana Critici Radio e Televisione
AN	Alleanza Nazionale
ARCI	Associazione Ricreativa Culturale Italiana
CGIL	Confederazione Generale Italiana del Lavoro
CONI	Comitato Olimpico Nazionale Italiano
DC	Democrazia Cristiana
DP	Democrazia Proletaria
EIAR	Ente Italiano Audizioni Radiofoniche
Fiat	Fabbrica Italiana Automobili Torino
FIO	Fondo Investimenti e Occupazione
FRG	Federal Republic of Germany
Fuori	Fronte Unitario Omosessuale Rivoluzionario Italiano
GDR	German Democratic Republic
LUCE	L'Unione Cinematografica Educativa
MSI	Movimento Sociale Italiano
NATO	North Atlantic Treaty Organization
PCI	Partito Comunista Italiano
PCUS	Partito Comunista dell'Unione Sovietica (CPSU)
PDS	Partito Democratico della Sinistra
PLI	Partito Liberale Italiano
PPI	Partito Popolare Italiano
PSI	Partito Socialista Italiano
RAI	Radio Audizioni Italia
RC	Rifondazione Comunista
SEI	Società Editrice Internazionale
SIP	Società Idroelettrica Piemontese
STET	Società Torinese di Elettricità e Telefonia
SVIMEZ	Associazione per lo Sviluppo Industriale del Mezzogiorno
UTET	Unione Tipografico-Editrice Torinese

Introduction: Approaches to Culture in Italy

DAVID FORGACS   ROBERT LUMLEY

THE title of this book, and its bringing together in one place subjects seemingly so diverse as anthropological fieldwork, film stars, gender relations, and the press, marks a new departure in work on Italy. Cultural studies is now well-established in the English-speaking world, both as a concept and as an area of knowledge in educational institutions, whereas in Italy as yet it has no exact counterpart. We hope this book will stimulate a critical reassessment of what 'culture' means in the Italian case and indicate new ways into the study of Italian culture and society.

Cultural studies is not so much a discipline as a cluster of disciplines. In Britain, where the term originated, and subsequently in other countries where it has been adopted, these disciplines have come to include literature, social history, media studies, human geography, cultural anthropology, and the sociology of deviance (for retrospective accounts see Hall 1980 and Turner 1991). Work in these diverse areas has been loosely unified by a common set of concerns: to deal with culture as a set of signifying practices and symbolic social forms; to look at a wide variety of cultural materials and avoid prior evaluative rankings of high and low; to bring new theoretical considerations to bear on the study of culture.

In Italy the term *studi culturali* is not used except as a rendering of the English term, which has entered Italian academic debate by a side door through translations or discussions of some influential British work on popular music, social rituals, and subcultures (for instance Frith 1978, Chambers 1985, Hall and Jefferson 1976, Hebdige 1979). This lack of terminological equivalence indicates that there is not an exact mapping of the field from the one country onto the other. This in turn is indicative of the fact that the intellectual traditions in the two countries and the ways in which institutions of learning and publishers' lists have divided up knowledge are different. Thus, there are in Italy about half a dozen degree courses in media studies or communication studies (*scienze della comunicazione*) as well as various courses in semiotics, cinema, and journalism, mainly in faculties of letters. Social history comes under *storia* or *discipline storiche*, studies of subcultures and deviancy under *sociologia*, studies of folklore and popular traditions under *antropologia culturale* or *etnologia*. Our book therefore links under the cultural studies umbrella disciplines and objects of study which in Italy would normally be thought of as unrelated to one another.

In Italian (see De Mauro 1987) as in English (see the entry on 'culture' in Williams 1976) it is conventional to distinguish two widespread current meanings of the word 'culture': a narrow one of intellectual activities, arts, and entertainments, and a broad one—which has gradually come into everyday usage from anthropology and ethnography—of a much more extensive range of practices characteristic of a given society, from its mode of material production to its eating habits, dress codes, celebrations, and rituals. Cultural studies deals with both these senses of 'culture'. But it also interrogates and deconstructs the distinction between them. For whether one limits the first, narrower sense of culture to 'high' culture (such as 'fine' arts, 'serious' music, or philosophy) or extends it to include 'popular' or 'mass' culture (such as comic strips and television talk shows), all of these activities need to be studied as a part of a wider set of social processes covered by the term 'culture' in the broader second sense. That is to say, they need to be understood not just in 'intrinsic' (aesthetic, intellectual, formal) terms but also sociologically and anthropologically in terms of such things as norms of social behaviour, the allocation of status and power in society, and the reproduction of values and beliefs.

Why, for example, do only relatively few people read philosophy or listen to and enjoy contemporary avant-garde music? Why do these same people often have high social prestige but not the highest incomes? Why, by contrast, do so many regular viewers of daytime television soap operas have both lower status and lower incomes? How does the watching of certain kinds of films or television programmes or the listening to a certain type of music or the way one dresses and eats relate to one's sense of belonging to a particular social group? The answer to all these questions is: because cultural practices are closely bound up with social differences, such as differences of class, gender, ethnicity.

The distinction between the two senses needs to be deconstructed for another reason: it has become eroded in practice by mass communications in contemporary industrialized or 'post-industrial' societies. So many everyday activities in these societies are now 'mass-mediated'—informed and influenced by images and values put in circulation in the media and advertising—that it is has become very difficult to sustain the old, and in any case questionable, analytical distinction between on the one hand the sphere of arts, ideas, and entertainment and on the other the sphere of social rituals, customs, and beliefs.

All these points apply as much to 'culture' in the Italian context as they do in other societies, since Italy too has moved, and very rapidly, into the post-industrial era. However, there are also some regionally specific features to the history and use of the term in Italian which it is important to introduce.

Concepts of Culture in Italy

If one traces the usage of the term *cultura* in Italian over the last century and a half, one finds that one of its most durable features is its strong association with education and literacy, and more generally with 'print culture'. Whether in the efforts by the ruling groups of the Liberal and Fascist eras (1861–1943) to restrict 'culture' to an élite by limiting access to the upper end of the education system, or in the efforts of opposition groups, like the Socialists in the period 1894–1925 or the Communists after 1945, to widen access to 'culture' by providing literacy schemes, reading circles, and other forms of educational provision to supplement the state schools, culture was seen as a value in itself, something which one either possessed or should aspire to acquire.

Historically, the identification of 'culture' with education and literacy, as well as with the high arts, seems to have been more resilient in Italy than in many other countries. A number of reasons may be suggested for this: the combination until the 1960s of restricted-access institutions of higher learning with low national rates of literacy and post-primary school attendance, particularly in rural areas; the prestige and durability of a humanist intellectual tradition—the neo-idealism associated particularly with the philosophers Benedetto Croce (1866–1952) and Giovanni Gentile (1875–1944)—which identified culture with intellectuals, cultural history with intellectual history. This tradition continued to hold sway over higher education and publishing in Italy until at least the mid-1960s (Croce left many pupils after his death) and was responsible, among other things, for the delayed reception in Italy of Anglo-American political science and sociology, which might have facilitated the development of an alternative definition of culture.

If it were not for the durability of these factors it would be hard to explain why the humanist-intellectualist concept of culture was so little shaken by the anti-fascist struggles and demands for widespread social change of the period 1943–7 and why it also partially survived a second wave of social protests in 1968–72. In the first case, one might cite as symptomatic of the conceptual continuity the call by Elio Vittorini (1908–66), in the first editorial of his journal *Il Politecnico* (29 September 1945), for a culture that would no longer 'console' people in their sufferings (as, he claimed, the writings of the European liberals and progressive Catholics had done up to the Nazi genocide) but would defend against and combat suffering. What Vittorini, who like many intellectuals in this period had gravitated to the Communist Party, meant by these rather coded remarks was that *intellectuals* had to play a more socially committed part, while retaining their right (as he argued subsequently in his open letter to the PCI leader Palmiro Togliatti) not to become mere pipers paid by political parties (Vittorini 1947: 106). The moment was indeed one of radical self-questioning of their social mission by intellectuals—assisted by a similar process taking place at the same time among intellectuals in other countries, like France, and by the first publication of extracts from the prison writings of Antonio Gramsci (1891–1937), which had theorized a new role for revolutionary intellectuals. But this self-questioning did not break the Crocean link between 'culture' and 'intellectuals'. If anything it reinforced it. Only on the fringes of this debate, and almost imperceptibly, was another concept of culture starting to emerge, namely that promoted by radical anthropologists and ethnologists like Ernesto De Martino and Alberto Maria Cirese. Their contribution is discussed in this volume by Paola Filippucci in Chapter 3, 'Anthropological Perspectives on Culture in Italy'.

That the same traditional link between culture, intellectuals, and book-learning should have persisted after 1968 is perhaps more surprising, given the extent of the counter-cultural movements in that period among students, workers, women, and youth and the growing attention to the power of the mass media. Yet it is significant that when, in 1975, one of the former activists and theorists of the new left, Alberto Asor Rosa, published a panoramic volume on the culture of post-unification Italy, it was a history of intellectuals and ideas reconstructed through texts, in particular those of social theory, politics, and literature (Asor Rosa 1975). There was no discussion of mass cultural forms like cinema or radio, nor of music or sport; nor, as one reviewer noted (Romagnoli 1977), of the 'middle-level' culture of minor intellectuals, of the popularizers of ideas, or of the more informal channels through which ideas circulated. However, just as in 1943–7, in 1968–72 different concepts of culture were starting to emerge on the edge of the academic mainstream.

'Popular Culture'

The traditional concept first began to be challenged both at the theoretical level and through empirical work in post-war studies of 'popular culture', including folklore studies, ethnography, and anthropology. These studies had already started developing in the nineteenth century (again see Filippucci, 'Anthropological Perspectives'), when they had been linked to Romanticism, nationalism, and the growing interest in the 'folk' or 'people'. But they took a new and more radical turn after 1945 with the reappraisal of marginalized and subaltern cultures. Here the posthumous influence of Gramsci was important, in particular his handful of prison notes on folklore (see Gramsci 1985: and for a good critical discussion, Cirese 1982), as was De Martino's pioneering work on the beliefs and practices of peasant communities in parts of the rural South (De Martino 1941, 1958). Indeed, the emergence of this radical work in folklore at the end of the war was inseparable from a political vindication of the communities and cultures of Southern Italy, an area which was once again coming to constitute a 'problem' or 'question' for the Italian state after its continued economic and political marginalization under Fascism (see John Dickie, 'Imagined Italies', and Gabriella Gribaudi, 'Images of the South', Chapters 1 and 4 in this volume).

Much radical anthropology and ethnography continued to privilege the South and rural Italy. Yet towards the end of the 1950s work in these fields began to focus on urban communities too—one important example was *Milano, Corea* (1960) a study of migrant communities in Milan undertaken at the height of the economic miracle by Danilo Montaldi, one of the pioneers of oral history in Italy, and Franco Alasia, a worker at the Breda factory in Milan who had attended the evening classes taught by the radical educationalist Danilo Dolci. Alasia collected the oral testimonies in the book and Montaldi wrote the analytical part. A more recent example of similar work is Alessandro Portelli's book on the town of Terni (Portelli 1985). Other key figures in the study of popular culture in this sense were Gianni Bosio, instrumental in founding the Istituto De Martino, a research base in Milan for the study of popular traditions, including a book and record library, and Roberto Leydi, an ethnomusicologist who has done invaluable work in recording, cataloguing, and analysing the popular music of various parts of Italy (see Chapter 19 below, Marcella Filippa's 'Popular Song'). It is significant that all of these intellectual activists belonged to the left wing of the PSI or other left groups outside of and critical of the PCI, which at that time tended to privilege the organized labour movement whereas they emphasized the importance of grass-roots movements and of marginalized social groups.

The guiding ethos of this highly politicized work on popular culture was powerfully stated by Luigi Lombardi Satriani at a conference in the late 1970s. Folklore studies was not, as he put it, 'just a collection of information about how Sardinian shepherds make ricotta with archaic equipment' (1979: 125). Anyone who entered this field had to make the choice either of adopting the standpoint of the dominant classes and their culture or taking the side of the dominated (1979: 126). With this conception of 'popular culture' the intellectual became what Bosio (1967) had called an *intellettuale rovesciato*, an intellectual turned upside down, the vehicle for the articulation of a creativity rooted in the subaltern classes of the countryside and the city. It was a conception sharply counterposed to the growing commercial culture of the period, usually referred to in Italy as *cultura di massa*. This dichotomy of traditional popular culture and modern commercial culture was also present in Britain and the United States but it was defined there differently and less dramatically (Baranski and Lumley 1990: 8–9).

Mass Culture, Media Studies, and Cultural History

In keeping with the ideas of Theodor W. Adorno and Max Horkheimer in their influential essay 'The Culture Industry: Enlightenment as Mass Deception' (1944), 'mass culture' was widely viewed from the 1950s to the 1970s, especially on the left, as inauthentic and as bringing about the commodification of all cultural life. This apocalyptic refrain, found in its finer manifestions in the writings of Franco Fortini (1965, 1968) and Pier Paolo Pasolini (1975), in fact fits into a longer tradition, as can be seen from the history of reactions by Italian intellectuals to cinema (Brunetta 1994) and subsequently to television (see Chapter 13 below, Elena Dagrada's 'Television and its Critics'). However, there were some individuals and centres of research that began in the 1960s to analyse 'mass culture' in its specific forms instead of indulging in outright political rejection or high moral outrage.

Pioneering work in the study of the mass media was done both by maverick individuals like Ivano Cipriani and Umberto Eco and through institutions such as the Istituto Gemelli in Milan, the first independent centre in Italy for mass communications research, which published the journal *Ikon*. The main cause of this new attention was the growing importance of the mass media themselves, particularly television, in the 1960s, and the sense that Italian society was changing more rapidly than ever before and needed to be analysed with new concepts and approaches. But the beginnings of media studies in Italy may also be linked to the belated eclipse of Crocean approaches to culture and the opening up to other schools of thought: linguistics (both European structuralism and American functionalism and pragmatism) and semiotics, sociology, structural and cultural anthropology. The 1960s in fact were the beginning of an extraordinary phase of receptivity in Italy to intellectual developments in other countries.

The role of Umberto Eco (b. 1932) in opening up areas of study from television audiences to cartoons and in elaborating a semiotic analysis of cultural products is already well documented, especially as his influence on the development of cultural studies in the English-speaking world is second only to that of Roland Barthes (see Eco 1994). For instance, the translation of his 'Towards a Semiotic Inquiry into the Television Message' was seminal (Eco 1972; Morley 1980). However, there is a danger in producing a kind of personality cult out of a single figure and it is worth drawing attention to Eco's important role in helping create an academic environment in which researchers and students would study mass culture—notably the Istituto della Comunicazione at the University of Bologna which he founded and directed until recently and where he holds a chair of semiotics—and to the degree to which his own writings have arisen from collective projects involving high-calibre scholars. In fact, his individual role, so important in the early years, has diminished with the growth since the 1970s of media studies in various centres. Some of the innovative television content analysis and audience research done under the auspices of the RAI (in the series 'Verifica dei programmi trasmessi') is internationally reputed. Semiotic analysis has built on a distinctively Italian focus on textual analysis (Bettetini 1979; Casetti and di Chio 1990) and a considerable body of work has been done on political controls over the media. The different stages in the development of media studies have been marked by particular attention to single media: firstly the press and subsequently (and overwhelmingly) television, with radio as a poor cousin and cinema occupying its own privileged niche. Since the 1980s analysis has turned increasingly on the interrelationship and synergy between the different media: the transformation of high art forms by industrialized culture (Rak 1981); the phenomenon of the best-seller and the tie-ins between publishing and other media (Grossi 1988); the adaptation of newspapers to television dominance (Castronovo and Tranfaglia 1994); the consumption of media and cultural goods as part of a continuum (Livolsi 1992); the formation of media empires and the development of corporate identities (Mosconi 1992). The methodologies and theoretical paradigms of media studies have also been critically reviewed in two excellent books by Mauro Wolf (1985 and 1992).

It would not be difficult to trace patterns that are also found in other countries and themes that have been researched elsewhere in the name of cultural or media studies. In part this is an effect of the internationalization of scholarship in these areas, through the development of conference networks, invitations to visiting scholars, and so forth, and in part the result of a felt need to confront issues arising from increasingly globalized communications. One sign of this in Italy is the widespread use of or adaptation of a specialist vocabulary drawn from English-language debates; for instance one manual of journalism (De Martino and Bonifacci 1990) includes the terms 'agenda setting', 'anchor man', 'antitrust', 'background', and 'backup'.

None the less there are features to the work on cultural formations in Italy that make it distinctive. Firstly, the study of culture has been heavily conditioned by politics. This is perhaps not surprising given the role of the parties in controlling public broadcasting, the strength of the Catholic and Communist subcultures, and the impact of extraparliamentary opposition, whether as social movements or as terrorism. Thus the focus on who owns and controls cultural industries has long been a central concern of analysts, and Silvio Berlusconi's entry into politics in 1994 merely gave it a new urgency. Studies of subcultures, whether of football fans (Dal Lago 1990), youth (Banfi *et al.* 1992; Canevacci *et al.* 1993) or feminists (Passerini 1991*a*), have shown the importance of 'political' languages and rituals. At the same time, there is a notable difference between the theses of the 1960s and 1970s, according to which mass culture was a manipulative agent of social control and conformity, and the more eclectic and culture-specific analyses which developed subsequently. A narrower definition of politics has also been replaced by a broader one in which gender and ethnicity are significant categories.

Second, some of the most interesting work has been done by historians of the modern and contemporary period. Histories have branched out to look at the ideologies of the school, minor writers and intellectuals, and middle-level élites (for instance Isnenghi 1979; Mangoni 1974; Lanaro 1979). Historical studies of small communities ('microhistories') using concepts drawn from cultural anthropology have offered new insights into the spatial dimensions of social and power relations (Gribaudi 1990; Bertolotti 1991), while analyses of the 'imaginary' have introduced questions about the relationship of cultural representations and political forms (Passerini 1991b). Little of this valuable work on cultural phenomena has been translated and it consequently remains largely unknown outside Italy.

The fact remains, however, that there is simply much less being done in these areas in Italy than in some other countries. There has been no equivalent boom to that of media and cultural studies in North America and Britain. Instead of colonizing other disciplines, those studying mass culture or subcultures have remained in often marginal positions within their own departments or faculties. In part this is because the sociological tradition in Italy in recent decades has remained relatively strong, in marked contrast to its crisis in the UK and North America. In part it is due to the rigidities of Italian educational institutions in which the concentration of power in academic fiefdoms has not yet been shaken by the incursion of market forces.

Organization of the Book

The material in *Italian Cultural Studies* is arranged thematically. We have deliberately avoided a structure based on a sequence of historical periods (for orientation and reference we provide in the Chronology a list of key political and cultural dates) and have chosen instead to highlight issues, debates, and approaches to culture which we consider to be of particular importance and value to those coming to this field for the first time. We asked our contributors to place their main emphasis on the period since 1945, but to add a historical perspective going back to Unification (1859–61) or even earlier wherever it seemed appropriate or necessary to the argument.

The book is divided into four Parts, each of which is prefaced by a brief introduction. The first Part, 'Geographies', critically discusses some of the ways in which Italy has been represented, both by Italians and by non-Italian observers. Anyone who works on Italy comes up frequently against a series of conventional or stereotyped notions, both in everyday 'common sense' and in academic scholarship, about the country, its people, and its institutions. Italy, it is widely claimed, is a nation culturally split between North and South; it is a country whose inhabitants have a weak national identity and a strong inward-looking attachment to the locality and the family; it is a unique and exceptional case of political maladministration and corruption. Yet, as the authors of the first four chapters point out, one needs to be wary of accepting these accounts uncritically; one has to look carefully at who is producing them, on the basis of what evidence, in comparison with what norms, and according to which values. The second Part, 'Identities', carries forward a theme from the first, namely how people in Italy identify themselves and are identified by others, but here the identities discussed relate to political affiliation, religion, gender and sexuality, and ethnicity. In the case of gender and ethnic identities, there has been a struggle to assert a right to be equal or a right to be different in the face of repression and discrimination. The third Part, 'Media', deals with the development of cinema, television, the press, and literature in the post-war decades. Here too, the intention of the chapters is not to provide a simple historical summary of what has happened but to open up new perspectives: a spatial analysis of the Italian media, which looks at the changing role of different cities as cultural centres and the media's role in creating a sense of the shape of the nation; a discussion of how far the Italian press constitutes an exceptional case; a parallel history of television and television criticism; an alternative account of post-war Italian literature that gives greater emphasis to writing by women. The final Part, 'Culture and Society', brings together analyses of different aspects of culture: consumption, the cultural policies of central and local government, stars and style, popular music and its relation to wider social processes.

Contributors to the book have provided their own guides to Further Reading, highlighting books and articles of special interest. At the end of each section is a short appendix called 'Analysis', containing discussions of specimen visual materials related directly to one or more of the preceding chapters. These are not intended in any way to be 'representative' of modern Italian culture, but serve as practical examples of the sort of concrete analysis that may be applied to cultural materials of diverse kinds: photographs, cartoons, magazine covers, frames from a film.

There are inevitably omissions in a book such as this and we make no claims to have included everything that may be considered of interest or significance to 'Italian cultural studies'. Sport is an obvious omission. The chapter on football which we commissioned was not able to be included, but it is our intention to incorporate it into a subsequent edition. However, if this book, for all its practical limitations, succeeds both in being informative about the culture of contemporary Italy and in indicating the diversity of meanings of culture and the many different ways into studying it, then it will have achieved its main aims.

References

ADORNO, T. W., and HORKHEIMER, M. (1944), 'The Culture Industry: Enlightenment as Mass Deception', in *Dialectic of Enlightenment* (London, 1979).

ALASIA, F., and MONTALDI, D. (1960), *Milano, Corea. Inchiesta sugli immigrati* (Milan).

ASOR ROSA, A. (1975), 'La cultura', in *Storia d'Italia*, iv (2). *Dall'Unità a oggi* (Turin).

BANFI, E. *et al.* (1992), *Il linguaggio giovanile degli anni novanta* (Bari).

BARANSKI, Z. G., and LUMLEY, R. (1990), 'Introduction' to Baranski and Lumley (eds.), *Culture and Conflict in Postwar Italy* (Basingstoke and London).

BERTOLOTTI, M. (1991), *Carnevale di massa 1950* (Turin).

BETTETINI, G. (1979), *Tempo del senso. La logica temporale dei testi audiovisivi* (Milan).

BOSIO, G. (1967), *L'intellettuale rovesciato. Interventi e ricerche sulla emergenza d'interesse verso le forme di espressione e di organizzazione 'spontanee' nel mondo popolare e proletario*, Lega di Cultura di Piadena (Cremona), Quaderno no. 3, May (cyclostyled).

BRUNETTA, G. P. (1994), *Spari nel buio. La letteratura contro il cinema italiano: settant'anni di stroncature memorabili* (Venice).

CANEVACCI, M. *et al.* (1993), *Ragazzi senza tempo* (Genoa).

CASETTI, F., and DI CHIO, F. (1990), *Analisi del film* (Milan).

CASTRONOVO, V., and TRANFAGLIA, N. (1994), *La stampa italiana nell'età della TV, 1975–1994* (Rome and Bari).

CHAMBERS, I. (1985), *Urban Rhythms: Pop Music and Popular Culture* (London).

CIRESE, A. M. (1982), 'Gramsci's Observations on Folklore', in A. Showstack Sassoon (ed.), *Approaches to Gramsci* (London), 212–47.

DAL LAGO, A. (1990), *Descrizione di una battaglia. Rituali del calcio* (Bologna).

DE MARTINO, C., and BONIFACCI, F. (1990), *Dizionario pratico di giornalismo* (Milan).

DE MARTINO, E. (1941), *Naturalismo e storicismo nell'etnologia* (Bari).

—— (1958), *Morte e pianto rituale nel mondo antico* (Turin).

DE MAURO, T. (1987), 'La nozione di "cultura"', in *L'Italia delle Italie* (Rome), 3–17.

ECO, U. (1972), 'Towards a Semiotic Inquiry into the Television Message' (1965), *Working Papers in Cultural Studies* (Birmingham).

—— (1994), *Apocalypse Postponed*, ed. R. Lumley (Bloomington, Ind., and London).

FORTINI, F. (1965), *Verifica dei poteri. Scritti di critica e di istituzioni letterarie* (Milan).

—— (1968), 'Introduzione', *Ventiquattro voci per un dizionario di lettere* (Milan).

FRITH, S. (1978), *The Sociology of Rock* (London).

GRAMSCI, A. (1985), 'Observations on Folklore' and 'Folklore', in D. Forgacs and G. Nowell-Smith (eds.), *Selections from Cultural Writings*, trans. W. Boelhower (London), 188–95.

GRIBAUDI, G. (1990), *A Eboli* (Padua).

GROSSI, G. (1988), 'Il libro nella sequenza multimedia', *Problemi dell'Informazione*, 3 (July–Sept.): 379–99.

HALL, S. (1980), 'Cultural Studies and the Centre: Some Problematics and Problems', in S. Hall, D. Hobson, A. Lowe, and P. Willis (eds.), *Culture, Media, Language: Working Papers in Cultural Studies 1972–79* (London).

—— and JEFFERSON, T. (1976), *Resistance through Rituals: Youth Subcultures in Postwar Britain* (London).

HEBDIGE, D. (1979), *Subculture: The Meaning of Style* (London).

ISNENGHI, M. (1979), *L'educazione dell'italiano. Il fascismo e l'organizzazione della cultura* (Bologna).

LANARO, S. (1979), *Nazione e lavoro. Saggio sulla cultura borghese in Italia 1870–1925* (Venice).

LIVOLSI, M. (1992), *Il pubblico dei media* (Scandicci).

LOMBARDI SATRIANI, L. M. (1979), 'Il folklore come cultura di contestazione', in R. Cipriani (ed.), *Sociologia della cultura popolare in Italia* (Naples).

MANGONI, L. (1974), *L'interventismo della cultura. Intellettuali e riviste del fascismo* (Bari).

MORLEY, D. (1980), *The 'Nationwide' Audience: Structure and Decoding* (London).

MOSCONI, F. (1992), 'Multimedialità e oligopolio', *Problemi dell'Informazione*, 17/1 (Jan.–Mar.): 73–103.

PASOLINI, P. P. (1975), *Scritti corsari* (Milan).

PASSERINI, L. (1991a), *Storia di donne e femministe* (Turin).

—— (1991b), *Mussolini immaginario* (Bari).

PORTELLI, A. (1983), 'Culture popolari e cultura di massa', in *Il mondo contemporaneo* (gen. ed. N. Tranfaglia), ii (10): G. De Luna, P. Ortoleva, M. Revelli, and N. Tranfaglia (eds.), *Gli strumenti della ricerca, II: Questioni di metodo* (Florence), 1470–90.

—— (1985), *Biografia di una città. Storia e racconto: Terni (1830–1985)* (Turin).

RAK, M. (1981) *La produzione dell'arte nella società industriale. Argomenti sul mutamento delle arti e in particolare della letteratura attraverso i materiali poveri della cultura di massa* (Palermo).

ROMAGNOLI, S. (1977), 'Una storia della cultura dell'Italia unita', *Studi Storici*, 18/2: 21–33.

TURNER, G. (1991), *British Cultural Studies: An Introduction* (Boston).

VITTORINI, E. (1947), 'Politica e cultura. Lettera a Togliatti', *Il Politecnico*, 35 (Jan.–Mar.): 2–5, 105–6.

WILLIAMS, R. (1976), Keywords: *A Vocabulary of Culture and Society* (London).

WOLF, M. (1985), *Teorie delle comunicazioni di massa* (Milan).

—— (1992), *Gli effetti sociali dei media* (Milan).

Geographies

Introduction

THIS opening Part introduces some of the ways in which Italy
has been represented, both by Italians and by non-Italians, and
offers ways of dealing critically with some of the more pervasive stereotypes. In the opening chapter, John Dickie poses
an apparently simple question—what, and where, is the Italian
nation?—and proposes an unorthodox answer. Italy, like all other
nations, is a 'social fiction'. It possesses no fixed identity or
stable boundaries; rather, different ideas of what Italy and Italian identity are have been evoked, modified, and challenged
over time. Dickie uses the examples of representations of Rome
and of the South to support these points. It is these imagined
Italies, he argues, that constitute the proper object of a critical
cultural analysis.

The drawing of comparisons between Italy and other countries has been integral to the process of defining it as a nation.
Since Unification, Italy's performance as a nation-state has been
measured, more often than not unfavourably, against that of
others, notably Britain, France, and Germany. Yet, as Michael
Eve argues in his chapter, when one makes comparisons, one
needs to be explicit about one's criteria and standards of measurement, reflect critically on one's own society, and avoid making reference to abstract models. In comparisons involving Italy,

frequent use has been made of a model in which a strong civic consciousness and a developed sense of the nation-state, said to be found in the 'mature democracies', are held to be lacking in Italy, where 'familism' and local identities allegedly hold sway. Eve links these points to recent discussions of corruption scandals in Italy and shows how a view has been produced in which Italian peculiarities have been turned into pathological abnormalities.

The central theme of the South is developed in two further chapters in this Part. In her discussion of anthropological work carried out in Italy since the nineteenth century, Paola Filippucci shows how the Mezzogiorno, for a long time the chosen site of ethnographic fieldwork, was treated as if it were a colonial or underdeveloped country and interpreted in terms of 'backwardness' and 'resistance' to modernization. This view was linked in turn to a conception of cultures as static and isolated, a conception which more recent anthropology has radically challenged. In her chapter on 'Images of the South', Gabriella Gribaudi examines the persistence of stereotypes over the last century and a half, showing how they were produced out of a series of negative comparisons with the North. Even today, as a result of the growth of these stereotypes, one finds some champions of the South and Southerners themselves believing notions—for instance that the patriarchal family is pervasive in the South—which are factually unfounded. It is significant in this respect that Edward Banfield's book *The Moral Basis of a Backward Society* (1958) is revisited in several chapters of this Part. It is a key text for understanding the development of a certain discourse on the South and on Italy more generally.

The official promotion of the Italian language has been crucial to the objective of 'making Italians' in united Italy since the time of Alessandro Manzoni. Yet Italy has remained uniquely plurilingual, with not only a very large number of 'Italo-Romance' dialects which are still used by many speakers (often now in alternation with one or other of the many regional and social varieties of Italian) but also a smaller yet still significant number of minority languages, including Greek, Albanian, German, and Ladin. Tullio De Mauro, in an influential essay of 1974 which has been abridged and updated for this volume (Chapter 5), sets out the key terms of a theoretical debate on language, and defends linguistic pluralism and diversity against the opposing tendency towards monism or homogeneity. For De Mauro, the linguistic diversity of the Italian peninsula and islands—so often used as a sign of a weak national culture—is actually the basis of a rich cultural pluralism.

Map 1. The twenty regions into which Italy is at present divided, with their capitals. After Unification (1859–61), the north-east border changed four times as a result of wars and treaties (1866, 1919–20, 1945–7, 1954) before assuming its present shape. A degree of political devolution to the regions was envisaged in the Constitution of the Italian Republic (1948) but came into force only in 1970. Fifteen of these regions have an ordinary statute (statuto ordinario); the remainder have a special statute (statuto speciale) which gives them a slightly greater margin of political and financial autonomy. These are the three border regions Valle d'Aosta, Trentino-Alto Adige, and Friuli-Venezia Giulia, all of which contain significant linguistic minorities, and the islands of Sicily and Sardinia. Each region is further subdivided into provinces (not shown—there are 95 in all, each with its own capital) and these are in turn divided into comuni (municipalities), the lowest tier of local government.

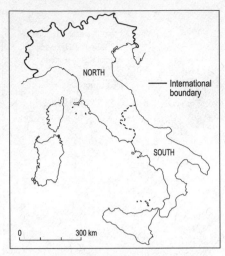

Map 2. A two-way division into North and South (Sicily and Sardinia belong to the latter): a division with a long history and strong ideological connotations

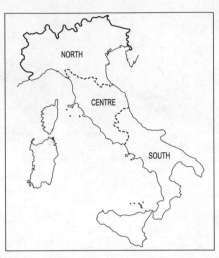

Map 3. A three-way division into North, Centre, and South, as used by the Istituto Centrale di Statistica (ISTAT) for its surveys

Map 4. A five-way division, sometimes used by ISTAT, involving a further subdivision of North and South

Maps 2–7 show other ways in which Italy may be subdivided within the same outer boundaries. Each map reflects a different judgement about inner divisions, either of a political or of a physical character, which are deemed significant. As a whole, they show the way that inner boundaries may 'move' as different discourses about the shape of the country are applied (see also the 'fantasy maps' reproduced and discussed on pp. 102–4 for some unorthodox products of the same procedure).

Source: Maps 1–7 reproduced from Russell King, *Italy* (London, 1987), 26 and 175.

Map 5. The 'three Italies': a refinement of the ISTAT categories introduced by Arnaldo Bagnasco in his influential *Tre Italie* (Bologna, 1977), which distinguished between a North-West with its older large-scale industry, a Centre and North-East with newer, dynamic small industries, and a South marked by slower economic development

Map 6. A common physical distinction between continental Upper Italy (Alta Italia), from the Alps to the Po basin, linked to the European land mass, the peninsula, and the islands

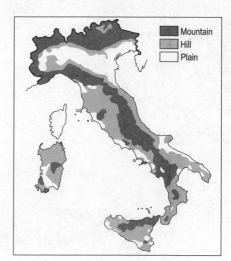

Map 7. Further physical divisions: another ISTAT model used mainly for settlement, population, and agricultural statistics.

Imagined Italies

JOHN DICKIE

The Historical Problem of Nationality in Italy

'WITH Italy made, we must now make the Italians.' This line, arguably the one most quoted in histories of modern Italy, was reputedly uttered by Massimo d'Azeglio in 1861. D'Azeglio's phrase (whether he actually ever said it in this form is doubtful) has been used to encapsulate the problem of 'nation-building' which faced the country's rulers (Soldani and Turi 1993: 17). Italy, as a state, had been forged by a small social group. The Italians, as a people, for the most part had little sense of loyalty to that state or to each other. How could they, indeed, when the vast majority of their number were illiterate peasants without the vote? Italy, it has been argued, was a state with little in the way of a nation on which to base its legitimacy.

The history of Italy since then has often been written as the history of the continuing failure to build a nation and create a proper relationship between the state and the people. Nearly 140 years after Unification, the level of education in Italy is now comparable with that in any other industrialized country. Italy is amongst the world's most powerful industrial economies. It has had universal adult suffrage for decades. Yet the impression that Italians are not 'Italianized' persists. It is often argued that an Italian's sense of geographical identity is more strongly based on a feeling of belonging to his or her town or village than it is on a sense of fellowship with other Italians. Unlike the citizens of other European nations, it is also maintained, Italians lack an underlying faith in the impartiality of the state: they see it as a bestower of favours to its friends rather than the guarantor of rights for all. The state, in turn, sees the people not as citizens but as political enemies, clientelistic allies, or obstacles to the working of the bureaucratic machinery. Recent political developments, in which even the spectre of Italy dividing has arisen, might be seen to support the impression that the Italians do not constitute a nation. Yet the most superficial observer of Italian culture cannot fail to note the patriotism which surrounds certain aspects of life in the peninsula, such as food and football. And how does one square the image of Italians as lacking a 'sense of the state' with, to take just one example, the formidable courage displayed fifty years ago by many Italians in the struggle against Nazism and Fascism from which the modern state emerged?

The concepts of 'state', 'people', and 'nation', all of them notoriously difficult to define, are at the centre of debates over Italian national identity. My concern here is to suggest how recent attempts to revise our understanding of what constitutes a nation can help clarify some of these issues. Nations, I will argue, are best thought of as *social fictions* rather than real entities. An understanding of nations along these lines can shed new light on the process of making Italians and, indeed, on what it means to be Italian. One of the major contributions which cultural studies can make to an understanding of modern Italy is to investigate the ways in which nationalism, as a form of political imagination and a set of social and cultural concepts, has interpreted change and registered its impact.

The Nation: Image and Reality

The nation is often taken to refer to the people who make up a modern society, as opposed to the state, by which is understood that society's public institutions. However, whilst those who use the language of nationalism might like us to believe that the nation and the people are the same thing, more often than not the term 'nation' is used in one of two ways which suggest that there is something of a gap between it and reality. Firstly, it disguises the fact that not everyone in a nation has the same interests. Does not a rich, white Frenchman have more in common with a rich, white Englishman than, say, one of his poor, black, female compatriots? Second, it is used to exclude certain groups from national status. A platitude like 'the British people are hard-working and honest' may well be a way of implying that those deemed lazy and dishonest are somehow un-British.

To confuse the nation and the population is also, crucially, to omit the dimension of feeling and thinking from nationhood. Nations cannot exist without the ideas and emotions people have about them. Benedict Anderson makes this point well: '[the nation] is *imagined* because the members of even the smallest nation will never know most of their fellow-members, meet them, or even hear of them, yet in the minds of each lives the image of their communion' (Anderson 1991: 6). However, in my opinion, Anderson's description of nations as 'imagined communities' does not go far enough because it does not take on board the full implications of the *diversity* of ways in which people imagine themselves as being or belonging to a nation. Within any group generally described as a nation there are a great many contradictory and incompatible ideas of what the nation is. The nation is not always imagined as a community or group. It can be given the attributes of a single person ('hoping', 'struggling', 'being reborn'); it can be confused with the state, or seen to be embodied in the landscape. Many writers have remarked upon the seemingly chronic woolliness which afflicts the terminology of nationalism in both everyday and academic usage (Hobsbawm 1990: 6, 24; Lanaro 1991: 358). Elements of disguise, exclusion, and vagueness are an integral part of the way discourses of nationality work.

We might conclude from these reflections that nations are some form of mixture of the imaginary and the real. But if they are, it is a mixture in which reality does not take the kind of precedence over image which common sense might presume. On the contrary, it is according to the ideas of the nation they have that people compete to determine whom the nation should include and exclude, where its frontiers should be, how it should be organized, and what values it should embody. The most successful state could not function without the unpredictable hotchpotch of ways in which its citizens imagine the state and each other; in our century, that imagining is most often conducted in the language of nationality. In a less well established state, where the relationship between the institutions and the mass of the citizenry is precarious or even hostile, the language of nationhood can have an important influence on the way certain sectors of the population, such as its rulers, formulate social problems, set goals, and motivate themselves. This was the case with Italy in the years after Unification.

Nationalist discourse can be thought of as providing a conceptual map of the world. As such it structures our perceptions and guides our actions, most notably in the political sphere, but also in culture, where we are used to studying in fields defined in national terms (Italian history, English literature, etc.). The impression that the map refers us accurately to something objective is partly due to the changes in human societies which have made it more reliable than the maps provided by, for example, religion. These changes include the diffusion of mass communications, the increase in our mobility across space and diverse social environments, urbanization, industrialization, the spread of 'impersonal' capitalist economic relations, and the growth of the modern state. However, more important in bolstering the credibility of nationalism is the fact that most people seem to *believe* in the kind of contours it projects onto the world. We have remade the world to fit with the map. This is not to suggest that nations are the product of our will. The realities which have been instituted in the name of the nation cannot simply be wished away. Just as importantly, the language of nationhood, like language in general, is handed down to us already endowed with an authority: this makes it difficult to change, oppose, or think without. We are made by the language of nationhood as much as we make it.

How to Imagine a Nation

Despite their great diversity, all forms of nationalism have one thing in common: they are always based on the assumption that the nation is a single, simple thing, such as a determinate group, 'race', or culture, which can be isolated from ideas and feelings. The ways in which this fiction can be perpetuated are potentially limitless. Here are just four of the most important.

First, one can produce a *narrative*, tell the nation's story—the tale of its birth, its struggles, and its triumphs. When one tells the story of something one implicitly endows it with an existence which can be isolated from passing circumstances: 'times change, but the nation remains essentially the same thing'. A few words suggesting a before-and-after story may suffice for a patriotic narrative: 'Italy has awakened' (i.e. Italy was asleep).

Secondly, one can invest in *symbols*. These symbols can be official, like flags, or unofficial, like the pizza or the bowler hat. They can be public (sports teams), and private (a favourite view or poem). The more things which are taken to symbolize the nation, the more likely it is to seem that there is something real which they symbolize.

Thirdly, one can imagine the nation as a *geographical space*. That space can then be filled with richly connotative land- or cityscapes (the leafy lanes of England, the Colosseum) and either redeemed or defended from invasion. Whilst a nation can certainly work without a territory to call its own (one only has to think of the patchwork of ethnic and national groups in Eastern Europe), the theme of territory is a very important one for national identity. A great deal of national self-esteem or aspiration is invested in territorial integrity and, more generally, in the imagining of the geographical space with which the nation is deemed to be coterminous. (I explore this particular way of imagining the nation in more detail below.)

Fourthly, the nation can be *set against* things, which are thus excluded from it. 'We', the nationals, can be defined against foreigners outside or criminals, subversives, and cynics inside. If the enemies against which the nation is pitted seem vivid and concrete, then the nation will seem equally real.

All these ways of fictionalizing the nation depend on differentiation, on defining the nation by what it is *not*. The effect of differentiation is obvious in the fourth case—the nation is what its enemies are not—but the other three also involve it. Narratives differentiate because they implicitly distinguish the nation from changing circumstances and thus seem to give it a reality independent of them. Symbols differentiate the things that represent the nation from the nation itself, the 'thing' represented; by doing so they again create the illusion of a real nation. Geographical images of nationhood depend on boundaries at which the nation inside and the foreign outside are distinguished. Nations need Others, images of what they are not. Nations are made at the conceptual boundaries beyond which that which is Other is deemed to lie.

Imaginary Geographies of Italy

The field of study opened up in the Italian case by this rethinking of nationalism includes all the images and texts in which the nation has been constructed and used to mean different things, at different moments, in different social contexts within the history of what is normally considered the 'single' nation of Italy. The woolliness of the language of nationalism forces us to concentrate both on teasing out the specific meanings which ideas of nationality have at given moments, and on examining the ways in which those ideas are related to real historical processes. Nationalism, like language, is intensely private; it provokes the most powerful of emotions: pride, nostalgia, fear, hope, embarrassment (Dickie 1995). Yet, also like language, it is very public in its collective and institutional manifestations. The study of the language of nationalism therefore requires sensitivity both to the details of individual instances of nationalism and to the broad patterns which a great many of those instances go to form; we must be prepared to study anything from flights of poetic fancy to the most mundane premisses of administration.

For these reasons, the examples in this section are necessarily somewhat disparate applications of a method of reading nationhood in general rather than an attempt to 'typify' or 'illustrate' the problem of Italian nationality. Nevertheless, in the history of any country, there are social problems in relation to which national identity tends to be particularly sensitized and important. Two geographical themes which have constantly brought national identity into question in modern Italy are Rome and the North–South 'divide'. In drawing attention to and exemplifying these themes, I shall try to illustrate the variety of levels at which the study of discourses of nationhood must be prepared to work, focusing mainly on one film in the case of Rome, and on much broader political discourses in the case of the North and the South.

Italy and Rome

In France—the implicit or explicit model for many accounts of the nation-state— Paris is the seat of government; it contains the largest concentration of population; it is the hub of the French economy; it is the centre of the country's academic life, artistic culture, sport, and tourism. Italy, by comparison, seems almost centreless. Its financial and commercial capital is Milan. Its industry tends to be concentrated in the triangle between Genoa, Turin, and Milan. Florence is at the heart of Italy's language and high culture. Tourists are as likely to be tempted by Venice as by

Rome. Naples had had a long history as a capital city before Unification. Many other cities had been the administrative centres of small realms and provinces. Turin was the political capital from the proclamation of the Kingdom of Italy in March 1861 until 1864. The dominance of Piedmontese personnel and administrative models was a feature of the establishment of the Italian state. When it was decided to transfer the capital to Florence, there were violent anti-government demonstrations in Turin (Candeloro 1968: 213–18). Rome only became the capital after being captured from papal rule in 1870.

The long history of Rome itself is far from being one with the history of the Italian nation or state. Before 1870, it was the capital of a theocracy rather than a secular state. Once robbed of its temporal power, the papacy barred Catholics from taking part in the political life of Italy at national level for many years. Rome has retained its role as the centre of Christendom. Few capitals have generated a field of connotations as complex as Rome, symbol at once of glory and decadence, transnational Christianity and national redemption, imperialism and civic republicanism. The idea of Rome has been the subject of a great deal of historical and critical literature, particularly on the nineteenth century (e.g. Chabod 1951: 179–323; Drake 1980; Sapegno 1986: 187–97; Springer 1987; Tobia 1991). The city has often been an emblem of the inadequacies of Italy's political system, and a focus for the citizens' resentment: the Lega Nord (Northern League) has recently made much political capital out of its image of *Roma ladrona* ('robber Rome') associated with 'Southern' corruption and the dead hand of the state. For all these reasons, the image one has of Rome inevitably says a great deal about the kind of Italian nation one imagines.

The transition from Fascism to the Republic was a period in which many of the central values of Italian society were remade and in which the imagery of Rome was especially problematic. Fascism had sponsored an aggressive, expansionist nationalism which made much of classical Rome's imperial grandeur. The centre of Rome itself was redesigned to fit with Fascist images. Many of the symbols of Fascist authority, such as the fasces themselves, were borrowed from ancient Rome. Patriotism and ideas of Rome had in a sense to be reclaimed from Fascist bombast after the fall of the regime. The forces competing to write the political and cultural ground rules of the new Italy had the awkward task of legitimating themselves in a language of nationhood which to some seemed discredited (Lanaro 1992: 5–163).

Roma città aperta (*Rome, Open City*), directed by Roberto Rossellini, was made in 1944, soon after the liberation of the city from Nazi occupation. One of the classics of neorealism, it tells the story of a working-class couple who, with a priest and a Communist resistance leader, are caught up in the struggle against the Nazis and Fascists (Bondanella 1983: 37–42; Forgacs 1990: 100–2). The title of the film is an ironic use of the definition of the city's status created at the capitulation of Italian forces to the Germans in September 1943: it was a definition never recognized by the Allies and ignored in practice by the Germans, who occupied Rome for the following nine months (Candeloro 1984: 226, 263). Individual cultural documents such as films can tell us a great deal about what being a national involves because they construct the nation in the ways outlined above (p. 22).

The opening sequence of *Roma città aperta* encapsulates its dominant system of *differentiation*. Singing German soldiers are seen marching across one of the city's most famous and popular squares, the Piazza di Spagna; they are seen as if spied in suspicion from down a dark street. The image is one of invasion, and it invites us to view the film from the perspective of those who have something to fear from the invader and who identify with the invaded space. The Nazis are, understandably enough, the film's central image of an evil Other. Many patterns of differentiation spring from this basic dichotomy, adding more nuances to the film's patriotism.

The image of Rome constructed by the film is predominantly that of a down-to-earth, working-class city: the antithesis of Fascist Rome. The heroes of the plot, particularly Pina (Anna Magnani) and Francesco (Francesco Grandjacquet), speak Roman dialect and are associated with the streets and tenements. This is decidedly *not* Rome as a prestigious capital of monuments and institutional buildings. Rome here *typifies* Italy rather than symbolizing it. The ordinariness of the city is brought into relief by the way in which the central characters, particularly Pina, are played off against Marina (Maria Michi), who betrays the resistance in return for drugs and glamorous trinkets. Marina does not speak dialect; her milieu is the theatre, her plush apartment, and the lounge of the Gestapo HQ. With her raucous American jazz, nylon stockings, and loose morals, Marina is associated with aspirations to a Hollywood lifestyle. As an image of Americanized culture, she is a representation of the inauthenticity which is the Other, the defining opposite, of what seem the genuine values and real problems of ordinary Romans.

The two central Nazi characters are seen in closed interiors and associated with a hostile surveillance of the city (Brunette 1987: 51): we first see Bergmann (Harry Feist), the Gestapo commander, against a map of Rome divided into administrative zones for security purposes (Figure 1); he then describes how he takes imaginary walks with secret police photographs as his guide. The contrast with the heroes' intimate knowledge of and involvement in the real city could not be clearer. Marina and the central Nazi characters serve as foils against which stand out the values of ordinariness, authenticity, and realism which the viewer is to impute to Rome, to the heroes, and, it might be added, to the film as a whole.

It is striking in a film as patriotic as *Roma città aperta* that on only one, fairly inconspicuous, occasion do any of the heroes mention 'Italians'. They invoke instead the ideals of 'charity', 'freedom', and 'justice'. The people who use the word 'Italians' with emphasis and frequency are the Nazis: 'how these Italians scream,' Bergmann remarks as he hears the cries of a tortured prisoner. As well as representing the Other of the Rome of Pina, Francesco, and Don Pietro, Bergmann is also the mouthpiece for a series of negative ideas of Italy from which we are left to infer more positive ones. Bergmann sees the Italians as weak and

Figs. 1, 2

cowardly, but his claim is clearly undermined by the bravery displayed by the heroes. The positive values created by Rossellini's film (authenticity, tolerance, freedom, a better future) are thus given subtly patriotic connotations. On the one hand, they are implicitly gathered under the heading 'Italy'. On the other, they are good because they are universal and not linked to any nation; because the characters who symbolize and advocate them never seem to think of them as Italian. The good thing about our capital city and our nation, the film seems to imply, is that they embody universal values which are not related to any nation; we can be proud of our nation because it is not nationalistic.

However, images of the nation are rarely, if ever, as tolerant and impartial as they claim: imagined nations have the effect of including some people and excluding others. The 'Italy' constructed in Roma città aperta is no exception. The film was made at a moment, before the establishment of Christian Democrat hegemony, when the unity of Catholics and Communists against Fascism and Nazism was a plausible patriotic rallying cry. But despite its message of solidarity between the forces of resistance, Roma città aperta does place a kind of popular Catholicism at the centre of its imagined nation. Images of Rome play their part in this Catholic emphasis. In the final sequence, a group of young boys troop away sadly after watching the priest, Don Pietro (Aldo Fabrizi), being shot (Figure 2). The boys themselves embody hope in the future. A panoramic shot of the city, the only one of its kind in the film, forms the background against which they are shown and invites a symbolic reading. The skyline is dominated by St Peter's, symbol of Catholic Rome (Figure 2). The film's stereotypical images of sexual 'deviance', associated with the weak or bad characters, are a starker instance of the creation of an imagined national space by the differentiation and exclusion of Others: the representation of Marina's immorality, Bergmann's effeminacy, and the lesbianism of his lieutenant, Ingrid (Giovanna Galletti), suggest that the film's patriotism has components which are less than broad-minded.

North and South

More than any other area of Italy, the South has been taken to emblematize the problem of state-formation since 1859. Still today, the power of organized crime in areas of the South dramatizes the failure of the idea of an impartial state to set down roots: remarks such as 'here it is as if we were outside Italy' (quoted in Bocca 1992: 28) have been commonplaces for over a hundred years. What such sentiments tell us is that the South and concepts of the South are profoundly implicated in definitions of the Italian national space. The Italy counterposed to the South in the sentence I have just quoted is an ideal, imagined country where, one assumes, clientelism and corruption do not appear. 'The South' also has flexible boundaries: it can include or exclude Rome, Sicily, and Sardinia, for example. But few geographical notions can have had such persistent stereotypical associations:

the South is where Italians, to say nothing of foreign travellers (Mozzillo 1964), have often found their favourite hackneyed images of exotic and/or primitive peasant cultures, dangerous and/or mysterious criminal practices (Mangiameli 1988). The South has been made into a theatre for the 'the shock of diversity', whether provoking moral indignation in the spectator, or a fascination for the picturesque (Bevilacqua 1993: p. xi). Journeys to the South have been woven into myths of the foundation and crisis of the nation (Isnenghi 1993). From street-corner prejudices to journalistic and academic discourse, the very diverse and changing range of problems within the South, such as those related to economic underdevelopment and organized crime, have too often been thought as the problem of the Otherness of the South, seen as an unchanging whole without internal differences (Donzelli 1990; see also Ch. 4 below, Gabriella Gribaudi's 'Images of the South', for an extended discussion).

In the history of Italy since Unification, stereotypes of the South as Other have assumed a particular importance in conceptions of political space at two moments which are separated by more than 120 years. The first was during the foundation of the united Italy after 1859. The second is the crisis of Italy's post-war institutions and the rise of the Lega Nord in the late 1980s and early 1990s.

In October 1860 Luigi Carlo Farini, a government envoy, wrote from the South to Prime Minister Cavour in Turin: 'What barbarism! Some Italy! [*Altro che Italia!*] This is Africa: compared to these peasants the Bedouin are the flower of civilized virtues' (Cavour 1952: 208). Farini, and with him many of Cavour's correspondents, portrays the South as an alien land, an Africa (Moe 1992). The opposition between Italy and the South is scored over oppositions between Europe and Africa or the Arab world, and between civilization and barbarism.

In April 1992 Umberto Bossi, the leader of the Lega Nord, commented on the parliamentary elections: 'The North has chosen federalism and Europe, the South has chosen Africa and Fascism' (quoted in *La Repubblica*, 7 Apr. 1992). Bossi here associates the South with Africa, linked implicitly to backwardness, and with Fascism, seen to be the centralizing antithesis of the Lega Nord's programme of federalism. But interestingly it is the North rather than Italy which is here defined against the South. In other words, where Farini, working to establish a national state, both assumes and reaffirms a certain definition of Italy, Bossi, working to establish a more regional form of state, projects a positive conception of the North. In each case a different concept of political territory is being brought into relief against the same stereotypical South-as-Africa.

It clearly suited the largely Northern Italian moderates after 1860 to have the South portrayed as a land in need of firm and even brutal government from outside. Yet their vision of the South as Other was also the product of a genuine crisis of understanding. They came to the task of governing the South with a particular model of the nation they meant to create, a nation which they associated with specific ideas of freedom, order, reason, legality, and civilization. When the situation in the South failed to fit in with that grid of concepts, it became defined as Other, as the theatre of serfdom, anarchy, irrationality, violence, and barbarism. The most dramatic example of this process is the bloody and drawn-out war waged by the Italian army in the South after 1860 against peasant 'brigands' (who were often nothing of the sort) (Molfese 1964). From the level of the legitimation of military policy, to that of the daily practices and experience of the officers involved in the fighting, the campaign was informed by the notion of the South as badlands where the normal rules of 'civilized' warfare did not apply, and where unconstitutional and downright brutal forms of repression were required. The 'brigands' themselves became powerful symbols of barbarism and irrational violence (Dickie 1992). One army officer referred to the locals as 'a population which, although in Italy and born Italian, seems to belong to the primitive tribes of Africa' (Bianco di Saint Jorioz 1864: 12). Paradoxically, therefore, the way that the representatives of the new national order conceived of the South as alien to an imagined Italian nation was part of the process in which it was incorporated into the Italian state.

The roots of the growth of a populist regionalism in the late 1980s in Northern Italy lie in the crisis of a traditional Catholic subculture; in the social upheaval brought by the breakneck economic acceleration and subsequent crisis in areas of 'diffuse industrialization'; in the inefficiency of Italy's administrative and political system. But the success of the Lega Nord is also due to the way it has managed to get people to think these political and social problems in territorial terms (Biorcio 1991; Cento Bull 1992; Diamanti 1993b: 3–16).

The home territory which the Lega Nord, and the various Leagues from which it grew, have claimed to represent is itself a perfect example of an invented political constituency. The boundaries of that territory have shifted over time, from just Lombardy and the Veneto to the 'North' as a whole, an area which has no historical precedents as a political entity, and no obvious or accepted boundaries. The criteria used by Bossi to define that territory have also shifted: from claims for a community based on a Lombard language and ethnicity, to a set of northern economic needs relating to stereotypical notions of a local culture of hard work (Diamanti 1993b). Bossi has, at times, used terms such as 'nation' and 'people'. Other Lega representatives have sought to explain what the North is by reference to ancient invasions by northern peoples or to a mixture of historical and ethnic traits which produce a 'non-Mediterranean' mentality (Vitti 1994; Miglio 1994).

The vagueness of the territory of the Lega Nord is one of the things which allows the party to become what has been called a political 'tram', on which a great variety of interest groups can travel (Diamanti 1993a: 125). But the most politically significant aspect of the imagined North is the hostile forces seen to lie beyond it. The Leagues have regarded themselves as merely a legitimate defensive response to 'outside' problems such as immigration and the central state. Amongst these Others in Lega discourse the South has been a constant presence, although its relative importance has fluctuated (Diamanti 1993a). Even when ethnocentric representations of the South are absent from official Lega discourse, they are none the less widespread amongst Lega supporters and those supporters see the Lega Nord as in some way giving political expression to their opinions on the South (Costantini 1994: 151–66). The South against which the North is defined in Lega discourse provides a powerfully charged emblem of threats which are seen to come from outside Lega territory (Diamanti 1993a: 51–3). Rising crime and drugs are thought through the issue of the Mafia. The dysfunctions of the state can be seen as the result of Southern clientelism and benefit dependency which contrast to 'typically' Northern self-reliance. Economic slowdown can be attributed to the way the South supposedly acts as a 'lead ball' tied to the feet of the North. A whole series of antithetical values are superimposed on the contrast between North and South: the people versus the politicians; the regions versus centralization; straight talk versus political jargon; the working population versus the spongers; the forces of change versus the corrupt establishment.

The Lega as a 'political entrepreneur' (Biorcio 1991: 38) is faced with a task, that of constructing a territorial consensus, which is analogous to the state-building project of Italy's first rulers. Ironically, very similar ethnocentric representations of the South as Other have been involved in both projects, despite their almost diametrically opposed political implications. But although the Lega Nord has argued for various forms of political separation from the South, it still *needs* the South in the sense that it is dependent on the otherness it projects onto the South to mobilize its supporters. In April 1993 the Lega organized a protest against a woman, a suspected *camorrista*, being kept in protective detention in Codognè (Treviso), one of *leghismo*'s strongholds. The *combined* sense of belonging and being under threat which such actions evoke is clear from the comments of Fabio Padovan, a parliamentary deputy of the Lega who was on hunger strike at the time: 'This land is ours and we will defend it tooth and nail' (quoted in *La Repubblica*, 27 Apr. 1993). Just as nationalists have done for centuries, Padovan is here conjuring up fears of invasion as a way of activating the boundaries of an imaginary geographical space.

Images of territory are important to state-building and belonging to a community. But there is no necessary referential relationship between those images and real geography: the North of the Lega is vague; the South was often conceptually excluded from the Italy into which it was being materially integrated after 1860. With those images of territory come a whole series of exclusions or differentiations, often in the form of stereotypes. But there is an ambivalence to the texts and images in which these differentiating gestures are made. Because the exclusion is conceptual it can never be complete: the nation always cleaves to that which it excludes. Each of the examples I have chosen exemplify that 'cleaving': the horror and fascination of the Italian troops for what they witnessed in the South 'infested' with brigandage; the Lega Nord's *need* for the enemies it loathes; *Roma città aperta*'s voyeuristic interest in the forms of sexuality which are represented by Marina, Ingrid, and Bergmann and which it portrays as deviant and dangerous. Imagining the nation is a task which is always prone to fantasy and anxiety.

Conclusions

How might an understanding of nations as social fictions shift the way we think about the problems of 'nation-building' in Italy (where the English term has also been adopted)? 'Nation-building' is a metaphor whose connotations of concreteness can be misleading. It is used in different ways: it can describe initiatives deliberately undertaken by the state to create a national community within its sphere of influence by, for example, improving communications or spreading propaganda through the education system; or it can describe a whole set of changes not entirely within the control of the state, such as migration, urbanization, and the spread of associations of citizens. The first point to make about 'nation-building' is that changes like these, whether controlled by the state or not, only provide the conditions in which people are *more likely* to think in the language of nationhood, to invest in it psychologically: this outcome is by no means inevitable and these circumstances are by no means the only ones in which nationalism is created (Lanaro 1991: 361–2). Second, quite what people do with the discourse of nationhood once they have learned to think in it is by no means always what the state might like them to do. Third, given the diversity and divisiveness of the different nations people can imagine, and given the incompatible interests that can be expressed in the same national terms, there is no reason why those who have been 'Italianized' should actually agree with each other. (Indeed, precisely because the nation is generally associated with impartiality and the collective good, the competition between different interests to speak on its behalf can be all the more fierce.) My fourth point is that the 'construction' of a national identity does not necessitate the 'destruction' of other identities. One of nationalism's most important effects is simply to create distinctions between 'us' and 'them'. The vague 'we' of the nation can overlap with the 'we' projected by other ideologies: we the believers in the true religion; we the Party; we the real men; we the proletariat; we the enterprising. Finally, because of its dependence on a shifting mosaic of images used at a variety of levels in society, even the nation conceived of as a form of social organization can never be 'built' once and for all. At the level of discourse, the 'building' of the nation is a constant process beset by ambivalence and vagueness, by fantasy and anxiety, by division and exclusion. The dream of the nation realizing itself in a solid, unanimous, inclusive, final form is a dangerous patriotic delusion.

On the basis of the redefinition of nations as social fictions, what sort of response might be offered to the questions with which this chapter began? Is Italy a nation? Is Italian national identity weak or strong? The only possible answer to these questions is, I am afraid, that it depends what one means by nation. If one means a body of citizens amongst whom affairs are conducted according to criteria of public impartiality, an ethos of mutual trust, and an underlying confidence in representative institutions, then one will be likely to conclude that Italian national identity is relatively weak. If one means a group of people with a common pool of historical experiences, a common language and culture, then one may conclude that Italian national identity is relatively strong. On the basis of what I have argued above, I would maintain that, inasmuch as discourses of nationhood are an important part of the way in which large numbers of Italians now think about themselves and about political, social, and cultural problems, the Italian nation could be considered strong. Nevertheless, the 'Italian nation' that the Italians and others imagine, the concepts of 'Italy' and the 'Italian people' that they use, are as 'weak', as discordant, slippery, and imprecise, as in any other language of nationhood. Furthermore, no national body politic, no national culture, can be created without the muddle of different concepts of the nation produced in discourses of nationhood. Those discourses render *all* nations weak, however one defines them, in the sense that they are inevitably unstabilizable, divisive, and open-ended.

Further Reading

Two general studies of nationalism written in English have been influential in Italy recently: E. J. Hobsbawm, *Nations and Nationalism since 1780: Programme, Myth, Reality* (Cambridge, 1990), and Ernest Gellner, *Nations and Nationalism* (Oxford, 1983). Hobsbawm's book is a useful history of nationalism in the modern era, even though there is some confusion in it between an assumed definition of nations as objectively identifiable 'ethnic/linguistic groups' (p. 182) and an understanding of nationalism as myth (p. 12). Many sociologists agree that modern forms of mass nationalism would not be possible without the social transformations associated with industrialization and the growth of the modern state which have revolutionized human mental horizons and made possible the organization of communities across extensive stretches of territory. Gellner's book provides a compelling account of some of these changes which, none the less, conflates nations with the societies that such changes have produced.

The recent political crisis in Italy has given rise to renewed reflection on the themes of national identity and citizenship. Gian Enrico Rusconi's *Se cessiamo di essere una nazione. Tra etnodemocrazie regionali e cittadinanza europea* (Bologna, 1993) is a wide-ranging account of the debate on nationality in Europe, with a particularly stimulating chapter on the Resistance in Italy. R. Cartocci, *Fra Lega e Chiesa. L'Italia in cerca di integrazione* (Bologna, 1994) advocates nationhood as model of social *integration*, though it fails to take proper account of the conflict, exclusion, and differentiation which inevitably accompany nation-building.

Homi Bhabha's 'Dissemination: Time, Narrative and the Margins of the Modern Nation', in H. Bhabha (ed.), *The Location of Culture* (London, 1994), is a difficult but influential account of the 'complex strategies of cultural identification and discursive address that function in the name of "the people" or "the nation" and make them the immanent subjects of a range of social and literary narratives' (p. 140).

References

ANDERSON, B. (1991), *Imagined Communities: Reflections on the Origin and Spread of Nationalism*, revised edn. (London).

BEVILACQUA, P. (1993), *Breve storia dell'Italia meridionale dall'Ottocento a oggi* (Rome).

BIANCO DI SAINT JORIOZ, A. (1864), *Il brigantaggio alla frontiera pontificia, 1860–63* (Milan).

BIORCIO, R. (1991), 'La Lega come attore politico: dal federalismo al populismo regionalista', in Mannheimer, R. (ed.), *La Lega Lombarda* (Milan), 34–82.

BOCCA, G. (1992), *L'inferno. Profondo sud, male oscuro* (Milan).

BONDANELLA, P. (1983), *Italian Cinema from Neorealism to the Present* (New York).

BRUNETTE, P. (1987), *Roberto Rossellini* (Oxford).

CANDELORO, G. (1968), *Storia dell'Italia moderna*, v. *La costruzione dello Stato unitario (1860–1871)* (Milan).

—— (1984), *Storia dell'Italia moderna*, x. *La seconda guerra mondiale, il crollo del fascismo, la Resistenza* (Milan).

CAVOUR, C. (1952), *Carteggi: la liberazione del Mezzogiorno e la formazione del Regno d'Italia*, iii. (Oct.–Nov. 1860) (Bologna).

CENTO BULL, A. (1992), 'The Lega Lombarda: A New Political Sub-Culture for Lombardy's Localized Industries', *Italianist*, 12: 179–83.

CHABOD, F. (1951), *Storia della politica estera italiana dal 1870 al 1896*, i. *Le premesse* (Bari).

COSTANTINI, L. (1994), *Dentro la Lega. Come nasce, come cresce, come comunica* (Rome).

DIAMANTI, I. (1993a), 'La Lega, imprenditore politico della crisi. Origini, crescita e successo delle leghe autonomiste in Italia', *Meridiana*, 16: 99–133.

—— (1993b), *La Lega. Geografia, storia e sociologia di un nuovo soggetto politico* (Rome).

DICKIE, J. (1992), 'A Word at War: the Italian Army and Brigandage 1860–70', *History Workshop Journal*, 33: 1–24.

—— (1995), '*La macchina da scrivere*: The Victor Emmanuel Monument in Rome and Italian Nationalism', *Italianist*, 14: 261–85.

DONZELLI, C. (1990), 'Mezzogiorno tra "questione" e purgatorio. Opinione comune, immagine scientifica, strategie di ricerca', *Meridiana*, 9: 13–53.

DRAKE, R. (1980), *Byzantium for Rome: The Politics of Nostalgia in Umbertian Italy, 1878–1900* (Chapel Hill, NC).

FORGACS, D. (1990), *Italian Culture in the Industrial Era, 1880–1980: Cultural Industries, Politics and the Public* (Manchester).

HOBSBAWM, E. J. (1990), *Nations and Nationalism since 1780: Programme, Myth, Reality* (Cambridge).

ISNENGHI, M. (1993), 'Dall'Alpi al Lilibeo. Il "noi" difficile degli italiani', *Meridiana*, 16: 41–59.

LANARO, S. (1991), 'Dove comincia la nazione? Discutendo con Gellner e Hobsbawm', *Meridiana*, 11–12: 355–66.

—— (1992), *Storia dell'Italia repubblicana. Dalla fine della guerra agli anni novanta* (Venice).

MANGIAMELI, R. (1988), 'Mafia a dispense, tra *fiction* e realtà', *Meridiana*, 2: 203–18.

MIGLIO, G. (1994), 'Nord e Sud: due Italie, due civiltà', interview in *Ulisse*, 12: 17–25.

MOE, N. (1992), ' "Altro che Italia!" Il sud dei piemontesi (1860–1)', *Meridiana*, 15: 53–89.

MOLFESE, F. (1964), *Storia del brigantaggio dopo l'Unità* (Milan).

MOZZILLO, A. (1964), *Viaggiatori stranieri nel Sud* (Milan).

SAPEGNO, M. S. (1986), ' "Italia", "Italia" ', in *Letteratura italiana*, v. *Le questioni* (Turin), 169–221.

SOLDANI, S., and TURI, G. (1993), 'Introduzione', in S. Soldani and G. Turi (eds.), *Fare gli italiani. Scuola e cultura nell'Italia contemporanea*, i. *La nascita dello Stato nazionale* (Bologna), 9–33.

SPRINGER, C. (1987), *The Marble Wilderness: Ruins and Representation in Italian Romanticism, 1775–1850* (Cambridge).

TOBIA, B. (1991), *Una patria per gli italiani. Spazi, itinerari, monumenti nell'Italia unita (1870–1900)* (Rome and Bari).

VITTI, M. (1994), 'Qualunque cosa decida Bossi a noi sta bene', interview in *Ulisse*, 12: 26–31.

Comparing Italy:
The Case of Corruption

MICHAEL EVE

THERE is a minor character created by Jerome K. Jerome who claims to speak fluent French but is not believed by his friends. The reason is that, whenever he is asked what the French for such-and-such is, a perplexed look comes over his face, and he replies that the French don't really have such-and-suches. The example is given of bed-and-breakfast. 'The French don't really have a word for bed-and-breakfasts' is the slightly uncomfortable reply. When one of the robust English friends asserts that they do, and that they are called *pensions*, the French-speaker defends himself by saying that a *pension* is 'not really the same thing' as a bed-and-breakfast.

Anyone who has more than a superficial knowledge of another language, or has lived in another country, is likely to have some sympathy with the French-speaker, and be less sure than his friends that the difficulty is just a disguise to cover up lack of knowledge. The downright, commonsensical attitude which assumes that there 'must be' essentially the same things in another society, and that it is only the details which differ, cannot be sustained for long. Although in some ways a bed-and-breakfast may be the same kind of establishment as a *pension* and perform the same kind of functions, its clientele, its owners, and the services it offers make it very different.

A similar kind of difficulty arises in comparative sociology. In this chapter I shall discuss the extent to which corruption among politicians and businessmen in Italy is 'the same thing' as corruption in Britain or the USA. The problem is not confined to corruption but is a general issue. Before moving on to the 'Tangentopoli' scandals of the 1990s, let us consider very briefly some other examples.

Some comparative studies adopt a somewhat similar stance to that favoured by the friends of Jerome's French-speaker, and play down the problems of differences in the content of the particular phenomenon studied in different countries, assuming that there is a stable core of sociological significance which makes comparison possible without extensive investigation of social context. Thus studies may measure, say, the percentage of the population in poverty, or the size of the submerged or 'black' economy in each of a number of different national states using a standardized definition of the phenomenon in question. A commonly used international definition of poverty, for example, is 50 per cent or less of average earnings in a particular nation. Yet application of this poverty line sometimes creates results which seem puzzling to those who are familiar with the situation in different countries, and this raises the question of whether it really is the same phenomenon which is being compared. It is not surprising therefore that debates on poverty in different countries often seem to be talking about quite different things. (For an example of differences in the academic debates in different countries, see the British, French, and Italian contributions in Negri 1990.) Likewise, 'small firms' or 'small farmers' may mean quite different things even in countries relatively similar to each other, such as the states of the European Union. Participants at international conferences may realize after a couple of days that in spite of using many of the same terms as their colleagues from another country, and citing many of the same authors, they are really talking about quite different types of things.

If we want to make truly meaningful comparisons, therefore, we cannot pretend that issues of comparability can be dispensed with merely by straightforward translations or standardized definitions. Results obtained on this basis should be the starting-point for analysis, not an end-point. We need to take into account a great deal of social context. This naturally makes the task of comparison much more complex; but it also makes it much more fruitful and stimulating. Delving precisely into the *difficulties* of comparisons can shed considerable light on both the social structures and the cultures of two different countries, and on the conceptual frameworks used to describe them.

In this chapter I shall try to make comparisons between Italy and other Western countries on the issue of corruption more meaningful by investigating the different social and legal contexts in which corrupt relationships between businessmen and politicians form. I should stress that my aim is by no means to downplay the seriousness of Italy's enormously widespread corruption; nor, certainly, to encourage the banal and false idea that politicians and businessmen are equally venial everywhere. However, in order to understand more thoroughly why corruption has been so difficult to eradicate in Italy, and what this tells us about Italian society more generally, it is necessary to dig further into what really makes Italy different from other Western countries. I suggest this is not just a question of 'more' corruption of the same kind, but rather of a whole different set of rules which lead politicians, businessmen, judges, and journalists to act differently in different nations. I try to show that a questioning and 'reflexive' type of comparison (see Bourdieu *et al.* 1968) which is attentive to its own categories can be useful here. A type of comparison, that is to say, which is aware that many of the categories commonly employed to conceptualize another society rest on implicit comparisons with one's own society which are naïve or partial. (To take a one-sentence example: many Anglo-American versions of the idea of Italian society as 'familistic' do not reflect sufficiently on the importance of kin links in Britain or the USA.)

Corruption in Italy attracts attention in the press and in academic studies not only because it is important in itself, but also because of what it seems to tell us about Italian society more generally. Widespread corruption has often been seen as confirming a series of related theoretical frameworks which portray Italians as particularly prone to 'particularism' and 'familism'—perennially subject to pressures to favour friends and relatives, and concomitantly incapable of adhering to the impersonal rules which are said to characterize a modern state. In the second half of this chapter, I discuss these influential ideas briefly and argue that, although they do point to genuinely important features of Italian society, in many circumstances they are blunt tools which can easily mislead. 'Reflexive' comparison of the type I recommend shows that 'particularistic' social arrangements (albeit of a different kind) also exist in, say, Britain or the USA (often implicitly taken to be more 'universalistic' societies). Reflection on this helps us to become aware of the limits of these concepts and avoid using them in a way which reinforces stereotypes.

Visibility

Before proceeding to some more basic exploration of differences in the social relations involved in 'corruption' in Italy and elsewhere, it will be useful to examine the issue of how we come to know about corruption in the first place, how it becomes 'visible'.

The social 'visibility' of an issue often varies greatly between countries. Awareness of this can prevent us from jumping to over-hasty conclusions—such as assuming that the amount of debate necessarily corresponds to the 'objective' size of a particular phenomenon. We cannot be sure a priori that the intensity of debate over corruption in a particular time and place, or the number of cases coming to light, varies simply with the seriousness of the underlying problem. More importantly, awareness of the gap which often exists between differing levels of visibility in different countries encourages us to investigate *why* visibility should be greater or less. It drives home the lesson that the information we have about a social phenomenon in two different countries is not just naturally 'given', but is socially constructed. Any social phenomenon, whether rape, child abuse, unemployment, fraud, or corruption, is raised to the status of a 'social problem' only when there are specialists who collect data, classify cases, and interpret evidence, fitting it into patterns. Corruption comes to light through the mediation of the law, judges, the police, colleagues, companies who complain, journalists, and so on. Yet all these institutions and professions operate differently in different countries. Investigating the mechanisms which render a phenomenon visible is thus a first step to becoming aware of the social context which gives it meaning. This does not mean that we will come to the conclusion that the special prominence of corruption in Italy is an optical illusion, merely the result of greater Italian sensitivity to the issue. However, investigation of how corruption comes to light provides a useful reminder that things may be more complex than they seem. We can therefore get away from the kind of oversimplified approach which simply sees different quantities of what is assumed to be essentially 'the same thing' in different countries (20 units of corruption in Britain, say, 100 in France, and 500 in Italy), and then hurries on to the more interesting task of explaining the causes of this difference (in terms, perhaps, of weak civic consciousness in Italy).

There is no doubt that corruption was a highly visible issue in Italy in the early 1990s. In February 1992 Milan judges issued arrest warrants for the first of a series of local politicians and businessmen. The statements made by these early victims of judicial scrutiny soon incriminated large numbers of others and the scandal—soon dubbed 'Tangentopoli' ('Kickbackopolis' or 'Bribesville': initially an allusion to Milan)—spread with incredible rapidity. The spectacular success of the Milan team spurred on judges elsewhere, and one after another the politicians who had dominated national politics over the previous decade came under investigation. Little more than a year after the first arrests, no fewer than a quarter of Italy's parliamentary deputies had received orders to testify, and the numbers were still increasing rapidly (Ricolfi 1993). The ranks of local politicians were similarly decimated and some of the cream of the country's business élite had seen the inside of a jail cell at least briefly.

Although corruption was right at the top of the agenda of Italy's major social problems in 1992 and 1993, this had not been so only a few years previously. An interesting newspaper interview with Giorgio Vitari, the investigating judge at the centre of an earlier corruption case which broke in 1983, compares the climate he and judges in the subsequent appeal case worked under and those experienced by the Tangentopoli judges:

everyone tended to play down the scale of things, whereas now all those involved confess right away and reveal the whole system. At that time we did not dream of tapping the telephones of politicians or ordering searches in the head offices of the big firms—not because we were particularly awed by them, but because politics and business still enjoyed credibility and respect. It is true there was already discussion of corruption, but in highly general terms. One did not think of a full-blown spoils system in local government. Now, evidently, certain obstacles obscuring things have disappeared. (*La Repubblica*, 21 Feb. 1993)

Vitari does not seem to have been an unusually timorous judge, but the daring raids into the sanctuaries of party headquarters and the head offices of Italy's leading firms (including Fiat, Olivetti, and Ferruzzi) which were ordered in the 1990s were simply inconceivable in his time. His case, for lack of other evidence, rested heavily on the verbose confessions of Adriano Zampini, an intermediary involved in arranging deals, collecting the money from businessmen, and handing it over to politicians. In the original trial, these were sufficient to convict nineteen of the twenty defendants. At appeal, however, reliance on Zampini's confessions was criticized, and all but seven of the convictions were quashed.

Vitari recalls the 'incredulity' he felt at the time and his feeling that his perception of the world was being rocked. For example, he remembers his initial disbelief when Zampini informed him that a Christian Democrat had passed on money to members of the Socialist–Communist ruling majority in the local council. In the early 1980s, this sort of collusion and co-operation between members of different parties seemed inherently implausible; the image of parties fundamentally opposed ideologically was still fresh in people's minds. Yet if this case had occurred in 1993, we can be virtually certain that no such doubts would have been raised. It is only now that we are more familiar with how politicians operated that this kind of detail does not undermine the credibility of statements. Many other details which Zampini recounted have been recounted by others in subsequent cases, and it is now evident that, far from being the inventions of a pathological liar, they form part of a common pattern.

Just ten years previously, however, the evidence often seemed far from conclusive. Vitari himself had his doubts; and the appeal judges had graver doubts, because they believed Zampini had lumped very different transactions together under the label of kickbacks—including some which were perfectly legal transactions. It should be remembered that the distinction between items such as consultancy fees and voluntary political contributions on the one hand and bribes on the other is not necessarily self-evident. The judges were not sure the facts before them amounted to a watertight case because their image of how politicians and businessmen operated did not contain the clear conceptual framework which judges (and even the public at large) had acquired by the 1990s.

In an international comparative perspective, it is worth considering a few of the mechanisms which make corruption visible. I am not suggesting that, if investigators in the United States or Britain worked under similar social and legal conditions as the Tangentopoli judges, the figures for corruption would leap enormously (although they might well move up a little). There is no real reason to doubt that Italy has been exceptional among Western nations in the extent of its public corruption. However, we should be clear that it is only under certain conditions—fostered partly by the awareness created by newspapers, academics, and political polemicists, by changes in the conceptions of how far it is acceptable for an investigator to go in probing suspicions, and by many other ultimately social factors—that many forms of corruption emerge to the light of day and are successfully

Fig. 3 The *bustarella* passing from hand to hand and getting smaller as it travels down the social scale. Many Italians do seem to conceive of their economy and their society as a long chain of personal transactions with many self-serving middlemen (*mediatori*) taking their cut on the way. In this cartoon, politicians are seen taking the richest pickings. Even though the waste associated with corruption accounts for a relatively small part of Italy's current economic crisis, it is not entirely insignificant, and is often popularly assumed to be a major factor.

proved in court. This doubtless explains why historical series of statistics on corruption among politicians (Cazzola 1988; Ricolfi 1993) show that there are sharp oscillations in the judicial figures, not entirely explicable in terms of real variations in corruption.

There are certainly large international differences in the powers and the expertise of investigating authorities. In Britain, for example, where it is the police who have responsibility for collecting evidence and preparing a prosecution case, resources devoted to fraud and white-collar crime in general, including therefore corruption, have traditionally been very limited (see Levi 1987; Croall 1992). Numbers in fraud squads have been very small and officers have very rarely stayed long enough to acquire specialized expertise. Because of the volume of work they are expected to undertake, the British police have remained largely reactive rather than proactive: 'they wait for complaints to arrive rather than seek out fraud' (Levi 1987: 121), and are thus particularly reliant on the 'victims' of fraud (including corruption) complaining and demanding prosecution. It is likely in these circumstances that the extent of corruption in Britain has been underestimated.

Institutional Rules Define What Is Legitimate

However, it would certainly be a mistake to think that the number of hidden cases which never come to light (what criminologists call 'the dark figure' of criminal statistics) is the only or even the principal factor behind national differences in the prominence of corruption. A more fundamental reason lies in the nature of the rules themselves. Is it true, as one or two more sophisticated politicians involved in corruption cases in Italy have professed, that half of what they were doing would have been perfectly legal anyway in any genuinely civilized country? Do not firms in other countries co-opt politicians onto their payrolls in the lobbying process? Are not political contributions by companies perfectly legal (and even tax-deductible) in many nations?

The self-interested comparison made by these politicians is disingenuous for a number of reasons, but it is interesting to consider where exactly the difference lies. Some overlap does exist. Although lobbying is usually thought of in terms of the representation of collective interests (the steel *industry*, for example, rather than a particular steel company), in reality not all cases fit this formula. Similarly, it seems reasonable to suppose that the lucrative posts on company boards of directors regularly given to British or American politicians (especially to those in governing parties with most influence over spending decisions) are not offered in exchange for any technical expertise but rather for their 'contacts' and inside knowledge.

None the less, a number of crucial differences do exist between patterns in Italy and those in Britain or the USA, for example in the degree and type of *social control* over unscrupulous behaviour present in different arrangements.

First of all, we should note that the very fact of illegality changes the nature of social relationships; this has been crucial in the case of corruption, as Pizzorno (1992) and della Porta (1992) have pointed out. At least in theory, a lobbying relationship, being legal, is open to public inspection and control (although, in reality, few relationships between a lobbyist and a politician are so transparent). On the other hand, illegal relationships, by definition, become open to public inspection only when they are uncovered by police and investigating judges. Another important feature of relationships which are illegal is that they tend to encourage the emergence of intermediaries and 'fixers', as the politicians and entrepreneurs concerned try to protect themselves. This encourages the formation of ever more complex networks of relationships and perhaps the formation of secret societies like Freemasons. Among politicians, 'specialists' tend to emerge, as a distinction is made between those who are prepared to get their hands dirty and those who are not. This has very clearly been the case in Italian politics, where large numbers of persons entered local or national politics not through any ideological motivation (indeed they may have been willing to change parties two or three times in order to advance their careers), but with the specific intention of using political positions as a way of accumulating wealth. These unscrupulous politicians often gained great power within their own parties (due to the numbers of clients they were able to attract), thus affecting the whole nature of the party itself. At the same time, the various intermediaries and fixers who sprang up tried to drum up business for themselves, thus encouraging the spread of corruption.

Another crucial feature of the corrupt relationships between firms and politicians in Italy is that they were essentially tit-for-tat deals without wider implications. In a bribery transaction, so much money is handed over in return for *this* contract, a bundle of notes in return for the bending of *that* regulation. Only rarely did the system of *tangenti* include deals which were not linked directly to specific favours. It does seem that towards the end of the 1980s, Socialist Party leader Bettino Craxi encouraged building contractors in the Milan area to make regular periodic payments, on the grounds that such payments would be less easily identifiable as bribes, but this scheme was simply a subterfuge. The bribes remained simply bribes, not elements of some more ambiguous relationship which might also involve some control over unscrupulous behaviour. It is interesting to compare the system whereby the Communist Party (PCI) obtained much of its financing. The PCI (and then its successor the Democratic Party of the Left (PDS)) received a significant part of its income from contributions from co-operatives with socialist or communist roots. It seems to have been tacitly understood that, in return, councillors in regions and communes would make sure that the co-operatives in question obtained a share of public contracts. However, in this relationship between these 'red' co-operatives and the PCI/PDS, there was no direct and explicit exchange. In contrast, it is clear from trial proceedings that, in most cases of bribes given by private firms, the object of purchase was in no doubt. We have, therefore, a crucial difference between a sale and a gift (see Davis 1992 for a review of conceptualizations of this distinction): with gifts there is no *immediate* reward, although in the long term reciprocity is expected. However, there is a major difference in the type of relationship between the parties to the arrangement. If a long-term relationship is to hold up, there must be a considerable degree of *trust* involved (see Gambetta 1988 on the significance of trust, including its significance in providing a basis for effective economic and political arrangements), and this cannot be created solely on the basis of immediate interest. It is no accident, therefore, that this kind of looser, more generalized exchange should form between groups like 'red' co-ops and the PCI/PDS, where even now there is a minimum of common ideological ground and where many links of friendship exist.

The difference is real, therefore, and has real effects on the type of work undertaken, on waste, on sense of responsibility and commitment to a collective interest. It is no accident that Emilia Romagna—where the Communists have been in power in local and regional government—has a reputation for efficient administration, notwithstanding the multiple links with favoured co-operatives. Co-operatives were therefore protected (at the expense of other firms which might have been able to obtain public contracts if there had not been this partial closure of the market); but at the same time they were evidently subject to social control which prevented them from exploiting the situation too extensively and constrained them to give reasonable value for money.

However, the differences at issue are differences in the type of social relationships linking firms and politicians—not simply a difference which can be captured in terms of a binary opposition between personal relationship and market competition. The same applies when comparison is being made not within Italy but internationally. It is certainly noteworthy that relationships between local and national politicians and businesses may sometimes be more intimate in Britain or the USA than in Italy. A good example is provided by local development agencies such as those organizing urban renewal. In Britain and the USA, where the idea of private–public 'partnership' in local development has been influential, it has been common to include directors of local companies (including development companies) in publicly funded bodies which have access to substantial government funds and wide powers to decide how development should proceed. Representatives of building companies may thus sit on local development agencies which decide the shape of a local town plan, infrastructures, industrial development, and even allocate individual contracts. This does not mean that representatives of companies will necessarily pursue their own interests, blindly. Indeed, it is probable that their very position in decision-making bodies will encourage them to pursue more general strategies where elements of general interest are well entwined with particular interests. This exploitation of the overlap between the interests of private developers and general community interests in urban redevelopment is, after all, the reason why governments in the United States and Britain have introduced legislation granting an important place (even majority control) on local development boards to private companies.

This kind of 'osmotic' relationship between contractors and political decision-making bodies is not necessarily inefficient. Investment in a local area may be encouraged—and at a cost to the community which is not excessive. It should be recognized, however, that this kind of arrangement probably constitutes a partial closure of access to contracts, or involves an advantage of some firms over others, at the very least in terms of information. In other words, it is misleading to portray companies present on development boards as representing 'the business community' in general, although this is the way things are usually presented in Britain and the USA. Members of development boards are in a position to decide on issues where different sections of the 'business community', and particular firms within it, have different interests. This is the sort of advantage companies in Italy pay bribes to receive. The two systems are by no means the same, socially, morally or legally, and are liable to have very different consequences. Yet the difference cannot be captured in over-simple terms of acceptance of impersonal 'rules of fair competition'.

Another type of relationship between business and politics is exemplified by a large company which, at the time of writing, seemed relatively untouched by the contracts-for-bribes exchange of Tangentopoli (although it was implicated in other kinds of cases), namely the Fininvest group headed by Silvio Berlusconi. Fininvest, whose interests range from television and publishing to urban development and supermarkets, was no less dependent on relationships with politicians than Italy's other major groups. Indeed, it was normally seen as having a *closer* and more symbiotic relationship—with one party in particular, the (notoriously corrupt) Socialist Party. Yet precisely because the relationship was unusually close, reciprocal favours do not seem to have normally flowed down the channel of direct monetary exchange. The Socialist Party seems to have defended Fininvest's interests by warding off the threat of effective anti-monopoly legislation in the media industry, and by providing crucial information in a variety of circumstances. In return, Fininvest media gave plenty of interviews with PSI spokesmen, appearances on popular entertainment or chat shows, prominent coverage of issues championed by the party, and reduced rates for election advertising. The total value of this relationship was no doubt considerably greater than the advantage gained by firms obtaining single profitable contracts in return for bribes. In 1994 the formation of a government headed by Silvio Berlusconi and containing three former managers and consultants of Fininvest as ministers or secretaries of state raised even more intriguing questions regarding relationships between government and a particular set of companies.

The various patterns of relationships between business—or rather, particular companies—and bodies having the power to allocate public contracts and decide development plans are all very different, with very different effects. They are similar to each other only in their failure to live up to an ideal of impersonal and anonymous market competition. As Sapelli (1994) has argued, corruption is one form in which firms establish an oligopolistic position, partially closing access to the market on the part of potential competitors. The other relationships referred to above also have oligopolistic consequences. However, my argument is that the differences between them are of great importance in that other effects (ranging from the tendency towards corruption spreading to the strength of informal controls requiring responsible behaviour) are very different. In order to explain why corruption has been such a problem in Italy, therefore, it is necessary to grasp the bases of these social relationships—rather than simply distinguishing between corruption on the one hand and respect for the law on the other. Genuinely comparative research needs to be carried out. The search for causes can only be really satisfactory if we are clear as to what it is that is being explained. It is not just 'more' corruption that marks out Italy, but the different context in which it takes place.

I hope it is clear that this in no way implies any kind of defence of what journalists are fond of referring to (perhaps prematurely) as 'the old regime' in Italy. The system was immensely damaging not only because it involved enormous waste but also because it virtually abolished normal politics, as the latter became less and less a question of competition between different interest groups and different programmes and more and more a struggle for control of a slice of the spoils system. In this way, the whole political system completely lost contact with shifts in political demand. So my argument is not in any way that different systems of relationships between politicians and businesses are at root 'the same'; but rather that they have to be understood as social systems.

A 'Weak Sense of the State'?

At first sight, the very widespread instances of corruption in Italy seem to provide obvious support for the influential thesis that civic consciousness is weak in Italian society. Political debate and private conversation regarding typical national failings often refer to a 'weak sense of the state'. This concept brings together a bundle of characteristics associated with a failure to internalize laws and to adjust one's individual behaviour to take into account the interests of one's fellow citizens. So phenomena as various as a proclivity to go through red traffic lights, tax evasion, or the forging of documents to obtain an invalidity pension on false pretences may all be cited as examples of weak internalization of the rules imposed by the national community and a disrespect for the law. As the phrase itself implies, this kind of free-riding behaviour is related, in this widely held conception of national character and national ills, to lack of loyalty to the national community. Loyalties to family and friends, or to the entourage of some influential leader, are said to squeeze out loyalties to the state and the wider community. Hence, when an opportunity arises to favour a friend at the expense of strangers, it is said that a high proportion of Italians will sacrifice the interests of those who are not personally known. Similarly, if there is a chance of using collective resources (whether municipal funds or the facilities of a hospital) to increase one's personal and family income, Italians are believed to be particularly tempted to take advantage. The supposedly late formation of Italy as a unified state is often cited as the background to this weak sense of identification with the national community (even though Italy is not a more recent construction than many other European states).

It is into this kind of framework which most analysts have fitted the 'Tangentopoli' corruption scandals. Thus Galli della Loggia sees corruption among national politicians as symptomatic of a whole society with very little resistance to corruption. For Galli della Loggia, therefore, the central question is why a sense of public morality and respect for the law has been so weak in Italy. He sees the root cause of the problem as lying in 'the absence or weakness of the tradition of the state and also of the community. The absence of a state tradition comparable, for example, to that of the great European absolutisms has meant an intrinsic weakness of the authority represented by the law' (1994: 235). The problem is thus set up as one of deep-seated *cultural and ethical attitudes* in individuals springing from a particular historical experience.

This kind of framework is extremely widespread both in everyday discussions and soul-searching over Italy's ills and in academic interpretations of Italian social and political structure. Banfield's (1958) description of 'amoral familism'—where individuals pursue their own interests, or those of their immediate family, at the expense of more general community interests, thus rendering a whole host of forms of social co-operation impracticable and inhibiting economic and political development—is still widely cited in Italy today. More recently, Tullio-Altan (1986) has criticized the 'disastrous' and wide-ranging consequences for Italian collective life and political institutions of excessive 'familism'. While distancing himself from Banfield and Tullio-Altan, Ginsborg (1990) has argued that the strength of loyalty to the family—and a parallel difficulty in making wider loyalties stick when these conflict with family loyalties—has remained one of the most persistent characteristics marking Italian post-war history. All these interpretations, in their different ways, stress the intrusion of 'particularistic' values—loyalties to families or to wider 'families' of friends, followers, and clients of patrons with access to resources—into the public realm.

It is important to note that this kind of framework is based on an implicit comparison with a type of society which is *not* particularistic and familisitic (or is less so), and where the 'sense of the state' is more deeply rooted in national consciousness. The terms of the comparison are to be found in those features which both Italians and foreign commentators have seen as distinguishing Italy from the 'advanced' liberal capitalist national states it has traditionally wished to emulate. At the same time, however, this comparison is not based on any empirical comparative research—but rather on an unexamined and idealized vision of the differences between Italy and the USA or the major states of northern Europe. Elements of stereotype in the visions the respective societies have of each other have been transferred into the conceptual framework which opposes particularistic to universalistic. At the same time, elements of idealization have become entwined with the framework because it is not only a scientific description of features of Italian society but also a *critique* of Italy's ills, and an appeal to an *ideal* of the state and of a 'modern' society which reformers have wished their society would live up to.

This implicit comparative background to concepts like particularism is rarely emphasized. It is, however, *intrinsic* to the framework of particularism that there should be a more universalistic pole to the continuum (see Landé 1977: 507 for an exposition which makes this explicit, and also makes it explicit that US society is the model for universalism).

Careful empirical comparison of patrimonial, clientelistic, or other particularistic patterns of social relations existing in Italy with the (quite different) patterns existing in Britain or the USA (perhaps the national societies most commonly taken as implicit terms of comparison) do not reveal any such stark dichotomy, nor indeed a continuum from more particularistic to more universalistic (see Eve 1993). What emerges is rather a variety of processes of exclusion and co-optation, of compromises over who competition will be opened up to—and in any case sets of thoroughly social relationships between players. These bear little resemblance to the idealized, impersonal relationships supposed to prevail in market societies and mature national states.

It is relevant to note in this context that corruption in Italy does not seem to be unambiguously associated with those features we might expect of a 'weak' or even 'absent' state. The importance of deals being *hidden* and *secret* was underlined earlier. However, if the fact that arrangements are illegal and therefore secret changes the whole nature of the relationship, as Pizzorno (1992) and della Porta (1992) argue, this implies we should direct our attention to the tendency (different from country to country) to make certain types of behaviour illegal. In particular, the formal refusal in Italy to countenance co-optation (US or British development boards being striking cases of co-optation), and the concomitant Italian insistence on universalistic criteria placing all firms on an equal footing in the competition for a contract, places large areas of behaviour out of bounds. Italian legislation attempts to regulate the granting of public contracts with very elaborate measures to prevent one firm gaining an unfair advantage. In other words, very universalistic procedures are expected of all concerned; it is expected that public officials and contractors are two completely separate parties who will act quite independently of each other. In Britain and the USA, expectations are evidently lower.

The general point at issue here is that comparison of the extent of corruption in different countries cannot be analysed independently of the laws which make particular forms of behaviour illegal. Sgubbi (1990) has argued that there has been an important extension in the kind of activities, especially economic activities, to which the criminal law typically applies. Traditionally, it was the lower working class whose marginal economic activities (from poaching to theft) were controlled by the criminal law. On the whole, the upper and middle classes were very much less likely to fall foul of the courts because their activities were self-regulated or at most regulated by the civil law. We may think of institutions like stock exchanges which have until recently been 'self-regulated' by club-like bodies with informal, flexible rules. The legal system (especially the criminal law) was rarely called in to regulate the conflicts which naturally existed. Some exchanges—notably London's—still maintain important elements of this pattern. Sgubbi argues, however, that in recent decades laws carrying criminal sanctions have affected more and more entrepreneurial activity. So the 'social risk' for members of the middle class engaged in business, or self-employed in the professions, has sharply increased. Sgubbi's argument is not intended to apply specifically to Italy (although his examples are taken from Italian law) and does not relate directly to the issue of corruption. However, it is useful to be reminded that the 'allocation' of the 'social risk' of becoming embroiled in the law is a social choice, liable to be different in different times and places.

In turn, this analysis requires focus on the struggles between different élites to impose laws which restrict the behaviour of others. It is pertinent to mention, for instance, that the chronic conflict and lack of trust among élites in Italy provides a background against which attempts have been made to safeguard the public interest via law rather than via informal regulation and tacit agreements between élites.

Inflexible, Impersonal Rules in Italy

There is little doubt that one of the most persistent paradoxes of Italian society is the coexistence of exceptionally rigorous and detailed laws and administrative regulation designed to prevent the interference of individual interests in public interests together with an exceptionally high incidence of precisely the kind of behaviour this mass of regulation is supposed to make impossible. Italian bureaucracy imposes a notoriously high number of requirements on those demanding a service or asking for a contract, in the attempt to ensure that those not entitled to the service, not best qualified to receive the contract, will not get it. In addition, rules governing officials are unusually strict—again Italian law and administration is particularly aware of the problem of controlling the controllers. Unfortunately, while all this inflexible regulation certainly does eliminate some forms of corruption, it often generates new opportunities for it. One of the most common kinds of corruption, in fact, consists of officials offering to overcome theoretically inflexible rules in return for suitable recompense (see Cazzola 1992 and della Porta 1992).

In countries where somewhat more flexibility is granted to public officials (i.e. they are trusted more), such as Britain, the USA, or even a traditionally centralized and bureaucratic state like France, conflicts between an official and a citizen can often be resolved more simply. An official with direct contact with the public may discover that someone does not have one of the required documents, or that some minor formality has not been observed; in many cases, this will be overlooked if it seems to be a mere formality and not a matter of substance. Or if the client is challenged he or she may at least be able to appeal to the official's sense of reasonableness. A supervisor may be called and asked to arbitrate, and sometimes the formal requirement will be waived. Client and officer are able to *negotiate* to a certain extent, and the two share to some extent a conception of what is 'reasonable' and rational and it is accepted that the official at the desk must, within limits, justify the reasonableness of a measure. The negotiation itself is part of this shared construction of sense of reasonableness.

In Italy, in contrast, much less freedom is given to officials either by written rules or by conventional working practices covering the implementation of the rules; hence the kind of minor negotiation which is often possible in other countries is not allowed, and is classified in the realm of illicit behaviour. Thus it is a fairly frequent experience for Italian citizens to queue for one of the numerous documents required by the bureaucracy (that is to say, the corpus of laws and administrative regulations which is in large part designed to discourage the abuse of state services by private interests) and find that they have to return empty-handed because they did not realize they needed another document. The clerk at the desk will throw up his or her hands in helpless sympathy; sorry, nothing to be done, rules are rules. The lack of *reasonableness* (a sense agreed on by both official and client) make this into a Kafkaesque situation. The official dissociates himself or herself from any identification with the rules—an external force without reasonableness—and hence is invulnerable to argument or persuasion. The only means of persuasion which does exist in these circumstances is a small bribe.

My own conversations with managers in Britain suggest that, in the field of relations between businesses and local authorities, there is often scope for negotiability and application of criteria of 'reasonableness'.

This is interesting because Italian analyses of corruption tend to indicate discretion in the hands of public officials as a factor encouraging corruption. Cazzola (1992: 7) sees discretion and negotiability as key features intrinsically associated with corruption, and implicitly identifies inflexibility with adherence to legality and thorough institutionalization of universalistic criteria ('sense of the state'). Many reformers take the same position when they call for laws so tightly drafted that discretion and interpretation are eliminated. Unfortunately, this is probably an impossible ambition—laws and rules can never directly *determine* behaviour—as Wittgenstein stressed. All law needs to be interpreted and implemented; so although every effort needs to be made to eliminate unnecessarily contradictory phrasing in laws, the totally unambiguous law seems a chimera—and thus a distraction from the attempt to impose more realistic controls.

Another feature which the comparison of behaviour in government offices in different nations highlights concerns the structure of responsibility. On the one hand, officials in the USA, Britain, or France seem to be more willing to take responsibility upon themselves. This might seem to reinforce the thesis according to which Italian employees of central or local government have a less thoroughly internalized 'sense of the state'. However, it might also be related to a different allocation of accountability. Chains of accountability often seem to be long in Italy, so that the heads of organizations and senior staff often seem to be held accountable—both politically and legally—for decisions taken lower down. If it is true that there is more of a risk that officials (including higher officials) may be made to pay for a mistaken decision, this would naturally encourage a literal and pedantic observation of rules, discouraging the institutionalization of a process of rational negotiation over what is 'reasonable'.

Another point to note is that the relative inflexibility (in theory) of many Italian authority structures may place powerful figures—socially powerful, but also people with considerable economic resources—in conflict with regulations. It seems to have been a characteristic of Italian legislatures over the past twenty years or so that they have been tempted to pass rigorous laws which place considerable burdens on economically or politically powerful actors; but then the power to enforce these apparently democratic laws is missing. In other words, there is a mismatch between real social power and formal power provided by the law.

None of these features—the perverse effects of heavy legal and administrative regulation, long chains of accountability, the attempt to extend state authority in the face of powerful interests—fit in with any *simple* version of the 'weak state' or lack of civic consciousness thesis.

So although frameworks which relate particularism or familism to a weak sense of the state are in many ways crucial for the understanding of contemporary Italy, they can be deepened considerably if comparison is made not with a stereotyped and sociologically unrealistic model (which is supposed to exist elsewhere in the civilized world but to be sadly lacking in Italy) but rather with real structures of authority, responsibility, solidarity, and power. In this chapter, I have argued that comparison which reflects problematically on the categories used can raise questions which challenge conventional conceptual frameworks. Comparisons with other nations are in reality difficult to avoid. Whether we are fully aware of the fact or not, comparative terms of reference orient the questions we ask and the analytical classifications we construct. Notions as widespread as 'modernization' and even many conceptualizations of 'the state' or 'the market' contain implicit comparisons with pre-modern situations where the state is not fully developed and the market not mature—comparisons which have their roots in comparisons between nations. It is better to make comparisons explicitly and methodically, using clear empirical examples, rather than risk using frameworks which contain elements of idealized contrasts or implicitly evolutionist binary distinctions.

Further Reading

Corruption has very frequently been at the centre of political attention in Italy, but there has been more moralizing about the issue than academic analysis. Newspapers are a good source for detailed accounts of 'the facts', as these emerge at trials or in political accusations. For the recent wave of scandals ('Tangentopoli'), newspapers published almost any day between mid-1992 and early 1994 contain several articles. Opinion articles in national newspapers like *La Repubblica*, *La Stampa*, or *Il Corriere della sera* are also a good source for understanding the kinds of terms in which corruption was discussed.

The sociologist Franco Cazzola has drawn on numerous newspaper accounts in *L'Italia del pizzo. Fenomenologia della tangente quotidiana* (Turin, 1992), to give a useful survey of the very various types of situation where bribes pass between public officials of one kind and another and members of the public, businessmen, etc. This book provides a good starting-point to get a feel of the practices and mechanisms at issue. Donatella della Porta's *Lo scambio occulto. Casi di corruzione politica in Italia* (Bologna, 1992) is perhaps the best empirical study and contains some penetrating analysis of its three local case studies. The book also contains a long introduction by Alessandro Pizzorno, which criticizes the tendency, dominant in American analyses of corruption (e.g. S. Rose-Ackerman, *Corruption: A Study in Political Economy*, (New York, 1978)), to study corruption in terms of the *opportunities* offered (e.g. the number of public contracts politicians have influence over). Pizzorno argues that cultural factors—affecting the willingness to give or accept bribes—are crucial as well. Another interesting case study is A.Vannucci, 'La realtà economica della corruzione politica, analisi di un caso', *Stato e mercato*, 34 (Apr. 1992). M. Maraffi highlights some theoretical issues in 'Politica corrotta o società corrotta?', *Polis*, 7/3 (Dec. 1993). Franco Cazzola bravely attempts to chart the quantitative extent of political corruption in various periods since Unification in *Della corruzione* (Bologna, 1988).

Edward Banfield, *The Moral Basis of a Backward Society* (Glencoe, Ill., 1958) is still a stimulating place to start to enter the wider debates, regarding what it is that widespread corruption tells us about the nature of Italian society. Chapter 5, in particular, offers examples of attitudes still widespread today (such as the assumption that 'all' politicians and public officials are liable to be corrupt) and an oft-cited set of hypotheses regarding the supposed lack of civic consciousness and excess of individualism and particularism in traditional Italian society. Banfield should definitely be read in conjunction with his critics; the 1976 Italian edition of the book, *Le basi morali di una società arretrata* (Bologna, 1976), contains a useful selection. On the background to political corruption in patronage politics in the South, see Gabriella Gribaudi, *Mediatori. Antropologia del potere democristiano nel Mezzogiorno* (Turin, 1980), and Percy Allum, *Society and Politics in Post-War Naples* (Cambridge, 1973).

In 'Le radici storiche della crisi italiana', *Il Mulino*, 352 (Mar.–Apr. 1994), E. Galli della Loggia argues that strong Catholic and Communist loyalties undermined commitment to the national state and identification with the *res publica*. On the general political preconditions favouring corruption, and the diffusion of corrupt attitudes see also A. Pizzorno, 'Le difficoltà del consociativismo', in *Le radici della politica assoluta* (Milan, 1994); and L. Cafagna, *La grande slavina* (Venice, 1993). Massimo Salvadori emphasizes the crucial importance of a 'log-jammed' political system encouraging the rise of unprincipled politicians in *Storia d'Italia e crisi di regime* (Bologna, 1994).

As for the general theoretical and methodological problems raised by comparing phenomena across different societies, the literature is immense. However, Neil Smelser provides a readable introduction to some of the issues: *Comparative Methods in the Social Sciences* (Englewood Cliffs, NJ, 1976).

References

BANFIELD, E. (1958), *The Moral Basis of a Backward Society* (Glencoe, Ill.).
BOURDIEU, P., CHAMBOREDON, J.-C., and PASSERON, J.-C. (1968), *Le Métier du sociologue* (Paris).
CAZZOLA, F. (1988), *Della corruzione* (Bologna).
—— (1992), *L'Italia del pizzo* (Turin).
CROALL, H. (1992), *White Collar Crime* (Buckingham).

Davis, J. (1992), *Exchange* (Buckingham).

della Porta, D. (1992), *Lo scambio occulto* (Bologna).

Eve, M. (1993), 'Paradigmi nazionali: percezioni del "particolarismo" in Italia e in Inghilterra', *Rassegna Italiana di Sociologia*, 34: 3.

Galli della Loggia, E. (1994), 'Le radici storiche della crisi italiana', *Il Mulino*, 352, Mar.–Apr.

Gambetta, D. (1988) (ed.), *Trust: Making and Breaking Cooperative Relations* (Oxford).

Ginsborg, P. (1990), *A History of Contemporary Italy* (Harmondsworth).

Landé, C. (1977), 'Group Politics and Dyadic Politics: Notes for a Theory', in Schmidt *et al.* (eds.) (1977).

Levi, M. (1987), *Regulating Fraud: White Collar Crime and the Criminal Process* (London).

Negri, N. (1990) (ed.), *Povertà in Europa e trasformazione dello stato sociale* (Milan).

Pizzorno, A. (1992), 'Introduzione. La corruzione nel sistema politico', in della Porta (1992).

La Repubblica (1993), 21 and 22 Feb.

Ricolfi, L. (1993), *L'ultimo parlamento* (Rome).

Sapelli, G. (1994), *Cleptocrazia. Il 'meccanismo unico' della corruzione tra economia e politica* (Milan).

Schmidt, S., Scott, J., Landé, C., and Guasti, L. (1977) (eds.), *Friends, Followers and Factions: A Reader in Political Clientelism* (Berkeley).

Sen, A. (1985), *Commodities and Capabilities* (Amsterdam).

Sgubbi, F. (1990), *Il reato come rischio sociale. Ricerche sulle scelte di allocazione dell'illegalità penale* (Bologna).

Tullio-Altan, C. (1986), *La nostra Italia. Arretratezza socioculturale, clientelismo, trasformismo e ribellismo dall'Unità ad oggi* (Milan).

3

Anthropological Perspectives on Culture in Italy

PAOLA
FILIPPUCCI

ITALY is in the interesting position both of having its own academic tradition of anthropology, part of which has studied Italian society and culture, and of being itself the object of anthropological study by foreigners, notably British and North Americans. In this selective review of studies of Italian culture by Anglo-American and Italian anthropologists, I shall explore some implications of this fact (for comprehensive reviews of Anglo-American anthropology see Cole 1977, Davis 1977, and Kertzer 1983, and of Italian anthropology see Grottanelli 1980, Saunders 1984, and Clemente *et al.* 1985). I shall show that Anglo-American and Italian anthropological studies of Italy form separate traditions, shaped by different political and ideological interests. Recently, however, the theoretical premises for a dialogue between them have developed, and this is likely to be beneficial to the understanding of contemporary Italian culture.

The study of culture is central to the project of contemporary social and cultural anthropology. In one early but still influential definition, culture is 'that complex whole which includes knowledge, belief, art, morals, law, custom, and any other capabilities and habits acquired by man as a member of society' (Tylor 1871; see also Singer 1968 and Beattie 1989). Anthropologists consider culture as a universal human endowment. At the same time, they seek to show that the meanings and values by which people live vary across space and time. The joint premiss of the unity of humankind and of the variability of its sociocultural creations underpins the comparative project of anthropology (see e.g. Marcus and Fischer 1986; Carrithers 1992).

Anthropologists study culture mainly by 'participant observation', living for a time with a group of people, joining in activities and conversations, and conducting systematic questioning and observation. Usually they work alone, with a relatively localized set of people, and for a short time-span. This method has historically been premissed upon, and has in turn encouraged, a view of culture as static, bounded, and internally homogeneous (cf. Fabian 1983). Recently, however, anthropologists have recognized the broader influences bearing upon even the most isolated societies (see e.g. Wolf 1982). Studies now stress heterogeneity, change, intercultural borrowing (Rosaldo 1989: 208), and the way people manipulate cultural forms in pursuing diverse and often conflicting interests.

Anglo-American Anthropological Studies of Italy

Anglo-American anthropology began as the study of 'non-Western' people, mainly indigenous inhabitants of European colonies and of North America (see Asad 1973; Kuper 1983; Marcus and Fischer 1986; Stocking 1982). The demise of colonial empires and the world-wide impact of industrial capitalism in the post-war period led anthropologists to recognize that Western and non-Western peoples participated in, and were often victims of, the same economic, political, and social processes (see e.g. Wolf 1982).

In the 1950s these processes were interpreted in terms of a transition from 'traditional' to 'modern' ways of life. Southern Europe was seen as 'half-way' along the path of modernization (Cole 1977: 358), combining nation-states, cities, and patchy industrialization with large rural populations, strong labour movements, and powerful religions. The assumption of incomplete modernization has coloured anthropological studies in this region until recently (see Herzfeld 1987; Piña-Cabral 1989). Anthropologists studying societies around the Mediterranean identified some distinctive cultural 'traits', including concern for 'honour', a form of social status based on the fulfilment of sexual roles (e.g. Peristiany 1965; Davis 1977; Gilmore 1987), strong subnational (localistic and regionalistic) identities (e.g. Pratt 1986), and preference for personalistic forms of political action, clientelism, and corruption (e.g. Gellner and Waterbury 1977). These 'traits' imply a limited separation of affective and instrumental relations in political, economic, and social life, necessary to 'modern' rational capitalism (e.g. Weber 1923—see Cole 1977; Davis 1977; Gilmore 1987; and the critiques by Herzfeld 1987 and Piña-Cabral 1989).

Interest in the cultural underpinnings of economic and social backwardness inspired early Anglo-American anthropology in Italy. Americans visited Italy in the 1930s to study the culture of origin of Italian immigrants (see Clemente *et al.* 1976:

262–3). After the war, the USA also sponsored research projects, mainly in the South, as part of the US plan of capitalist reconstruction of Italy (see e.g. Ginsborg 1990: 78–9; Clemente *et al.* 1976: 262). Friedmann, who worked in Matera, in the Basilicata region, in 1950–5, coined the term *la miseria* to denote the culture of Southern peasants. This 'way of life' and 'philosophy' was compounded of resignation and attachment to values like virginity and honour, 'pitiful attempts' to uphold individual and collective dignity in the face of economic, political, and social deprivation (Friedmann 1957, reprinted in Clemente *et al.* 1976: 287–99). This outlook in turn allegedly explained Southern peasants' resistance to 'modernization'. Culture was linked to Southern Italy's 'backwardness' also by the American sociologist Edward Banfield, who studied a village in Basilicata (Banfield 1958). For Banfield, the backwardness of the South was explained by a 'traditional' ethos, which he called 'amoral familism'. This, he claimed, made peasants 'maximize the material, short-run advantage of the nuclear family' (1958: 83), thereby inhibiting the co-operation and solidarity basic to 'modern' political and economic life. Both Friedmann and Banfield depicted peasants as prisoners of their culture. The latter was treated, especially by Banfield, as a factor independent of material conditions.

Banfield's theory has long been discredited (but see Tullio-Altan 1986; see also Gribaudi, 'Images of the South' and Eve, 'Comparing Italy', Chapters 4 and 2 of this volume). However, the main themes of his book, namely the cultural role of the family in Italy, and the cultural construction of the public/political domain, dominated subsequent Anglo-American anthropological research in Italy. Banfield's idea of 'familism' was challenged by Silverman (1968), who saw Southern peasants' exclusive attachment to their nuclear family as an effect, not a cause, of their poverty. Landless peasants were unable to support the large families which were to be found in areas of peasant ownership and long-term tenancy, such as Central and Northern Italy. Later studies have also documented 'extended' family patterns in parts of the South where there are smallholdings (Douglass 1980, 1991; Galt 1991*a*, 1991*b*). Davis (1973), on the other hand, found the nuclear family to be the ideal form in Pisticci (Basilicata) in the early 1960s. This was not, however, a 'traditional' trait of local mentality, but the recent outcome of changing inheritance practices in new economic conditions. In the 1960s, co-residence of several generations, residential clusters of kin-related nuclear families, and kin co-operation were also a frequent outcome of property distribution and strategies of socio-economic advancement. Ties of neighbourhood and godparenthood were evidence of solidarity beyond the family. On the other hand, Belmonte (1979) found in a Neapolitan slum that extreme poverty induced such desperate dependency among kin that even nuclear families fell apart under the strain. Finally, Pitkin (1985) showed how 'nuclear' and 'extended' family forms may be used flexibly in changing circumstances. He recorded a shift from nuclear to extended family arrangements as three successive generations of one family moved from utter poverty in Calabria in the 1920s to relative affluence in Abruzzo in the 1970s. This recent work sees family form as the outcome both of people's cultural expectations about what family 'is', and of choices they make in the light of perceived opportunities in changing circumstances (see also Kertzer 1984).

Banfield's idea of the centrality of the idea of the family as a frame of social reference in Southern Italy was also explored by studies of 'honour' (*onore*). This is a kind of prestige based on the performance of ideal sexual roles, in which males are typically enjoined to defend their own and their family's reputation by ensuring the chaste behaviour of their kinswomen (see e.g. Peristiany 1965; Schneider 1971; Davis 1977; Blok 1981; Gilmore 1987). In Italy the main study was conducted by Jane and Peter Schneider in western Sicily in the late 1960s (published 1976—see also Schneider 1971; Giovannini 1981). The Schneiders identified *onore* as one of three key 'cultural codes', developed as adaptive responses to the island's historical experience as a 'colony' of successive empires (Roman, Spanish, Euro-American capitalist). First, they argued, lack of state regulation under the Spanish had given rise to *furberia* (cleverness), which legitimated the ruthless pursuit of individual interest. Then, in the absence of generalized trust, makeshift coalitions to further political or economic interests were formed which made reference to the code of *amicizia* (friendship). Finally, *onore* developed as a strategy of resistance to attempts by State and Church to control family affairs and resources (see also Schneider 1971). These codes persisted, the Schneiders argued, because they were upheld by successive 'broker' strata (lately, the Mafia) mediating between peasants and the state and market. The Schneiders also noted in passing (1976: 94) that the 'honour code' may always have been flexibly used, publicly upheld but privately contradicted. By the 1960s, it was also receding in the face of 'alternative cultural codes' from Northern Italy (1976: 227). These remarks suggest that the Schneiders' treatment of 'Sicilian culture' in terms of 'codes' is overly rigid. A more historical approach suggests that cultural forms are strategically used in changing circumstances and to express different interests; this kind of approach may require narrower geographical and temporal frames (see Piña-Cabral 1989: 404). The latter characterized Davis's study of honour in Pisticci in the 1960s, where 'honour' is described as a kind of status that is the means of allocating material resources and social prestige to individual men in the public arena, on the basis of their performance as providers and defenders in the domestic sphere (Davis 1969, 1973, 1977). The question of why public status and domestic performance, and social prestige and sexual roles should be thus linked, has recently been tackled by Goddard (1987) in a study of Neapolitan working-class women. She found that women and men shared a concern with female chastity in terms of male 'honour' and female 'shame'. At the same time, women controlled their own sexuality, manipulating the norms to their own advantage (e.g. by becoming pregnant to hasten a marriage). Goddard suggests that ideas about honour and shame are related less to women's individual worth than to group identity, of which women are carriers. Women are associated with the family, focus of a defensive identity opposing working-class Neapolitans to traditionally exploitative spheres 'outside': the state, the market, Northern Italy. Women's chastity comes to symbolize variably inclusive collective identities (familial, class, and regional) in a historical context of inequality. While broadly following the Schneiders' argument, Goddard concentrates on the contradictions between norms and practice. She treats honour and shame as manipulable categories, part of an ideology that uses historically constituted and contested ideas about maleness and femaleness in ordering the social world (cf. Cowan 1990).

A focus on cultural strategies in historically and socially specific settings is found in other recent studies of sexual and gender roles in Central and Northern Italy. Counihan (1985) interpreted gender symbolism in a Sardinian carnival, when working-class men dress as grieving mothers, as an expression of their anxieties about social and economic inferiority in the village and in the nation. Maher (1987) looked at how women dressmakers crossed class boundaries by manipulating their sexuality in early twentieth-century Turin. Yanagisako (1991) studied successive generations of owners of family firms in Como, showing how the interests of men and women in these families have come to conflict in changing economic, political, and legal circumstances, and now threaten the firms' continuity. Historically specific 'gendered interests' are here seen as a crucial dimension in shaping families as concrete social configurations at each point in time.

The second major focus of research by Anglo-American anthropologists in Italy has been politics. In the South, research has concentrated on the role of local élites as political and economic patrons and mediators between locality and state (e.g. Blok 1974; Schneider et al. 1977; Weingrod 1977). This was linked to the personalistic focus of grass-roots political culture, manifested in phenomena like clientelism and the Mafia (see Blok 1974; Boissevain 1966; Davis 1973; Schneider and Schneider 1976, 1983 discussed above). The assumption of a uniformly clientelistic South was challenged by White (1980), comparing two villages in the Fùcino basin. She found that the inhabitants of Luco, overwhelmingly PCI/PSI voters, opposed clientelism, whereas those of Trasacco, DC voters, practised it. White linked these attitudes to divergent historical experiences. The Trasacchesi had always been tenants of large landowners, whose paternalism later made the villagers attuned to the DC's idiom of mediation and clientelism. The Luchesi, on the other hand, had been smallholders and fishermen, until the Fùcino lake was drained in the nineteenth century, when they were forced into tenancy. They experienced this as a brutal imposition, and were later receptive to the language of struggle of the Socialist Party and later the Communist Party. This study shows the importance of local history and what people make of it, in accounting for present 'cultural' features like clientelism.

The role of élites as mediators was also discussed in Central and Northern Italy, mainly in relation to representations of collective identity (local, ethnic, and political party). So Silverman's study (1975) of a village in Umbria discussed the local notion of civiltà, a combination of courtesy, generosity, attention to formalities, appreciation of high culture, aptitude at public speaking and socializing and respect for one's inferiors, all seen as characteristic of 'urban' living. *Civiltà* was expected particularly of exponents of the local upper class. For Silverman, the origin of the notion of *civiltà* lay in the paternalistic relationship between town-based landlords and rural *mezzadri* (sharecroppers), from the sixteenth to the early twentieth century (see also Silverman 1977b). Local landowners, who were literate and had personal connections among state and church officials, acted as mediators in peasants' dealings with officialdom. In this context, social superiority became identified with education, verbal and social skills, and knowledge of etiquette, and those in turn with 'urban' life. By the time of Silverman's fieldwork, in the 1960s, the gap between urban and rural living was closing, with universal literacy, a higher standard of living, and improved communications. State officials and political parties had become the new patrons and mediators between local people and the state (see also Silverman 1977a). Thus, Silverman concludes, the connotations of *civiltà* discussed in the book were 'the cultural consequences of an urban past' (1975: 234), that would soon disappear.

This conclusion is challenged by studies showing the ideological role of localism and notions of urban excellence in contemporary contexts. Pratt (1973, 1980, 1984, 1986) has noted the Christian Democrats' use of a 'city-centric' idiom in local propaganda in Tuscany between the 1950s and 1970s. For Pratt, territorially defined interests are central to the political debate in contemporary Italy because of the importance of the *comune* and other levels of local government (the province, the region), and because of the DC's role as mediators between locality and state. The idea of locality also enabled the DC to stress shared interests, against the left-wing idiom of class conflict (see Pratt 1986; also 1984).

While Pratt looked only at official political language, Kertzer looked at the interplay of official and grass-roots representations of community and locality through party political allegiance. In a suburb of Bologna in the 1970s, Kertzer showed how the struggle between the Catholic Church and the Communist Party for ideological supremacy was played out in people's daily lives (Kertzer 1980). The Communist Party provided the symbolism of community solidarity, but the Church was a central reference point through its control of marriage, baptism, and funerals. Kertzer's is one of the few Anglo-American anthropological studies in Italy specifically to consider religion and belief (see also Christian 1984; Holmes 1989). In this case, people were shown to make 'ideological' choices on the basis of social considerations, for instance Southern immigrants seeking local integration by joining the PCI.

Another focus of research has been ethnic identity. Cole and Wolf (1974) linked social and cultural patterns to ethnicity in a study of adjacent villages in Trentino Alto Adige, respectively Romansch- and German-speaking. In the 1960s, the German-speaking inhabitants of St Felix developed local assets (tourism, farming), and had a strong attachment to local civic institutions and associations. Villagers in Romansch-speaking Tret, on the other hand, were attracted by urban lifestyles, and left the village in search of socio-economic advancement. Cole and Wolf explained these contrasting local responses to the same conditions by the villages' different historical experience of political participation in the nation-state, which affected the authority structure of the family, patterns of inheritance and intra-community relations. They thus showed how past and present interpenetrate, and questioned polarized oppositions of 'traditional' and 'modern' in accounting for ethnic feeling. This is also the thrust of Holmes's (1989) study of Friuli, where small cultivators striving to keep their land have been moving for centuries be-tween farming and wage labour, locally and abroad, daily or seasonally. Making a living in a fluid, fragmented, and until recently harsh economic environment, these peasants gave meaning to their experience by constructing a separate iden-tity around the Friulian language, religious practices, and folk beliefs, and the routine of farm life. Their forays into the wage economy did not threaten, but on the contrary helped to preserve, this cultural separateness. The latter has remained even though Friulians have now entered the consumer culture of present-day Northern Italy; indeed, local specificity is now celebrated, notably by a regionalist movement born in the mid-1960s among the urbanized young. Holmes's study is particularly compelling at a time of flourishing regionalism in industrial Northern Italy, showing how the 'traditional' may be formulated as people pursue their own interests in very 'modern' circumstances. A similar conclusion was reached by Poppi (an Italian with a British Ph.D.) after he looked at two Carnivals in the Val di Fassa, Trentino (Poppi 1983). He showed how the form of the festivals is ma-nipulated by locals, to be more or less 'traditional', as they formulate a separate Romansch local/ethnic identity in the context of social and economic changes in the valley. The appeal to 'tradition' and to an idealized image of past community in the context of social and economic change is also explored in my own work (likewise included under this heading because of my British anthropological train-ing). I look at how people in a 'modern' (industrialized, well-connected) north-east Italian town selectively reformulate the past, strategically opposing a 'good' past to a socially fragmented present, as they make a living in present economic, pol-itical, and social circumstances.

Overall, recent Anglo-American studies of politics, family, and gender challenge the polarized opposition between 'traditional' and 'modern' that underlies the 'Mediterraneanist' perspective. This perspective strongly coloured earlier studies, which were mainly set in rural or small-town and Southern locales (see Kertzer 1983; Davis 1977: 163). Although these were carried out in years of radical social, economic, and cultural transformation (see e.g. Ginsborg 1990: 186 ff.), change was rarely built into their descriptions. While authors noted in passing, usually in the conclusion, that things were changing, the body of their texts gave a picture of stability and continuity, reinforced by the anthropological convention of writing in the present tense (see e.g. Fabian 1983). Culture was often treated in terms of rigid 'codes' or syndromes. Earlier studies also made crude distinctions between 'élite' and 'grass-roots' ideas, failing to consider the role of 'culture' as a means of drawing fine social distinctions, in years of great socio-economic mobility.

Assumptions about 'Mediterranean' backwardness also inspired the overall focus on family and politics. Interest in politics may also be related to Cold War pre-occupations with consensus in a country that was a key NATO outpost (cf. Cole 1977). The relative neglect of religion (but see Wolf 1984) is harder to account for. Finally, until recently, Anglo-American anthropologists have by and large failed to take into account the fact that Italians too observe their own culture anthropologically (but see Kertzer 1983; Kertzer and Saller 1991; Tentori 1990; Galt 1991a). To their work I turn next.

Italian Anthropological Studies of Italy

Anthropological studies of Italian culture by Italian scholars in the twentieth century belong to two theoretically and thematically distinct disciplinary traditions: 'folklore' and 'cultural anthropology'. Let us consider these separately.

'Folklore' studies began in the nineteenth century, as a subdiscipline of *antropologia* (which focused at that time on the study of the physical configuration and evolution of the human species), with the aim of studying the culture of the lower strata of Italian society. Before Unification, folklorists collected popular poetry as evidence of a 'shared literary homeland' prefiguring the political one (Berchet, quoted in Cocchiara 1981: 63, see also 52 ff.; Lombardi Satriani 1979a: 42). After Unification, concern about the conditions of the mass of the population encouraged folklorists to study other aspects of popular culture, like family forms (see Lombardi Satriani 1979a; Cirese 1976: 128–30; Manoukian 1988).

Popular cultural forms were seen as survivals of earlier ways of life, preserved in the countryside, less affected by 'modern' influences (namely revolutionary ideologies—see Cirese 1985: p. xii; Cocchiara 1981: 193 ff.; Clemente *et al.* 1985: 97 ff.; Carpi 1981: 455–65; Lombardi Satriani 1979a: 45–9). Bound by fixed 'customs', the people were excluded from history, identified with the artistic and political creations of urban and bourgeois 'Italian civilization' (Bollati 1983: 85–6; cf. Smith 1981: 90; Hobsbawm 1983: 2–3; Cocchiara 1981: 164 ff. and 204; Clemente *et al.* 1985: 97 ff.). For the eminent folklorist Giuseppe Pitré, the 'people's' 'life, history, memories, and institutions' were radically different from those 'of their dominators' (1868, quoted in Lombardi Satriani 1979a: 49; see Cocchiara 1981: 153 ff.). This separation acquired a geographical dimension, since folklore studies concentrated in the South, that was represented as rural, archaic, and immobile, in contrast to a modern and innovative North. Many folklorists were exponents of the Southern upper class, who may have stressed their society's 'traditional' features in resisting incipient economic and social modernization (Lombardi Satriani 1979a: 62).

Folklore studies remained the main anthropological discipline in early twentieth-century Italy. Elsewhere, interest in non-Western peoples and in the generalizing and comparative study of humans was stimulated in practice by colonial expansion and, theoretically, by evolutionism (see e.g. Asad 1973; Kuper 1983, 1988). Italy's colonial expansion was limited. More importantly, theoretical and methodological reform were discouraged by the combined influences of the Catholic Church and of the idealist philosopher Benedetto Croce (see Clemente *et al.* 1985: 13 ff., 97 ff.). The Church opposed evolutionism, maintaining that humans, endowed by God with free will, could not be studied according to the mechanical laws of nature and chance (Clemente *et al.* 1985: 54–6, 63). Similarly, Croce considered all 'naturalistic' disciplines to be inadequate for grasping the uniqueness and individuality of human experience. The latter could only be comprehended through history, which revealed the development of the human spirit in the world (see Edwards 1967: 23–4; Clemente *et al.* 1985: 5 ff. and 70 ff.; Grottanelli 1980: 230 ff.). Following Croce, folklorists returned to 'popular poetry', in search of a 'simple' aesthetic (see Clemente *et al.* 1985: 18 and Cocchiara 1981: 187 ff.).

In the 1920s and 1930s, 'folklore' studies were also encouraged by the Fascist regime. A campaign for a 'return to traditions' (1929) was part of its reorganization of working-class leisure (see de Grazia 1981; Puccini and Squillacciotti 1979: 81 ff.). The regime sponsored folklore publications, festivals, and exhibitions, and the revival of (often invented) 'local traditions', with the aim of 'mobilizing the greatest possible civic participation' (de Grazia 1981: 210). Making local identities an object of consumption in mass leisure may be linked to the regime's bid to present locality as a model of interclass unity, template for the Fascist 'corporative' state (see de Grazia 1981: 210, 214—but see also Puccini and Squillacciotti 1979: 83). The physical branch of anthropology was instead drawn upon to present Mussolini's colonial and expansionistic aims in the Mediterranean, and later his adherence to Nazi doctrines, as practical applications of the findings of pure science (see Puccini and Squillacciotti 1979: 70, 84; Tullio-Altan 1983: 114–17; Lospinoso 1975–6: 163). The work of physical anthropologists was enlisted to demonstrate the superiority of the (invented) 'pure Italic/Mediterranean race' over foreigners (notably black Africans), and internal minorities (notably Jews). This racist framework coloured studies of the indigenous people of Fascist Italy's new African colonies (see e.g. Lospinoso 1975–6).

Despite their association with the regime, folklore studies survived into the post-war period partly because of the influence of the Marxist thinker Antonio Gramsci, who wrote short notes on the subject during his imprisonment by the Fascist Special Tribunal (see Gramsci 1985: 188–95; cf. Cirese 1976). Influenced by Croce, Gramsci was interested in the role of ideas and of human subjectivity in socio-economic change (see Femia 1981: 1, 61 ff.; Joll 1977: 85; Tullio-Altan 1983: 127). He therefore argued that successful domination of one class over others depended not solely on force or economic supremacy, but on the imposition of a system of moral, political, and cultural values which he called 'hegemony'. 'Folklore', Gramsci wrote, was 'a view of the world and of life', specific to the 'instrumental and subaltern classes of every form of society that has so far existed' (Gramsci 1985: 189). It may include elements derived from the past and present world views of 'the cultured parts' of societies, but it was also formulated in response to the historical experience of oppression, forming a kind of rudimentary class consciousness ('protest' or 'progressive' folklore—see Cirese 1976: 88). For Gramsci, folklore was a poorly articulated view of the world which would eventually have to give way to a more coherent one as the masses achieved political supremacy and hegemony (Gramsci 1985: 189–91; cf. Cirese 1976: 89). Gramsci thus linked culture to historically specific social strata and saw it as a weapon of social and political struggle. In his work, the nineteenth-century idea of the separateness of popular culture gave way to the idea of cultural stratification. Dominators and dominated did not inhabit separate histories, but had different perspectives derived from their unequal positions within the same history. In this way the category 'folklore', appropriated by the Fascist regime in countering class-based ideologies, was reformulated by Gramsci in the context of class struggle.

Gramsci's notebooks were published in Italy in 1948–51, as many Italian intellectuals drew on Marxism to fashion a national culture based on the 'realistic' apprehension of the country's social conditions, formerly obscured by Fascist rhetoric (see e.g. Salinari and Ricci 1980: 1447; Tullio-Altan 1983: 119). The study of 'popular culture' acquired political connotations as the PCI tackled the issue of the peasants' role in the struggle, during years of peasant and worker agitation (see e.g. Ginsborg 1990: 122 ff., 188 ff.). Folklore was seen as a potential basis of an autonomous culture for the 'proletariat' struggling for hegemony (see Clemente et al. 1976: 115 ff.). It was in this climate that the anthropological work of Ernesto De Martino began. A Socialist and later Communist Party activist in his native Basilicata, De Martino witnessed the Southern peasants' struggle to transform their own lives (De Martino 1980: 165). He became critical of those, like Carlo Levi, who saw peasants as locked in an archaic culture (see Levi 1945; Pasquinelli 1977: 11; Clemente et al. 1976: 145 ff.). De Martino aimed instead at studying peasants as subjects in their own history (De Martino 1941; Clemente et al. 1976: 27; Clemente et al. 1985: 3 ff.; Cases 1973).

De Martino sought to contribute to the 'Southern Question' by compiling a 'religious history of the South' (De Martino 1980: 165). He focused on practices marginal to official Catholicism, which he saw as 'relics' of former belief and ritual systems, including dominant ones. Their continuation in the present, he argued, exposed the 'internal limits' both of high Catholicism and of modern, bourgeois, Western culture (1959: 11, 25–6; 1980: 153). Thus, for instance, De Martino linked the practice of ritualized funeral weeping, traceable to classical times, in contemporary Southern Italy to the extreme material deprivation of the peasants (De Martino 1958, 1980: 186–202). Constantly aware 'of the limited efficacy of human action' (1980: 196–7), the peasants had a fragile sense of self, in danger of 'floundering' at times of crisis, like the death of kin. This condition of psychological misery particularly affected women, who were even more oppressed than men in this socio-economic context. Ritualized weeping was a technique to alleviate self-destructive impulses unleashed by grief, containing psychological collapse

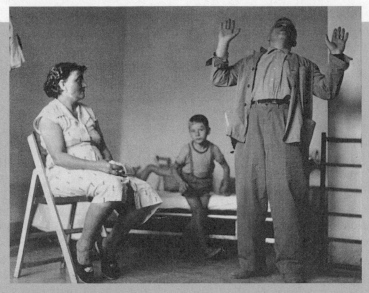

Fig. 4 Ernesto De Martino was one of the few anthropologists working in Italy to use photographs as a form of ethnographic documentation, notably in *La terra del rimorso* (1961), in which he recorded the practices associated with *tarantismo* in Puglia. Here he is seen in 1959 with a woman affected by a tarantula bite. His exuberant gestures and the woman's placid attitude blur the distinction between observer and observed. This was itself a key element in De Martino's anthropological fieldwork: 'One must go from house to house, seek out those who are most reluctant, who are sometimes the best [informants]: women, who cannot face the social risks of public meetings, and those who live in the countryside, the elderly, the sick. But above all one must find the path of a simple human relationship, and enter that exact point where one can be with them, in the same history.'

(1980: 197–202). The role of rescuing the threatened self in a crisis was attributed by De Martino to other popular ritual practices, like magic (De Martino 1959), and the dance of the 'tarantula cult' in Puglia (1961). In the latter, men and women are cured of recurrent spells of possession ('dance'), triggered by the (imagined) 'bite' of a mythical spider, associated with St Paul. The 'dance' is neither a physiological reaction to spider bites, nor a psychological disorder, but a culturally specific, symbolically coherent response to personal crises, particularly those arising from the onset of puberty and the control of erotic desire in the context of Southern peasant society's regulation of sexuality and marriage. In linking the personal/ psychological and the collective/social self, De Martino was influenced by Gramscian Marxism, but also by existentialism, psychoanalysis, and Crocean idealism (see Tullio-Altan 1983: 120; cf. Clemente *et al.* 1976: 22). Like Gramsci, De Martino saw 'folklore' as a rudimentary form of class consciousness, to be transcended as the masses become emancipated (see Cases 1973: p. xxviii). De Martino, however, saw this mainly as a spiritual process, and only marginally addressed its socio-economic dimension (see Cases 1973: p. xli; Clemente *et al.* 1976: 28).

The socio-economic context of 'subaltern' cultural forms was instead central to the work of folklorists in the 1960s and 1970s. The failure of the 1950s peasant revolts and ensuing mass migration from the South during the 'economic miracle' (see Ginsborg 1990: 310 ff.) focused the debate about popular culture among left-wing intellectuals on the danger of 'cultural homogenization' in consumer society (e.g. Pasolini 1975). Scholars began to conduct folklore studies in urban as well as in rural locales. So Lucio Lombardi Satriani studied the occurrence of 'archaic' Southern peasant cultural forms in 'modern' socio-economic conditions. For instance, he interpreted the enduring relevance in the South of complex funerary rituals and beliefs as a way of claiming a privileged relationship with death, tabooed by 'official' culture. Appropriated through memory and mediumship (which brought the living and the dead into direct contact), death becomes a foundation of antagonistic identity (Lombardi Satriani and Meligrana 1989). For Lombardi Satriani, however, folklore cannot be considered a priori as oppositional. As a subordinate form in a class-stratified society, it may be turned to the advantage of the dominant. Accordingly, he showed how a popular idiom of localism and social justice was appropriated to conservative ends by local right-wing administrators during the revolt in Reggio Calabria in 1970–1 against the Government's decision to make the rival city of Catanzaro the regional capital (1971, reprinted in Lombardi Satriani 1979*b*). Lombardi Satriani also noted that, following massive outmigration towards Northern Italian and European cities, 'the South is no longer in the South': bearers of folklore are now migrants, factory workers, students and the young (Lombardi Satriani 1979*b*: 66). In a study of university students' protest in Rome and Naples in 1977, Lombardi Satriani suggested that 'youth subculture' more or less consciously retrieved expressive forms and institutions of Southern peasant culture (1979*b*: 26 ff.) in rejecting 'bourgeois' values. Its use of 'peasant' themes may be explained by the fact that many of the students were the children of

Southern emigrants. Their protest exploded as the economic crisis threatened to disappoint their expectations for a better future (see Ginsborg 1990: 358 ff.). So Lombardi Satriani showed how the cultural forms of 'traditional peasant Southern culture' may be appealed to by different social groups in changed socio-economic circumstances. He identified folklore with those forms, however, and held their content to be stable.

This contrasts with Cirese's mainly theoretical contribution, which argues that a phenomenon is not 'popular' because of its origins or content but because of the social stratum it is associated with and its position in relation to other socially connoted cultural facts (Cirese 1978: 15). The object of folklore studies must be cultural forms associated with all 'subaltern' strata (1978: 13–14). Those forms may be imposed by dominant strata, but the subaltern may also manipulate and subvert them, and formulate autonomous ones, in response to their concrete conditions of existence (1978: 23). Cirese's theory is illustrated by Lanternari's work on the revival of 'traditional' festivals, music, and religious practices in Italy in the 1960s (Lanternari 1976). He indicated that 'archaic peasant' cultural forms, from 'folk' dress and music to magic and charismatic religion, may become commodities consumed by bourgeois audiences, and/or be appropriated by youth and new religious movements, symptoms of a bourgeoisie in crisis seeking 'self-identification and self-determination' by drawing on 'pre-bourgeois' themes and symbols (see also Lombardi Satriani 1974). Popular protest, meanwhile, may be expressed through new cultural forms, consciously opposed to bourgeois ones (Lanternari 1976). In the 1960s and 1970s, the latter idea also inspired folk singers and research groups (like the Istituto De Martino and Roberto Leydi's group in Milan, and the Folkstudio in Palermo), to record and perform protest songs and popular theatre (see Cusumano 1981: 261–2; Clemente *et al.* 1985: 231–2). These initiatives saw 'folklore' as the culture of all subaltern classes, not just of Southern peasants. Since the 1970s, however, the focus of folklore studies has largely shifted back to the rural South (e.g. Bianco and Del Ninno 1981; Lanternari 1984). Folklorists continue to use a simplified representation of socio-cultural stratification (e.g. juxtaposing 'subaltern' and 'hegemonic'), and the notion of 'popular culture' has not been redefined to tackle central aspects of contemporary Italian culture like television, football, or fashion.

The anthropological study of urban, 'bourgeois', and 'modern' culture was initiated earlier by exponents of the second strand of Italian anthropology, *antropologia culturale*. Its roots lay in US anthropology in Southern Italy in the 1950s (Clemente *et al.* 1976: 264). Tullio Tentori, who worked with Friedmann in Matera (see above, p. 54), was among the young Italian scholars who defined the aims of *antropologia culturale* in a 1958 'memorandum'. They advocated the anthropological study of complex societies, including Italy. Influenced by North American anthropology's interest in 'culture' and by Croce's focus on subjectivity, they set out to study the 'value orientations' developed as individuals live in changing social and economic contexts (see Tentori 1979: 112; Saunders 1984:

453–4). They also called for anthropologists to become involved in the formulation of social policy (see Tentori 1979: 118; Clemente *et al.* 1976: 262; cf. Pasquinelli 1979: 71).

Tentori's published work includes 'community' studies of Matera and Bologna (Tentori 1971*a*, 1976; Tentori and Guidicini 1972), using ethnography, oral history, and archival data to describe the 'traditional' lifestyles of, respectively, Matera's *galantuomini* (notables), peasants, shepherds, and artisans; and a working-class district of Bologna. In Matera, Tentori considered local representations of social stratification, and emerging class consciousness among the lowest strata. In Bologna, he described the changes in 'community life' caused by industrialization and urban renewal in the late 1960s. In a more ambitious bid to take on the complexity of Italian society, Tentori later conducted broad-ranging surveys of the political attitudes of university students, the position of women in Italy, the Italian family, ideas about food and nutrition in Trentino, and middle-class aspirations (see Tentori 1970*a*, 1970*b*, 1972; Marazzi 1973: 640–1; Saunders 1984: 460).

A comparable focus on 'values', and broad-ranging survey methods also characterize the work of Carlo Tullio-Altan. Following Croce and later De Martino, Tullio-Altan became interested in the role of non-rational forms of knowledge (e.g. mythical and religious) in dealing with individual and collective crises (1992: 143, 207–8). In practice, his research has focused on what he sees as the contemporary 'crisis' of Italian society. In a vast survey of young people's attitudes throughout the 1970s, he found that the majority, mainly from Southern, rural, and less privileged socio-economic backgrounds, upheld 'traditional values', including 'an attitude favourable to authoritarian political and social arrangements', 'ethnocentrism', and 'familism' (see Tullio-Altan 1974; Tullio-Altan and Marradi 1976). For Tullio-Altan, these formed a 'syndrome of socio-cultural backwardness'. They signalled the persistence in contemporary Italy of the familistic values and the localistic structure of medieval communal society, unchallenged by the 'fundamental European cultural revolution' of the Reformation (Tullio-Altan 1986: 239). This syndrome, he argued, underpins the populism and transformism that have characterized Italian political ideologies since national unification (Tullio-Altan 1986). Tullio-Altan's characterization of Italian culture in terms of a syndrome recalls the Anglo-American 'Mediterraneanist' perspective. The influence of North American cultural anthropology (compounded by Crocean idealism) is also evident in his focus on values and ideologies at the expense of socio-economic factors.

A critique of this approach from within *antropologia culturale* is contained in the work of Amalia Signorelli, who follows Marx in arguing that culture is embedded in objective economic, political, and social relations of domination (Signorelli 1977: 99). Signorelli explored the relationship between cultural categories, like familism, and structural factors. In a study of Italian, mainly Southern, migrants who had subsequently returned from abroad, Signorelli found that most had seen migration as the only way of changing their condition. Abroad, facing discrimination by the receiving culture, migrants constructed their self-esteem around strong family ties and their ability to labour and save for the family (1977: 116 ff.). This enabled many to realize an aspiration of 'returning' to build a house in their place of origin. The house symbolized economic well-being, partly countering the sense of dependency on patrons, experienced by returnee migrants looking for a job (1977: 168 ff.). At the same time, investment in real estate prevented the revenues from migration from boosting the local job market (1977: 186 ff.). Thus people's choice to change their lot by migrating ended up perpetuating the objective causes of their 'choice', serving the broader productive system's need for a mobile labour force. While treating migrants as 'cultural subjects' (1977: 91), Signorelli showed the extent to which their perceptions were formulated in the context of, and perpetuated, existing socio-economic structures. In a later study, Signorelli considered patron–client relations in Calabria 'from the clients' point of view', showing that people condemned clientelism even as they relied on it, under the guise of 'friendship' and 'kinship' (Signorelli 1983: 18, 51). People's clear sense of equal rights was offset by their blaming instead the 'local mentality' for the lack of infrastructure and opportunities. Local politicians justified in the same way their bestowing jobs, services, and resources as 'favours'. While ostensibly critical, by seeing 'culture' as an independent factor accounting for local problems, people ended up perpetuating the conditions of clientelism. The cultural context of clientelism and shifting local ideas of collective and individual interests is also explored in the work of Gabriella Gribaudi, based on fieldwork and archival research in Eboli, Campania (see G. Gribaudi 1980, 1990). Gribaudi is one of many Italian historians who draw on anthropology in studying recent social and cultural change, historical memory, and gender (see e.g. Accati 1992; M. Gribaudi 1987; Melograni 1988; Passerini 1984; Portelli 1991; Siebert 1991 and 1994).

The influence of Marxism, and of Gramsci's theory of hegemony, colours policy-related studies of the ideological role of public services by 'cultural anthropologists'. Research has covered attitudes towards schooling among the illiterate, towards municipal housing in Emilia-Romagna, and towards hospital care among doctors and hospitalized heart disease patients (Harrison and Callari Galli 1971; Berardi et al. 1974; Callari Galli et al. 1988). Callari Galli has also looked at schooling in the urban North, as a cultural practice implicitly inculcating class and gender roles (Callari Galli 1975 and 1979; Callari Galli et al. 1989; Callari Galli and Saitta 1990).

In sum, *antropologia culturale* began in the context of the explicitly anti-Communist US-sponsored programme of capitalist modernization of Italy, and was influenced by American cultural anthropology and by Croce to stress cultural over social and economic factors. This is perhaps reflected in research methods relying mainly on questionnaires and surveys rather than 'participant observation', effectively abstracting values and ideas from the social contexts of use (but see Marazzi 1973). More recent work, however, has been influenced by Marxism to seek the socio-economic context of ideas. The study of 'folklore', on the other hand, has been in the post-war period linked to the cultural policy of the PCI, and has had a clear Marxist matrix, stressing the material aspects of human existence.

However, it has also carried the legacy of Gramsci, including his interest in the role of ideas, derived from Croce. So, ultimately, both Croce and, to a lesser extent, Marx have influenced both strands of Italian anthropology, like the rest of twentieth-century Italian 'high' culture (see e.g. Clemente *et al.* 1976: 260–1). This gives those two strands a certain unity, despite the fact that, in the post-war period, they have been associated with opposed ideological camps (see Clemente *et al.* 1976: 259 ff.). This is evidence of the ongoing interplay between the study of culture and national culture itself. The anthropological study of Italian culture by Italians is a distinct, 'national' project in that it has been at once shaped by, and involved in shaping, Italian culture since the nineteenth century (see Gerholm and Hannerz 1982).

Conclusions

Despite some one-way influence and limited cross-fertilization, Anglo-American and Italian anthropology have run separate projects in Italy. Anglo-Americans have focused on small communities, and tended to treat local cultural forms as homogeneous and fixed. By playing down Italy's history and social and cultural complexity, they have studied Italy more as an 'exotic Other' than as part of 'the West' (see Herzfeld 1987). This perspective has only recently been challenged, in the wake of a broader critique of the discourse of 'otherness' in anthropology (see Herzfeld 1987; Piña-Cabral 1989; and e.g. Marcus and Fischer 1986; Rosaldo 1989). One outcome has been an interest in anthropology 'at home', both in the Anglo-American 'core', and in the Southern European and Third World 'periphery' by 'native' researchers (see e.g. Jackson 1987; Strathern 1992; Bouquet 1993; Gerholm and Hannerz 1982). Italians, for their part, have long worked 'at home', at first focusing on subordinate social strata, treated as 'Other' in the context of a process of national unification that resembled colonization, with an élite bringing 'modern' political, economic, social, and cultural forms to 'backward' regions and strata. As those strata became protagonists of the country's transformation, Italian anthropologists realized, sooner than their Anglo-American counterparts, that 'otherness' implies inferiority (see Saunders 1984: 461; De Martino 1941; Lanternari 1974; Remotti 1990). They became interested in how, in a complex society, culture is dynamic, both shaped by and shaping socio-economic stratification. This perspective may be seen to converge with the current Anglo-American interest in the cultural construction of individual and collective selfhood as historical process (e.g. Strathern 1988; Cowan 1990). Together, these two disciplinary traditions suggest an agenda for anthropologists of any nationality working in contemporary Italy: namely, to study how people use cultural forms as they make daily sense of their diverse, often contradictory experiences in a social, political, and economic context in confusing motion. This may help to answer the urgent question of why in Italy these cultural strategies lately appeal with alarming frequency and force to the idea of bounded, internally homogeneous frames of identity from which 'Others' (be they Southerners, African immigrants, women, the handicapped, squatters, or Communists) are to be excluded. The answer to this question ought to be formulated by a discipline of anthropology that, by being open to the sustained cross-fertilization of diverse and equally valid intellectual traditions, challenges the viability of cultural closure in any form.

References

ACCATI, L. (1992), 'Il marito della santa', *Meridiana*, 13: 79–105.

ASAD, T. (1973), *Anthropology and the Colonial Encounter* (New York).

BANFIELD, E. C. (1958), *The Moral Basis of a Backward Society* (Glencoe, Ill.).

BEATTIE, J. (1989), *Other Cultures* (London and New York).

BELMONTE, T. (1979), *The Broken Fountain* (New York and Guildford).

BERARDI, R., CALLARI GALLI, M., CUPPINI, G., and HARRISON, G. (1974), 'Casa dolce casa', *Parametro*, 31, Nov.: 22–30.

BIANCO, C., and DEL NINNO, M. (1981) (eds.), *Festa, antropologia, semiotica* (Florence).

BLOK, A. (1974), *The Mafia of a Sicilian Village* (Oxford).

—— (1981), 'Rams and Billy-Goats: A Key to the Mediterranean Code of Honour', *Man*, NS 16: 427–40.

BOISSEVAIN, J. (1966), 'Patronage in Sicily', *Man*, NS 1: 18–33.

BOLLATI, G. (1983), *L'italiano. Il carattere nazionale come storia e come invenzione* (Turin).

BOUQUET, M. (1993), *Reclaiming English Kinship* (Manchester).

CALLARI GALLI, M. (1975), *Antropologia e educazione* (Florence).

—— (1979), *Il tempo delle donne* (Bologna).

—— and SAITTA, L. R. (1990), *Cultura e infanzia* (Modena).

—— COLLIVA, C., and PAZZAGLI, I. (1989) (eds.), *Il rumore silenzioso* (Bologna).

—— DALLA VOLTA, S., HARRISON, G., and TERRANOVA, F. (1988) (eds.), *Scegliendo la qualità* (Milan).

CAPLAN, P. (1987) (ed.), *The Cultural Construction of Sexuality* (London and New York).

CARPI, U. (1981), 'Egemonia moderata e intellettuali nel Risorgimento', in Vivanti (1981), 431–71.

CARRITHERS, M. (1992), *Why Humans Have Cultures* (Oxford).

CASES, C. (1973), 'Introduction', in De Martino (1973), pp. vii–xlviii.

CHRISTIAN, W. (1984), 'Religious Apparitions and the Cold War in Southern Europe', in Wolf (1984), 239–66.

CIRESE, A. M. (1958), *La poesia popolare* (Palermo).

—— (1976), *Intellettuali, folklore e istinto di classe* (Turin).

—— (1978), *Cultura egemonica e culture subalterne* (Palermo).

—— (1985), 'Sulla storiografia demo-etno-antropologica italiana', in Clemente *et al.* (1985), pp. ix–xvi.

CLEMENTE, P., MEONI, M. L., and SQUILLACCIOTTI, P. (1976) (eds.), *Il dibattito sul folklore in Italia* (Milan).

—— LEONE, A. R., PUCCINI, S., ROSSETTI, C., and SOLINAS, P. (1985), *L'antropologia italiana. Un secolo di storia* (Bari).

COCCHIARA, G. (1981), *Storia del folklore in Italia* (Palermo).

COLE, J. W. (1977), 'Anthropology Comes Part-Way Home: Community Studies in Europe', *Annual Review of Anthropology*, 6: 349–78.

—— and WOLF, E. R. (1974), *The Hidden Frontier* (New York and London).

COLLIER, J., and YANGISAKO, S. J. (1987) (eds.), *Gender and Kinship* (Stanford, Calif.).

Counihan, C. M. (1985), 'Transvestism and Gender in a Sardinian Carnival', *Anthropology*, 9/1–2: 11–4.

Cowan, J. K. (1990), *Dance and the Body Politic in Northern Greece* (Princeton).

Cusumano, A. (1981), 'Post-fazione', in Cocchiara (1981), 249–63.

Davis, J. (1969), 'Honour and Politics in Pisticci', *Proceedings of the Royal Anthropological Institute*.

—— (1973), *Land and Family in Pisticci* (London and New York).

—— (1977), *People of the Mediterranean* (London, Henley, and Boston).

DE Grazia, V. (1981), *The Culture of Consent: Mass Organization of Leisure in Fascist Italy* (Cambridge).

De Martino, E. (1941), *Naturalismo e storicismo nell'etnologia* (Bari).

—— (1951), 'Il Folklore progressivo', *L'Unità*, 28 June.

—— (1958), *Morte e pianto rituale nel mondo antico* (Turin).

—— (1959), *La terra del rimorso* (Milan).

—— (1961), *Sud e magia* (Milan).

—— (1973), *Il mondo magico* (Turin).

—— (1980), *Furore, simbolo, valore* (Milan).

Diamond, S. (1980) (ed.), *Anthropology: Ancestors and Heirs* (The Hague).

Douglass, W. A. (1980), 'The South Italian Family: A Critique', *Journal of Family History*, 5: 338–59.

—— (1991), 'The Joint Family in Eighteenth-Century Southern Italian Society', in Kertzer and Saller (1991), 286–303.

Edwards, P. (1967) (ed.), *The Encyclopedia of Philosophy* (London and New York).

Fabian, J. (1983), *Time and the Other: How Anthropology Makes its Object* (New York).

Femia, J. V. (1981), *Gramsci's Political Thought* (Oxford).

Filippucci, P. (1992), 'Presenting the Past in Bassano', Ph.D. thesis (Cambridge).

Galt, A. H. (1991*a*), *Far from the Church Bells* (Cambridge).

—— (1991*b*), 'Marital Property in an Apulian Town during the Eighteenth and Early Nineteenth Centuries', in Kertzer and Saller (1991), 304–20.

Gellner, E. (1983), *Nations and Nationalism* (Oxford).

—— and Waterbury, J. (1977) (eds.), *Patrons and Clients* (London).

Gerholm, T., and Hannerz, U. (1982), 'Introduction: The Shaping of National Anthropologies', *Ethnos*, 1: 5–35.

Gilmore, D. D. (1987) (ed.), *Honour, Shame and the Unity of the Mediterranean* (Washington).

Ginsborg, P. (1990), *A History of Contemporary Italy: Society and Politics 1943–1988* (London).

Giovannini, M. J. (1981), 'Woman: A Dominant Symbol within the Cultural System of a Sicilian Town', *Man*, NS 16: 408–26.

Goddard, V. (1987), 'Honour and Shame: The Control of Women's Sexuality and Group Identity in Naples', in Caplan (1987), 166–92.

Gramsci, A. (1985), *Selections from Cultural Writings*, ed. D. Forgacs and G. Nowell Smith (London).

Gribaudi, G. (1980), *Mediatori* (Turin).

—— (1990), *A Eboli* (Padua).

Gribaudi, M. (1987), *Mondo operaio e mito operaio* (Turin).

Grillo, R. D. (1980), '*Nation*' and '*State*' in Europe (London).

Grottanelli, V. L. (1980), 'Cultural Anthropology Reconsidered', in Diamond (1980), 221–42.

Harrison, G., and Callari Galli, M. (1971), *Né leggere né scrivere* (Milan).

Herzfeld, M. (1987), *Anthropology through the Looking Glass* (Cambridge).

Hobsbawm, E. (1983), 'Introduction: Inventing Traditions', in E. Hobsbawm and T. Ranger (eds.), *The Invention of Tradition* (Cambridge).

Holmes, D. R. (1989), *Cultural Disenchantments* (Princeton).

Jackson, A. (1987), *Anthropology at Home* (London).

Joll, J. (1977), *Gramsci* (Glasgow).

KENNY, M., and KERTZER, D.I. (1983) (eds.), *Urban Life in Mediterranean Europe* (Urbana, Ill., Chicago, and London).

KERTZER, D. I. (1980), *Comrades and Christians* (Cambridge).

—— (1983), 'Urban Research in Italy', in Kenny and Kertzer (1983): 53–75.

—— (1984), *Family Life in Central Italy* (New Brunswick, NJ).

—— and SALLER, P. (1991) (eds.), *The Family in Italy* (New Haven and London).

KUPER, A. (1983), *Anthropology and Anthropologists* (London).

—— (1988), *The Invention of Primitive Society* (London).

LANTERNARI, N. (1974), *Antropologia e imperialismo* (Turin).

—— (1976), *Folklore e dinamica culturale* (Naples).

—— (1984), *Preistoria e folklore: tradizioni etnografiche e religiose della Sardegna* (Sassari).

LEVI, C. (1945), *Cristo si è fermato a Eboli* (Turin).

LOMBARDI SATRIANI, L. (1974), *Folklore e profitto* (Florence).

—— (1979*a*), 'Realtà meridionale e conoscenza demologica: linee per una storia degli studi demologici dagli anni post-unitari alla conquista della Libia', *Problemi del Socialismo*, 16: 41–66.

—— (1979*b*), *Rivolta e strumentalizzazione* (Milan).

—— and MELIGRANA, M. (1989), *Il ponte di S. Giacomo: l'ideologia della morte nella società contadina del sud* (Palermo).

LOSPINOSO, M. (1975–6), 'Etnologia e fascismo: il caso del convegno "Volta"', *La Critica Sociologica*, winter, 36: 147–64.

MAHER, V. (1987), 'Sewing the Seams of Society: Dressmakers and Seamstresses in Turin between the Wars', in Collier and Yanagisako (1987), 132–59.

MANOUKIAN, A. (1988), 'La famiglia dei contadini', in Melograni (1988), 3–60.

MARAZZI, A. (1973), 'La ricerca antropologica sul campo in Italia: alcuni dati e alcune considerazioni', *Rassegna Italiana di Sociologia*, 2: 625–42.

MARCUS, G. E. (1983) (ed.), *Elites: Ethnographic Issues* (Albuquerque, N. Mex.).

—— and FISCHER, M. M. J. (1986) (eds.), *Anthropology as Cultural Critique* (Chicago and London).

MELOGRANI, P. (1988) (ed.), *La famiglia italiana* (Bari).

PASOLINI, P. P. (1975), *Scritti corsari* (Milan).

PASQUINELLI, C. (1977), *Antropologia culturale e questione meridionale* (Florence).

—— (1979), 'Simmetrie tra antropologia culturale e marxismo', *Problemi del Socialismo*, 16: 47–76.

PASSERINI, L. (1984), *Fascism in Popular Memory: The Cultural Experience of the Turin Working Class*, trans. J. Bloomfield and R. Lumley (Cambridge, 1987).

PERISTIANY, J. G. (1965), *Honour and Shame* (London).

—— (1976), *Mediterranean Family Structures* (Cambridge).

PIÑA-CABRAL, J. DE (1989), 'The Mediterranean as a Category of Regional Comparison: A Critical View', *Current Anthropology*, 30/3: 399–406.

PITKIN, D. S. (1985), *The House that Giacomo Built* (Cambridge).

POPPI, C. (1983), 'We are Mountain People', Ph.D. thesis (Cambridge).

PORTELLI, S. (1991), *The Death of Luigi Trastulli and Other Stories* (New York).

PRATT, J. C. (1973), 'Friends, Brothers and Comrades', Ph.D. thesis (Sussex).

—— (1980), 'A Sense of Place', in Grillo (1980), 31–43.

—— (1984), 'Christian Democratic Ideology in the Cold-War Period', in Wolf (1984), 213–37.

—— (1986), *The Walled City* (Göttingen).

PUCCINI, S., and SQUILLACCIOTTI, M. (1979), 'Per una ricostruzione critico-bibliografica degli studi demo-etno-antropologici nel periodo tra le due guerre', *Problemi del Socialismo*, 16: 69–93.

REMOTTI, F. (1990), *Noi, primitivi* (Turin).

ROSALDO, R. (1989), *Culture and Truth* (Boston).

SALINARI, C., and RICCI, C. (1980), *Storia della letteratura italiana*, iii (Bari).

SAUNDERS, G. R. (1984), 'Contemporary Italian Cultural Anthropology', *Annual Review of Anthropology*, 13: 447–66.

SCHMIDT, S. W. *et al.* (1977) (eds.), *Friends, Followers and Factions* (Berkeley).

SCHNEIDER, J. (1971), 'Of Vigilance and Virgins', *Ethnology*, 9/1: 1–24.

—— and SCHNEIDER, P. (1976), *Culture and Political Economy in Western Sicily* (New York, San Francisco, and London).

———— (1983), 'The Reproduction of the Ruling Class in Latifundist Sicily', in Marcus (1983), 141–68.

———— and HANSEN, E. (1977), 'The Role of Elite and Non-Corporate Groups in the European Mediterranean', in Schmidt *et al.* (1977), 467–81.

SIEBERT, R. (1991), *E' femmina però è bella* (Turin).

—— (1994), *La donna, la mafia* (Milan).

SIGNORELLI, A. (1977), *Scelte senza potere. Il ritorno degli emigrati nelle zone dell'esodo* (Rome).

—— (1983), *Chi può e chi aspetta* (Naples).

SILVERMAN, S. (1968), 'Agricultural Organisation and Social Structure, and Values in Italy: Amoral Familism Reconsidered', *American Anthropologist*, 70: 1–20.

—— (1975), *The Three Bells of Civilization* (New York and London).

—— (1977a), 'Patronage as Myth', in Gellner and Waterbury (1977), 7–19.

—— (1977b), 'Patronage and Community–Nation Relationships in Central Italy', in Schmidt *et al.* (eds.), 293–304.

SINGER, M. (1968), 'The Concept of Culture', *International Encyclopedia of the Social Sciences* (no place given).

SMITH, A. D. (1981), *The Ethnic Revival* (Cambridge).

STOCKING, G. W. (1982), 'Afterword: a View from the Center', *Ethnos*, 1–2: 172–86.

STRATHERN, M. (1988), *The Gender of the Gift* (Berkeley).

—— (1992), *After Nature* (Cambridge).

TENTORI, T. (1970a), 'Atteggiamenti degli studenti alla vigilia dell'occupazione dell'Università a Roma', *Rivista di Sociologia*, 8: 109–38.

—— (1970b), *La donna in Italia* (Rome).

—— (1971a), 'Il sistema di vita della comunità materana', in Tentori (1971), 99–185.

—— (1971), *Scritti antropologici* (Rome).

—— (1972), *La famiglia italiana* (Rome).

—— (1976), 'Social Classes and Family in a Southern Italian Town: Matera', in Peristiany (1976), 273–86.

—— (1979), 'Note e memorie per una discussione sulla impostazione della antropologia culturale in Italia negli anni '50', *Problemi del Socialismo*, 16: 95–122.

—— (1990) (ed.), *Antropologia delle società complesse* (Rome).

—— and GUIDICINI, P. (1972), *Borgo, quartiere, città* (Milan).

TULLIO-ALTAN, C. (1974), *I valori difficili* (Milan).

—— (1983), *Antropologia* (Milan).

—— (1986), *La nostra Italia* (Milan).

—— (1992), *Un processo di pensiero* (Milan).

—— and MARRADI, A. (1976), *Valori, classi sociali e scelte politiche* (Milan).

—— and SCARTEZZINI, R. (1992) (eds.), *Una modernizzazione difficile* (Naples).

TYLOR, E. B. (1871), *Primitive Culture* (London).

VIVANTI, C. (1981) (ed.), *Storia d'Italia. Annali 4. Intellettuali e potere* (Turin).

WEBER, M. (1923), *General Economic History* (London).

WEINGROD, A. (1977), 'Patrons, Patronage and Political Parties', in Schmidt *et al.* (1977), 323–37.

WHITE, C. (1980), *Patrons and Partisans* (Cambridge).

WOLF, E. R. (1982), *Europe and the People without History* (Berkeley).

—— (1984) (ed.), *Religion, Power and Protest in Local Communities* (The Hague).

YANAGISAKO, S. J. (1991), 'Capital and Gendered Interest in Italian Family Firms', in Kertzer and Saller (1991), 321–39.

4

Images of the South

GABRIELLA
GRIBAUDI

THE Southern question (*questione meridionale*) continues to be discussed as though one were dealing with clearly defined objects rather than a set of controversial historical constructions (Cafagna 1994). This chapter starts from the conviction that the objects can only be understood if we analyse the processes through which their image has been created, processes in which the dialogue between North and South has played a crucial part. The particular conditions in which this dialogue has been conducted have reflected the imbalance between the two parties involved. It may seem obvious that the idea and therefore the identity of the South of Italy (*Sud, Mezzogiorno, Meridione*) has been moulded through its dialogue with the North, yet the various works which have been published on this subject rarely take this factor into consideration.

An identity is the product of a comparison. Whenever one imagines an 'Other', one starts with categories and images which reflect the culture of the society in which one was born and lives, and one translates that Other into familiar terms. North and South have interpreted each other through scientific paradigms and pre-existing stereotypes; they have exchanged images and interpretations, fashioning their respective identities by reflecting one another. If one ignores this element, these interactive mechanisms which have created the images, and fails to place them in their cultural and historical context, one will understand little about the questions relating to the history of the South. The South is much more than a geographical area. It is a metaphor which refers to an imaginary and mythical entity, associated with both hell and paradise: it is a place of the soul and an emblem of the evil which occurs everywhere, but which in Italy has been embodied in just one part of the nation's territory, becoming one of the myths on which the nation has been built.

In 1860, the lands belonging to the Kingdom of the Two Sicilies which became part of the unified nation were in a weak position and were obliged to measure themselves against cultural and economic models based on profoundly different societies. This argument could be applied to the whole of Italy (Agnew 1994), but it has particular relevance in explaining the situation of the *Mezzogiorno*. The region's identity was in fact based on negation, on what it lacked in relation to the ideal model: a bourgeoisie, an entrepreneurial class, middle strata, individualism, group solidarity. The cultural features of Southern Italy had great difficulty in obtaining any positive recognition in the founding myths of the Italian nation, apart from abstract references to its Greek and Roman past. Its history was treated as a dark age, whose worst expression was to be found in its rule by the Spanish viceroys and the Bourbons. Meanwhile, nineteenth-century Italy sought the roots of a possible national identity in the history of the medieval city-states and the Renaissance, with its art, its great men, and the Italian (Tuscan) language. Naturally, the South was excluded from this history and the models to which it appealed. The classical ideal expressed by the Florence of the Medici constituted a positive ideal for the nation and one which every community in Italy had to measure up to. This attitude was found in *Napoli a occhio nudo* by the Tuscan writer Renato Fucini, who belonged to the circle of Pasquale Villari, a prominent writer on the South (see Fucini 1878), and in the concluding remarks of Benedetto Croce's *Storia del Regno di Napoli* (1925)—in many ways a reassessment of the history of the South:

It has been said that 'Italy ends at the Garigliano', and such is the opinion of travellers and tourists coming from the northern and central regions, who expect to find great natural beauties and ruins of Greek and Roman antiquity but none of the glorious monuments of Italian history or the works of a famous school of art such as they have admired elsewhere. Beside the masterpieces of Tuscan, Lombard, and Venetian artists that were created or brought here by chance, they find, for the most part, secondary works, ostentatious rather than of intrinsic worth. Historians of classical Italian literature, also, are little concerned with southern Italy, which boasts of no Dante, Machiavelli or Ariosto. The South is almost extraneous to the second wave of civilization (the first being that of ancient Rome) which radiated from the Italian peninsula between the beginning of the communes and the height of the Renaissance. (Croce 1925: 232)

It is also significant that after 1946 the South was excluded from the myth on which the Italian Republic was founded, that of the 'resistance'. While in the North a part of the population had fought in 1943–5 against German domination and what remained of Italian Fascism, the South had been subjected to Allied

Fig. 5 'Views' of southern Italy became popular in the late nineteenth century as collectables for a middle-class public who felt competent to appreciate their 'picturesque' quality, composition, and technique. This engraving by Ballerini of a *cantina* (basement) in Naples, which originally accompanied an article by Carlo Del Balzo in the weekly magazine *L'Illustrazione Italiana* (published by Treves, Milan), condenses various stereotypes of the genre into a single image: the flasks of wine, the *maccheroni* eaten with the fingers, the guitar, the dark seductive young women, the nursing mother, the barefoot children and general atmosphere of idleness (*dolce far niente*). Other recurrent Neapolitan figures were street vendors, beggars (*lazzaroni*), and musical story-tellers (*cantastorie*). These images powerfully reinforced existing assumptions about the quaintness, backwardness, and immobility of southern Italy.

occupation. Thus once again the citizens of the South found themselves obliged after the war to celebrate and mythologize an event—the resistance—in which they had not been able to participate. The continued support for monarchism in the South—the extreme defence of the nation's identity through the sovereign— and the subsequent powerful attachment to local myths and identities can perhaps be explained by the inability to identify with events and actions which could not be experienced at first hand.

Unification and the Late Nineteenth Century

When the Piedmontese administrators went south, they carried these images with them. The South was a happy land, kissed by the gods, favoured by the climate and the fruitfulness of the soil. Yet violence and anarchy reigned there because of the former rulers, the Bourbons. The good, rationalizing, honest Piedmontese administration was going to solve everything. Once the tumour of Bourbon corruption had been cut out, everything would return to the gentle and happy state promised by the natural environment. When the Piedmontese realized that the Southerners were rebelling against them and rejecting them, they changed their tune and reverted to the idea of a paradise inhabited by devils: the South as a happy land rendered unhappy by men. Civilization had to be imposed on the inhabitants even at gunpoint, otherwise the tumour represented by the Southerners' behaviour would grow and infect the rest of the nation (Moe 1992). The conflict between the two parts of the country increased in the early years after Unification. The ruling class of the North showed a total lack of understanding of the culture and institutions of the South. There was also the problem of obtaining popular legitimation for the new political system, which added to existing and long-standing problems like brigandage, dealt with by military occupation. In this case, as Moe has shown, the image of the Southerners as devils was particularly suited to the measures taken against them. It was in this period that the theoretical construction of Italian dualism originated. A series of images settled in national public opinion. Photographs of brigands in prison or hanging from the scaffold, and tales of their actual or alleged barbarity, circulated around the country, and lent credibility to the demonic image of the *Mezzogiorno*. This image was soon to receive a further decisive confirmation in the form of positivist racism.

The coming to power of the Left in 1876 marked the entry of the Southern ruling classes into national political life. However, politics came to be dominated not by the élites who had played a leading role in the Risorgimento but by groups who defended narrow local interests and used local factions to support this or that party. At this point, a number of Southern intellectuals, who had placed their hopes in intervention from outside and in the adoption of rational models, began criticizing both the government, for its continuing failure the tackle the most serious problems of the South, and Southern society itself, which in their eyes was proving incapable of pursuing modern and dynamic objectives. It was from these reflections that *meridionalismo*—the body of expertise on the Southern question—began to develop.

The early *meridionalisti*—Pasquale Villari, Giustino Fortunato, Leopoldo Franchetti, and Sidney Sonnino—were all positivists and ardent supporters of the unitary state. They were above all tireless analysts of the *Mezzogiorno*—they wanted to understand it and make others understand it, without glossing over anything. They thought that the ruling class of a state which had the extremely difficult task of bringing together such heterogeneous regions had to be in full possession of the facts, so that it could intervene in an equitable and rational manner. Their intention was to combat ignorance about the South and offer a true image in its place.

Their books were mainly based on enquiries carried out in the field. They yielded a body of empirical and sociological information which constitutes the richest collection of social analysis carried out in Italy in the late nineteenth and early twentieth century. Of course, it was a positivist myth to believe that once truth emerged from the abyss of ignorance it would inexorably win out. This myth was to be shattered a thousand times over when it came up against political expediencies. Yet these intellectuals were struggling against some of the most negative features of Italian humanistic culture—unstructured reasoning, the discussion of grand principles without reference to everyday realities, taking decisions without knowing the relevant facts (see e.g. Villari 1875 on the civil service, the army, and the reason for its defeat in 1866). They placed the utmost faith in the state's institutions; in the debate over the organization of the civil service they supported a centralist model.

According to Fortunato, Sonnino, and Franchetti, the greatest limitations on the Italian South were on the one hand the poverty and ignorance in which the mass of the people were kept, and which made them incapable of defending themselves and asserting their own interest, and on the other the predatory nature of the ruling classes which further contributed to the poverty and ignorance. This led to the other great battle of those who took up the cause of the South: the battle over the social question, which aimed to explain the reasons for the disturbances and rebellions, to open the eyes of those in government to the real condition of the population, and to force them to adopt a more responsible and enlightened attitude. It was an era of considerable social enquiry, to which Pasquale Villari's circle in Florence gave a decisive contribution. Naturally they focused on the most dramatic problems: urban poverty, the peasantry working on large estates, and Mafia violence. The images were vividly presented and marked by stark contrasts, for instance between urban poor and élites, peasants and landlords.

The denunciatory tone naturally accentuated the contrasts and obscured the intermediate features. Other factors contributed to the rigid perception of class structure in the South. The campaign against the protectionist policy for wheat production led people to overestimate the power and the role of the large landowners, and those who knew little about the question were led to think of the

South as one vast wheat-growing estate. Moreover, the scientific paradigms of the nineteenth century were unable to grasp the phenomena of social fluidity and mobility. All this contributed to the constructon of a rigid and dichotomized image of the social and economic reality of the *Mezzogiorno*.

The idea that Southern society was incapable of self-rule and that the endemic corruption could only be corrected through a powerful initiative from central government is the other great theme that was filtered by the tradition of nineteenth-century *meridionalismo* and has survived into the present. It is interesting to note that a few *meridionalisti* dissented from this view and put forward alternative interpretations and solutions. Napoleone Colajanni, for example, argued that it was precisely the supremacy of the bureaucracy, an uncontrolled and uncontrollable power, which generated corruption. He criticized what he defined as 'fiscal inequality', and claimed it was caused by the state, which 'because of its absurdly centralized organization, acts on the periphery like a suction pump, which only returns a tiny part of what it absorbs' (Colajanni 1894: 42). Gaetano Salvemini, a federalist (a member of the Socialist Party, then after the First World War of the liberal-socialist Partito d'Azione) noted for his attacks on the Giolitti government and his savage descriptions of the Southern élites, was convinced that the political control exercised by the prefects over local government and the centralization of the civil service were the fundamental cause of corruption. Similar positions were adopted shortly afterwards by Luigi Sturzo (a Sicilian priest and Catholic political activist, founder in 1919 of the Partito Popolare Italiano) and Guido Dorso (like Salvemini, an activist in the Partito d'Azione), but they had little influence on political debate and were destined to be ignored. Even now, such opinions have difficulty in gaining currency in the South.

At the same time that *meridionalismo* was fighting its battle, positivist theories on race were being extensively developed. Alfredo Niceforo, Paolo Orano, and others may now seem very distant, but reading them a hundred years on one realizes that their ghosts live on in certain expressions and arguments used today. It has never been sufficiently stressed how late nineteenth-century racism profoundly influenced 'common-sense' social categories and how it continually resurfaces in new forms. Common opinion (and, unfortunately, some academic circles too) still attributes the same characteristics to Northerners and Southerners as Niceforo, who used the then current terms 'Aryans' (*Ari*) and Mediterraneans. The dark Mediterraneans are individualists and in consequence their society is 'fragmented' or 'disaggregated'. The peoples of the North, on the other hand, have collective consciousness and therefore social organization, institutions, and discipline. Neapolitans, dissolute and weak by nature, are a 'popolo-donna', a female people, while the others are 'popoli uomini' (Niceforo 1898: 293).

In their context these statements might appear amusing but if one thinks of passages one has read, conversations heard in the street, on television or even in learned discussions of the *Mezzogiorno*, one cannot fail to notice the similarities. I remember a discussion in 1992 in *La Repubblica* about the fact that in the North people follow the dictates of the father and in the South the dictates of the mother: the male principle and the female principle, very much like Niceforo's male/female distinction. We shall meet these stereotypes again below in relation to the concept of 'amoral familism'.

Racist positivism had a powerful resonance in the Socialist Party. Its arguments were used to explain, for example, the party's limited success in the South: the causes were not its own political errors but the congenital inability of Southerners to accept the discipline of an organization and their anarchic individualism, which made them disorderly, liable to rebellion, and unsuited to long-term political preparation (Niceforo 1901). Filippo Turati, leader of the reformist wing of the Socialist Party, described what he saw as the struggle characterizing Italy:

A struggle between the feudal Middle Ages, which dominates the South and whose tentacles reach out into the entire Italian countryside, and the beginnings of the modern age and industrialization which are dawning in the more civilized and cultured districts, especially in the North. Between these two civilizations, or rather, between an incipient civilization and that putrid barbarity, the battle lines are now drawn. There are two nations in the nation, two Italies in Italy, each one fighting for supremacy. (Turati 1895: 79)

Salvemini left the Socialist Party because of its widespread anti-Southernism, while Colajanni rebutted one by one the arguments of the racists and the Socialists.

From 1900 to 1945

A distinctive role in the history of the Southern question was played by Francesco Saverio Nitti, who was of the same generation as Salvemini and Colajanni, and belonged to more or less the same part of the political spectrum, that of Radicalism. He was perhaps the figure who most vigorously defended the South's history and interests. His theory was that Italian unification had been created at the South's expense, by squandering its immense financial resources and thus preventing it from developing independently through its own energies (Nitti 1958). He was convinced that the state had to intervene actively with an industrial policy which would correct the imbalance which had been created. He was the only one of the *meridionalisti* to address the question of industrialization and the only one to hold important government posts (Barbagallo 1984).

Around Nitti gathered a group of specialists—engineers, agronomists, financial experts—of considerable standing and of radical-socialist inspiration, many of them Southerners. Together they played a crucial role in government economic policy in the first two decades of the twentieth century. They believed the state had to intervene directly in favour of the industrialization of the South itself, in order to compensate for the tendency in the economy to channel resources and capital towards the North. Very little has been said about this group of specialists, and the tradition of *meridionalismo* has not taken up their cause with much vigour. There are many reasons for this, but the distortion and debasement of their ideas and efforts by Fascism and later the Christian Democrats certainly played a part. The Fascist regime carried through some of the land reclamation projects they had devised (specifically for the purpose of generating hydroelectric energy), but instead of using them for a radical transformation of the South's industrial infrastructure, it made them part of its 'ruralization' or back-to-the-land policy, thus depriving them of all their revolutionary content (Barone 1986). In the period since 1950 their ideas became the symbol of a system of political patronage which made the South even more dramatically dependent on the North than before.

There were, however, some fundamental problems with the reformers' theoretical and practical framework itself. They were guided by an Enlightenment notion, which had already inspired other Southern reformers, that the state could and should act for the good of its subjects, by interpreting progressive reason and imposing it on a blind and unruly population which was incapable of pursuing its own best interests. Behind this view lay a deep mistrust of the local ruling class, which they believed had to be circumvented. They were unable to identify anyone at local level who could mediate and interpret their plans for innovation.

During this period, Dorso, Sturzo, and Salvemini were looking at the problem of the ruling classes and Southern pride. The 'parasitic oligarchies of the North' (Dorso 1924: 217) had subjugated the Southern ruling classes, dragging them down to the condition of lazy and corrupt agrarian rentiers. Dorso and Salvemini were both convinced that the South could only reassert itself by being autonomous from central government, and that it was the duty of political activists, 'an élite which may be small but which had clear ideas and an unrelentingly critical role' (Dorso 1924: 35), to make sure that the Southern upper and middle classes who were wavering between reaction and progress swung towards the latter. These classes had the extremely important historical task of completing the 'unfinished revolution of the Risorgimento' and thus of bringing about a real unification of the country, one which involved the mass of the people. But this could only be achieved after a phase of vigorous assertion of Southern autonomy. In Dorso's words:

The people of the South need to win self-government, and develop practical solutions which openly reject the requirements of paternalism. . . . Italy has now existed for seventy years, and no one is suggesting it should be broken up; its unity has been considerably reinforced in the recent war, which saw sons of all its regions fighting and dying side by side. . . . But it is precisely these common services and sacrifices which have given the people of the South the right to demand the destruction of the old economic and political order, which the Northern oligarchies have used to create a veritable dictatorship at the South's expense, bleeding it dry economically and failing to educate it politically. (Dorso 1924: 216–18)

Sturzo had expressed himself in a similar vein in 1901: 'Leave us in the South to govern ourselves, plan our own financial policy, spend our own taxes, take responsibility for our own public works, and find our own remedies for our difficulties; . . . we are not schoolchildren, we have no need of the North's concerned protection' (Sturzo 1901).

In the years following the First World War, a period of acute social crisis, when new groups and movements sought access to power at local and national level, the problem of the ruling classes became strikingly evident and demanded a more up-to-date analysis of the class structure. Dorso's and Sturzo's writings were the first to deal with these issues in a non-stereotypical way, and they could have led to a more accurate analysis and a deeper understanding of the social reality had subsequent events not contributed to marginalizing these problems and preventing rigorous scientific analyses. First, the decisive influence of idealist thought on both right- and left-wing Italian culture (Gramsci and his influence on the Communists will be discussed below) was a considerable obstacle to the development of the social sciences. Then, the Fascist regime contributed not only to halting political and economic development, but also to remodelling the image of the South on old stereotypes.

Fascism was born in the North, and initially had difficulty implanting itself in the South, as Dorso pointed out (1924: ch. 6). It was in fact the bloc of Northern moderates who attacked the interventionist policy in the South advocated by Nitti and his followers (Barone 1986). As we have noted, land reclamation for the generation of energy and industrialization was transformed into 'land reclamation for ruralization'. During the economic crisis of the late 1920s, as had happened so often before in the history of the South, capital flowed back to the North, along with control of the economic system. Even the civil service, which after the Italian state's initial 'Piedmontese' phase had been dominated by Southerners, was now 'Northernized', in that the functionaries brought into the state apparatus by the Fascist Party were mainly of Northern origin (Salvati 1992). The South's dependence on the North increased. Whereas in the North the Fascist regime played a partly modernizing role, at least on the ideological level, in the South its message was populist and ruralist. This produced a very serious setback in the relationship of citizens to public institutions and the state. Mussolini's populism was particularly influential on the working classes of Naples, whose culture was rooted in the historical memory of the great Bourbon court (Varvaro 1990). Mussolini became the new sovereign-father, unaware of the misdeeds of his underlings, to whom people appealed for justice (this influence continued to be felt after the Second World War, when the people of Naples supported Achille Lauro, a populist and monarcho-fascist, as mayor). Moreover, the new élites also used the Fascist regime to attack the old liberal élites, justifying their actions in the name of the struggle against patronage and corruption, and depicting Fascism as a system of arbitration and pacification (Gribaudi 1990). The idea that only a strong authoritarian state could eradicate corruption and endemic violence became increasingly entrenched.

The Period of the Republic: Intervention in the South and New Stereotypes

After the crushing defeat of the Partito d'Azione in 1947 and the political splitting of Italy between Catholics and Communists, regional autonomy and federalism completely disappeared from the debate on the *Mezzogiorno*. Instead Nitti's idea of the state's promotional role was taken up and reinterpreted by the Christian Democrats. Intervention by the DC-led governments operated exactly in the manner which had been so fiercely criticized by Sturzo, Dorso, and Salvemini, and it exacerbated the South's dependency on central government intervention. Ideological use was made of some of the images of the *meridionalisti*, which were mixed with the modern doctrines of economic backwardness.

The debate started at the end of the 1940s with the theme of backwardness. It was a theme that had already been present in the Enlightenment and in nineteenth-century conceptions of the South, but it took on a new lease of life in the theories of development of the1940s and 1950s. The international political scene had emerged shaken after the Second World War, with traditional colonialist policies in crisis. The problem for the advanced countries was now that of developing international markets by stimulating internal demand through credible development plans. The USA undertook to give considerable financial aid to the war-torn economies of Europe. In Italy, US influence was of considerable importance in the development of state intervention in the South. It operated at a theoretical level through the example of Roosevelt's 'development areas' and in practice through the consultancy of American experts, on loan first to SVIMEZ (Associazione per lo Sviluppo dell'Industria nel Mezzogiorno) and then to the Cassa per il Mezzogiorno (Gribaudi 1980; Cafiero 1987). The old images of Southern 'lag' were transferred to the new concept of underdevelopment. Economists and sociologists were brought in to define the economic features of the *Mezzogiorno* (analysed through a series of variables such as income, consumer demand, supply of capital) and measure its distance from the model of growth societies. In other words the debate was about how to trigger development in a society which was considered to be still at zero level. The South was once again a land without history, in a state of nature. This ideology chimed to perfection with the interests of a political leadership—the DC and its allies—which founded its legitimacy and power on state intervention (Gribaudi 1980 and 1990).

At the same time the response from the left and centre was weak. It was limited to the slogan of modernization from above and proved incapable, except during the brief period of the peasant struggles of the late 1940s, of evoking or recreating any form of positive identity. The cultural reference point for the Communist Party was Gramsci's essay of 1926 on the Southern question (Gramsci 1971) which, in stark contrast with the autonomist arguments of Dorso and Salvemini, identified a single way forward in the struggle against a nationally 'unitary' capitalist system, namely a solid alliance between Northern workers and Southern peasantry.

In this alliance, however, in line with the Marxist model, it was the working class that was to play the hegemonic role, that of a conscious and modernizing vanguard. For Gramsci, comparing the complicated and uncertain social composition of the South, which he described as 'una grande disgregazione sociale' ('a great social disintegration') with the clear class boundaries of Turin, the only possible salvation lay in accepting the solid leadership of the Northern working class.

It is extremely illuminating on this point to look at the controversies in the late 1940s and early 1950s over the writings of Ernesto De Martino, Carlo Levi, and Rocco Scotellaro (collected in Clemente, Meoni, and Squillacciotti 1976 and in Angelini 1977). A first debate after the appearance of De Martino's *Il mondo magico* in 1948 was followed by another after the posthumous publication of two books by Scotellaro (1954a, 1954b), the young Socialist mayor of Tricarico in Basilicata. It was Carlo Levi who had discovered and supported Scotellaro, and Levi's *Cristo si è fermato a Eboli* was also brought into this second debate. These authors were all very different from one another, but what they had in common was the desire to interpret the popular culture of the South. Their books raise complex problems which I cannot deal with adequately here. The idea of the peasant world as an enclosed and uniform whole is not convincing; nor is the way the peasant from Basilicata or Calabria is made into a symbol of a human condition of pain and oppression, which almost becomes a universal category in the case of De Martino, who looks at superstition and magic in relation to an argument about the crisis of reason. These were, however, important attempts to understand a culture from within, restore a measure of dignity to it, and get inside what we would nowadays call its intrinsic rationality.

Their critics, however, challenged the legitimacy of the whole operation, flatly rejecting any possibility of saving a world they considered an anachronistic relic and an obstacle to the reawakening of the Southern masses. They argued therefore—and on this point Crocean idealists and Marxist historicists were in agreement—that it was a world which had to be rejected without half measures. Today, it is astonishing to read the arguments used by critics of the time who accused De Martino, Scotellaro, and Levi of irrationalism (Croce 1949), of populism (because they had not 'sufficiently acknowledged the special role of the working class' and its vanguard function in relation to the Southern masses: Luporini 1950), of appealing to the popular and the primitive (Fortini 1950), and of diverting the Southern masses from their alliance with the working class (Alicata 1954). The whole debate was off the mark, and it drove the authors themselves, in order to defend themselves from the accusations of obscurantism and conservatism, to look for explanations and propose solutions which were not always in harmony with their own analyses. In the end, their true message was obscured, their images were recuperated within the ideology of backwardness, put on one side, and used to describe an archaic world which needed to be superseded. They thus had the effect of confirming one of the many stereotypes about the *Mezzogiorno*: that of its immobility and exclusion from history.

Shortly afterwards, Edward Banfield's work on 'amoral familism' arrived in Italy from the United States. The concept was used by Banfield to explain the principal characteristic of the society he studied, a poor and isolated village in Basilicata, where he lived with his family for a year. He also proposed it as a more general analytical category with which to interpret the causes of Southern Italy's backwardness as a whole. *The Moral Basis of a Backward Society* appeared in English in 1958 and was translated into Italian in 1961. It made an important contribution to the cultural debate of the 1960s on the question of backwardness and its causes and, like other studies of the time, it attempted to respond to the questions posed by Third World aid policies. Banfield, an anthropologist and political scientist, asked what mechanisms existed for allocating and redistributing resources and power in societies dominated by scarcity, and whether the values attached to these mechanisms were an obstacle to development and modernization.

The term 'amoral familism' designates a form of behaviour directed solely towards the pursuit of the good of the family, understood here in the more restricted sense of parents and children. It implies therefore an endemic inability to act for the common good—what is popularly called a lack of civic consciousness. It is related to societies where the fundamental unit is the nuclear family and more complex forms of social organization are absent. It is often associated with centralized and authoritarian states which discourage the growth of intermediate institutions of government between state and citizens. Its original causes include poverty, authoritarianism in social relations, and above all the absence of the extended patriarchal family, a complex organization capable of producing and disseminating throughout society organizational ability, a sense of collective duty, and the practice of co-operation and solidarity. Such was the picture drawn by Banfield and such were his categories, which produced a heated debate when his book appeared.

It is extremely instructive to retrace the chain of reasoning which led the paradigm of amoral familism to become so firmly established because it provides a close-up view of how a stereotype gets constructed. Amoral familism was stripped of its descriptive and scientific content, and it became used to mean simply the tendency of Southerners to favour the family group; as such it was identified as one of the major causes of clientelism or patronage. In this way, the strength of the family was linked to the persistence of 'tradition', and tradition, in turn, to the extended patriarchal and patrilinear family, dominated by the blood tie. This view was partly the natural effect of a simplistic idea of how family groups developed in the West, an idea which has held sway over sociological and historical analyses for a long time, and has been propagated through the mass media, taking root at all levels of society. This is the idea that in 'traditional' peasant societies the extended and patriarchal family is predominant, and that with the transition to so-called modernity the family becomes nuclear, kinship ties slacken, and choices become individualized. Thus, in this reworking of Banfield's concept, Southern society, already considered 'backward' and 'traditional' according to one powerful stereotype, now also becomes patriarchal. Hence Banfield's argument was unwittingly turned on its head, the prevalence of the patriarchal family was identified as the reason for the strength of kinship, and its pervasiveness in the social and political fabric and the category of amoral familism was misused. The experts in the field are practically the only ones who avoid this mystification.

At the same time, this stereotyped perception has coincided with another, which is closer to Banfield's original idea: that of a fragmented South, lacking valid principles of social organization, dominated by extreme individualism, riven by the war of all against all, incapable of creating permanent group identities—the South of the Mafia and competition over limited resources. This image is all the more tenacious because it has been superimposed on older perceptions: consider the statement by Niceforo quoted above. Thus there is a principle of order (the patriarchal and hierarchical family typified by subordination of its members to the group strategy) and a principle of fragmentation and disorder. Nobody seems to notice the contradiction between these two images.

The history of the concept of amoral familism illustrates well the processes by which the image of the *Mezzogiorno* has been constructed. Both within the South and outside, the image of backwardness has been adopted. Empirical data have been inserted into this framework, and if they have not fitted they have been adapted, reinterpreted, or ignored. An identical phenomenon, the patriarchal family—commonly associated with underdevelopment—goes unnoticed if it relates to a society in the North, whereas it is immediately considered and presented as part of an integrated perspective if it relates to the South. Thus the representations of patriarchal families in the Veneto or Tuscany are neutral facts not worthy of mention, while similar images referring to the South make a powerful impression on public opinion, confirm the mental model, and lead to its perpetuation.

These images are constructed within the North–South dialogue, but Southerners are the first to believe them and appropriate them. In the past, I have examined students of contemporary history at the University of Naples on a text which amongst other things dealt with the family in European history. I tried many times to ask students what type of family they thought was prevalent in Southern society, and they all replied: the patriarchal family. Anyone who has observed and studied Southern society impartially knows very well that the patriarchal family practically does not exist there (if one excludes bourgeois and aristocratic families of the nineteenth and early twentieth century, which were in any case patriarchal throughout Europe at that time). They would also know that women have a 'traditional' power there which is unquestionably greater than that of other Italian women—division of wealth between the sexes according to an equitable method, careful protection of the dowry throughout a woman's life and its direct inheritance by her children, enormous moral and contractual power within the family, and so forth. But the everyday image is filtered or even obscured by a conviction rooted in the naturalness of common opinion. This opinion is confirmed by interactions with a North which is admired and turned into a myth.

When we interpret something 'unknown', we do so by inserting it into the system of meanings of a culture accumulated in a specific historical context and in the course of our own life. Often we select only that information which fits into our pre-established image. In this way, the representation is reinforced in a vicious circle, it becomes a reality inasmuch as the person who is its object accepts it, and if he or she is weaker, ends up taking it on and identifying with it. I have often heard things which I myself experienced as a girl in a large city of the North described as examples of the startling conditions in which women live in the South: sexual taboos, the difficulties of communication between generations, the impossibility of going out in the evening, fear of one's neighbours. These features were probably common to the whole of Italy in a specific generation, but when they are combined with the term *Mezzogiorno* they take on a very different meaning and manage to convince Southerners, who cannot easily make comparisons, that they are living in a unique situation of centuries-old inferiority. Interaction does not automatically mean understanding, as can be seen from the terrifying ethnic conflicts which are devastating part of Eastern Europe. From this point of view, the faith the advocates of *meridionalismo* placed in a peaceful osmosis between cultures based on mutual knowledge has proved to be a great illusion.

Although the conflict between North and South in Italy has not ended in bloodshed, it is developing in a similar manner to that in Eastern Europe. The integration between the two areas is very considerable: one need only consider all the intermarriages between Northerners and Southerners, the assimilation into the Northern cities of the Southern migrants of the 1950s and 1960s, the high number of Southerners amongst the Italian ruling class, not only in the ranks of the discredited state bureaucracy (in Milan, for example, there is a substantial group of company directors who were born in Naples and graduated there). Despite all this, there is currently a marked return to the divisive arguments of the nineteenth century, but with even greater malice. Integration has not diminished the negative stereotype. This new situation has been brought about by political events, vested interests, and problems of national leadership, and the North/South cultural categorization has provided an ideal vehicle for rekindling conflicts and channelling hatreds. The image of the South has entered a perverse circle in which it is increasingly stereotyped.

Further Reading

A good starting-point for an examination of representations of Southern Italy is provided by the classic texts of the *meridionalisti*, notably Giustino Fortunato's *Il Mezzogiorno e lo Stato italiano* (Bari, 1911), Pasquale Villari's *Le lettere meridionali* (Naples, 1979; first published 1875), Guido Dorso's *La rivoluzione meridionale* (Turin, 1977; first published 1924), Francesco Saverio Nitti's *Scritti sulla questione meridionale* (Bari, 1958), Gaetano Salvemini's *Scritti sulla questione meridionale* (Turin, 1955), and Antonio Gramsci's 'Alcuni temi della questione meridionale' (1926), in *La costruzione del Partito Comunista (1923–1926)*, (Turin, 1971), 137–58—for an English translation see Gramsci, *Selections from Political Writings 1921–1926*, trans. and ed. Q. Hoare (London, 1978), 441–62; an abridged version is in D. Forgacs (ed.), *A Gramsci Reader* (London, 1988). For an influential if dated survey of this literature, see M. Salvadori, *Il mito del buongoverno* (Turin, 1960).

Carlo Levi's *Cristo si è fermato a Eboli* (trans. F. Frenaye, *Christ Stopped at Eboli*, 3rd edn., London, 1967) and Edward Banfield's *The Moral Basis of a Backward Society* (Glencoe, Ill., 1958) have both been touchstones. The latter has been much contested and there are much finer anthropological studies such as John Davis's *People of the Mediterranean* (London, 1977) and Anton Blok's *The Mafia of a Sicilian Village* (Oxford, 1974). For the post-1945 period as a whole, see Manlio Rossi Doria's *Scritti sul Mezzogiorno* (Turin, 1982) and Gabriella Gribaudi, *Mediatori* (Turin, 1980). On Naples, see P. A. Allum, *Politics and Society in Postwar Naples* (Cambridge, 1973) and Allum's interview with Giuseppe Galasso, *Intervista sulla storia di Napoli* (Bari, 1978). Studies of communities include Fortunata Piselli's *Parentela e emigrazione* (Turin, 1981) and G. Gribaudi, *A Eboli* (Padua, 1990).

More recent 'revisionist' currents in historiography in Italy have questioned many of the premisses about Southern 'lack of development'; for instance, Carlo Trigilia's *Sviluppo senza autonomia* (Bologna, 1992). An important role has been played by the journal *Meridiana*, launched in 1987, and by its publisher, Donzelli, whose list includes titles such as Piero Bevilacqua's *Breve storia dell'Italia meridionale dall'Ottocento a oggi* (Rome, 1993).

References

AGNEW, J. (1994), 'Italia arretrata, Europa moderna', *Il Mulino*, 351.

ALICATA, M. (1954), 'Il meridionalismo non si può fermare a Eboli', *Cronache meridionali*, 9.

ANGELINI, P. (1977) (ed.), *Dibattito sulla cultura delle classi subalterne* (Rome).

BANFIELD, E. (1958), *The Moral Basis of a Backward Society* (Glencoe, Ill.).

BARBAGALLO, F. (1984), *Francesco Saverio Nitti* (Turin).

BARONE, G. (1986), *Mezzogiorno e modernizzazione* (Turin).

CAFAGNA, L. (1994), *Nord e Sud* (Venice).

CAFIERO, S. (1987), *Tradizione e attualità del meridionalismo* (Bologna).

CLEMENTE, P., MEONI, M. L., and SQUILLACCIOTTI, M. (1976), *Il dibattito sul folklore in Italia* (Milan).

COLAJANNI, N. (1894), *In Sicilia* (Rome).

—— (1898), *Settentrionali e meridionali* (Milan and Palermo).

CREUZÉ DE LESSER, A. (1806), *Voyage en Italie et en Sicile en 1801 et 1802* (Paris).

CROCE, B. (1925), *History of the Kingdom of Naples*, trans. F. Frenaye (Chicago, 1970).

—— (1949), 'Intorno al magismo come età storica', in *Filosofia e storiografia* (Turin).

D'ELIA, C. (1995), *Bonifiche e Stato nel Mezzogiorno 1815–1860* (Naples).

DE MARTINO, E. (1948), *Il mondo magico* (Turin).

DORSO, G. (1924), *La rivoluzione meridionale* (Turin, 1977).

FORTINI, F. (1950), 'Il diavolo sa travestirsi da primitivo', *Paese Sera*, 23 Feb.

FUCINI, R. (1878), *Napoli a occhio nudo* (Turin, 1976).

GALASSO, G. (1969), *Croce, Gramsci e altri scritti* (Milan).

GRAMSCI, A. (1971), 'Alcuni temi della questione meridionale' (1926), in *La costruzione del Partito Comunista* (Turin), 137–58.

GRIBAUDI, G. (1980), *Mediatori. Antropologia del potere democristiano nel mezzogiorno* (Turin).

—— (1990), *A Eboli. Il mondo meridionale in cent'anni di trasformazioni* (Venice).

LEVI, C. (1945), *Cristo si è fermato a Eboli* (Turin).

LUPORINI, C. (1950), 'Intorno alla storia del mondo popolare subalterno', *Società*, 1.

MOE, N. (1922), 'Il Sud dei piemontesi (1860–61)', *Meridiana*, 15.

NICEFORO, A. (1898), *L'Italia barbara contemporanea* (Milan and Palermo).

—— (1901), *Italiani del Nord e Italiani del Sud* (Turin).

NITTI, F. S. (1958), *Scritti sulla questione meridionale* (Bari).

SALVATI, M. (1992), *Il regime e gli impiegati* (Rome and Bari).

SALVEMINI, G. (1900), 'La questione di Napoli', in *Scritti sulla questione meridionale* (Turin, 1955).

SCOTELLARO, R. (1954a), *Contadini del sud* (Bari).

—— (1954b), *E' fatto giorno* (Milan).

STURZO, L. (1901), 'La questione del mezzogiorno', in *La Croce di Costantino*, ed. G. De Rosa (Rome, 1958).

TURATI, F. (1895), 'Tattica elettorale', in *Critica sociale* (Milan, 1959).

VARVARO, P. (1990), *Una città fascista. Potere e società a Napoli* (Palermo).

VILLARI, P. (1875), *Le lettere meridionale* (Naples, 1979).

Linguistic Variety and Linguistic Minorities

TULLIO DE MAURO

SOME years ago a so-called confidential report to the Italian Minister of the Interior mentioned a teacher working in a modern Greek community in Southern Italy, who took the trouble to print, and to have others print, material in modern Greek, in order to keep alive that ancient and noble linguistic tradition. The report added that the teacher did indeed do all these things, but (and the 'but' was, and still is, in the so-called confidential text) he was nevertheless a good citizen, a good Catholic, etc. What mechanisms were at work in the head of the *carabiniere*, or whoever wrote the report for him? What interests are threatened by the fact that local papers are being printed in modern Greek and ancient linguistic traditions are being kept alive? We would need to search long and hard among sophisms and schematisms of every kind to find the military and economic interests that are jeopardized by asserting the linguistic rights of a few thousand Italian citizens who, in Southern Italy, speak not only Italian and the local Romance dialects, but also the modern form of Homer's ancient language.

In the head of the *carabiniere* there were neither military alarms nor economic concerns. There could only have been the deep, instinctive conviction that those who speak differently from others can be suspected of not being good citizens, good Catholics, etc. Linguistic diversity is a strangeness, and it legitimizes any other suspicion, even though the honest writer of the report wished to forestall any possible suspicion. The fact remains that an implicit, deep, unassailable conviction exists that, in the end, speaking in a different and particular way compared to others is a very strange thing. At higher social and cultural levels, the *carabiniere*'s conviction still exists, though in more disguised forms: it is shown by the annoyance with which many people approach discussions on linguistic rights. Aren't there more serious, more important things to do? What do these people want? Why on earth do they worry about some tens, perhaps even some hundreds of thousands of people, on an issue as irrelevant as their way of speaking? In the age of interplanetary travel, why waste time on the German spoken by the descendants of miners from the late Middle Ages, or on the heirs of farmers imported by some Prince of Aragon?

Perhaps those who think otherwise, those who are aware of the present cultural and political importance of recognizing the rights of ethnic and linguistic minorities, have not done all that they could and should have, in order to make finally clear the theoretical and scientific arguments that could help our choices on the matter in one direction or the other.

That is the reason for this attempt. Before providing some data concerning the present condition of minorities in Italy, I shall examine some questions of a more general theoretical nature on the subject of linguistic, cultural, and ethnic diversity.

Types of Language Variation

When confronted by linguistic facts, modern philosophical and scientific thought is caught in a contradiction. On the one hand, there is factual evidence which proves the permanent presence of what we call *plurilingualism*. This has at least two aspects. The first is plurilingualism *within* each language, or *internal* plurilingualism. What we consider to be and define as 'a language' is in reality an open and changing collection of facts. The sets of words, endings, conjunctions, word order, etc. which are known to all those who identify themselves as users of a language, but who have different levels of education or income, different work experience, etc., are sets which overlap to a greater or lesser extent, but which do not coincide. There are variations corresponding to differences of social class (*diastratic* or social variation), differences of geographical area (*diatopic* or regional variation), and difference between the usage of different generations at any moment in time (*diachronic* or temporal variation). The social, geographic, and temporal variations of each language together form its internal plurilingualism. The existence of this plurilingualism is evident even in the ancient world, and is widely confirmed in modern times by the development of studies and modern techniques of recording, analysis, and organization of socio-linguistic facts, as well as by the increasing complexity of industrial societies, which have encouraged the growth and, through the mass media, the increasing obviousness of these variations.

The second kind of plurilingualism is the *external*. Across historical time and ethnic space the human species has used language sets which were completely different from each other or had very little overlap; in other words, people have spoken and speak languages that differ from each other.

It seems clear that a relationship between internal and external plurilingualism exists. Even on the most empirical level, it is difficult to count the exact number of different languages in the world because of the mixture of the two kinds of plurilingualism. When can one say that two language sets A and B stop being internal variants of the same language and become two different languages? But the most important point to make here is that, for as long as people have reflected on linguistic reality, there has been both internal and external plurilingualism—the first consisting of more or less noticeable variations of a linguistic heritage which is recognized by both speakers and observers as being somehow one, and the second consisting of the multiplicity of different languages spoken by humanity.

As well as the evidence of internal and external plurilingualism, our culture also provides evidence of the ability to transcend plurilingualism. By common experience, the obstacles to communication linked to internal plurilingualism can be overcome in that it is possible for people to understand each other in some way. Differentiation within a language (endolinguistic differentiation) is quite real, but it is continually being transcended by the shared ability of people to understand each other even between disparate sets of language, and by the tendencies of the various language sets to become unified and standardized. This is all the more evident if from the point of view of practice we move to that of linguistic reflection. The recording of endolinguistic variety is possible, and has methodical substance, inasmuch as it fits inside the framework of the recognition of a shared linguistic nucleus. We can speak of educated or popular French or Italian, Northern or Southern French or Italian, spoken by the old or the young, in so far as, somehow, we recognize the existence of *one* French language, *one* Italian language. Endolinguistic diversification or internal plurilingualism therefore fits inside the fact and the recognition of *linguistic communion*.

We can make similar considerations about external plurilingualism, the diversity of languages. Both the existence of exolinguistic diversity (differences between languages) and the experience of overcoming it in two ways, translation and the learning of other languages, are part of the historical experience of humanity. Translation or translatability is possible because the human brain is able to learn more than one language. The existence of individuals who are able to command several languages at the same time is also part of our oldest historical memories and of shared experience. Therefore exolinguistic diversity, no less than endolinguistic diversity, fits within a uniting framework, our shared ability to use several different languages.

The historical world, the world of nations, is therefore sending us a contradictory message: on the one hand the message of internal and external plurality of linguistic reality, on the other hand the message that this plurality can be transcended, that linguistic experience can be unified beyond its diversity. The history of a language like Latin is emblematic of this: it is the history of the changelessness by which a language that can be considered the same lasts, in written documentation, from remote texts of the late sixth century BC to recent examples in Church use by the Roman pontiffs, through a vast production of literary, legal, scientific, and philosophical writings. It is also the history of continuous change, temporal, social, and geographic differentiation, to and beyond the limits of fragmentation into different linguistic traditions, those of the disparate neo-Latin languages, both national and subnational, of widespread communication and dialects. It is the history of the gathering, over more than two thousand years, of different peoples around the same language, within which they recognize themselves and each other, often abandoning other languages to do so; and it is the history of the birth, from a single matrix, of a varied and composite family of dialects and languages. A history of a multiplicity that cannot be reduced, and a community that cannot be disregarded.

Relativism and Universalism

The paradox we have outlined is real. We are aware of it on an intellectual level, on the level of reflected and documented awareness, but first of all we experience it in linguistic reality, in society. The national spirit, which that great theorist of the contradictions which make up linguistic reality, Ferdinand de Saussure, called with good-humoured irony *l'esprit de clocher*—the spirit of the belltower—has been a powerful ally of external plurilingualism throughout human history. The great demographic, economic, technological, and social upheavals which have characterized the most recent centuries of human history have seemed on several occasions to be on the brink of wiping out ethnic distinctions, of bringing about the unification of all nations and all languages into a single undifferentiated reality. But this has never happened. Instead, we have under our eyes the increasingly intense revival of national and linguistic diversity.

But other forces have been exercised for opposite ends. The need to widen collaboration to ever-broader groups, which human beings seem to carry within themselves as part of their genetic heritage, has driven peoples of different languages to use a shared instrumental language, and this has happened from ancient times, from the beginning of the culture of cities in the ancient Near and Middle East. The need of single peoples, which developed autonomously, was often mixed with imposition by economic necessity or, often, by brutal imposition on the part of a stronger people. In particular, the modern European world, after the rise of the great national states, has experienced phenomena of linguistic violence, attempts to wipe out national identity, to destroy ethnic, linguistic, and cultural identity which have gone as far as the horrors of pogroms and genocide.

Even within single linguistic communities contradictory forces are at work. On the one hand, powerful dominant groups have often sealed their power by marginalizing the various linguistic realities which differed from their own, by using acceptance of a preferred linguistic norm as a shibboleth, as a pass that gives access to the ruling classes. On the other hand, the social division of work and the dispersion into environments differentiated by human geography have formed the basis of the spread and success of differentiated sociolects—socially distinct ways of speaking.

The contradiction in social reality between forces tending towards internal and external linguistic differentiation and forces tending towards homogeneity has been paralleled since ancient times on the level of intellectual knowledge. The history of linguistic research and theory is the history of the juxtaposition, the alternating supremacy, the balancing, of directions of study and overall visions which at times stress the importance of diversity, at times the importance of homogeneity inside a linguistic reality.

Twentieth-century linguistic studies have manifested the greatest extremes in this regard. On the one hand, there has been the success of an ideology which has been called relativistic, and which finds its most rigid expression in the work of Benjamin L. Whorf. According to this ideology, our thinking, knowledge, and experience are supposedly surrounded by and caged inside the structures of each language. Since these structures diverge from one another, to each language there supposedly correspond cultures and ways of life which are incommensurable with and impermeable by each other. On the other hand, the recurring philosophical inclination to deny importance and value to linguistic variations in order to leave space only to unity, to linguistic identity, has found its most coherent and rigid development in the linguistic universalism theorized and ardently preached by Noam Chomsky. Chomsky does not deny the existence of variations within the same linguistic community and the existence of different languages but, together with his followers, now divided into different schools of thought, he tries to drive variations and differences towards the sphere of execution of superficial aspects. Thus, if one compares languages to fruit, the 'deep' flesh or pulp (consisting of syntactical and grammatical rules for Chomsky, and of reference and semantic rules for many of his followers) is supposedly universal and what varies is only the skin and the way the people bite and chew the language.

Considered in general, Whorfian relativism and Chomskian universalism have at least one characteristic singularly in common. According to both points of view, human beings are in a subordinate relationship with the given fact of linguistic structures, whether these are divergent from one language to the other or universal. Human beings do not make and speak languages, but obey them, are made by them and, so to say, are spoken by them.

Something of the kind is not unthinkable. In fact we find that in many of the systems in our communications universe, whether they have a finite number of signs or an infinite number (but whose relations can nevertheless be reduced to a finite number of basic units of calculation), the user is outside the process of assigning value to the sign. A system of road signs or shipping signals, like a classification and filing system, or algebra, or any other system of calculation, are communication systems which have been constructed precisely in order to generate signs whose value is independent of the condition of the users. In such systems, the performance of the person producing or receiving a sign is in effect external to the value of the sign. This independence of the process of assigning value to the sign from its use and from the users' conditions makes it possible, in the case of communication systems which are not historical, natural languages, to entrust production, reception, coding, and decoding to machines and calculators.

For natural languages, however, the repeated failure of attempts at mechanical translation and the theoretical difficulty of reducing the creation of language signs to an ideal automaton suggest that the automatic nature of the processes of production and reception of the signs of verbal language is merely partial. In reality, in producing and receiving a linguistic sign, automaticity operates only on the most superficial, exterior aspects, while semantic and syntactic aspects see the constant intervention of non-automatic subjectivity, which is not foreseeable by users. The appeal to the user is a constant of the production and reception of the sentences and texts of a language.

The appeal to the user, to the conditions in which the productive or receptive use of the sign takes place, combines with an important characteristic of the meaning of linguistic signs and the words of which they consist: indeterminacy. The semantic values of words are subject to unforeseeable fluctuations, with the result that existing words may at any time potentially be taken out of use and new ones may need to be introduced. Unlike the constituent units of street signs or systems of calculation or of classification, the vocabularies of historical-natural languages are, therefore, typical *creative* sets, with contents which can vary widely according to the kind of users, their social, regional, and temporal placing.

Non-specialist readers will be able to see that the social, geographic, and temporal variations which were my starting-point do not lie outside the reality of a language, but are part of its function. A verbal language is *the sum of these variations*. Unlike non-verbal languages, it is characterized by a continuous creativity, a constant drive towards innovation. This makes a language flexible enough to be used as a code of communication for the most varied technologies, sciences, and experiences of human communities.

This is the reason why a language can become deeply rooted in the culture of a population, and vice versa. But it is also the reason why, thanks to the same drive for innovation, a language can become detached from one culture and go on to express a different one, just as the same culture can be expressed through more than one language. The incessant drive for innovation which characterizes historical-natural languages is evidently what lies at the origin of language change, of the transformation of languages through time and space until they become distant and different from each other.

The Rights of Languages

Having briefly outlined this theoretical background, we may now deal with the factual evidence of internal and external plurilingualism from a standpoint which enables us to criticize, from a theoretical point of view, the errors both of linguistic nationalism and of the oppression and destruction of national identity. For both these policies protect words and languages, but *not their users*. Nationalism claims to protect each language against all the others, and by this claim it tries to make languages inflexible. It tries to preserve cultural situations by putting them, metaphorically, in a museum, removing them from the life that comes from cultural exchanges with the rest of the world. In the most extreme cases, it creates ghettos which may perhaps save some mummified languages, but which condemn their speakers to isolation and stasis. As for the policies which attempt to destroy national identity by imposing a single language at another language's expense, their violence is evident. But, beyond the examples of obvious violence and oppression, there is also a range of examples of hidden violence. Even if it were possible to carry out a total unification of humanity in a common language, uprooting the forest of differing idioms inherent in the varied world of nations, the constant drive towards innovation could not fail to create, all over again, a multiplicity of linguistic traditions from the heart of this hypothetical single and universal idiom. These new traditions could only be stifled at the cost of forcing all users into a condition of oppression which would be more than just linguistic.

Just as relativism and universalism turn out to be, on the theoretical level, enemy brothers with an important trait in common, so too do linguistic nationalism and linguistic imperialism on the level of possible policies. In order to become established, both nationalism and imperialism must decide to limit and stifle the ability to change, the ability to experience history in human beings, so that within each community (in the case of nationalism) or on the whole planet (should the plans of imperialism be realized) everyone should speak in the same way once and for all. In short, the error which, paradoxically, nationalistic and de-nationalizing tendencies share is that of watching languages and ignoring users, the concrete individuals who speak, and their rights.

As soon as we choose to give priority to human beings, however, the picture of possible linguistic and cultural policies changes. It is no longer a question of choosing in a detached way which language the inhabitants of a place must speak for the salvation of their kind (from a nationalistic or micronationalistic perspective) or for the greater glory (or efficiency) of the dominant people and their dealings (from the point of view of imperialism or, at any rate, of the oppression by one nationality of other nationalities). The question, which naturally requires a remarkable change in mentality and habits by the ruling classes who might wish to consider it, becomes: *what language or what languages do the inhabitants of a place want to speak?* And therefore, more concretely, what is the real language set in which they meet and communicate locally? Are there any other language sets which they consider to be useful in their life or which they are already actually using, and if so what are they?

If we adopt this standpoint, then cultural institutions in the wide sense of the term—schools, the mass media, and so forth—will no longer act like heavy tanks advancing out from a more or less distant centre which claims uniqueness for itself, flattening any cultural and linguistic diversity they find in their path. They will become instruments that respond to the need for culture of the populations in the way that these populations perceive them, develop them, and shape them, including through time.

Plurilingualism in Italy

The populations gathered within the present borders of the Italian Republic experience, more than those of other European countries, and perhaps more than those of any other country in the world of similar geographical and population size, a native condition of internal and external plurilingualism, which is well rooted in history and in the present-day social reality. In Italy one finds together idioms belonging to very different linguistic families or groups—Germanic, Illyrian-Albanian, Slav, Greek, Indo-Aryan, and neo-Latin. Almost each one of these groups is present through different idioms: the Germanic group through both Alemannic and Bavarian-Tyrolean dialects; the Slav group through Slovenian and Serbo-Croat; the Latin group through almost all its known subgroups: Ibero-Romance, Gallo-Romance, Rheto-Romance, Italo-Romance. Plurilingualism reaches its peak in the Italo-Romance group, which is fragmented into a multitude of dialects—the 'Italian dialects'—which are very strongly differentiated and very viable, being used, even today, by more than 60 per cent of the population and, in fact, being used exclusively, that is, not alternating with Italian or another language, by 14 per cent of the population (1991 figures).

This rich plurilingual picture is deeply rooted in the history and social reality of the populations who live inside the present borders of the Republic. Within this picture we can make out the threads of the evolution of Italian history through the centuries. The origins of Italy's complex ethnic plurality undoubtedly lie in its physical shape and geographical location. It is divided internally by natural barriers, but at the same time because of its coasts and mountain passes and its position it has been traversed from the most distant prehistoric times by peoples and trade moving back and forth between the Euro-Asiatic East and the Atlantic and between northern Europe and the southern Mediterranean. This complex ethnic plurality characterized pre-Roman Italy from the beginning of the first millennium BC, especially when compared to the other large natural areas of Europe, which were ethnically much more homogeneous either because they were more sheltered from penetration by other populations or, on the other extreme but with a similar result, because they were crossed by swift waves of migration which did

Map 8. The regional dialects and minority languages of Italy

not leave any autonomous ethnic trace. At the time of the rising power of the Roman Republic in the third century BC, we find a highly composite ethnic picture deeply rooted in Italian soil: non-Indo-European peoples with various linguistic traditions, such as Ligurians, Etruscans, Rhaetians, Piceni, Punics, Sards, can be found beside Indo-Europeans whose traditions and provenance are even more varied, such as the Gauls and Veneti in the North, the Umbrians, Latins, and Oscans in the Centre, and the Oscans, Greeks, Messapics, and Latino-Siculans in the South. The federal policy of the Roman Republic, its relative linguistic toler-ance towards its confederates, the Greek–Latin bilingualism not only of the ruling and the intellectual classes, but also of considerable numbers of slaves, were rea-sons why the linguistic Latinization of Italy and of the largest islands off its coasts did not cause the destruction of the country's original linguistic variety. In the Middle Ages, the political fracturing of the country, the centuries-long domination by peoples from outside it (Arabs followed by Normans in the South; Goths, then Longobards and Franks in the North and Centre; Byzantines in several Adriatic and southern regions), and the supranational nature of the Pope's power at once reinforced the persistence of the ancient traces of ethnic and linguistic plurality and added new elements.

The protection of the country's linguistic variety, which is required both by United Nations documents and by the Constitution of the Italian Republic (Article 6 of which reads: 'The Republic protects linguistic minorities by means of special provisions') means in Italy the protection of a plurality which is a precious original characteristic of the history of the peoples who lived in Italy. We recognize, in the pluralism of the present, the precious sign of a long, rich civil and cultural history.

With the quantitatively and qualitatively very significant exceptions of the Slovenians, South Tyrol Germans, and part of the Ladins who are included in territories which are now Italian as a result of the extension of the northern and eastern borders of the Kingdom of Italy after the First World War, the other communities whose speech differs from the mass of Italo-Romance dialects are situated in the places where their history has kept them ever since their origin, or where it has carried them by their own choice. These origins and choices are closely intermixed, for good or ill, with the history of the populations who speak Italo-Romance dialects.

The different genesis of the present communities whose language is other than Italo-Romance, and therefore who all deserve equally to be included among the linguistic minorities whose protection is guaranteed by Article 6, should be kept in mind in order to understand both the different extent of the problems they face and pose, and, from a more strictly linguistic point of view, the different extent of their linguistic difference. In the case of the Slovenians of Venezia Giulia (the area round Trieste in the north-east) and the South Tyrol Germans of the Trentino (round Trento) and the Ladins of the neighbouring Alto Adige—they were incor-porated into Italy's borders as a result of the settlement following the First World War. Even after the fall of the Fascist regime, which tried to destroy the sense of nationality of these communities and did not hesitate to persecute them, Italian central administrations have had a discriminatory attitude towards them. Yet among Germans and Slovenians the sense of ethnic and linguistic difference from the Italian populations is very much alive, as is the awareness of their belonging to linguistic and national traditions other than the Italian ones. This has led the linguistic minorities of north-east Italy to create their own cultural and political organizations. The linguistic situation reflects this separateness, in that in the two largest communities Italianisms are rare. The fact that the Ladins of Alto Adige, if they abandon Ladin, opt for German rather than Italian, is particularly interesting. The history of the other communities which speak languages that are not Italo-Romance is very different. As their history has mingled with that of populations who speak Italo-Romance, so their speech has followed the same evolutionary lines as the Italian dialects.

The Italo-Romance dialects have undergone a twofold change which started in the first twenty years of the twentieth century and has continued after the stasis of the Fascist period. First, their conditions of use have changed: from being used in an almost exclusive way by most of the population in all social relations except when writing, dialect has gradually become the speech used only in the most informal, most private, relationships, such as within families, particularly among elderly people. As the areas of dialect use have become more limited, the use of Italian has gradually spread. Secondly, the dialects have been invaded by an ever-increasing number of words, constructions, and pronunciations of Italian origin. In short, both the speakers and the idioms have become Italianized.

The same twofold change can be found in the communities whose language is not Italo-Romance. Occitans and Franco-Provençals in Piedmont, Walser (or Waldensians) from the Monte Rosa, Germans from the areas around Vicenza and Verona, Friulians and Ladins from outside the Alto Adige, Serbo-Croats from Molise, Catalans and Sardinians, modern Greeks from Calabria and Puglia (Apulia), Albanians from Molise to Sicily, Rom (travellers), especially when settled—all these people have tended to use Italian in increasingly wide contexts. And, at the same time, their speech has opened to numerous borrowings from the vocabulary and syntax of Italian and the Italo-Romance dialects, as a consequence of the cultural pressure applied by Italian institutions and by the profound integration with the populations speaking Italo-Romance dialect.

The historical movement of past centuries has erased or restricted the areas where plurilingualism was most prominent. Of the area of Greek culture in Southern Italy, which was still quite extensive in the late Middle Ages, only the two above-mentioned linguistic islands—those in Calabria and Puglia—still remain, and only the expert eye of linguists and philologists can discern the presence of Longobards and Goths in place names, from Sgurgola to Atripalda, and in the vocabulary. Another language that used to be widely spoken, almost as a native language, as the everyday language of culture among the urban bourgeoisie in the eighteenth and nineteenth centuries and which today has lost this function and vanished, is French. Only in the Valle d'Aosta, where linguistic protection does not cover the native Franco-Provençal but does cover French, has the use of French survived, under conditions that a hundred or a hundred and fifty years ago were typical of aristocratic, middle-class, and even lower middle-class drawing-rooms, from Naples to Venice, from Milan to Palermo, and even to small urban centres. The principal traces of this almost naturalized French in Italy are dialect borrowings and adaptations.

A stronger resistance through the course of history has been put up by the Jewish-Romance languages, particularly the Jewish-Roman dialect, a variety of Roman dialect with strong archaic tendencies which has survived in the ancient Jewish community in Rome (the most ancient in the world, brutally attacked by the Nazis, it reassembled after 1945 and is today flourishing again), with a wealth of lexical elements borrowed from Hebrew and inserted into the Romance structure.

What I have said so far should not lead the non-specialist to think that there is nothing left of the plurilingualism of the Italian populations except ruins. Of course, compared to the situation as it must have been in the later centuries of the Middle Ages, the character of the non Italo-Romance traditions has become weaker. Nevertheless, these traditions are still strong, and there is no country in Europe which has such a wide variety of native plurilingualism.

Out of nineteen regions plus two provinces with a special statute, fifteen are directly affected by the native, original presence of non-Italo-Romance communities. Let us look at the list: Valle d'Aosta (Franco-Provençal for the majority of the natives, Alemannic German for the Walser, native French for the urban middle class, and French learned at school by all those whose native language is not Italian and who attend school); Piedmont (Provençal or Occitan, Franco-Provençal, German for the Walser, Sinto for the Rom); Lombardy (Sinto); Trento (Bavarian German for the so-called Mòcheni, in Folgària etc., Ladin in Fassa and Moena); Bolzano (German, Ladin in Gardena and Badia, Sinto estrekaria); Veneto (German in the Belluno, Verona, and Vicenza area, Ladin in the Belluno area); Friuli-Venezia Giulia (German in the Udine area, Slovenian in Trieste, Friulian in Gorizia and Udine); Abruzzo (Albanian, Romany); Molise (Serbo-Croat, Albanian); Campania (Albanian); Puglia (Albanian, Franco-Provençal, modern Greek); Basilicata (Albanian); Calabria (Albanian, modern Greek, Provençal, Sinto); Sicily (Albanian); Sardinia (Logudorese and Campidanese, Catalan).

One should add that sizeable Friulian, Sard, Albanian, and modern Greek groups have settled outside the land of their origin, in the large urban centres of Northern Italy such as Turin and Milan (Sardinians, Friulians), of Central Italy, such as Rome (modern Greeks, Albanians), of Southern Italy, such as Palermo (Albanians), and in minor cities like Salerno (Albanians), Reggio Calabria (modern Greeks). Even if we omit these migrant groups and restrict our calculation to those who both live in the area where they were born and speak (according to census data and objective research, carried out by the Study Centre of the Italian Parliament, among others) non-Italo-Romance languages, Italian citizens whose native language is not

Italo-Romance number two and a half million. For all these people, with the exception of the people of Valle d'Aosta, the Germans from Bolzano, and the Slovenians from Trieste and Udine, Article 6 of the Italian Constitution has been without validity. As far as they are concerned, the governments and parliamentary majorities which have followed each other for nearly fifty years have all treated this article as if it were a dead letter.

The complexity of the Italian linguistic situation, the tangle of different ethnic and linguistic traditions which are often consistently present *outside* their territory of origin, makes the prospect of legislative action in favour of linguistic minorities problematic, if such action is founded only or mainly on protections or concessions connected to the territory itself. One might say that even this kind of legislation is preferable to the limited legislation which the Italian authorities were obliged to develop, under pressure from the events of the war and their international consequences, in favour of the people of Valle d'Aosta, the Germans and Ladins in Bolzano, the Slovenians in the two provinces of Trieste and Gorizia. Nevertheless, if one wants laws that will provide complete protection for linguistic minorities, one needs to bear in mind what I have tried to show here, namely that the kind of legislation which guarantees linguistic rights only inside certain geographical areas would trample on the rights of the largest Albanian nucleus, which is now in Palermo, of the largest modern Greek nucleus, in Reggio Calabria, of the sizeable Sardinian and Friulan nuclei in Turin and Milan, and so forth. Moreover, such legislation would run the risk of remaining ineffectual with regard to the more recently formed minorities that are becoming established in Italy, where the 1970s witnessed the influx of between four hundred and six hundred thousand workers from the Balkan and Arab states, from the Philippines, and elsewhere.

Besides, this question does not concern Italy alone. Throughout the European Union large 'islands' containing speakers of languages other than the local have formed, owing to the settlement of immigrant workers. European legislation aiming to protect the linguistic rights of the population could not ignore this without riding roughshod over the concrete linguistic rights of millions of workers.

Cultural institutions—the media, the performing arts, and especially schools—will form the battleground on which the fight to protect and promote the linguistic rights of coexistent groups in contemporary Europe and, more generally, in the present world will take place. And, as I have argued and shall repeat by way of a conclusion, the protection of linguistic rights does not mean merely a mechanical reversal of the linguistic and cultural oppression which many peoples suffer today as part of policies of micronationalistic exclusivism. If what is worth protecting is not micronationalistic pride, but the real freedom to recognize oneself in a native linguistic heritage in order to make it the starting-point for the development of wider communicative abilities, then a democratic linguistic education, one based on the respect of the pupils' linguistic identity and openness to the linguistic and cultural heritage developed by the peoples of the world, particularly in the most widespread international languages, is the most adaptable and widely effective instrument for the reclaiming of the primary human right to speech.

Further Reading

There is not a great deal available in English on linguistic variety and linguistic minorities in Italy. For a lively and lucid introduction, see Anna Laura Lepschy and Giulio Lepschy, *The Italian Language Today* (2nd edn., London, 1988), notably Part One, 'The Linguistic Situation in Italy', and Martin Maiden, *A Linguistic History of Italian* (London, 1995), Chapter 5. The latter also contains an extensive bibliography. See also U. Ammon (ed.), *Status and Function of Language and Language Varieties* (Berlin and New York, 1989), especially the essay on the sociolinguistics of contemporary Italian by G. Berruto, and Geoffrey Hull's *Polyglot Italy* (Carlton, Victoria, 1988). On the Italian dialects, see M. Maiden and M. Parry (eds.), *The Dialects of Italy* (London, 1996). In Italian, Tullio Telmon, *Le minoranze linguistiche in Italia* (Alessandria, 1992) is recommended. On the debate in Italy about legislation to protect minority languages, see T. De Mauro, 'Una legge per le lingue', *La Rivista dei Libri*, Sept. 1992, pp. 12–14, and Oct. 1992, pp. 11–13.

For a history of the Italian language since Unification that puts linguistic developments in a social, political, and cultural context, see Tullio De Mauro, *Storia linguistica dell'Italia unita* (3rd edn., Rome and Bari, 1993). For a history of the development of Italian in the various regions, see Francesco Bruni (ed.), *L'italiano nelle regioni. Lingua nazionale e identità regionali* (Turin, 1992). For perhaps the best recent survey of varieties of Italian, see Alberto Sobrero, *Introduzione all'italiano contemporaneo. La variazione e gli usi* (Rome and Bari, 1993).

For the theoretical positions of Chomsky and Whorf mentioned in this chapter, it is best to read them directly: see Noam Chomsky, *Language and Problems of Knowledge: The Managua Lectures* (Cambridge, Mass., 1988), and Benjamin L. Whorf, *Language, Thought and Reality: Selected Writings* (Cambridge, Mass., 1956).

Fantasy Maps

JOHN DICKIE

As citizens of nation-states, we all have imaginary maps which we draw according to the different meanings the nation and places within it have for us. Despite their comic exaggeration, the two maps reproduced here are indicative of the place that the South often occupies in many imaginary geographies of Italy.

The first is a cartoon by Giorgio Forattini originally published on the front page of *La Repubblica* on 18 September 1990. The shaded regions are Campania, Calabria, and Sicily, where the problem of organized crime is at its most serious. The warning sign reads 'Beware!!! You are entering the area where they kill children.' The events which provoked the cartoon are indeed shocking. In three days in the Naples area, two young boys had been killed in separate incidents involving the Camorra. But while we might well share Forattini's outrage, we should be careful to interrogate the way it is expressed. What is striking about the map of Italy here is that it is upside down when compared to present-day cartographic conventions. This inversion seems to push the South further away from the reader, thereby reinforcing the stereotype of the South as a land of extremity, somehow removed from Italy. The cartoon also reduces the complex problem of organized crime to an emotive geographical opposition between 'healthy' Italy and areas 'infected' with the Mafia and Camorra. It could be seen as providing a catchy visual encapsulation of a misguided understanding of the problem of organized crime according to which the Mafia and Camorra are restricted to the South and organized crime typifies Southern society as a whole. However, as a number of articles also published in *La Repubblica* at the time make clear, the persistence of organized crime cannot be explained without reference to the failings of the *national* state.

Fig. 6

The second cartoon map shows a much more extreme version of the same division between Italy and the South. Its origins are more mysterious: it seems to have circulated rather in the fashion of an 'urban myth' between offices and friends in 1990. The image suggests that 'The complete solution to all our [i.e. Northern Italians'] problems' would be to separate North and South with a 'liberation channel' patrolled by 'Southerner-eating' sharks (*squali 'mangiaterün'*) and piranhas. The *Mezzogiorno*, which here begins just below Florence, would be renamed 'The island of "New Africa"'. The channel is reinforced on either side by protective barriers two kilometres high—an 'electronic [electric?] border' and a 'laser border' which operates automatically when an 'African islander' approaches. It would be difficult for overtly prejudiced material of this kind to get access to the public domain. The unofficial channels in which the drawing was distributed, as well as affording the protection of anonymity, endowed the map with the comic energy derived from breaking the taboo against regional prejudice which is operative in the public media. The image may not have been produced by supporters of the Lega Lombarda/Lega Nord, but it may be considered typical not just of the attitudes to the South current at that time but also of the way the *leghisti* saw themselves as puncturing discredited official pieties about regional differences.

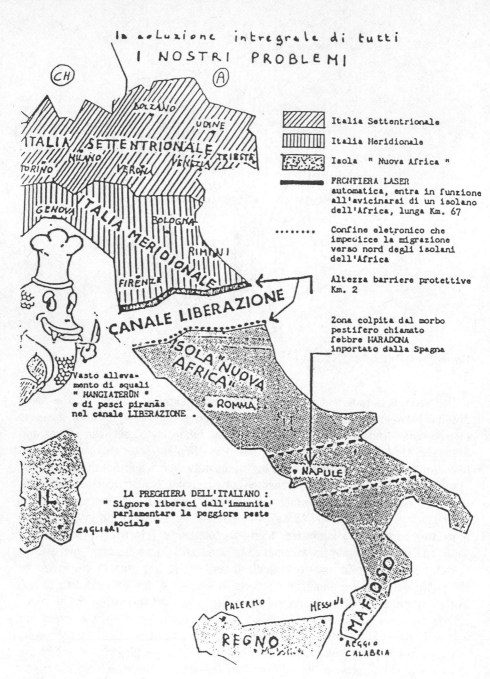

Fig. 7

Identities

Introduction

PART II examines, in historical perspective, some of the main changes in identities that have taken place in contemporary Italy. Simon Parker analyses the demise of the political sub-cultures which re-emerged after the Second World War—Catholic, Marxist, and 'lay'—and their replacement by weaker but more numerous types of associationism in which a sense of political belonging is no longer dominant. Rather, politics has tended to become a spectacle, with citizens as onlookers, not participants. Religious identity has declined too, despite the force of cultural inertia and countervailing movements for renewal within the Church. In the process, as Jeff Pratt shows, Catholicism has shifted its centre of gravity from community-based traditions towards individual voluntarism.

The political and religious identities linked to the main sub-cultures have been sanctioned by history and tradition, and change within them has often been expressed as a return to or recovery of past practices. By contrast, the feminist and gay and lesbian politics of the 1970s presented themselves as inventors of identities. In Italy it is perhaps in this decade, celebrated as well as analysed by Luisa Passerini, that the freedom to create oneself was announced as a political project. There was, however, a double evolution in sex and gender identities: on the one hand towards greater parity, and on the other towards a greater recognition of difference. For immigrants from the countries of the South, too, the struggle over identity has involved simultaneous calls for equality of citizenship and respect for cultural diversity. Vanessa Maher looks at how ethnic minorities in Italy have struggled to represent themselves in the face of government authorities and local populations that have sought to lump them together using labels that deny their identities. The response to their presence reveals latent or manifest forms of racism with roots in the Fascist period, together with memories of the persecution and discrimination experienced by Jews in Italy and by Italian migrants abroad.

Political Identities

SIMON PARKER

'POLITICAL IDENTITY' is a term that has only recently entered the language of the social and political sciences, even though the idea of 'man' as a political subject can be found in the classics of European civilization. Aristotle wrote (1905: 28): 'it is evident that the state is a creation of nature, and that man is by nature a political animal. And he who by nature and not by mere accident is without a state, is either above humanity, or below it.' According to W. J. M. Mackenzie, the phrase 'political identity' was invented 'in or about 1960' by the American political scientist Lucian Pye, who 'deliberately adapted it from the usage of Erik Erikson, who began to write about the crises of "personal identity" in or about 1946. Erikson in turn acknowledges two lines of descent in the development of his ideas; one of them from Freud and the Freudians, the other from the native American school of personality and culture' (Mackenzie 1978: 49). An important contribution to the understanding of identity was provided by Erving Goffman, whose work on social interaction offered an explanation for the importance of 'role assimilation' for an individual's self-projection in a given social environment (see Giddens 1987). Identity involves a combination of agency and ascription; we make choices about who we are, but who we are is also determined by how others see us.

In fusing the concept of the political with that of the personal we arrive at a modern definition of political identity, one which places an individual's sense of political being alongside that of other 'identities' such as those of nation, race, gender, language, culture, religion, class, and sexuality. Such identities will often cross-cut one another and one may serve to reinforce or to weaken others. Thus while there is an increasing acceptance that 'the personal is the political' and that political behaviour is not just an activity delegated to parties and party leaders, it is also true that politics is a continual struggle for resources and power played out within the confines of civil society and organized through the institutions and apparatuses of the nation-state. As such politics can appear to be remote, impersonal, and alienating.

It follows, then, that political identity is not simply defined by an individual's sympathies or hostilities towards a given set of parties and political movements, even though such sentiments will be an essential component of political behaviour in a more general sense. Rather, the constitution of the polity (how it is structured socially and economically, its main regional and cultural divisions, the key historical processes that helped to shape its political institutions) creates a series of 'instances' where the vertical ordering of society (individual, family, workplace, neighbourhood, locality, region, nation) interacts with horizontal cleavages (class, religion, language, race, culture) to form complex patterns of *identification* in which we may identify with a number of different political formations in a variety of social instances. Whether identification is passive or active, negative or positive, it can often usefully be analysed in terms of particular 'subcultures' where identification *with* or *against* something is as, if not more, important than the identity *of* someone.

Subcultures as Sources of Political Identification

In Italy subcultures have been generally regarded as more important than powerful cleavages such as class. Subcultures are 'ecological' features of political systems, meaning that they exist in a reasonably distinct and bounded geographical area where one or more 'cultural types' are homogeneously dominant. Concentrations of, for example, particular religious communities or occupational groups may give rise to a specific kind of polity that has little in common with a neighbouring area where these features may be quite different. The stronger the endogenous presence of such socio-economic and cultural types, and the more articulated their community representation (in terms of associations and institutions such as sports clubs, local newspapers, youth groups, etc.), the keener, it is argued, will be the sense of political identification with the subculture (Trigilia 1986).

The post-war period in Italy gave rise to the development of three main subcultures—lay, Catholic, and socialist/communist—that had their origins in the opposition to Fascism and the war of national liberation. However, the roots of these subcultures can be traced back to the birth of the Italian nation itself in the mid-nineteenth century. During the Risorgimento, Italian nationalism was closely associated with republicanism and anticlericalism because the autocratic division and rule of Italy had been conducted by the Catholic Church and 'foreign' monarchs for many centuries. Not surprisingly it was also from these privileged élites that the most powerful opposition to Italian unification stemmed. With the annexation of the former papal states to the Kingdom of Italy and the incorporation of Rome (1870), Church hostility to Italy's political leaders intensified. The papal *non expedit* of 1871 forbade Catholics to participate in politics at the national level (though they could go to the polls or run for office at municipal level) and the Vatican refused to recognize the legitimacy of the Italian government. The Roman aristocracy even took to wearing black in permanent mourning at the Church's loss of its temporal powers.

An essentially anticlerical nationalist 'lay' culture with strong roots in the regions of the North and Centre thus found itself in conflict with a newly politicized Catholicism, stripped of its earthly powers and contemptuous of Italy's fledgeling democracy. The devout Catholics who remained loyal to the Holy See began to organize themselves as families and consumers, as farmers and industrial workers, and as teachers and students, with the intention of preserving a social milieu that was able, until the advent of Fascism, to maintain its way of life with little state interference.

The rebirth of democratic Italy after the fall of Fascism in July 1943 was the occasion for a reassertion of the political subcultures that had remained dormant under Mussolini's dictatorship. The early liberation of Southern Italy by the Allies gave the recrudescence of political life an important twist, for Sicily and the South were spared the bloody civil war that bitterly divided the peoples of the Centre and North (Pavone 1991). Here the Communist Party and its Socialist allies fought side by side with the bourgeois radicals of the Action Party and with anti-Fascist Catholics. This *camaraderie de guerre* was to be short-lived, however, and by 1947 the Communists and Socialists had been ejected from Alcide De Gasperi's first post-war coalition government.

The legacy of the war and the Resistance thus had a markedly different geographical impact on Italy, and this was most clearly demonstrated in the strong support for retention of the monarchy during the referendum of June 1946 in the Southern and Island provinces and the overwhelming support for a Republic in the industrial towns and cities of the North (Lanaro 1992: 203). Thus since its inception the Italian Republic has been heavily segregated along geopolitical lines. The central regions of the north (Emilia-Romagna, Tuscany, the Marches, Umbria) where the Communists and Socialists had led the Resistance were predominantly left-of-centre, the South and Islands and the smaller towns and cities of the North mostly backed De Gasperi and the centre-right.

Changing Political Identities

Italy's 'national revolution' was only a partial, or 'passive' revolution (Gramsci 1971: 106–14), and for reasons that we have already noted, the lack of common purpose with the national ideal has made it very difficult to transcend the particularities of Italy's historic and geographical divisions (see John Dickie's contribution to this volume, Chapter 1). Inevitably this lack of national cohesion has structured the relationship between citizens and state which has rarely been one of voluntary and mutual recognition. Instead, reconciliation has often proceeded on a quid pro quo basis brokered by certain political parties that have acquired powerful and exclusive rights of intermediation. The American political scientists Gabriel Almond and Sidney Verba argued that strong identification with a particular party or ideology was typical of Latin countries where the civic culture was weak (Almond and Verba 1963). Mature democracies, they claimed, were composed of citizens who did not have a priori and fixed political beliefs; instead they used their powers of discrimination and reason to make the best available choice.

Until recently, Italian electoral behaviour appeared to confirm Almond and Verba's assessment of Italy as a 'Latin' political culture. Mannheimer and Sani found in the mid-1980s that as many as 60 per cent of Italians belonged to one or other of the socialist/communist or Catholic subcultures (Mannheimer and Sani 1987). The subcultures have traditionally generated what Parisi and Pasquino have called the *voto di appartenenza*—the 'vote of belonging' (Parisi and Pasquino 1977). It is, they argue, an affirmation of the subjective identification with a political force that is shared by one's own social peer group, and it is based on an organic relationship of identification rather than on simple representation.

According to this view the act of voting is a behavioural ritual that reconfirms one's membership of the wider network of like-minded individuals. Such political behaviour is characterized by a strong sense of duty and obligation and an indifference to the timing and nature of the elections. The subcultural voter seems mostly indifferent to the nature of the contest and is 'inelastic' in her or his political choices. If an electoral market-place existed in Italy in the first two decades after the Second World War, it appears there were few stalls to choose from and that the majority of the customers went back to the same stall-holder again and again, seemingly oblivious to the ringing imprecations of their competitors.

The Cold War era was associated with a party system described by Sartori as 'polarized pluralism' and which was characterized by a large number of parliamentary parties, and by significant support for 'extreme' parties, especially on the left (Sartori 1976). These 'extreme poles' (the PCI and the neo-Fascist MSI), except on rare occasions, remained formally excluded from power by a permanent if frequently changing coalition of 'centrist' political forces led by the Christian Democrats. However, these sharp divisions that resulted from the externally imposed polarities of the Cold War of the 1940s and 1950s slowly began to yield to a more transversal political culture that corresponded more closely to the contours of political and economic power in Italy itself.

From the time of the 'economic miracle' in the late 1950s, Italian society had been undergoing a profound and sustained process of modernization and secularization (Mannheimer and Sani 1987), and it was not a coincidence that the

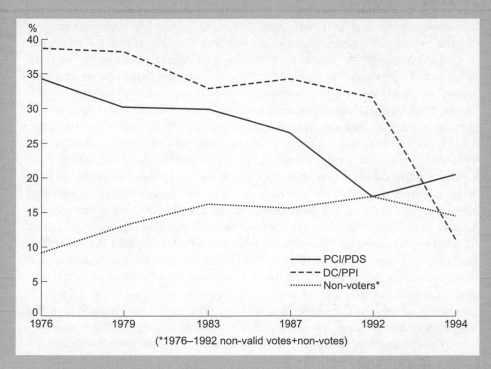

%
40

35

30

25

20

15

10

5

0

1976   1979   1983   1987   1992   1994

(*1976–1992 non-valid votes+non-votes)

PCI/PDS
DC/PPI
Non-voters*

Fig. 8 DC/PPI and PCI/PDS % share of the vote for the Chamber of Deputies, 1976–1994.

first centre-left government in 1963 saw the Socialists join the executive at a time when organized labour had found its voice again after a long period of relative inactivity (Ginsborg 1990: 264). As the era of consociational democracy (or reciprocal power-sharing) began, the polarized pluralism that Sartori saw as characteristic of the Italian polity became less polarized and increasingly consensus-driven, particularly at the élite level (Sartori 1976; Putnam *et al.* 1993). Aggregate support for the two largest political parties (the PCI and the DC) continued to decline from 1976 onwards (see Figure 8), while the vote concentration index fell from 0.284 to 0.151 between 1976 and 1992 (the maximum value being one and the minimum being zero) revealing an increasing electoral fragmentation (Agosta 1994: 20). In the 1980s party identification remained important, but the 'idealistic basis' of popular politics seemed almost to disappear. For the left as well as for the centre and right, the discussion centred on technocratic priorities rather than on the reordering of society on the basis of a qualitatively different set of ethical principles. In other words, while on the surface strong party loyalties appear to have been sustained throughout the 1970s and 1980s, the nature of this support had changed. Instead of seeing political parties as a collective reality that confers as well as reflects political identity, voters have increasingly related to parties as vehicles for representing delegated interests (Palma 1993). Indeed the analysis of the 'new' PSI electorate of the 1980s confirmed the existence of a professional middle class that no longer shared the politico-religious affiliations of its parents, an observation that held true for younger voters in general. Meanwhile, the growth of the PSI in the South confirmed a different process, the establishment of the Socialists as an 'exchange party' (see below) capable of negotiating with voter-clients as effectively as their Christian Democrat coalition partners (Merkel 1987).

The Tangentopoli corruption scandals certainly accelerated the process of dealignment in the Catholic and lay subcultures, but the very practice of politics in the 1980s was the expression of a deep-seated cynicism that extended far beyond the restricted world of the political class to include large parts of Italian civil society. Political exchange certainly took place, but it was not the democratic exchange that the founders of the 'Civic Culture' school had in mind (della Porta 1992, 1996). The school's most recent interpreter, Robert Putnam, has written of the Italy of the 'civic community' where traditions of social solidarity and collectivism have been maintained in the face of royal and ecclesiastical absolutism and despite twenty years of Fascist dictatorship. According to this view, efficient and honest government at a local level is seen as the product of a 'civic-mindedness' the antique roots of which date from the time of the medieval city-states (Putnam *et al.* 1993). This is not typical of a great many regions, however, and even Putnam's positive portrayal of Lombardy is vitiated by the revelations of the 'Mani Pulite' judges making Milan's claims to be the 'moral capital' of Italy somewhat debatable. Italian exceptionalism, which had been increasingly contested by political scientists in recent years (Furlong 1994), suddenly assumed a fresh relevance as the effects of the end of the Cold War began to be felt.

Political Identities in the Post-Cold War Era

After the 1989 collapse of East European communism, Italy began to experience a series of tremors in its political geology which by 1993 had become a full-scale earthquake. The then Communist Party secretary, Achille Occhetto, decided that the PCI could not continue in its present guise: that its name, its programme, and its organization would have to change if it was to remain a major force in Italian politics. By 1991 the party had been renamed the Partito Democratico della Sinistra (PDS) and the opponents of the change who wanted to preserve the ideology and symbols of Italian Communism left to form Rifondazione Comunista (RC), which attracted members and support from other far-left groups such as Democrazia Proletaria.

Another new party, La Rete, was established in 1991 by the ex-Christian Democrat Leoluca Orlando, who for a short time succeeded in supplanting his former party as the main force in the city council of Palermo, the Sicilian capital. Orlando's supporters came from a variety of backgrounds; they included the university and high school students of *la pantera* ('the panther')—a protest movement that opposed the privatization of the university system—radical Catholics disillusioned with the complacency and corruption of the DC's left-wing, anti-Mafia voters in general, and radical figures in the Church itself such as the Jesuit priest Ennio Pintacuda.

In the general election in the spring of 1992, the PDS and RC performed less well than they had in previous elections, but the 'bedrock' of support for the ex-communists proved to be stronger than many catastrophe theorists predicted (see Figure 9). The former leader of the Socialist Party, Bettino Craxi, confidently prophesied the disappearance of communism and its replacement by a new moderate left led by himself. Instead Craxi has seen his own political career and the party he helped to build into one of the most powerful coalition forces in Europe completely destroyed by corruption scandals.

The Rise of the *Leghe*

However, the main beneficiaries of Tangentopoli have undoubtedly been the *leghe*, the regionally based 'leagues' of Northern Italy that are grouped collectively under the title Lega Nord, the most important of which is the Lega Lombarda (Lombard League) led by Umberto Bossi and generically referred to as *la Lega* (Diamanti 1996). It is difficult to synthesize the Lega's ideology since Bossi's leadership is characterized by a robust and frequently contradictory populism. The Lega Lombarda has maintained a highly ambiguous position in relation to national unity; in the late 1980s and early 1990s Bossi took an extreme position and called for the secession of Northern Italy from what he saw as the corrupt and Mafia-riddled Roman nation-state. Subsequently his position has become more ambiguous, and he has invoked the federalist and autonomist ideas of Carlo Cattaneo (whose

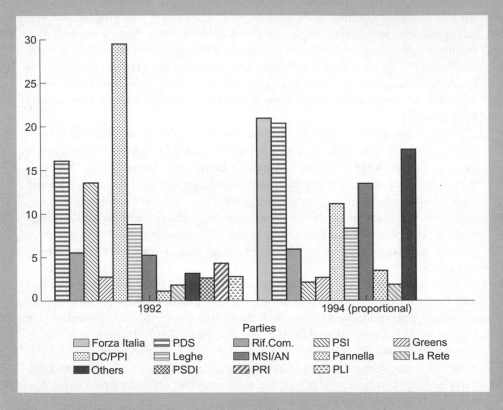

Fig. 9. Elections to the Chamber of Deputies—% of votes cast, 1992 and 1994.

writings are in fact a far cry from Bossi's 'ethno-federalism'). Bossi's criticism of the existing Italian party system and state apparatus owes much to the Lega's ex-ideologue, Gianfranco Miglio, who has proposed the establishment of a small number of largely self-governing macro-regions (Miglio 1991: 144). However, the Lega Nord's Roberto Maroni, who became the Republic's first non-Christian Democrat Minister of the Interior in Berlusconi's Government, has shown no great enthusiasm for the federalist project, although Bossi continues to insist that a new federal constitution is the League's primary objective.

Several sociologists and political scientists have tried to define the electorate of the Lega, but there is a lack of consensus on whether the party is attracting those on the political right, those who are disillusioned Catholics who no longer feel that they can support the DC, a 'submerged' and neglected electorate that saw its values unreflected by any of the existing parties, or simply protest voters against the entire political system. There are components of all these groups in the Lega electorate, but the presence of ex-DC supporters is particularly important, as is the large following the Lega has among the young—especially those without high school diploma or university degrees (Diamanti 1991). But can we say that there exists a distinctive Lega identity in the sense that we have understood Communist and Catholic identities? In other words, what does it mean to be *leghista*?

A series of questions was put to Northern Italians in 1992 in an attempt to describe the political profile of the typical Lega voter. The questions dealt with taxation (it would be better if the taxes we pay are spent on our own region), education (it would be better if schoolteachers came from the region they taught in), political parties (the traditional parties argue among themselves, but basically they are all the same), immigrants (non-European immigrants do not integrate easily because they are different from us), regionalism (the North, the Centre, and the South are very different, and it would be better if they had more autonomy from one another), and marriage (it would be better if people married those from their own part of the country).

On these questions the Lega voter is to be found almost exactly at the centre of the political spectrum, and is a long way from the extreme positions taken by MSI voters. On a scale of 1 (far left) to 10 (far right), the Lega voter scores 5.2, the (ex-) Christian Democrat voter 5.5, while the MSI voter scores 8.3 (Mannheimer 1993). Indeed Bossi recognizes this by invoking the values of the Resistance and anti-Fascism as part of the democratic make-up of the Lega. It is reasonable to assume therefore that it was political opportunism rather than ideological affinity that prompted Bossi to join the 'Forza Italia/Polo della libertà' ticket in the parliamentary elections of March 1994, a political position that Bossi was happy to confirm during the course of the parliamentary election campaign (*La Repubblica*, 14 Mar. 1994) and later to repent.

The Political Market-Place

The success of Berlusconi's Forza Italia (effectively a creation of his marketing company Publitalia) in the first parliamentary elections to be held under a predominantly majoritarian electoral system suggests that these new political identities are far from solid. Rather the cultural, economic, and social profile of the Lega Nord's electors may have remained the same but these voters are not so much loyal to a party, even one led by the charismatic figure of Bossi, as to a set of beliefs and fears which can be easily articulated by a 'party' that with the resources of Diakron (Berlusconi's market research organization) is able to alter its message to suit public opinion literally on a daily basis (McCarthy 1996).

This process is not new in that there has always been a 'political market' where electors provide a 'demand' for government and political parties furnish 'offers'—the programme or philosophy that will potentially direct that government's activities. Under the previous electoral system it was possible to nominate several candidates in order of preference and frequently the number of preference votes a candidate received determined whether or not he or she would be elected. This system allowed a semi-clandestine parallel market to evolve in what might be called the 'derivatives' of power. The 'exchange vote' allowed politicians to 'sell' state resources or various types of decisions, preferments, and placements to mediators—often party officials, local notables, or frequently powerful criminal 'families' in return for a guaranteed number of preference votes (Parker 1996).

This practice was not universal, it was a strong feature of the faction-riven DC in the South and of the rival currents of the PSI almost everywhere, but it was hardly in evidence in the parts of Italy that Robert Putnam has most identified with the 'civic culture'. In observing that these 'civic' regions have traditionally been administered by the former PCI, it is worth remarking that the tradition of democratic centralism would have made it very difficult for PCI politicians to imitate the exchange vote practice because of the party's long-term ban on internal factions and Communist (and now to a lesser extent PDS) career politicians' greater sensitivity to the moral vigilance of the party's base (Magna 1983). While the 1991 referendum abolished the multiple preference vote and undoubtedly paved the way for the majoritarian ('first-past-the-post') electoral system that was overwhelmingly approved in the referendum of 18 April 1993 and was first applied in the parliamentary elections of March 1994, the wholesale shift of support away from the DC to the Forza Italia/Alleanza Nazionale ticket in parts of the country where vote-trading was most evident raises doubts whether the *voto di scambio* has disappeared for good (McCarthy 1996).

Fragmentation and Continuity

As I suggested in the introduction to this chapter, because human actors are often negotiating several different types of conflicting identities, it is perilous to characterize individuals as uniquely liberal, conservative, Catholic, secular, or socialist. This does not mean that there are not voters who strongly identify with a particular political formation, but we must distinguish between those for whom a sense of political belonging is a central, important, and conscious feature of their life and the vast majority for whom it is not. Here we need to make a subtle but vital distinction between what Max Weber called 'politics as a vocation' and what (after Guy Debord) we might call 'politics as spectacle'. For the former, participation in the political process is to enter the rather closed world of the politically initiated. Even collecting signatures on a petition requires commitment and a certain amount of specialized knowledge that few citizens possess. For the great majority who do not fall into this category, however, politics is experienced as an essentially passive activity that is almost entirely dependent on media representations of political monologues or interviews between politicians and journalists. Much more significant for the average person's self-image have been the processes of social and cultural change that affected Italy in the 1980s and early 1990s.

Public disillusionment with the political process reflected in falling electoral turnout and party membership was symptomatic of a decline in 'strong political attachments' which could be observed throughout the Western democracies in this period. This in itself is not surprising if one considers the diminishing importance of class as a major political cleavage and the increasing gap between those employed in regular, well-paid occupations and those who are either without work or in part-time, temporary, and low-paid employment. What has been called the 'two-thirds, one-third society' (Therborn 1986; Galbraith 1992), with the socially and economically excluded third increasingly taking on the features of an 'underclass', has had major consequences for the appeals made by political parties and the demands made on these same parties by the electorate. In particular it has made the 'friend/foe' dichotomy that Carl Schmitt identified as the basis of political subjectivity much more problematic (Schmitt 1976).

In the past the organized working class had a strong sense of 'them and us', but the decline in trade union membership and the greater importance of non-unionized small firms in the labour market has meant that the workplace solidarity of the 1960s and 1970s has been all but lost (Accornero 1992). The Southern migrant workers no longer form a separate and potentially militant subclass within the industrial cities of the North, and persistently high levels of unemployment as elsewhere in Europe have discouraged trade unions from taking industrial action which might result in redundancies or plant closures. The demise of the PCI has also meant that an explicitly 'workerist' politics (i.e. one based on the political centrality of the male, industrial worker) is upheld only by Rifondazione Comunista—the hard-left party that broke away from the PDS in 1991 and which in 1994 had the political support of only around 6 per cent of the electorate.

The service sector, by contrast, has seen a major expansion throughout the postwar Republic (see Table 6.1), but the structure of tertiary employment is very different from manufacturing industry. White-collar jobs are increasingly dominated

Table 6.1. The changing class structure of Italy, 1951–1983 (%)

	1951	1971	1983	Change 1951–83
Bourgeoisie	1.9	2.5	3.3	+1.4
Urban middle class	26.5	38.5	46.4	+19.9
Private-sector white-collar	5.2	8.7	10.2	+5.0
Public-sector white-collar	n.a.	11.0	15.8	n.a.
Artisans	6.0	5.3	5.8	−0.2
Small farmers	30.2	11.9	7.6	−22.6
Working class	41.2	47.1	42.7	+1.5
Farm labourers	11.8	6.1	4.0	−7.8
Industrial workers	22.9	31.1	26.1	+3.2
Workers in commerce, transport, and other services	6.5	9.9	12.6	+6.1

Source: Paolo Sylos Labini, *Le classi sociali negli anni '80* (Rome and Bari, 1986).

by women, few of whom are unionized or in secure full-time employment (Rossi Doria 1994). The nature of white-collar employment almost invariably requires a face-to-face relationship with managers and employers and this inevitably results in a greater degree of control over the employees. Although some sociologists have sought to portray these white-collar workers (*impiegati*) as a 'new working class', surveys consistently reveal that they persistently identify with parties of the centre and right rather than with the left and that their values are highly aspirational—in other words they do not want to overthrow the boss; they want to *be* the boss. The extent to which this managerial philosophy has been internalized by Italy's *impiegati* is hard to judge, but there is no doubt that Forza Italia's supporters shared Berlusconi's belief in strong management as necessary to the efficient functioning of any organization (whether it be a football team or a nation-state).

In the past Italy has been a country where at least the rhetoric of social solidarity was invoked both by the ruling Christian Democrat Party and the Communist opposition—although its practical application in terms of social policy was harder to discern (Ginsborg 1994a). Consequently the Thatcher–Reagan ideology of the 1980s with its contempt for 'welfarism' was not part of the political vocabulary of old-style DC leadership. However, this did not mean that the neo-liberal values that had won support from large sections of the new middle class had failed to have an impact in Italy. The Socialists under Bettino Craxi consciously adopted a quasi-Thatcherite language, winning favour with the young professionals who were to swing behind the 'politics as business' credo of Silvio Berlusconi's enterprise party. Craxism may have disappeared, but the values that it articulated are much more in evidence at every level of government than they were in the past.

It is also not difficult to see in the massive rise in support for the neo-Fascist MSI/Alleanza Nazionale in the 1994 parliamentary elections (especially, but not only, in the South and Rome), the political articulation of a petty bourgeois nostalgia for order and authority that had been rather overshadowed in the First

Republic by the DC's obsession with political consensus-building and the art of non-decision-making. Thus the social and economic fragmentation of contemporary Italy has revealed the persistence of attitudes and values among a large number of centre- and right-oriented voters that have remained salient despite the declining presence of the social institutions that have been their traditional custodians—most notably the Church.

Yet the restructuring of social relations in Italy since the early 1980s has not all been in one direction. The continuing and rising importance of assocational life in this period suggests that Italians are drawn together for other reasons than work and consumption. Antonella Meo reveals that associationalism (since Tocqueville's time long considered an index of any civilized democracy) actually increased by 2 per cent in the early 1990s with respect to the mid-1980s (Meo 1994). No fewer than 21 per cent of adult Italians belong to an association of one kind or another and more than half of these participate in voluntary groups. Another important observation is that, while in the past such voluntary activity had been almost exclusively organized by Catholic organizations, in recent years the ideological motive has been replaced by a desire to contribute to the life of the community outside the confines of 'formal politics' and working life. Contrary to what one might imagine, the 'volunteers' tend to be reasonably high-earning males in early middle age. Not only does this confirm the idea that the new *dopolavoro* is a therapeutic antidote to the stresses and contortions of modern Italian life, it also suggests that Italy is witnessing the steady abandonment of 'strong' or party-based political activity in favour of a much weaker, more varied and dynamic form of social self-realization. But for the many Italians, who instead preferred to remain within the privatized domain of the family and the small screen, the reflecting sky of Berlusconi's virtual politics offered an immediate and attractive alternative to the dour, elliptical, and discredited *partitocrazia* (rule by parties) of the First Republic.

Conclusion

Berlusconi's triumph in the 1994 parliamentary elections would not have been possible without support from the old regime (and in particular Berlusconi's close friend Craxi), thus allowing him to control all three of Italy's private national television channels, and a large part of the newspaper and magazine sectors. Neither could an 'instant' party which was formed only three months before the elections have won such a large consensus without the collapse of the old centre-right parties, leaving lifelong Christian Democrats with the unattractive prospect of an Italian government under the control of the former Italian Communist Party. Nevertheless, Berlusconi's victory would seem to confirm an earlier observation that while *partitocrazia* dominated the headlines throughout the 1980s, Italian civil society had become increasingly oriented to the values of spot advertising, a fantasy world of game shows and Brazilian soap operas that had long ago supplanted the moral universe of the Church in the collective imaginary, but which needed the legitimation of the Christian Democrats' delegitimation finally to speak its name.

The new political geography that resulted from the March 1994 elections is a complex one and the politically distinct contours of Italy's subcultures have (the old 'red belt' notwithstanding) given rise to a 'marbled' landscape of voter orientations that vary considerably in their concentrations (see Maps 9–12). Large parts of the South have 'opened' to the left, while the Northern voters, at least in the constituency ballots, shunned candidates from the left and centre almost everywhere. The largest remnant of the DC, the Italian People's Party (PPI) did particularly badly, as did Mario Segni's reformist Catholic Patto per l'Italia, both falling victim to a squeeze from the right-wing 'Polo' and the left-wing Progressive Alliance. Electoral systems are always distorting mirrors of the body politic, and while the right certainly benefited from the majoritarian system, the local elections of November 1994 which saw Forza Italia's vote cut in half are a pertinent reminder of the volatility of electoral politics in the Second Republic (see Figure 10).

Whether the fall of Silvio Berlusconi's government at the end of 1994 and the subsequent return of a 'technocratic' administration under Berlusconi's former finance minister Lamberto Dini can be seen as a turning-point or a temporary setback for the new right coalition will remain open to debate for some time to come. But what the political crisis that began in earnest in 1992 has proved is the durability of traditional forms of political action. After the 1994 general election there were even more political parties represented in Italy's parliament than under the 'old regime', leading to greater fragmentation and less political direction at national, regional, and local level than ever before. Political dirty linen is now no longer washed *a casa*, within the close confines of the party leadership, but openly in parliament, where across the political spectrum party group leaders find it increasingly difficult to 'whip' their members into line even in major votes of no confidence.

The continuing impression of a national political class operating under conditions of imminent and often actual crisis does nothing to encourage the renewal of political life in Italian civil society itself. But despite the decline in traditional forms of political activity, there has been no appreciable drop in public participation in citizens' initiatives—ranging from support campaigns for the victims of the civil war in Bosnia to the rather less edifying neighbourhood protests at the presence of 'clandestine immigrants' in the larger Italian cities.

Whether the defenders of Italy's 'civic virtues' will win out against a *qualunquista* populism that always seems to flourish at times of political uncertainty and change must, however, remain an open question. Yet in the face of attacks from the Lega Nord aimed at its political unity and even greater pressure from Berlusconi and his supporters on its judicial integrity, the First Republic has proved remarkably resilient, and its 'virtuous minorities', in Paul Ginsborg's telling phrase, still command broad respect and consent (Ginsborg 1994c). It would seem that the polarization is now

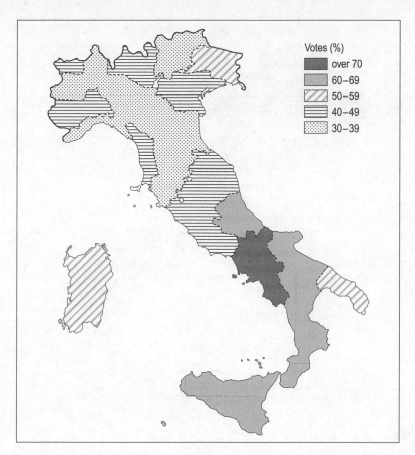

Map 9. Elections to Chamber of Deputies, 1992. Four-party coalition (DC, PSI, PLI, PSDI)

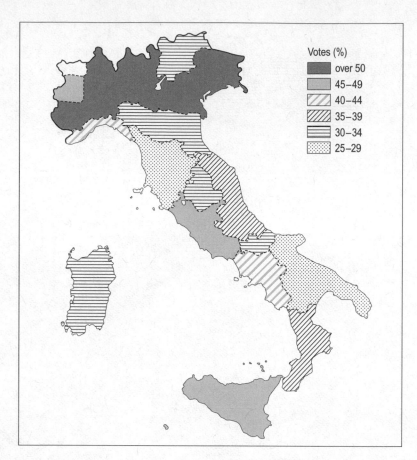

Map 10. Elections to Chamber of Deputies, 1994 (proportional). Polo della libertà/Polo del buon governo (Forza Italia, Lega, AN)

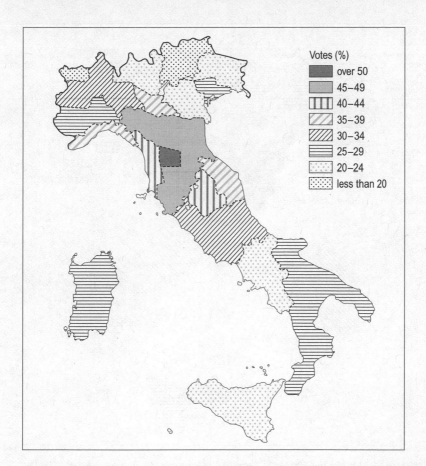

Map 11. Elections to Chamber of Deputies, 1987. The left (PCI, DP, Greens)

Votes (%)
- over 50
- 45–49
- 40–44
- 35–39
- 30–34
- 25–29
- 20–24
- less than 20

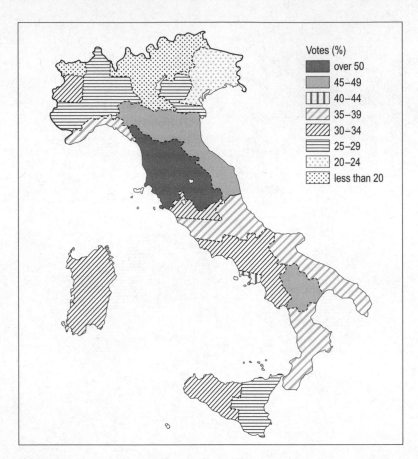

Votes (%)
- over 50
- 45–49
- 40–44
- 35–39
- 30–34
- 25–29
- 20–24
- less than 20

Map 12. Elections to Chamber of Deputies, 1994 (proportional). Progressisti (PDS, PSI, RC, Greens, Rete, AD)

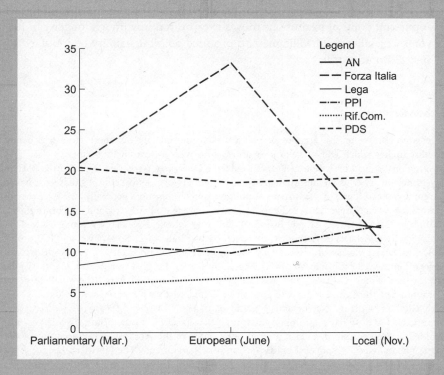

Fig. 10 Movement of the vote among Italy's six top parties in 1994.

no longer between the Cold War-imposed dichotomy of communism and anti-communism, but between an authoritarian-enterprise conservatism and a social-liberal democratic reformism. Neither of these two competing camps has yet succeeded in winning the consensus necessary to 'fix' the still developing photograph of Italy's new republic. But as the convergence of the European Union's economic and political institutions moves ever nearer, how much longer can Italian voters' inability or unwillingness to produce political stability be indulged by the new European order?

Further Reading

There is no comprehensive account of political identities in Italy, but there are a number of specialist studies which will be helpful for those who wish to investigate further.

On regional subcultures, Robert Putnam's *Making Democracy Work: Civic Traditions in Modern Italy* (Princeton, 1993) is an important study of the variety of political cultures that exist in the different regions of Italy. For a treatment of political subcultures more generally, Aris Accornero's *L'identità comunista* (Rome, 1983) is the most comprehensive study of rank-and-file communism, although its interest is now largely historical. On the Catholic side, Percy Allum's essay 'Uniformity Undone: Aspects of Catholic Culture in Postwar Italy' in Z. G. Baranski and R. Lumley (eds.), *Culture and Conflict in Postwar Italy* (Basingstoke and London, 1990), 79–96, deals with relations between the Church and practising Catholics in the post-war period. Carlo Trigilia analyses the 'white' (Catholic) and 'red' subcultures of the 'third Italy' (the small business communities of the Centre and North-East) in his *Grandi partiti e piccole imprese* (Bologna, 1986). Judith Chubb's book on Naples and Palermo, *Patronage, Power and Poverty in Southern Italy* (Cambridge, 1982), remains an important study of political life in the South. Ilvo Diamanti's sociology of the Lega Nord, *La Lega* (Rome, 1992) is one of the most influential accounts of the League phenomenon. A shorter English version of his argument, 'The Northern League from Regional Party to Party of Government', can be found in S. Gundle and S. Parker (eds.), *The New Italian Republic: From the Fall of the Berlin Wall to Berlusconi* (London, 1996).

The far right has traditionally been a neglected area of study in Italian political science, but Piero Ignazi's *Il polo escluso. Profilo del Movimento Sociale Italiano* (Bologna, 1989) is a useful insight into the world of the MSI. A more recent study by the same author on Alleanza Nazionale is contained in I. Diamanti and R. Mannheimer (eds.), *Milano a Roma. Guida all'Italia elettorale del 1994* (Rome, 1994). In English, L. Cheles, R. Ferguson, and M. Vaughan (eds.), *The Far Right in Western and Eastern Europe* (London and New York, 1995), contains two useful chapters on the Italian Far Right—a historical study by Robert Chiarini and Luciano Cheles's analysis of Gianfranco Fini's propaganda drive. Ruzza and Schmidtke's chapter 'Towards a Modern Right: Alleanza Nazionale and the "Italian Revolution"', in Gundle and Parker (1996), also charts the rise of Fini's MSI and its reincarnation as Alleanza Nazionale.

The Forza Italia phenomenon has produced a large number of newspaper and magazine articles but so far little in the way of in-depth studies. Patrick McCarthy's essay 'Forza Italia: The New Politics and Old Values of a Changing Italy', in Gundle and Parker (1996), seeks to explore Berlusconi's political venture in terms of the language of consumer culture, while Renato Mannheimer's essay 'Forza Italia', in Diamanti and Mannheimer (1994) provides a detailed analysis of the Forza Italia electorate in the March 1994 general election.

For a compelling history of the protest movements of the 1960s and 1970s which inspired the 'new politics' of environmentalism, feminism, pacifism, civil liberties, and gay rights, see Robert Lumley's *States of Emergency: Cultures of Revolt in Italy from 1968 to 1978* (London, 1990). Judith

Adler Hellman's *Journeys among Women: Feminism in Five Italian Cities* (Cambridge, 1987) is based on conversations with mainly PCI-oriented feminists and their attitude to politics and power relations in general in Italian society.

A very useful encyclopedia of contemporary Italian life is Paul Ginsborg (ed.), *Stato dell'Italia* (Milan, 1994). It contains short sections on many themes which touch on political identity, from historical sketches of each of the regions to analyses of new political parties and the impact of feminism and consumer culture on contemporary Italian society. The yearbook on Italian politics *Italian Politics: A Review*, currently published by Westview, is a valuable source on political events and trends and contains a helpful chronology.

References

Accornero, A. (1983) (ed.), *L'identità comunista* (Rome).

—— (1992), *La parabola del sindacato: ascesa e declino di una cultura* (Bologna).

Agosta, A. (1994), 'Maggioritario e proporzionale', in I. Diamanti and R. Mannheimer (eds.), *Milano a Roma. Guida all'Italia elettorale del 1994* (Rome), 15–27.

Almond, G., and Verba, S. (1963), *The Civic Culture: Political Attitudes and Democracy in Five Nations* (Princeton).

Aristotle (1905), *The Politics*, trans. B. Jowett (Oxford).

della Porta, D. (1992), *Lo scambio occulto. Casi di corruzione politica in Italia* (Bologna).

—— (1996), 'The System of Corrupt Exchange in Local Government', in Gundle and Parker (1996).

Diamanti, I. (1991), 'Una tipologia dei simpatizzanti della Lega', in R. Mannheimer (ed.), *La Lega Lombarda* (Milan), 159–90.

—— (1996), 'The Northern League from Regional Party to Party of Government', in Gundle and Parker (1996).

Furlong, P. (1994), *Modern Italy: Representation and Reform* (London).

Galbraith, J. K. (1992), *The Culture of Contentment* (London).

Giddens, A. (1987), 'Erving Goffman as a Systematic Social Theorist', in *Social Theory and Modern Sociology* (Cambridge), 109–39.

Ginsborg, P. (1990), *A History of Contemporary Italy: Society and Politics 1943–1988* (Harmondsworth).

—— (1994a), 'La famiglia italiana oltre il privato per superare l'isolamento', in Ginsborg (1994b).

—— (1994b) (ed.), *Stato dell'Italia* (Milan), 284–90.

—— (1994c) (ed.), *Le virtù della Repubblica* (Milan).

Gramsci, A. (1971), *Selections from the Prison Notebooks of Antonio Gramsci*, ed. and trans. Q. Hoare and G. Nowell-Smith (London).

Gundle, S., and Parker, S. (1996) (eds.), *The New Italian Republic: From the Fall of the Berlin Wall to Berlusconi* (London).

Lanaro, S. (1992), *Storia dell'Italia repubblicana. Dalla fine della guerra agli anni novanta* (Venice).

McCarthy, P. (1996), 'Forza Italia: The New Politics and Old Values of a Changing Italy', in Gundle and Parker (1996).

Mackenzie, W. J. M. (1978), *Political Identity* (Harmondsworth).

Magna, N. (1983), 'Dirigenza e base', in A. Accornero (ed.) *L'identità comunista* (Rome).

Mannheimer, R. (1993), 'L'elettorato della Lega Nord', *Polis*, 7: 253–74.

—— and Sani, G. (1987), *Il mercato elettorale. Identikit dell'elettore italiano* (Bologna).

Meo, A. (1994), 'Le associazioni volontarie e il volantariato', in Ginsborg (1994b), 284–90.

Merkel, W. (1987), *Prima e dopo Craxi. Le trasformazioni del PSI* (Padua).

Miglio, G. (1991), *Una Costituzione per i prossimi trent'anni* (Rome and Bari).

Palma, S. (1993), 'L'identificazione di partito in Italia. Due indici a confronto', *Rivista Italiana di Scienza Politica*, 23/2: 349–79.

Parisi, A., and Pasquino, G. (1977), 'Relazioni partiti-elettori e tipo di voto', in Parisi and Pasquino (eds.), *Continuità e mutamento elettorale in Italia* (Bologna), 215–49.

PARKER, S. (1996), 'Electoral Reform and Political Change, 1991–1994', in Gundle and Parker (1996).

PAVONE, C. (1991), *Una guerra civile* (Turin).

PUTNAM, R., with NANETTI, R., and LEONARDI, R. (1993), *Making Democracy Work: Civic Traditions in Modern Italy* (Princeton).

ROSSI DORIA, A. (1994), 'Una rivoluzione non ancora compiuta', in Ginsborg (1994b), 262–72.

SARTORI, G. (1976), *Parties and Party Systems* (Cambridge).

SCHMITT, C. (1976), *The Concept of the Political* (New Brunswick, NJ).

THERBORN, G. (1986), *Why Some Peoples Are More Unemployed than Others* (London).

TRIGILIA, C. (1986), *Grandi partiti e piccole imprese* (Bologna).

Catholic Culture

JEFF PRATT

CATHOLICISM permeates Italian cultural life. Its presence is striking in the black hoods and haunting chants of a Good Friday procession, less conspicuous in the dusty olive branch tacked to a stable wall, hidden in the amulet pinned under a lapel. It is manifest in the teachings about human nature which prepare a child for First Communion, and at a more abstract level its influence can be discerned in many currents of Italian intellectual life. There are non-Catholic populations in Italy: small historic communities of Jews and Protestant Waldensians, and more recently agnostics and atheists who have broken with the Church, growing numbers of Jehovah's Witnesses, and Muslims from the Third World diaspora. However, Catholicism has a position of overwhelming dominance within Italy, and has generated an enormous variety of cultural forms. This chapter can only describe a few of these, and will do so by following a historical sequence.

There are two interconnected problems in trying to analyse this phenomenon. First, when the vast majority of Italians declare themselves to be Catholic, how can we decide what part of their lives is significantly shaped by that identity? There is a 'minimalist' answer to this, privileged by some who study the sociology of religion, which is to draw attention to rates of Church attendance, and to thought and behaviour in a formal religious setting. This answer, however, underestimates the way

Catholicism has influenced the lives of its adherents and Italian society. On the other hand there are also difficulties in claiming that everything a Catholic thinks and does is a manifestation of Catholic culture. Even if we do find a solution to the problem of labelling the various dimensions of cultural life, we encounter the second problem: how can we create order out of the variety and heterogeneity of precepts, teachings, and practices which have been identified as part of Catholicism? If we treat them all as equal, this rubs against an intuitive sense that the celebration of the mass is a more central part of Catholicism than the use of a religious amulet as protection against the evil eye. But on what grounds can we claim that the former is more central, and how do we generalize this?

I shall be using a particular framework for handling the two problems of placing 'boundaries' around a cultural tradition, and of weighing the different experiences which constitute it. The starting-point for this analysis is the formal organization of the Church, which brings us immediately to the crucial issue of authority within the Catholic tradition. The Church endows some people with authority, and in turn they recognize particular beliefs, practices, and experiences as authoritative or authentic. This leads on to the issue of how the variety of religious practices (from baptism to the invocation of saints) are conceptualized within Catholicism, and the suggestion that however much the Church emphasizes its eternal properties, we are not in fact dealing with a static culture but with a process. The account also suggests that this process can only be understood if we recognize the power dimension of cultural life: that the Church is constantly struggling to achieve and defend hegemony within Italian society. This shifts the focus away from attempts to define the boundaries of Catholic culture towards the problem of understanding the way the Church tries to control and influence Italian cultural life.

The life of the Church is structured around the distinction between clergy and laity. The clergy have two main functions: they are the essential mediators between the human and the divine, and they establish orthodoxy in all spiritual and moral matters. The first role of the priesthood is in the mediation of the gift of God's grace (*grazia*) through the sacraments, which are at the heart of Catholic theology, and also of most people's understanding of themselves as Catholics. There are seven sacraments in all, starting with baptism, which involves spiritual birth and entry into the Christian community. Penance, communion, confirmation, and extreme unction are available to all, but there is also a choice between a vow of celibacy and (for men) the sacrament of Holy Orders (leading to the priesthood), and the sacrament of Holy Matrimony. This choice establishes the distinction between clergy and laity, and the two roles are clearly contrasted in theological terms. The purpose of matrimony for the laity is the physical procreation of children, while the clergy are celibate fathers to their flock, to whose spiritual life they minister.

The theology of grace is complex, but in simple terms there are two main channels between the human and the divine, and they give rise to two very different forms of religious practice. The first are the sacraments, which are rigidly defined by the Church (for example at the Council of Trent in the sixteenth century) and can only be administered by the clergy. Sacraments are concerned above all with salvation and are the most universal aspect of the Church. Thus it is of great importance that the sacraments are administered in exactly the same way wherever there are Catholics. Indeed until the Second Vatican Council in the early 1960s they were always administered in the same language, Latin, the loss of which some still resent.

The second main channel of grace is represented by Mary and the saints, who may be invoked for help by all Catholics to intercede with God, and who in popular practice may be credited with considerable autonomy as spiritual figures. The Church also controls these channels of grace in the sense that the Vatican has a whole series of procedures for the canonization of saints, the promotion or demotion of their cults, and the definition of the attributes of the Virgin Mary, for example the Dogma of Immaculate Conception in 1854, or the Assumption of Mary in 1950. However, it is a different kind of control from that over the sacraments, in two ways. First, the laity have access to these intercessors without passing through the priesthood; secondly, in its procedures the Church is often responding to demands formulated by sections of the laity, for example for the recognition of the occurrence of miracles. There is a more dialectical relationship between the clergy and the laity: a movement between the experiences of the laity, the hierarchy's judgements on that experience, and its orthodoxy, followed often by proselytizing action to spread the cults which it has approved.

These two channels of grace correspond to two focuses of religious practice: first, sacramental religion directed towards the salvation of all believers and very standardized in its form; and secondly the cult of the saints, which may sometimes have salvatory purposes but which is generally associated with requests for intercession with the problems of this world. Saints are associated with a variety of identities: they may be patrons of villages, towns, regions, or nations, or of particular occupational groups, or be associated with particular kinds of problems or illnesses. In contrast to the more universal dimension of Catholicism, centred on unchanging salvatory practice, here we find an enormous and evolving repertoire of practices concerned with temporal issues. There are in effect two subjects of religious practice: the individual soul which all humans possess, and the socially defined individual who participates in religious practice as a mother or father, Milanese or Neapolitan, carpenter or farmer.

The human head of the Church, the Pope, is elected by a college of cardinals, and below him superiors appoint inferiors down to the level of the parish priest. This chain of command (the Apostolic Succession) is concerned both with the right to administer the sacraments and with teaching and the maintenance of orthodoxy. Both aspects are highly centralized. The establishment of dogma and doctrine is the prerogative of the Pope and the Councils, but the elaboration of teaching passes right down the hierarchy. Bishops and priests, in pastoral letters and from pulpits, expound on basic matters like the sanctity of life, the indissolubility of marriage, the importance of the family for a moral existence, as well as on current political evils and Catholic social doctrine. I shall return to some examples of this teaching below.

Overall the Catholic Church as an organization rests on a rigid distinction between clergy and laity, has a theory of mediation, is sacramental, centralized, hierarchical, and concerned with orthodoxy. All these aspects set it apart from the Christian traditions which developed out of the Reformation. Alongside the Church itself there exist a mass of flanking organizations for the direct mobilization of the laity, such as Catholic Action, the organization set up after Italian Unification to counter the secularization of society. These organizations make up what has been called the 'Catholic World', and constitute a powerful structure which attempts to shape the culture of Italian society and maintain consent to the Church's authority. These comments are not intended to prejudge the issue of whether this power is a means to a spiritual end or, as its critics claim, has become an end in itself, nor do they imply a reductive argument that every aspect of Catholic culture can be analysed in terms of a power strategy. However, the Church has at various points in its history seen all other intellectual and political traditions as its enemies: Protestantism, the natural sciences, liberalism, socialism. It has engaged in tireless ideological work to combat rival cultural traditions and maintain its own hegemony. In order to maintain its position, the Church has also, since the Concordat with the Fascist State in 1929, sought closer relations with Italy's government, and it gave virtually unconditional support to the Christian Democrats, Italy's ruling party from 1945 to 1994. In this way the Church has tried to guarantee the position of Catholicism in Italian society (in family law or education) and to combat the Church's enemies. However, and this is a point of major importance, the Church's position within Italian society has been transformed by its political engagement.

We shall return to the political aspects of the Church's activity, but first we need to explore some of the ways in which Catholicism permeated Italian life in the early post-war period. It was a predominantly rural society, where peasant culture and Catholicism meshed in many contexts. Church teaching provided many of the basic conceptions in a cosmology of ideas about human agency, natural forces, fortune and misfortune. God's grace was invoked when the priest made the annual blessing of all the houses of his parishioners before Easter, and later blessed the fields of the village. A whole range of practices grew up to deal with misfortune (*disgrazia*), from the ringing of church bells to avert storms, to exorcism, or the invocation of particular saints specializing in help with bodily illness, or the ubiquitous St Anthony for the sickness of animals. In part these practices slipped out of the control of the clergy. The olive branches blessed by the priest in the Church celebrations of Palm Sunday might be conserved by a family as a kind of good-luck charm to be employed at critical moments in the annual farm cycle. Other objects blessed in Church, together with religious formulas and imagery, were used by laity faced with misfortune in private acts of divination and curing. Here we are in the presence of magical practices whose interpretation has generated controversy. Certainly there are parallels between these practices and those of non-Catholic peasantries, while some have seen their presence as a survival from a pre-Christian culture which the Church has been unable to eradicate. Ernesto De Martino in his brilliant study *Sud e magia* (1959) contests this view and attempts to show that there has been a dialectic between the Church and non-Christian conceptions, a dialectic in which the Church emerged hegemonic. He does at least show that, far from being survivals, these magical practices show a fundamental continuity with central parts of Catholic theology, for example with the rite of exorcism which is part of baptism, and in constructions of time, space, and agency which shape the Mass.

A second dimension of cultural life is identity, the way in which conceptions and practices developed by the Church in its teaching, in the sacraments and other rituals, generate or shape specific social identities. This happens at many different levels, of which the most basic is human identity itself. Gramsci and others noted how the word *cristiani* was used in many parts of Italy to refer to a human being, typically in contrast to an animal. Christians are all baptized and receive a baptismal ('Christian') name, chosen from the calendar of saints, and that saint's name day (*onomastico*) is celebrated by everybody called, for example, Giuseppe or Anna in preference to the individual birthday. Through baptism, all human beings have both a natural and a spiritual birth, which leads eventually to the possibility of sin, and a consciousness of good and evil. This consciousness, the rituals of penance and communion and teachings on salvation, provide people with a framework for thinking about the morality of their actions, the state of their conscience, the significance of life and the hereafter.

Catholic teaching about salvation involves belief, and hence the possibility of doubt. More striking are the matter-of-fact areas of certainty, the unquestioned assumption that it is normal to be Catholic, to be baptized, to be married in Church, and that these are preconditions for a moral life and moral judgement. These assumptions were of course grounded in the everyday social life of towns and villages, where they were enormously powerful in the post-war period, such that a refusal to participate in the life of the Church transformed a person's social status, and for a long time carried a very high cost. These general notions about humanity and morality were also structured by gender, and this is another level at which we find the impress of Catholic culture on social identities. Gender roles were a major theme in Church teaching, from the great encyclicals on spiritual and social matters down to the sermons of a parish priest on Sundays. They legitimated, for example, an explicitly patriarchal construction of male identity, in terms of the 'natural' authority the male head should exert over the family, and the qualities he should possess as a father. For women, the flowering of devotions to the Blessed Virgin Mary, and a complex of beliefs around virginity and motherhood, created both an ideal of love and devotion and a problematic construction of women's sexuality which has been extensively analysed (e.g. Parsons 1964; Davis 1984).

Teachings on morality have long focused primarily on the control of sexuality, on the sanctity of the family and the special quality of the relationships within it. The family is considered a unique institution: created by God, with the Holy Family as a model, the Church has consistently stressed the inalienable rights of the family as a 'true society' with its own property rights and patterns of authority which no State should restrict. The Church has consistently stressed the special quality of relations within the family, and these teachings, which became an important theme in post-war political life, were widely shared. They represent the basic axioms which generated judgements about how people behave in the personal domain and, although some are now increasingly contested, they remain deeply rooted in Italian culture.

Catholicism also provided the framework for the articulation of other forms of identity based on territory. In many parts of Italy people have a very strong sense of pride and identification with the town or village of birth, there are names and stereotypes for these regional and local identities, and in a number of areas it was the Church which provided the focus for many of the large-scale activities which brought a village together as a collectivity. The village patron saint, with its statue, cult, and processions, provided one way in which a village collective identity was articulated, and was sometimes only part of an elaborate hierarchy of linkages between protector saints, with their pilgrimage sites, and geographical regions. The prominence of these Church-sponsored events in the social life of a locality varies between regions, and reflects the long-term pattern of more or less 'devout' or 'anticlerical' traditions in the religious geography of the country. In rural Italy (and elsewhere in Catholic Europe) we generally find that where there is a relatively egalitarian society of smallholders and farmers (in the north-east, the mountains, and parts of the South) the Church maintained considerable hegemony over all local forms of organization, whereas in areas with a class structure polarized between landlords and labourers or sharecroppers (for example in Central Italy), the Church in the twentieth century tended to lose its hegemony over the poorer sections of society, and we find less enthusiasm for these large scale external cults (cf. Stern 1975).

Political Involvement

The Cold War produced a profound change in Italian Catholicism. The broad government coalition of 1945–7, which had pushed through a new constitution after the collapse of Fascism, was split, and the election of 1948 was fought between two broad alliances, that of the Popular Front, which included the Communist Party, versus the DC and its allies. The election was fought not just for control over the state but to determine the position Italy was to occupy within the emerging world order, and, it was said, for the heart and soul of the Italian people. The Church committed itself totally to this political contest, and its organizational and ideological support was crucial to the victory of the DC. Parish priests emerged as the focal point of electoral politics: they assiduously instructed their parishioners to 'vote for the Cross', while the Catholic hierarchy organized a network of 'civic committees' which ran a massive propaganda campaign alongside that of the DC. The approval of the local hierarchy and a reputation as a devout, practising Catholic were necessary for any prospective party candidate.

Italian society was further polarized when in 1949 the Pope declared an Anathema against all those who supported Marxist-inspired political parties, in effect those of the Popular Front. Exclusion from the life of the Church was very selective in practice: prominent party activists might be denied access to the sacraments unless they publicly renounced communism, but not the bulk of supporters. Other forms of discrimination, such as the refusal to bless the house of leftist leaders in Lent, might be even more effective than suspension from the sacraments in underlining their exclusion from the moral community. It was part of a Catholic programme of integralism, a strategy to bring the whole of Italian society 'back to Christ', and eliminate any space for those who supported non-Catholic traditions. It legitimated a policy of excluding the left from positions in the state, and in the hands of the local civic committees was also designed to marginalize 'non-Catholics' in all spheres of public life.

This totalitarian design had lasting consequences for the Church and was carried forward in a long and complex ideological battle which redefined the characteristics of Catholic identity. The battle was fought out using all the media: sermons, rallies, radio, cinema, newspapers, and, most strikingly, wall-posters. As I have shown elsewhere (Pratt 1986, chapter 8), during the Cold War great emphasis was given to those dimensions of Catholic teaching and practice which could be defined in antithesis to communism. The struggle between the two was represented as a fight between Christian good and evil and drew on an enduring iconographic tradition for its imagery. Catholic forces were represented pictorially as the Archangel Michael or other figures of strength and purity, communism by the Angel of Death, masked devils, demons, and animals. In this ideological battle the economic interests at stake took second place to the institution of the family, which as we have seen was portrayed as the foundation of a Christian society. The Church was the creator and defender of the family, recognizing its unique and sovereign status, whereas under communism the moral and sacred ties of family life were destroyed, people's loyalty and allegiance were to the state, divorce and free love were encouraged. It was argued that support for communism was incompatible with being a Catholic on the grounds that communism was fundamentally hostile to family life.

If the Church represented the Cold War as part of the eternal struggle between good and evil, it was also grounded in place and time. It was a struggle for the soul of Italy, and the ideological themes already mentioned were combined with appeals to defend the home town and the nation from the barbarian hordes: Catholicism was a central component of Italian identity, communism was an external threat. The time was the apocalypse: the final separation of good and evil. A series of images from the Book of Revelation were used to invoke a sense of impending doom, a feeling that Italy was at a crossroads facing either salvation or perdition. This was a far-reaching cultural movement which utilized many elements of what Gramsci called the 'common-sense' level of ideological life: everyday conceptions and practices surrounding gender, the family, local identities and loyalties, of human beings as *cristiani*. They were elaborated and systematized into a representation of Italian society and its internal divisions, so that everyday experience became part of the political fault line in a nation at a turning-point in its history.

This evolution of Italian Catholicism had its own dynamic. Effectively the Church was saying that in order to be a Catholic you had to follow the political directives of the clergy and support the Christian Democrats. The Popular Front were rejecting the authority of the Church; they were following a political doctrine which was materialistic and atheist in its principles, and had to be excommunicated from the life of the Church and excluded from civil society. This was an alienating message for the majority of the left, for example for the sharecroppers in the communist heartlands of Central Italy. These people were neither atheists nor devotees of free love. They married in Church, baptized their children, placed a high value on family life, and participated in many of the same devotional practices as other Italians. Yet now they were being defined as not true Catholics and were being asked to choose between Church and Party. Integralism, working in conjunction with developments on the left, proved a double-edged sword. The totalizing ambition to lead all political life back to a religious purpose was an all-or-nothing strategy, and its failure reinforced the secularizing trends within Italian society. Some broke with the Church and no longer recognized its authority in any domain of life. A larger number recognized it only in a restricted domain of 'religion' and personal morality, separate from the social and cultural domains in which the Church had once been hegemonic. Its position was diminished.

The Cold War continued to shape Italian politics into the 1970s and 1980s, both in the composition of government coalitions and in covert action. However, within the Church a thaw did follow the election of Pope John XXIII in 1958 and the calling of the Second Vatican Council in the early 1960s. In political terms this Council was seen as an 'opening to the left': the Anathema against communists was lifted, and while support for the DC continued, integralist policies fell out of favour, and in their place came support for the possibility of dialogue with non-Catholic traditions.

The Second Vatican Council represented a renewal of the Church, an attempt to respond to the forces that were changing society and to reconsider the position of the Church in an evolving international context. At a purely theological level the innovations were complex because, although there were no changes in dogma resulting from the Council, there were many changes in practice and in emphasis. Perhaps the most striking and the most contested was the introduction of the vernacular instead of Latin into the celebration of the sacraments. For the first time during the mass the priest was speaking the same language as the laity, and this together with other changes in the form of the ritual can be seen as reducing the distance between the two. The distribution of mass sheets, the use of deacons from the laity to read the lessons, choral singing, the offer of wine as well as the wafer to communicants, all these increased the level of participation in the service. Some of these changes were optional, resisted by some clergy and embraced enthusiastically by others as a way of breaking with an authoritarian model of the priesthood and creating another, that of a servant going out into the community, offering spiritual sustenance wherever it was needed. As a new generation of priests emerged from seminaries where the teachings of Vatican II had taken root, there emerged a concern not just to reduce the distance between laity and clergy, but to change the prevalent conception of God as a remote figure. Emphasis shifted from God the judging Father to God the loving Son, who makes himself available to us through the sacraments, and can be approached in prayer: here a switch from the formal personal pronoun *Voi* to the informal *Tu* was advocated.

These changes have been called a Christocentric shift within Catholicism, that is, a renewed emphasis on the teachings of Jesus Christ and on his sacrifice at the core of religious life. This involved also a reminder of his commandment to love one's neighbour (*il prossimo*) and that a Christian life is lived not just through private acts of devotion and the sacraments, but in acts of love, charity, and fellowship with other human beings. The implementation of this teaching varied greatly according to the inclinations of the clergy and the sociological characteristics of the parish. In the words of one parish priest I interviewed in the 1970s, 'some clergy moved rapidly towards the construction of a truly Christian life amongst the most committed.' They had organized lay groups for study, discussion, and charitable works, and even played down the private act of confession except for the graver sins, in favour of a stress on that part of the mass where all those present express contrition so that (to quote from the same priest): 'it is clear that sins are not only sins against God, but also against one's brothers, against one's fellow men.' Others moved more slowly and found little enthusiasm for these newer forms of worship amongst their parishioners.

The other dimension of the changes introduced by Vatican II was the devaluation of the 'external cults' focusing on the power of the mediating figures, Mary and the saints. There was a review of the historical evidence for the existence of many saints whose names, images, and relics were venerated in countless churches and chapels throughout the country: the review led to the ejection of some from the canon of saints and the 'demotion' of others as patronage figures. Elaborate symbolic forms which had, for example, accompanied the celebrations of the Easter cycle began to drop out of general usage in the 1970s. Local clergy also began to withdraw their support from many popular forms of celebration—those

Fig. 11 A procession winds it way through a Lucanian village in the 1950s. Processions carrying statues of Christ or Mary to celebrate major events in the liturgical cycle, or of local patron saints on their feast day, are still an important part of Italian religious practice, especially in the South. These processions are an enactment of relations between the human and the divine, and at the same time establish various social identities: here both the village as collectivity, and the division between men and women within it. Pinning money to a religious icon is part of a transaction with the divine, and may also reflect competition for social status within the village.

that mobilized parish populations for *feste* which included a procession with a saint's statue or other religious images and which often also included a great deal of locally generated ritual and symbolism.

The clergy offered a variety of justifications for these changes. There was the already mentioned stress on the teachings of Christ and on the desirability of a universally conceived charity as a higher priority than the veneration of religious figures who act as patrons. The clergy also questioned the motives of those who participated in these cults: parishioners were apparently unconcerned with the spiritual significance of the events: they did not go for 'religious' reasons at all, but out of social convention. As one priest said to me in 1975, 'we are moving towards a conception of a more restricted Church, concentrating on the devout', rather than organizing activities with an unclear religious purpose for everybody in the locality. These reforms did not receive the unanimous support of the laity. Not everybody may have been familiar with the details of the Miracle of Bolsena and the history of Corpus Christi celebrations, but villagers in many parts of Italy had participated enthusiastically in the processions and elaborate flower decorations which marked it as a day of *festa*. Some laity felt that it was their *festa*, and there was irritation with clergy who withdrew their support and destroyed the tradition. Other reforms provoked more than irritation: when doubts were raised about the efficacy and importance of San Gennaro, the focus of an immensely popular cult in Naples, there was such an outcry that the ecclesiastical authorities had to backtrack rapidly.

These reforms took place in a society still absorbing the disruptions of Italy's economic miracle, which had moved millions of families from South to North and from rural to urban occupations and environments. Alongside the geographical and social mobility there was the beginnings of a decline in an authoritarian and patriarchal model which had characterized relationships in the family, the workplace, and between citizens and state functionaries. Religious forms premissed on a bounded and stable community, on the household as economic enterprise, on a fixed division of labour, and on a deferential recourse to powerful patrons in the face of adversity were obviously losing much of their meaning in the society which had emerged. The loss of meaning was not total: it applied more to the younger generations than to the older ones, and did not preclude revivals which, for example, used old ceremonies to revalorize local identities with a new (and changed) significance. However, overall the Church had clearly set itself the task of renewal, even if the precise relationship between economic and religious change needs careful analysis in the different domains of social life.

Forms of Catholicism which had permeated and shaped many social identities —those of parents, villagers, or farmers—and which had operated through ritual acts and symbolic forms lost their resonance and were replaced by a view of religion as concerned essentially with inner states. Those who attend a procession out of 'habit' or 'convention' are described by clergy as not being religious. What is required is faith, not 'external' adherence but 'inner' commitment, conscious articulation, and the choosing of a religious style of life. Church weddings had been standard and unquestioned; now they became a choice, and greater emphasis was given to the spiritual preparation of the betrothed and their commitment to the meaning of the sacrament. There was a general shift from traditions, embedded in particular social contexts whose existence was normally unquestioned, to a more universalistic ethos based on individual conscience and agency. Douglas, who has explored this aspect of the Vatican II reforms using Bernstein's distinction between elaborated and restricted codes (Bernstein 1971), has also suggested that they represent a marked shift towards middle-class values in the forms of religious practice favoured by the clergy (Douglas 1973).

We have seen that twice in the post-war period the Church developed new strategies to conserve consent in the face of major changes. The first time it defined true Catholicism in terms of obedience to the political directives of the clergy, the second time it modernized its liturgy and priorities in relation to the secular forces within Italian society. In both cases the strategy seemed to acknowledge that some sections of society would remain outside its influence, but that it would recreate its hegemony over a 'moral majority' of Italians. In each case, a decade later the Church appeared to be in a weaker position than before.

Family life is one key sector where this is apparent. There have been massive changes in family life following from new employment patterns, education, and the diffusion of feminist aspirations, but the Church has tried to hold constant some moral principles through an uncompromising reaffirmation of basic teachings. One is its insistence that the purpose of the sexual act is procreation—hence its opposition to contraception and homosexuality. In the case of contraception the situation is complicated by the fact that even in peasant Italy forms of birth control had been widely practised, but new technology made them much more effective, and the heartland of Catholicism now has the lowest natural reproduction rate in Europe—only immigration prevents an overall population decline. However, the two body-blows to the Church's hegemony in the moral sphere were over divorce and abortion. First the Christian Democrats, who provided the Church's guarantee that the Italian government would not pass laws in conflict with basic Catholic dogma, was unable to prevent the passing of laws which permitted divorce (1970) and legalized abortion (1978). In both cases a Church-backed coalition emerged determined to repeal these laws through referendum campaigns in 1974 and 1981, and these became highly charged crusades demonstrating the Church's authority over the laity. Majority support did emerge in the traditional areas of strength in the North-East and the South, but in the country as a whole both referendums were lost.

If much of the Church's moral teaching is ignored in practice, its legitimating presence is still widely accepted in rites of passage focused on family life. In the boom years which made parts of Italy as prosperous as any in Europe, baptism, First Communion, and weddings became the occasion for massive expenditure: Church decorations, elaborate hospitality, the exchange and display of gifts could easily cost a year's income. The bedecked child making her first contact with the Eucharist is often blinded by flashguns and distracted by the whir of camcorders immortalizing the event. The Church still retains an effective monopoly on these large-scale family rituals, even as it becomes less clear what is being sacralized.

On the political front the Church's support for the Christian Democrats scarcely wavered in all the post-war years. That does not mean that all clergy conformed. Throughout the period there have been priests who have taken a more radical view of their society and their role: worker-priests, organizers of community initiatives amongst the deprived, including more recently homeless immigrants, figures like Padre Balducci in Tuscany, or the Palermo Jesuits who took a stand against the Mafia. These figures have often had a considerable impact at the local level, but this has also usually been without the support of the hierarchy in general and has sometimes brought them close to rupture with the Church. The majority continued, if less enthusiastically, to back the DC through the political stasis of the 1980s, as the smell of corruption spread through the body politic. Only in the 1990s, with the collapse of communism and with it one of the DC's main ideological justifications, has significant political movement re-emerged. The collapse of the DC means that the Church has had to review its relationship with party politics, and will find it difficult to re-create a unified Catholic party which obtains consent in both the North and the South of the country. A more distanced and flexible strategy will be necessary.

Does this mean that Catholic culture is everywhere in terminal decline, politically impotent, and significant only in private spirituality and the public celebration of wealth? Not entirely, in the first place because the rhythm of change in this area of cultural life is much slower than in the fashion industry: a group or a generation socialized into particular religious practices do not automatically abandon them the next season. Somewhere in Italy it is possible to find all the previously mentioned facets of Catholic culture very much alive today: magical curing practices, the belief that all communist women are immoral, flourishing and evolving saint cults, lay groups devoted to charity. Secondly, there have been movements of renewal even as the proselytizing fervour of Vatican II was diluted in the 1970s, and many of them have found inspiration in the figure of Pope John Paul II, elected in 1978. A man of strong convictions forged in the Cold War experience of Poland, he travels widely and uses his mastery of the media to create a contact with the laity which bypasses the hierarchy and projects a message of a Church confident in its truths and triumphant against its enemies.

The largest renewal movement in contemporary Italy is Comunione e Liberazione, whose foundation in 1969 in Milan predated the election of John Paul II by nearly a decade. An organization of devout laity with spiritual leadership from powerful sections of the hierarchy, its contours are rather complex. It emerged first on the political scene as a radical force, bringing news of the liberation struggles of Catholic peasantries in Latin America and denouncing the corruption and loss of spiritual purpose in the Italian political establishment. It used the weight of its preference votes to elect its own members of parliament from the Christian Democrat lists, obtained support from amongst the party notables like Giulio Andreotti, and became a relatively integrated pressure group, with an occasionally provocative stance.

At the grass-roots level Comunione e Liberazione is strongest in the North and in the towns, and especially in the universities, where it has eclipsed the left as the major political force. For young students leaving their homes in rural areas and small provincial centres, Comunione e Liberazione offers a network of assistance and welcomes recruits into wholesome social activities, parties, outings, music, all pervaded by an active Christian evangelism. It echoes an earlier integralist Catholic project, both in the desire to lead the world back to Jesus Christ and in the fact that, once drawn in, participants spend their entire social lives surrounded by fellow members, and shun non-Christians. It is one of a long stream of lay organizations that the Church has promoted since the nineteenth century, and may gain renewed prominence as Catholic politics are reshaped.

In this chapter I have concentrated on the political dimension of Catholic culture, both in terms of national government, and in terms of wider strategies of the Church to consolidate its power. There were two key periods in this abbreviated history, moments when the Church, while speaking the language of universalism, tried to reinforce its hegemony within Italian society, in effect by abandoning its influence over part of it. The first was when the Church fused religion and politics in the Cold War crusade, the second when it downgraded community-based traditions of religious practice in favour of individual voluntarism. At the end of each period Catholic culture was less powerful, in the sense that it influenced fewer people, over a smaller part of their lives. This does not contradict the existence of vibrant Catholic movements amongst some parts of the laity, or preclude their growth in a period of crisis. In discussing the change and decline of Catholic culture in the context of Italian society I have treated the Church as the active subject, attempting to shape political or moral life. However, it should be clear, from the brief comments on the politics of the Cold War, or on the transformations wrought by the economic miracle, that it is also possible to reverse the perspective and analyse the way forces within Italian society have shaped its Catholicism.

Further Reading

There is not an extensive literature in English dealing with Italian Catholic culture from the perspective of everyday experience and practice, partly because anthropological field research has rarely focused directly on Catholicism. Jeff Pratt's *The Walled City* (Göttingen, 1986) contains one chapter on the changes in grass-roots religious practice in Tuscany, and a second on the links between this and political ideology. Sydel Silverman analyses Catholic festivities and the life-cycle in Umbria in *The Three Bells of Civilization* (New York, 1975), while David Kertzer's study *Comrades and Christians* (Cambridge, 1980) gives a good picture of the Church's presence in Bologna. The essay by Ann Parsons, 'Is the Oedipus Complex Universal? A South Italian

Nuclear Complex', in W. Muensterberger and S. Axelrad (eds.), *The Psychoanalytic Study of Society* (New York, 1964), offers a provocative and stimulating insight into the connection between Catholic practice and gender identity in urban Naples, while that by Christopher McKevitt, 'San Giovanni Rotondo and the Shrine of Padre Pio', in J. Eade and M. J. Sallnow (eds.), *Contesting the Sacred* (London, 1991), analyses the impact of devotion to Padre Pio on the social fabric of a town in Puglia. Doug Holmes's monograph on Friuli, *Cultural Disenchantments* (Princeton, 1989), includes a fascinating account of the relationship between folk religion and the Church, though much of it deals with the Counter-Reformation and draws on Carlo Ginzburg's celebrated study *I benandanti* (translated as *The Night Battles*, Baltimore, 1983). For a rather different kind of discussion, focusing mainly on the political dimensions of the Catholic subculture, see Percy Allum, 'Catholic Culture', in Z. G. Baranski and R. Lumley (eds.), *Culture and Conflict in Postwar Italy* (Basingstoke and London, 1990).

Italian studies of Catholic practice belong to a slightly different intellectual tradition which bridges anthropology, folklore, and popular history. The key figure here is Ernesto De Martino, who did much research on popular religiosity in the South. His *Sud e magia* (Milan, 1959) is short and dense and poses fascinating questions for any anthropologist or historian interested in popular culture. De Martino's colleagues and students have continued to explore these themes, and Alberto Maria Cirese's *Cultura egemonica e classi subalterne* (Cagliari, 1973) provides a useful overview of this school and references to some of their rather specialist publications. An example of this kind of research is Alfonso di Nola's study of religious cults in the Abruzzi, *Gli aspetti magico-religiosi di una cultura subalterna italiana* (Turin, 1976). In a different vein, there are many interesting remarks about Catholicism and culture in the post-war period scattered in Silvio Lanaro's *Storia della Repubblica italiana* (Venice, 1992).

There is a range of English-language writings on the Church's role in Italian party-political life. Three recent general works which include such discussions are Paul Ginsborg, *A History of Contemporary Italy: Society and Politics 1943–1988* (Harmondsworth, 1990), David Hine, *Governing Italy* (Oxford, 1993), and Paul Furlong, *Modern Italy* (London, 1994). Finally, for those interested primarily in the more universal aspects of Catholic theology, the most accessible starting-point would be a good missal, or the English translations of Papal Encyclicals published by the Catholic Truth Society (London).

References

BERNSTEIN, B. (1971), *Class, Codes and Control* (London).
DAVIS, J. (1984), 'The Sexual Division of Labour in the Mediterranean', in E. Wolf (ed.), *Religion, Power and Protest in Local Communities* (Berlin).
DE MARTINO, E. (1959), *Sud e magia* (Milan).
DOUGLAS, M. (1973), *Natural Symbols* (London).
GUIZZARDI, G. (1976), 'The Rural Civilization, Structure of an "ideology for consent"', *Social Compass*, 23: 197–220.
PARSONS, A. (1964), 'Is the Oedipus Complex Universal? A South Italian Nuclear Complex', in W. Muensterberger and S. Axelrad (eds.), *The Psychoanalytic Study of Society* (New York).
PRATT, J. (1986), *The Walled City* (Göttingen).
STERN, A. (1975), 'Political Legitimacy in Local Politics: The Communist Party in North-Eastern Italy', in L. M. Blackmer and S. Tarrow (eds.), *Communism in Italy and France* (Princeton).

8

Gender Relations

LUISA PASSERINI

THIS chapter deals with two types of relations: that between women and men, particularly as these relations are defined in law, and that between individuals of either sex and the forms of masculinity and femininity which are produced at various times as cultural stereotypes and customs. In post-war Italy both types of relations underwent great processes of change in the 1950s and 1960s which culminated explosively in the 1970s. In turn, events and processes in the 1970s provided the starting-point for new developments which are still going on. In this perspective, the 1970s are historically central for the theoretical and historical definition of gender relations in the Italian case.

Italy is particularly interesting for this theme because of a historically specific accumulation of contradictions. In the twenty years after 1945 the lives of large masses of people were changed by the very rapid transformations taking place in the economy and society, with internal migrations moving them to different areas of the country and new sectors of employment. The vast cultural changes of this period brought people of many different regions and dialects into contact with one another. At the same time, there were important developments in education —the raising of the minimum school-leaving age to 14 (1962), the entry of increasing numbers of girls and women into second-ary and higher education—which were compressed into a rela-tively short period and occurred later compared with countries of older capitalism. All these processes had an enormous cultural impact on the people who lived through them. Gender was deeply involved, though not always in a visible way.

The stage on which these changes took place was a country of patriarchal traditions, imbued with the Mediterranean stereotype of a privileged relationship between the mother and the male child, on which Catholicism and Fascism had insistently played, in different ways, to establish their ideological domination. On this stage, women had increasingly become protagonists: during the Second World War they were involved in (sometimes against) the Resistance to the Nazis and Fascists; in the 1940s they became voters for the first time; in the 1950s they were workers and consumers; in the 1960s protagonists of education and sexuality. In the 1970s, all these ways of being actors of history came to the fore and were discussed in their rights and wrongs for both sexes.

Gender relations operate on different levels, and there may be contradictions between them at any given time. In this chapter, I shall be concerned with two main levels, between which there is a marked divergence. The first is the level of laws, norms, and institutions. Here one discerns in the 1970s a distinct movement towards *parity* or formal equality between women and men. The second is the symbolic level, including politics, culture, and pyschology. On this level in the 1970s there was a marked process of *differentiation* or pluralization in gender relations, towards a greater recognition of difference in the gender system and in sexual identities. These two processes are always interconnected but perhaps they are not always so synchronized as they have been in the Italian case. This fact enables us to observe that in Italy, because of its specific accumulation of contradictions, the dialectical relationship between equality and difference with regard to gender is particularly evident not only on the theoretical level but also historically.

Equality Within the Law—and Beyond

From the point of view of our present concerns, the decade opened with the parliamentary vote of 1 December 1970, which, after a hundred years of unsuccessful efforts (see Stella Richter 1976) approved legislation in favour of divorce. The very next day, a committee was set up to campaign for a referendum to overturn the new law, and although the legalization of divorce was approved by the Constitutional Court on two separate occasions, in 1971 and 1973, the referendum was eventually held on 12–13 May 1974. The Christian Democrat leader Amintore Fanfani mounted a violent anti-divorce campaign: the Communists feared that the time was not yet ripe for the Italians (and especially the Italian working class) to face such a battle: but the new law survived, by a majority of 59 per cent to 41 per cent.

Almost exactly a year later, on 19 May 1975, legislation reforming family rights was passed (Law 151, *Riforma del diritto della famiglia*). The laws covering this area at the time dated back to 1942, in other words they had been passed by the Fascists. On 9 December 1977 legislation covering equal rights at work was passed (Law 903, *Parità di trattamento tra uomini e donne in materia di lavoro*): this outlawed all discrimination on grounds of sex in the workplace.

The decade ended, from our point of view, with the referendum of 17–18 May 1981 to repeal the law on the protection of maternity and the termination of pregnancy (Law 194, approved on 22 May 1978). Abortion rights were preserved, the two proposals for change being rejected respectively by 88.5 per cent (the proposal of the Partito Radicale) and by 67.5 per cent (the amendment put forward by the anti-abortionist Movimento per la Vita).

These pieces of legislation and the referendums that accompanied them mark a period during which the major shifts of custom and sensibility that had occurred during the preceding decades found visible reflection in the domain of legal rights. The reform of family law is of particular significance, both theoretically and historically, in that it draws directly upon the most progressive aspects of the Constitution of the Italian Republic which came into force on 1 January 1948. Article 3 of the Constitution asserts the equality of the sexes:

All citizens are invested with equal social dignity and are equal before the law, without distinction as to sex, race, language, religion, political opinions, and personal or social conditions.

It is the duty of the Republic to remove all economic and social obstacles which, by actually limiting the freedom and equality of citizens, prevent the full development of the human being and the actual participation of all citizens in the political, economic, and social structures of the country.

Article 29 of the Constitution proclaimed that marriage partners were equal within the family; Article 37 established equal rights, including the right to equal payment, in the workplace; Article 48 confirmed women's electoral status; and Article 51 their full entitlement to take up public and elective office. However, other Articles of the Constitution (29, 30, and 31), referring to family life, continued to consign women to a position of inferiority. This contradiction bespeaks the dissonance between women's equality (or at any rate a tendency towards their equality) in the public sphere, and their subordination in the private sphere, which has been an enduring feature of Italian history (see Rossi-Doria 1994; also Boccia and Peretti 1988 and Bonacchi and Groppi 1993).

Moreover, for a long time many of the more egalitarian provisions of the Constitution were more or less dead letters. It was only in the mid-1960s that certain rulings of the Constitutional Court began to show a less conservative temper and a new concern with real sexual equality (one example was the 1968 ruling that the provision of the 1942 civil code making a husband's adultery less significant than a wife's was in breach of the principle of equality). Reform of family legislation, advocated from 1970 onwards, was delayed until 1975 because of the opposition to full recognition of political and legal equality of the sexes (Fortino 1981).

In these circumstances, the advent of divorce was a major breakthrough, in that it 'privileged spontaneous affection over formal constraints' (Rodotà 1976), and called in question the traditional image of the family as sacred and inviolate. It was the first legislative step towards freedom, within an institution hitherto governed by authoritarian and hierarchical principles (Barbiera 1976). The divorce referendum gave vital further impetus to moves towards bringing the law into line with society's requirements, leading Parliament to understand at last that Italian citizens not only supported the dissolubility of marriage, but were also strongly in favour of reforming legislation on the family (Santangelo 1976). The enthusiastic and spontaneous public demonstrations which greeted the referendum results demonstrated the breadth of popular support for the new law, which was seen as bringing Italian society up to date and liberating it from oppressive rules.

The reform of family law asserted the judicial and moral equality of the marriage partners, abolishing or amending provisions that had enshrined the husband's dominance (such as those which asserted his ultimate authority, and his wife's obligation to make her home with him wherever he might choose to reside). Where the 1942 civil code had made the husband head of the family, the reforms spoke of marriage as conferring equal rights and duties upon wife and husband alike. Under the new law, which recognized the wife's domestic labour (of which no account had previously been taken), property was seen as held in common. Husbands were no longer expected to support their wives: rather, each partner was to contribute to the maintenance of the family, from their own means and by their own labour inside or outside the home. Dowry payments, meanwhile, were abolished, putting an end to a custom linked to individual property ownership within marriage and to the notion of marriage as an exchange between two groups transacted in the person of the woman.

Reform gave rise to a new vision of the family as an association of equals, a community in which parity, not hierarchy, was the rule. Each parent was accorded equal rights and duties in respect of their children, and the recognition of natural children was facilitated by measures which gave parents equal rights and duties in respect of their offspring whether legitimate or illegitimate (Bessone *et al.* 1980; Cuocolo 1989; Schwarzenberg 1975). Cohabitation between a child's natural parents became accepted: the 'natural family' was recognized, as an arrangement that derived not necessarily from legal matrimony, but from the fact that the parents lived together (Santangelo 1976).

One highly controversial provision of the new law allowed for judicial intervention where there was disagreement between the partners: either partner could invoke this simply by making a request and no formalities were involved. Some commentators have seen this as a recognition of the fraught nature of conjugal relations. Certainly the new provision marked the end of an era in which the governance of family life had been a matter entirely for the family itself: now, the silence and secrecy of the domestic sphere were being broken (Mattone and Ruggiano 1977).

None the less, elements of inequality remained in Law 151. One instance of this is the fact that under the new law the wife is expected to take the husband's surname (though she can seek judicial authorization not to use it, if by doing so she would risk serious harm), and the children take the father's name. From the logical and juridical standpoint of formal equality, nothing justifies this privileging of the name of the husband/father (Fortino 1981).

It is generally agreed that the Italian legislature thus took on board the deep-seated change in values that had occurred, and that it largely, though not entirely, undertook the task of doing away with role divisions and hierarchy within the family. Some commentators also trace to this period the establishment, among the most progressively inclined social groups, of ways of living which broke with the sexual division of labour, with its allocation of domestic work to the wife and leadership to the husband, in favour of a relationship of equality in everything pertaining to collective life. Be that as it may, in everyday life parity remained a prize to be fought for, and this required alliance and collaboration not only among family members, but between the judiciary, with its new powers, and those who had customarily been most disadvantaged within the family (Mattone and Ruggiano 1977).

The second half of the 1970s also saw the closing of the gap between Constitutional principle and legal fact as regards equality at work. There was one statutory regulation (Law 1204, passed in 1971, concerning the protection of working mothers), but up until 1977, when Law 903 was finally approved, international conventions and European community law, although formally ratified in Italy, had no effect there. Here too, new legislation implemented what was proclaimed in the Constitution, superseding the old practice by which equal pay was given for work regarded as of equal value. From 1960 onwards, both case law and international directives tended increasingly to regard any attempt to compare the value of work performed as an irrelevance when it came to determining the levels of pay for women and men workers: the law thus confirmed a growing agreement that the correct principle was for equal pay to be made for the same kind of work, regardless of the value of the product.

Law 903 (Articles 1, 2, and 3) prohibits all discrimination on the basis of sex as regards the availability of work, rates of pay, access to qualifications, permanency of employment, and promotion. Of particular interest is the recognition (in Article 7) of the right of fathers as well as mothers to be absent from work in order to look after children—and not just children by blood: adoptive children, and other children for whose care the worker is responsible, are included. Here the law goes at least some way to accepting the feminist argument that simplistic distinctions between maternal and paternal roles have been linked to stereotypical notions of femininity and masculinity.

Law 194, on the termination of pregnancy, resembled the other laws we have been reviewing in that it gave legal recognition to an existing situation—in this case the widespread practice of illegal abortion. It differs from these other laws, however, in that, whereas they may be held to reduce the legal differences between the sexes, Law 194 actually increases them, for instance in allowing the father/ husband to be consulted only if that is the woman's wish (Cuocolo 1989). Indeed, although the decision to terminate her pregnancy does involve the woman in observing certain checks and limits, Law 194 regards her as the principal author of that decision: the family counselling services introduced in 1975 under the management of the Italian regions are charged with providing her with information and assistance. It should be noted that the Italian women's movement, despite profound underlying differences between its constituent groups, was very largely united, during the run-up to the law's enactment, in pressing for free and readily obtainable abortion. Where particular groups (such as Rivolta femminile) disagreed, this was because they did not want the powerful charge which female sexuality represented for patriarchal society to be defused in the rush for abortion rights. From this perspective, the law as approved certainly set limits to women's right to choose: Article 4 allows voluntary termination of pregnancy during the first ninety days when 'the woman can show cause why continuation of pregnancy or the birth of the child would entail a serious risk to her physical or mental health', and Article 9 allows medical and ancillary workers to refuse on grounds of conscience to take part in abortions.

Law 194 highlights the question of the relationship between equality and difference and of their dialectical interconnection, which must be grasped if either term is to be correctly understood. To achieve equality before the law and equality of rights, it is necessary first of all to abolish major discrepancies between the rights of women and those of men, but it is then also necessary to recognize gender difference and differences between individuals. Some rulings of the 1970s, bearing on the question of sexual identity, offered partial recognition of this (see Falzea 1982). A number of pertinent disagreements emerge here: for instance, between those who regard sexual identity as wholly determined by physiology and those who see psychological orientation as crucial (Garutti and Macioce 1981). These can have important consequences, as in determining the conditions for valid marriage (which for the law include difference of sex), or in considering requests made by transsexuals for the correction of the gender attributed to them by the law. Law 164 (of 1982), and a subsequent ruling of the Constitutional Court (1985), indicate that sexual identity can be rethought, as the liberty for individuals to choose their own sexual identity when it becomes necessary to do so (Fortino 1990).

It is along these lines that we must approach the question of the protection to be afforded to sexual difference, which includes the question of how sexual freedom is to be protected both positively and negatively—an area, as Lagostena Bassi argues (1993), in which Italian law is deficient. Some have argued that the achievement of parity within the framework of existing jurisdiction does not free women as subjects from their subordination: rather, it is claimed, they must inaugurate a completely new way of conceiving the relations between subjects, both in public and in private (Fortino 1990; Libreria delle donne di Milano 1987).

However this debate may develop, and even if the law does evolve in ways that allow it to take account of gender difference, it is still important, for several reasons, to record these steps towards equality. First of all, the record illuminates an important phase in gender relations in Italy: here, the 1970s bear the marks of the long-standing battle between women and men, but they also show how individuals came together in a new spirit of co-operation, accepting and valuing one another's otherness, seeing the Other as the counterpart of the self. Secondly, this progress towards equality makes it incontestably clear that femininity and masculinity cannot be defined once and for all; on the contrary, they are subject to constant negotiation and adjustment, as individuals relate both to various forms of collective life and to other individuals. Thus, if we follow the road of equality far enough, we come in the end to the point where gender difference, and individual difference, must be recognized and welcomed. Equality remains the common aspiration of humanity—all those born of women—but 'humanity' must itself be differently understood and defined in different historical periods and situations.

Gender Difference and Individual Difference

Gender-based political movements can influence gender relations both indirectly and directly. Indirect influences are, in my view, greatly more important, in their effects on culture and custom, especially in a country such as Italy where, whatever conflicts may have raged beneath the surface, the public sphere has been dominated by traditions of masculinism and patriarchy. In reviewing the history of the movements of the 1970s, we can identify a number of significant themes in regard to relations both between and within the sexes.

Italian feminism of the 1970s was diverse and various; indeed, a readiness to acknowledge this (despite serious conflicts), and a disavowal of any pretence to unanimity, was one of its strengths. However, despite this diversity, all those involved shared, explicitly or implicitly, and even when relations with men and with institutions were at stake, one common assumption—namely, that women were seeking to act as integral subjects towards one another. The movement was understood to be a movement which sought to discover and affirm female subjectivity. Whether or not it proved possible to do away with the mediation of men, women within the movement saw themselves as women, laying claim to a gendered identity and seeking to understand and live out that identity (*Memoria* 1987; Passerini 1991).

Radical feminist groups theorized both a woman-centred way of living and practices of speech and bodily expression which involved separation from men. The birth of the Italian women's movement can be dated to July 1970, when the manifesto of Rivolta femminile was posted up in the streets of Rome and Milan. The manifesto began by proclaiming that women cannot be defined in relation to men and cannot discover themselves by way of masculine models, and it concluded by stating 'comunichiamo solo con le donne' ('we communicate only with women'). The movement as a whole accepted separatist premises, even if some saw these as tactical, others as strategic. It is notable that twenty years later the young women of the student movement of 1990 criticized separatism, an essential aspect of 1970s feminism, as dogmatic, holding that it was not indispensably necessary to a feminist practice (Capussotti 1993).

In the context of 1970s Italy, feminist separatism made a considerable impact in both concrete and symbolic terms. Only a fairly small number of women put their separatist principles into practice, but these separatist groups were active in more than a hundred cities and towns. Their members were drawn overwhelmingly from intellectual circles, where there was a conflict between progressive and emancipatory tendencies on the one hand and the traditional role still ascribed to women on the other (see Ergas 1986). The effects on gender relations were felt both within the couple and in social life, and above all in the cultural sphere: symbolic and signifying practice was altered in particularly important ways, but much of this change took place only during the subsequent decade, one example being the work of the Commissione Nazionale per la Realizzazione della Parità tra Uomo e Donna, which oversaw the publication in 1986 of a text edited by A. Sabatini on non-sexist language, *Raccomandazioni per un uso non sessista della lingua italiana* (for a discussion in English, see Lepschy 1991).

Another important development in the sphere of culture was the growth of women's writing, in a range of forms, from narratives to diaries to journalism (see Del Bo Boffino 1986). This drew on, at the same time as it radically renewed, a long tradition of women's participation in literary work. When the movement was at its height, there was a great flowering of women's writing and feminist writing, born of the sense that women now had the chance to produce and express new forms of thought (Rusconi 1988). On the one hand, female voices came from the experience of consciousness-raising groups, from the pages of the new women's periodicals (*Effe*, *Sottosopra*, *Differenze*), and from feminists' encouragement to one another to take their old writings out of the closet or to embark on fresh ones; on the other, women's literature showed itself more and more aware that this was its cultural context and its new character. There was a complex interplay between these dimensions, a matter not of causal relationship but of common participation in the process which was creating language, values, and consciousness.

Important novels of the 1970s include Dacia Maraini's *Donna in guerra* (1975), Carla Cerati's *Un matrimonio perfetto* (1975), and Gabriella Ferri's *Un quarto di donna* (1976). Each in its different way tells the story of how bonds deriving from traditional gender relations are undone. Their protagonists feel less and less interest in being part of a couple which is not unhappy, but in which the relationship is emptied of meaning as a new female subjectivity comes into being. In this literature women's deepest subjectivity depends upon a moment of solitude (as has been noted by Amateis 1991), a characteristic very clearly revealed in the final pages of all three books: 'Now I am alone and I must begin everything over again' (*Donna in guerra*); 'I shall never be the same again, but I want to be myself' (*Un matrimonio perfetto*); 'Who knows what will become of me, scattered as I am amidst these great virtues, in this dawn of ideals which is still too much a dawn' (*Un quarto di donna*).

It is the sense of a beginning which animates this writing, as it makes bearable these moments of solitude. It is matched by a diction which is often plain, a preference for the everyday and the bodily, a quest for the degree zero of writing and of life (see Nozzoli 1977). In the decade which followed, women's literary and autobiographical writing continued to grow impressively in energy and in quantity, engendering whole series of works, publishing houses, and bookshops—and giving rise, too, to a body of critical and reflective commentaries (Cutrufelli 1988; see also Hallamore Caesar, 'Post-War Italian Narrative', Chapter 14 in this volume).

Moments of solitude may be foregrounded in the literary record, but in the documents of the new feminist movement they are few and far between. The latter refer above all to the rise of new relationships between women: relationships in the context of the collective and the group (it was in the years between 1971 and 1976 that women for the first time organized collective holidays, meetings, and conferences). Feminist publications celebrate the discovery of the other woman, of other women, of their speech and their bodies, in the almost stifling immediacy of the collective, where the individual is brought back to her personal relationship with her mother. As sexual difference was acknowledged and valued, differences between individuals blossomed too, but the politics of the feminist groups of the 1970s attributed little worth to the latter. However, the end of the decade saw the end, too, of 'the illusion that the project of the individual could be identical with that of the group' (Di Cori 1989).

Women's scholarly, journalistic, and essayistic writing of the 1970s deserves a special study to itself. We can do no more than mention a few milestones, works produced outside the movement itself: Chiara Saraceno's *Dalla parte delle donne* (1971), Elena Gianini Belotti's *Dalla parte delle bambine* (1973), Franca Pieroni Bortolotti's *Socialismo e questione femminile in Italia* (1974). The year 1976 saw the publication of Laura Balbo's *Stato di famiglia*, and a volume of testimony entitled *La resistenza taciuta*—the 'silenced' wartime resistance of twelve women partisans from Piedmont. Lea Melandri's *L'infamia originaria* came out in 1977, Marina Mizzau's *Eco e Narciso* in 1979. Even this tiny selection shows the diversity of fields in which women were working: sociology, history, literature. As women made their presence felt (both quantitatively and qualitatively) in the world of publishing, the boundaries of gender shifted in the cultural sphere—and a huge new market was created. All this, by highlighting the growing creativity of women, highlighted also the contradictory fact that they received little institutional recognition; it fostered closer ties between members of the same sex, but it sometimes sharpened conflicts between women and men in the public sphere.

Memories and oral histories confirm that great changes in relations between women followed in the train of 1970s feminism. In life histories collected in the second half of the 1980s and the early 1990s, the theme recurs again and again (see *Archivi orali*). This change took diverse forms, but in the great majority of cases a central theme is the making and celebration of relationships between women (relationships of friendship and love, and of professional collaboration, many of which were to endure during the years to come), or else the forging of symbolic links with cultural forms in which women had found, and were finding, self-expression. This was something relatively new in Italian culture, as is shown by the frequent references to Virginia Woolf, perhaps the most favoured figure of inspiration and guidance even though she came from a foreign cultural tradition.

Limited though they were to certain sectors of society, and to women of the rising generation, these changes in women's perception of themselves, and in their relations with each other, had their effect on men too. L. Ellena's pioneering researches indicate that for those men who were in closest contact with the women's movement the 1970s were a turbulent decade, in which they felt estranged and ill at ease, at a loss for a common language, and full of envy. Life history sources, memoirs, and diaries of the period all suggest that men at this time were baffled by questions of gender relations, and fell silent (see Monico 1977; Segre 1977).

In the early 1970s, homosexuals came out in Italy too. Just as men had participated in some of the late-1960s groups which were forerunners of feminism (such as the 'Demau' group, which set out to demystify patriarchal authority: see Calabrò and Grasso 1985), so heterosexual women participated in some of the homosexual men's groups of the early 1970s. The homosexual movement echoed many of the practices of feminism—the collective-based structure, the emphasis on beginning with the personal, the critique of psychoanalysis, the celebration of the body and sexuality, the critique of the bourgeois family and of formal politics. From June 1972, Fuori (Fronte Unitario Omosessuale Rivoluzionario Italiano—the united Italian homosexual revolutionary front: *fuori* means 'out') published their 'monthly magazine of sexual liberation', also called *Fuori!* In its pages we find all these themes, and others, addressed in direct, impassioned and unsparing words and images. Heterosexual intellectuals, such as Fernanda Pivano, contributed to the journal, and one feature, which appeared over the name 'Myriam Quarzo' (pseudonym of Myriam Cristallo), was billed as 'A heterosexual woman speaks to heterosexual men'. However, *Fuori!* remained geared more to the needs and feelings of gay men than to those of lesbians.

Fuori embarked on a 'critique of normality', based on a critical consciousness that went 'well beyond the problem of homosexuality'. This drew upon the tradition of left intellectual culture, and referred, in a more or less critical spirit, to the works of Marx and Freud, Adorno and Sartre. The movement proclaimed the New Revolutionary Homosexual, who while he criticized the limited nature of class politics, preferring a trans-class approach, none the less emphasized economic and social oppression and paid attention to such questions as homosexuality in the factory. The publications of the movement (for instance, the selection of

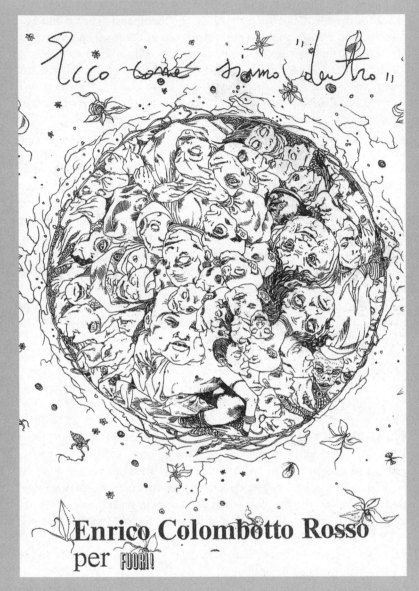

Fig. 12 This picture was drawn for the magazine *Fuori!* in 1970. It expresses the complex and innovative nature of the gay movement's cultural activity at the time. The artist, Enrico Colombotto Rosso, who was born in Turin in 1925, is a painter and stage designer whose work is known for the way it combines elegance and exquisiteness of touch with the treatment of subjects such as the concentration camp, physical deformity, and dementia. This particular image contains many of the motifs that recur in Colombotto Rosso's work and that relate to Fuori's concerns: the lack of innocence of childhood, the intertwining of suffering, masculinity, and sinister playfulness, and the promise of something embryonic free of illusions about the future.

material reprinted from *Fuori!*) offer a generalized critique of the violence of the capitalist world. The year 1975 saw the murder of Pier Paolo Pasolini, who was recognized by homosexual culture as one of its own, and served as a grim reminder of the daily violence surrounding gay men's lives.

Overall, the platform of Fuori bears the marks of the universalism of that time. The gay movements of the 1990s, in their more articulate and more searching discussion of the issues, have left such positions to one side, when they do not criticize them as paternalistic: now gay men favour an overtly separatist celebration of homosexual pride. The basic theoretical claim of Fuori was that 'homosexual desire is universal'; this was combined with a critique of capitalist domination, and the importance of homosexuality was conceived within the terms of 'human emancipation'. The rise of the women's movement was welcomed: new forms of intersubjectivity were to be created, which would lead to a new understanding between human beings. This basic framework of ideas is carefully developed in Mario Mieli's important work *Elementi di critica omosessuale* (1977).

The publications of the Fuori group showed this tendency to universalism in the welcome they offered to feminist statements and writings. The need for an alliance with the women's movement was proclaimed. In reality, however, attempts to form concrete alliances were rare, and often unsuccessful. One such attempt was made in the Milan conference of October 1972, where a meeting, or encounter, was staged between feminists and gay men: those lesbians who were present raised their voices in protest, feeling that they were not made fully welcome by feminist groups, but equally unhappy with the idea of being somehow bundled together with the men of Fuori. Towards the end of the decade lesbian groups emerged, rooted in an awareness of the gender-specificity of their position, and sustaining an autonomous network of groups and publications which was none the less connected to the women's movement (see Pomeranzi 1989). However, the debate on political lesbianism within the women's movement went back much earlier: it ran in parallel with discussions about the rediscovery of the daughter's relationship to the body of the mother, in the radical feminist groups of Turin and Milan which were linked to the French 'Psychanalyse et politique' movement.

It is important to register the considerable impact which these homosexual and lesbian movements and individuals had upon Italian culture and politics, through their writings and their public acts (demonstrations, critical interventions, conferences on homosexuality). The homosexual orientation of many prominent people, especially in the world of culture and the arts, had for years been a well-kept secret: when they came out, habits of behaviour and expression were transformed. Aspects of Italian life which had been present for a long time could now speak and be spoken of, and the consequence was an outbreak of conflict, but also a developing movement of solidarity both between and within genders.

Conflict was, perhaps inevitably, one aspect of the new forms of intersubjectivity. Once women stood as autonomous subjects no longer amenable to male mediation, they discovered new kinds of internecine discord and competition. Given the lack of fully formed democratic traditions in Italy, it was to take some while before such tensions could be handled in a spirit of civil disagreement and mutual respect. Some men, too, underwent profound, or at any rate spectacular, mutations: acknowledging the rights of the body, they declared themselves to be homosexuals, bisexuals, transsexuals—in any case, very definitely sexual beings, unmasking the false universalism of the category 'man' and questioning the privileged position accorded to the male in spheres such as politics, the academy, and the military.

The women's movement and the homosexual men's movement of the 1970s were both located primarily in intellectual, middle-class circles. For all that, their advent marked a point of no return for gender relations, public and private, in Italy. They differed in their extent and in their longevity, the women's movement enjoying wider and more sustained support, and concrete alliances were barely realized between them. But this does not affect their substantial convergence in many important respects.

A Provisional Afterword

A consideration even of the two limited domains surveyed here confirms that the 1970s were indeed crucial years for the history of gender relations in Italy. Long-standing tensions and dynamics came to the surface, expressing themselves both in legislation and in the sphere of symbolic representation (in politics and culture), and this led to far-reaching changes in the ways people spoke and behaved. Looking back twenty years later, it is not easy to draw up the balance sheet: further research is needed both on the 1970s and on the subsequent decade, in which many of the new tendencies grew stronger, but in which others were decidedly reversed. Some of the laws passed in the 1970s were little used in practice (the legislation allowing fathers leave of absence to care for children is a case in point), and this reluctance shows how slow the pace of change has been in some areas. The search for an authentic mutual intersubjectivity grounded in an awareness of gender has known setbacks, for instance in the rise of certain right-wing women who apply their determined managerial skills to themselves as well as to their political and business empires. Such women regard feminism, and their own femaleness, as irrelevant to their public personalities. This was exemplified, to take one instance, in the speech made by Irene Pivetti of the Lega Nord when she was elected President of the Chamber of Deputies (equivalent to the Speaker of the House of Commons in the British Parliament) after the 1994 general election. She defined herself using masculine forms ('cittadino', 'cattolico') rather than their readily available feminine equivalents (the text is taken from *L'Avvenire* of 17 April 1994):

come cittadino e come Presidente della Camera mi inchino alla Corte Costituzionale e mi impegno alla rigorosa osservazione del mio mandato istituzionale. . . . Come cattolico . . .

non posso non affidare la mia opera in questo Parlamento e, nella preghiera, alla volontà di Dio, a cui appartengono i destini di tutti gli Stati e della storia.

None the less even a superficial glance at contemporary Italy cannot but register profound changes which have been inspired by, or have come in reaction to, the experience of the 1970s. Many young heterosexual couples have relationships in which tasks are shared more collaboratively than they used to be. It has grown easier for couples to live together without being married. There is greater freedom for lesbian and gay male relationships, though more for the latter than for the former. Women have become more visible in a range of places and situations, and more visible to one another. For all that, Italy remains a country in which gender relations are still often formed in the mould of an underlying masculinism— old-fashioned or newfangled, covert or manifest—and this masculinism both sustains old traditions and invents new ones. In the confusion and disillusionment of the 1990s, we do well to remind ourselves of the irreverent energies which broke through twenty years ago. That remembered passion can encourage us to take stock of our own times, and to press once more for a recognition both of equality and of difference, between the sexes and between individuals.

Further Reading

There is practically nothing in English on gender relations in Italy. Some historical works on Italian feminism are of indirect relevance, such as Judith Adler Hellman's *Journeys among Women: Feminism in Five Italian Cities* (Oxford, 1987), or Paola Bono and Sandra Kemp (eds.), *Italian Feminist Thought: A Reader* (Oxford, 1991). See also Lesley Caldwell's 'Italian Feminism: Some Considerations', in Zygmunt G. Baranski and Shirley Vinall (eds.), *Women and Italy: Essays on Gender, Culture and History* (London, 1991).

On the juridical aspects, some information can be found in the chapter on 'Italy' by B. Sgritta and P. Tufari, in R. Chester (ed.), *Divorce in Europe* (Leiden, 1977), 253–82, and in V. Librando's discussion of 'Italian Law' in A. G. Chloros (ed.), *The Reform of Family Law in Europe* (Deventer, 1978), 151–82.

On the history of legislation, the relevant texts (all cited in the references to this chapter) are those by Bessone and others and by Cuocolo, and the articles by Fortino. On the history of the gender movements, see Calabrò and Grasso (1985), Crispino (1989), Mieli (1977), and Passerini (1991); and see *Memoria*, 19–20.

As for the other sources, the *archivi orali* cited in the text are collections of feminist life histories (both on tape and transcribed) which may be consulted in the Department of History at the Università degli Studi di Torino and at the Centro di Documentazione delle Donne in Bologna (for the latter collection, see *Il movimento delle donne in Emilia-Romagna. Alcune vicende tra storia e memoria (1970–1980)*, published in Bologna in 1990).

Issues of the magazine *Fuori!* may be consulted in the Fondazione Penna in Turin: I am grateful to the Fondazione Penna for having put them at my disposal. A selection of articles has been published in Angelo Pezzana (ed.), *La politica del corpo* (Rome, 1976) with an introduction by Alfredo Cohen: Pezzana and Cohen were both involved in the Fuori group during its years of activity.

References

AMATEIS, M. (1991), *L'amore al femminile. Trasformazioni del discorso amoroso in scrittrici italiane 1968–1988*, Tesi di laurea in Metodologia della ricerca storica, Facoltà di Magistero, Università degli Studi di Torino.

BALDARACCO, E., D'AMBROSIO, F., and BUSCAGLIA, M. (1976) (eds.), *Maternità cosciente. Contraccezione e aborto* (Milan).

BARANSKI, Z. G., and VINALL, S. W. (1991) (eds.), *Women and Italy: Essays on Gender, Culture and History* (London).

BARBIERA, L. (1976), 'Divorzio e nuovo diritto di famiglia', *Il Diritto di Famiglia e delle Persone*, II semestre: 1247–62.

BESSONE, M., ALPA, G., D'ANGELO, A., and FERRANDO, G. (1980), *La famiglia del nuovo diritto* (Bologna).

BOCCIA, M. L., and PERETTI, I. (1988) (eds.), *Il genere della rappresentanza*, suppl. to *Democrazia e Diritto*, 1, Jan.–Feb.

BONACCHI, G., and GROPPI, A. (1993) (eds.), *Il dilemma della cittadinanza. Diritti e doveri delle donne* (Rome and Bari).

CALABRÒ, A. R., and GRASSO, L. (1985) (eds.), *Dal movimento femminista al femminismo diffuso* (Milan).

CAPUSSOTTI, E. (1993), *Memoria e oblio del movimento femminista nelle donne della Pantera a Torino*, Tesi di laurea in Metodologia della ricerca storica, Facoltà di Magistero, Università degli Studi di Torino.

CICIONI, M., and PRUNSTER, M. (1993) (eds.), *Visions and Revisions: Women in Italian Culture* (Providence, RI, and Oxford).

CRISPINO, A. M. (1989) (ed.), *Esperienza storica femminile nell'età moderna e contemporanea*, ii (Rome).

CUOCOLO, F. (1989), 'Famiglia: I. Profili costituzionali', in *Enciclopedia giuridica* (Rome).

CUTRUFELLI, M. R. (1988), *Scritture, scrittrici* (Milan).

DEL BO BOFFINO, A. (1986), *I nostri anni settanta. Come le giornaliste hanno raccontato il femminismo* (Milan).

DI CORI, P. (1989), 'Il movimento cresce e sceglie l'autonomia 1974–79', in Crispino (1989).

ELLENA, L. (1994), *Storia e soggettività delle donne a Torino: sguardi incrociati maschili e femminili, 1970–1980*, Tesi di laurea in Metodologia della ricerca storica, Facoltà di Magistero, Università degli Studi di Torino.

ERGAS, Y. (1986), *Nelle maglie della politica. Femminismo, istituzioni e politiche sociali nell'Italia degli anni '70* (Milan).

FALZEA, A. (1982), 'I fatti giuridici della vita materiale', *Rivista di Diritto Civile*, 472–90.

FORTINO, M. (1981), 'Parità dei sessi', in *Enciclopedia del diritto*, xxxi (Milan).

—— (1990), 'Sesso (Diritto vigente)', in *Enciclopedia del diritto*, xlii (Milan).

GARUTTI, M., and MACIOCE, F. (1981), 'Il diritto alla identità sessuale', in *Rivista di Diritto Civile*, 273–94.

LAGOSTENA BASSI, T. (1993), 'Violence against Women and the Response of Italian Institutions', in Cicioni and Prunster (1993).

LEPSCHY, G. (1991), 'Language and Sexism', in Baranski and Vinall (1991).

Libreria delle donne di Milano (1987), *Non credere di avere dei diritti* (Turin).

MATTONE, S., and RUGGIANO, M. G. (1977), 'L'intervento del giudice nella famiglia', in *Democrazia e Diritto*, 1: 197–203.

Memoria. Rivista di storia delle donne (1987), special issue on *Il movimento femminista negli anni '70*, 19–20.

MIELI, M. (1977), *Elementi di critica omosessuale* (Turin).

MONICO, C. (1977), *Mia cara, da un marito compagno* (Turin).

Nozzoli, A. (1977), 'Sul romanzo femminista italiano degli anni settanta', in *Nuova Donna Woman Femme*, 5.

Passerini, L. (1991), *Storie di donne e femministe* (Turin).

Pomeranzi, B. (1989), 'Pratiche politiche tra donne. Il separatismo lesbico', in Crispino (1989).

Rivolta Femminile (1970), *Manifesto* (Rome).

—— (1971), 'Sessualità femminile e aborto', in *Scritti di Rivolta Femminile* (Rome).

Rodotà, S. (1976), 'La riforma del diritto di famiglia alla prova. Principi ispiratori e ipotesi sistematiche', in *Il nuovo diritto della famiglia*, 3–30 (Milan).

Rossi-Doria, A. (1994), 'Le donne sulla scena politica', in F. Barbagallo (ed.), *Storia dell'Italia repubblicana*, i. *La costruzione della democrazia* (Turin).

Rusconi, M. (1988), 'Nuovi percorsi tra esperienza e scrittura', in Cutrufelli (1988).

Santangelo, S. (1976), 'Alcuni aspetti della riforma del diritto familiare particolarmente significativi sul piano giuridico-sociale', in *Il Diritto di Famiglia e delle Persone*, II semestre: 1264–72.

Schwarzenberg, C. (1975), 'Una famiglia nuova', in *Il Diritto di Famiglia e delle Persone*, II semestre: 573–7.

Segre, S. (1977) (ed.), *L'antimaschio* (Milan).

Stella Richter, G. (1976), *L'istituto del divorzio in Italia e l'esperienza giuridica dei principali ordinamenti europei* (Milan).

9

Immigration and Social Identities

VANESSA MAHER

OVER the last twenty years, there has been a flow of immigrants into Italy from the South of the world. There is uncertainty over their numbers: the 1992 census figures put them at around 500,000, but the figures are not reliable (see Table 9.1). It is clear that the lobbies for greater or lesser provision for immigrants or more or fewer restrictions on immigration can use these figures to justify a variety of policies. There are also many people without permits to stay (around 200,000 according to some estimates). They are often called *clandestini*, although it is more appropriate to call them 'irregulars', since most of them have been registered on entry or at some point during their stay. The total number of recent immigrants amounts to no more than 1.8 per cent of the Italian population, a much smaller percentage than that found in Germany, France, or Britain, but their presence has caused a degree of 'social alarm' which can only be explained by taking into account the historical circumstances in which the immigration has taken place. The political circumstances, public debate, and actual situation of the immigrants is constantly changing. Only a foolhardy analyst would claim to have grasped the whole picture, and it is tentatively that I proffer the following observations.

Table 9.1. Foreign residents in Italy as at 31 December 1992 by source country and region

(a) First twenty source countries

Country	Number	% of total foreign residents
Morocco	95,741	10.34
USA	62,112	6.71
Tunisia	50,405	5.44
Philippines	44,155	4.77
Germany	39,629	4.25
Yugoslavia	39,495	4.21
Albania	28,628	3.09
Great Britain	28,087	3.03
Senegal	27,572	2.98
France	25,396	2.74
Egypt	23,515	2.54
China	21,417	2.31
Poland	21,221	2.29
Brazil	18,751	2.02
Switzerland	18,225	1.96
Sri Lanka	17,242	1.86
Romania	16,443	1.77
Greece	16,256	1.75
Spain	15,566	1.68
Somalia	14,973	1.61
TOTAL	624,829	67.36

(b) Main source regions

Region	Number	%
European Community (EC)	146,772	15.88
Western non-EC countries	33,420	3.62
Eastern non-EC countries	131,496	14.20
Non-European developing countries	530,165	57.30
Non-European developed countries	83,319	9.00
TOTAL	925,172	100.00

Source: Giovanna Zincone, *Uno schermo contro il razzismo. Per una politica dei diritti utili* (Rome, 1994), 84.

'In-Group' and 'Out-Group': Definitions of Immigrant

The years leading up to the formal ending of the Cold War were marked, in Italy, by the erosion of the political alignments which since the Second World War had been organized round the issue of communism and anti-communism. The process of European unification appeared to gather speed. Despite the boom in public and private spending in Italy during the 1980s, there was a rising tide of political discontent, fuelled by the ineptitude and corrupt dealings of a generation of politicians and public officials suspected of having subordinated the interests of the general public to those of political parties, or even to those of subversive and criminal organizations. The Lega Lombarda and other leagues (later unified as the Lega Nord) proposed that Italy should become a federation of three separate states, so that the prosperous Northerners could make their own European alliances and should not have to contribute to the maintenance of the weaker and racket-ridden South. This was only one symptom of a crisis in the relationship of Italians with the state and above all with a nation whose premisses, outlined in the Constitution of 1948, conferred on them the status of citizens of a democracy (Rusconi 1993).

The emergence of restricted regional 'identities' or fictive 'ethnodemocracies', which reflect a widespread estrangement from national politics, is paralleled by a more general tendency in some sectors of the population to draw sharper lines between the 'in-group' and the 'out-group'. The sectors most concerned are old people, young people from disadvantaged groups and the urban periphery, people in small towns. These groups are particularly worried by their precarious grasp on resources, such as jobs, housing, and welfare provision, and by the shortcomings of the state.

The process of 'out-group' definition has been intensified by the arrival of Filipino, Middle Eastern, and African immigrants, who are obviously foreign in appearance and habits; but this coincidence should not distract us from the fact that the reaction to the immigrants is grafted onto a restrictive redefinition of social boundaries. The Lega Nord took up a position, first, against the 'parasitic' South and only later against the new immigration. Categories of exclusion such as *ebreo* (Jew), *zingaro* (gypsy) or even *marocchino* and *africano* (once used of Southern Italians), have called into new salience elements of the Italian population such as Jews and Southern Italians whose participation in the state and in the nation had become a matter of course. Although the objects of actual racial violence are the immigrants and the nomads, they are also called by the names of other groups, some of them Italian, whose identity and rights are thus called into question. The new wave of domestic and sexual violence against women, which often goes unpunished, and the proposals to bring back the brothels, in order to 'control' immigrant prostitutes, remind Italian women too of their precarious hold on citizenship. Awareness of the social dangers presented by this combination of circumstances has encouraged Catholic organizations, local authorities, and many Italians of different political and religious persuasions to defend the immigrant cause. The perception that the very 'morality' of the post-war democratic settlement is at stake emerges from the writings of many Italian intellectuals (Rusconi 1993).

My analysis is from the vantage point of the Northern industrial city of Turin, known for the Fiat engineering works, the number and efficacy of its Catholic charities, and for the massive immigration from Southern Italy in the 1960s. I have been living in Turin for the past sixteen years and between 1988 and 1991, as part of a mixed team of immigrant and Italian research workers, I carried out research on the 'new' immigration (IRES-Piemonte 1991).

The arrival in Italy, between 1975 and 1990, of nearly a million immigrants from over a hundred African, Middle Eastern, Asian, and Latin American countries caused some consternation in a period of widespread unemployment among Italians. However it was soon evident that they were finding jobs in the informal labour market—picking tomatoes for the Southern canning industry, working as domestic servants for Italian families, taking on jobs in dangerous and polluted work environments such as chrome or tanning factories, and above all in the building industry with its high accident rate. Others became street-pedlars or washed windscreens at the traffic-lights as they waited for a job.

The laws on immigration of 1986 (Law 943) and 1990 (Law 39, known as the 'Legge Martelli'), the first since 1931, made some progress towards providing immigrants with a legal status, and many employers took them on with regular contracts and social security contributions. However, all those who arrived after 1990 were unable to obtain a legal permit to stay, and so remained ineligible for all except irregular jobs and the living conditions which went with them. The government took few steps to meet the emergency, and was content to leave the job of organizing canteens, dormitories, health care, and further provision for the immigrants first to the efficient Catholic charities, such as Caritas, and then to the local authorities.

The racist and xenophobic reactions of Italians to the new immigration were similar to those in many other European countries during the twentieth century. Immigrant lodgings were burnt to the ground in more than one episode; young thugs attacked and knifed Moroccans and Senegalese in Florence in 1989, and killed a South African refugee, Jerry Masslo, in Campania. Many newspapers introduced a new column entitled 'La caccia al nero' (Hunting down blacks) which has had many racist crimes to report over the last five years. Attacks on Senegalese and Moroccan pedlars and campaigns against them by Italian shopkeepers in several Italian cities brought home the point. Italians could no longer be characterized as just *brava gente* (decent people), erstwhile victims of other people's racism.

On the other hand, the speed, generosity, and highly articulated nature of the voluntary effort (particularly in Turin) to meet the immigrants' needs and to reduce the impact of any racist backlash has few parallels in other European countries. The voluntary activities were carried out with little detailed knowledge of how other countries had organized the reception of immigrants and in the absence of appropriate state legislation or funding. Quite often the initiatives of Catholic charities, trade unions, or other voluntary organizations were co-ordinated with those of the local authorities whose decisions anticipated or went beyond those of the central government. A first wave of Catholic or municipal reception centres and services for immigrants was reinforced, with the help of immigrant leaders and associations, by a second wave of voluntary initiatives which promoted the perception of immigrants as people who, on the one hand, were being denied their civil rights, but who, on the other, were contributing something of value to Italian society. Immigrants were not just 'people needing help'. Now there were groups for the legal defence of immigrants, Italo-immigrant cultural associations, groups to promote multicultural education in schools, trade union offices for immigrants, and so on. It was sometimes pointed out that the effect of immigration on the economy was positive given the low Italian birth rate and the ageing native population.

Attention was turned to changing immigrants' relationship to those state institutions which had remained essentially discriminatory and to enhancing the visibility of immigrants in prestigious positions. Immigrant associations and local authorities promoted several EC-funded courses in 1992 and 1993 to train highly educated immigrants as 'cultural mediators' in the social services. Since then the local authorities, schools, health and social services have organized a large number of courses on immigration for their own employees and some of the 'cultural mediators' have been called upon to give lectures based on their professional experience. An association of Italian and immigrant women founded an Intercultural Centre in Turin in 1993, one of whose aims was to promote entrepreneurship among women immigrants (IRES-Piemonte 1994).

Italians as Emigrants and the Experience of the New Immigration

The new immigrants are very different from the Italian emigrants of the late nineteenth and twentieth century of whom a large proportion were (until 1910) young, unmarried males, many of them from the countryside and illiterate. Apart from the fact that the new immigrants come from far away and are non-European, about 50 per cent of them are women, many come from cities, and up to half have at least a secondary school diploma. They are probably older on average than the Italian emigrants were, since they include people who left their countries because of wars and political repression, as well as many divorced and widowed women (Reginato 1990: 117–37). In spite of these differences, during the 1980s Italians implicitly or explicitly referred to their co-nationals' migratory experience when attempting to understand or express an opinion on the new migration. Associations and local government departments, originally set up to safeguard the interests of Italian emigrants, turned their attention to the new immigrants.

Temporary and seasonal emigration, particularly by skilled masons and decorators, has been a 'normal' feature of the life of many parts of Northern Italy since the seventeenth century (Albera 1989). But the massive and unprecedented exodus of millions of Italians from all regions which took place between 1875 and 1975 was often followed by the permanent settlement of the migrants in the Americas, in Australia, or in Northern Europe (see Figure 13).

However, for many years, emigration was temporary, families were left at home, and about half of the emigrants to the USA returned to Italy after a few years. This 'commuting' pattern of emigration, with its pre-eminent concern for local community networks, social events, and economic activity rather than national ones,

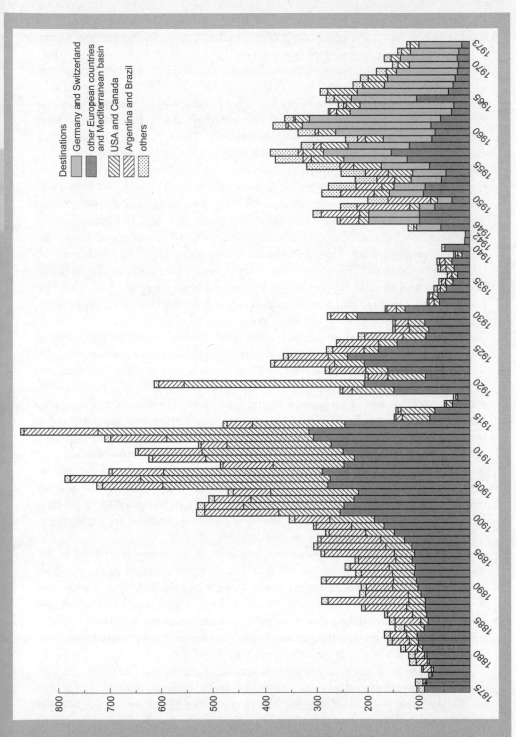

Fig. 13. Italian emigration abroad 1875–1973, with destinations (thousands).
Source: Atlante, vi, of *Storia d'Italia* (Turin 1976), 732–3.

may have had long-term effects on Italian social structure. In this connection we might consider phenomena such as the tendency to regional endogamy, the vitality of local dialects, and the mediation of access to the labour market and to state services by personal contacts (Nelli 1983).

In the industrial cities of the North such as Milan and Turin the new immigration evoked the traumatic experience of internal migration in the 1950s and 1960s, which began with the arrival of refugees from the Veneto, fleeing the disastrous floods which had devastated the Po Delta in 1953, and was followed by the 'Great Migration' from the South to the North. In the space of fifteen years whole villages disappeared from the map of Southern Italy, while Turin and its hinterland received nearly a million newcomers, including men with families, who transformed it into the 'third largest Southern city' (Fofi 1964: 22). The parallels with the current experience of non-European immigrants are often pointed out: the illegal exploitation of Southern workers, the hostile attitudes of the resident population which made it difficult for Southerners to find housing and regular employment. Even the areas of the city in which they first settled are now frequented by non-European immigrants. Recently these areas have become very dilapidated, the scene of drug-trafficking and petty crime.

Although most immigrants are in regular work, there is no doubt that many of those without are sucked into illegal rackets: drug-pushing, prostitution, and the managing of teams of young pedlars. In Turin it has been estimated that there are nearly one thousand Nigerian and East European prostitutes, who work under threat of violence and in particularly brutal conditions. There are also large numbers of Moroccan (male) child and teenage pedlars. Immigrants are easy scapegoats for whoever wishes to avoid tackling the structural reasons for the persistence of widespread corruption and crime. The social segregation of many immigrants in marginal and dangerous occupations, their greater vulnerability to discrimination, blackmail, and violence is a fact which official policies have done little to counter. Many immigrants languish in Italian gaols for lack of permits or on drug charges. In Turin half the inmates of the young offenders' prison are immigrants, imprisoned for drug-peddling or petty theft.

The drug traffic existed long before the arrival of the new immigrants, as the Turin Prefect (who is responsible for public order) was quick to point out after public protests in Porta Palazzo, the main Turin street market. The immigrants, he said, could not be blamed for the disorder there. They could be seen doing a hard and honest job washing down the pavements or preparing the market for the next day. Thirty years ago there were Southern Italians on the pavements, now they were behind the stalls (see also Frandino 1994).

It appears from a study on attitudes towards the immigrants in Piedmont that Southerners with an experience of emigration are no more favourable than others to the settlement of non-European immigrants (IRES-Piemonte 1992). This is probably related to the fact that although many of the first-generation Southern immigrants consider themselves integrated, they are still more vulnerable than other groups and occupy lower positions in the labour market (IRES-Piemonte 1992: 72–94; Virciglio 1991).

There are currently only around 70,000 non-European immigrants in Turin and its Region (Piedmont), with 15,000 in the city itself—less than 5 per cent of the numbers who came from the South in the 1950s and 1960s. However, the reference to Italian migration is rarely explicit or analytical in purpose. It is 'subliminal' and arises less from reference to real experience than from the suppression of memory. In the same way, the 'memory' of Italian colonial wars and occupation seems to have been suppressed and to have left a residue of stereotypes (Del Boca 1993: 158). When in the early 1970s immigrants first started arriving from the Horn of Africa, a former Italian colony, it was evident that few Italians had any explicit knowledge of or curiosity towards the societies from which they came. Immigrants had to deal with stereotypes created during the Fascist Ethiopian campaign. For example, the song 'Faccetta nera' (Little black face) associated Ethiopian women with slavery, which the Italian soldiers promised to replace with the 'slavery of love' (Del Boca 1992: 287). Indeed the institution of *madamismo* or temporary marriage with Ethiopian women was widespread (Carter 1992: 133). Is it a coincidence that almost the only jobs for immigrant women are those for domestic servants and prostitutes?

The somewhat misleading image of the migrant as a young single male is derived from a stereotyped view of earlier emigration by Italians as well as from the literature on North African migration to France or Pakistani migration to Britain. However, the prevalence of this stereotype may account for the fact that for a long time no arrangements were made to meet the needs of immigrant women, particularly those with children, despite the fact that they are a majority among the newcomers. In 1990 there were around 500 beds for men in municipal and charitable reception centres, but none for women. In 1990 social workers on a training course denied that there were any women among the immigrants. It is true that, through religious agencies, many immigrant women quickly found domestic work and so became invisible, but the lack of accommodation for them meant that they were forced to 'live in', always at their employers' beck and call, and board out their children in religious hostels (Olivero 1990). The immigration of family members is notoriously difficult, and most women are in Italy on their own and not as 'wives'.

Ethnicization and Symbolic Systems

It appears that Italian perceptions of the immigrants, who come from over a hundred countries, and two-thirds of whom are from the South of the world, particularly the Maghreb, West Africa, the Philippines, and Latin America, are filtered through a small number of symbolic categories: *marocchino, zingaro, meridionale*

(Southern Italian), *ebreo*, *africano/negro*. All these 'common-sense' categories suggest exclusion from the moral community rather than serving to identify any particular group, and to this extent they are something more than stereotypes. However, like all symbolic systems they operate at the level of unconscious or implicit knowledge and are impervious to evidence about the real nature of the people to whom they are applied. Indeed they are sometimes used interchangeably, the connotations of one category applied to another, and so on. Thus the term *marocchino* may be used to indicate immigrants in general, or Senegalese or Iranians. In ways redolent of nineteenth-century Orientalism (Said 1978: 99), the images of Moroccan and Jew are superimposed on each other. 'Moroccans to the gas chambers', reads one wall slogan.

On the other hand, a Calabrian worker from the Fiat works remembered how the Southern Italian immigrants were called *marocchini* in the 1950s, twenty years before the first Moroccan immigrants were seen in Italy. The new immigrants are called (benevolently) 'swallows', just as the Italian immigrants were called 'birds of passage' in the USA. Moroccan interviewees complain that they are often called *zingari*, which they consider insulting. Recently the habit of the police in some cities of shaving the hair off nomad (Rom) girls so that they looked like holocaust victims caused a scandal in the press. However, the same 'common-sense' categories are widely used in the media and even creep into sociological treatises.

These categories raise a number of questions concerning the way symbols are created and modified over time. In this instance, they appear to be the residue of a complex and selective social amnesia. Benedict Anderson, who insists on the 'imagined' nature of national communities, cites the nineteenth-century writer Ernest Renan who pointed out: 'The essence of a nation is that all the individuals in it must have a lot of things in common, and also that they must have forgotten a lot of things' (Anderson 1983: 13). The imagery evoked by the new immigration does not have an empirical referent. It is dissociated from its historical context. A sort of collective amnesia has swallowed up the experience of Italian emigration, of Italian colonialism, of Fascism, the knowledge of the complexity of Italian society itself. The residual imagery serves only to create boundaries between the newcomers and the host society. During our research on migration to Turin we discovered that immigrants were irritated by the fact that Italians had only a few large categories for identifying them: Moroccan, African, Oriental. The immigrants themselves insisted on the great variety of countries from which they came, on the fact that within every country there were different regions, societies, social classes whose inhabitants were culturally heterogeneous and who, as migrants, established different kinds of relationship with the host society. They attributed the Italian categories to 'ignorance' and 'mental laziness'. However, I am increasingly convinced that these categories have a place in a system of symbolic classification which is little affected by mere information. A Kurdish interviewee recounted a conversation with a bartender who asked him and his friends where they came from. 'Iraq, Lebanon, and Greece' was the reply. 'Oh, you're all African

Foto: Raúl Cocule

Con la collaborazione di:
Commissione Regionale per le Pari Opportunità
Associazione Produrre e Riprodurre
Cooperativa "La Talea"

OKOT
e SEMI di ZUCCA

Fig. 14 A still from a video about the lives and relationships of immigrant women, produced by the 'La Talea' Cooperative based at the Alma Mater Women's Multicultural Centre in Turin. Although the video is 'fictional', its representation of experience, whether of work or of personal relationships, is 'truer' than the large number of pictures of grim-faced men that recur in the press. The latter are often a reflection of the photographers' fears. News photographs of immigrant women are rare (it is usually prostitutes that are pictured), despite the fact that they account for over half the immigrant population in Italy.

then', exclaimed the bartender (IRES-Piemonte 1991: 172). In this case 'African' means 'from far off' and may equally be used of Sicilians.

In recent years there have been signs that many immigrants have decided to adopt as their own the identity of 'African', which they originally rejected as a source of confusion and de-personalization. For example, women from Cameroon, Kenya, Zaïre, Senegal, and Somalia (who previously knew little about one another's countries) have formed an African women's co-operative which does home-catering. The revival of these categories of exclusion leads to the 'ethnicization' (Zincone 1994) not only of immigrants but also of those Italians who feel themselves under threat from racism and misogyny. They feel a loss of social but also of state protection. The new 'ethnicity', with its identification of internal and external enemies, posits a hierarchy of social groups which is anything but spontaneous, and which official initiatives (or their omission) sometimes make more rigid.

The last few years have seen street demonstrations in several cities, to demand police intervention against drug-dealers and petty criminals or prostitutes, all of whom are identified with immigrants and provide a pretext for racist violence. In a series of episodes between February and June 1994, bands of young 'Nazi-skins' from the outskirts of Rome knifed a Tunisian whom they called 'dirty Moroccan', beat up a Congolese student and three Senegalese whom they called 'dirty negroes'. Others from their neighbourhood explained: 'We hunt down Moroccans and Poles' (though none of the victims belonged empirically to one of these categories), and accused them of 'touching the girls' and 'taking the bread out of our mouths'. On all these occasions, when the young thugs were arrested, their parents and neighbours protested to the police that they were good boys—'bravi ragazzi . . . figli di mamma' (La Repubblica, 1994; Fuccillo 1994).

This situation brings to mind the institutional licence which young men have always enjoyed in rural and even urban Europe. As Emrys Peters pointed out for Wales in the 1930s, the violence of young men against outsiders, single women, and people considered sexually immoral was often an interpretation of the sentiments of their parents, who as responsible householders could not themselves engage in open conflict but were ready to excuse the actions of the 'young hotheads'(Peters 1972). Thus while many Italians of these and other neighbourhoods pay lip-service to the condemnation of racism, they nevertheless condone violence against immigrants. We have seen that symbolic categories with their fictitious and menacing ethnic valency may produce reactions in ethnic terms on the part of the people who are their object. The victims were not 'real' but 'symbolic' Moroccans, nomads, and Jews but the use of these categories to attack 'outsiders' has a a negative effect on real Moroccans, nomads, and Jews as well.

The New Salience of Italian 'Marked' Groups

The relationship between nomads or 'gypsies' (they are officially called *nomadi*, commonly *zingari*) and the Italian citizenry is an extremely negative one. The *nomadi* belong to several linguistic and cultural groups (Sinti, Roma Rom, Rom°, Sinte) and some have several passports. There are about 80,000 in the whole of Italy, some of Italian but most of Balkan origin. They live in appointed caravan sites on the edges of the cities, sometimes deprived even of running water and electricity, let alone the normal city services such as rubbish collection. Indeed Piasere describes for Verona how the nomads' request for a site near a tap is usually disappointed and how the municipalities assign to them a field near a rubbish tip. If there is not one already, the townspeople soon build one up, so that the notion, emerging from every Council minute, that 'nomads mean lack of hygiene and the spread of disease' becomes a self-fulfilling prophecy (Piasere 1989). Camps are often subject to racist attacks, whose perpetrators are rarely discovered. Many nomads who have accepted a sedentary way of life live on public subsidies as well as on begging and the sale of goods (Piasere 1991). Others continue to follow a nomadic way of life. Even as young children, the females are visible because they dress in a colourful way and beg in the streets, offering to tell your fortune. The men are indistinguishable in attire from the local population and trade in all kinds of metals.

'Three were sitting self-consciously in the tram and talking. After they got off, a middle-aged woman exploded: "They shouldn't let them travel on the tram. They're so dirty and then we have to sit on those seats. They should walk."' Nomad women and children play provocatively on the superstition and fear of the non-nomad population, who consider them dirty and dangerous and attribute to them all the burglaries they hear about. The ideas of dirt, pollution, and danger are common features of those stereotypes which express intentions of exclusion and social distance, and are common tropes in the discussion of immigrants (Okely 1983).

Our second category, Southern Italians (*meridionali*) were perceived by Northerners as having 'barbarous' attitudes to women, including their own wives, and as being bad-mannered, ignorant, delinquent, violent, and liable to have too many children (Fofi 1964: 253). This stereotype has much in common with the way Italians were viewed in the USA and may indeed have developed there at a time when Northern Italians were anxious to distinguish themselves from their less fortunate co-nationals in the eyes of potential employers and landlords. Some of the negative judgements made of the Southern workers in Turin came from civil servants of Southern origin who had preceded them to the North. However, Fofi's important study of immigration to Turin pointed out that the reciprocal judgements of Southerners and Northerners, however hostile and prejudiced, showed that the two categories were in constant contact. (Nowadays, the Lega Nord includes a certain number of people of Southern origin among its adherents.)

This is not the case with the new immigrants. A recent study in Turin points out that not many Italians, apart from their employers and civil servants, have direct dealings with immigrants (IRES-Piemonte 1992: 182–4). The visibility of non-European immigrants, nowadays called *extracomunitari* and often referred to as a 'problem', contrasts with the invisibility of European and North American immigrants who are an unmarked category (though Polish men are the target of racist attacks). According to 1989 estimates based on the number of permits to stay issued to foreigners, Europeans were 43 per cent of the total and Americans (from the North and South and including many people of Italian descent) another 19.2 per cent, but they seem to elude the marking which labels the non-Europeans as troublesome outsiders. In one primary school, children's essays showed that they thought the term *extracomunitari* meant 'outside the community' or 'beyond the pale', instead of its real meaning of 'people who do not come from European Community countries'.

The Jewish colony in Rome is said to date, like the Christian one, from the first century AD but the antiquity of its settlement has not prevented Jews from being considered a group apart. From the fifteenth until the early nineteenth century they were mostly confined to ghettos on the outskirts of the cities and to certain occupations, such as usurer, prohibited to Christians. They could not own land and they did not intermarry with the Gentiles. They were also blamed by Catholics for the crucifixion of Christ and were subject in some periods to forced conversions and public pillory. However, there is no history of pogroms in Italy (Milano 1992; Fubini 1993). Since the Fascist Anti-Semitic Laws of 1938 onwards and the death of over 8,000 Italian Jews in Nazi concentration camps during the war, the problem of Italian anti-Semitism has been amply debated in the media, thanks to the writings of Primo Levi and others (Bravo and Jalla 1994). However, a number of 'revisionist' theories, casting doubt on the extent of Nazi crimes, and a recent outbreak of anti-Semitic violence in Rome brought to light the widespread ignorance among young people of the role of anti-Semitism in contemporary history (Cavallieri 1994). Yet in fact, true to our hypothesis of 'suppressed memory', some of the current racism towards immigrants takes Nazi anti-Semitism as its model. At the same time, anti-Jewish activities seem to have intensified among groups and in areas most hostile to the new immigration.

Many Jewish intellectuals have made common cause with the immigrants in their call for a 'plural society'. They claim that the demand for mere equality has undermined the right to 'difference' in post-Enlightenment Europe. In particular, the argument in favour of the Jewish right to religious difference lends itself to that in favour of religious tolerance towards Muslims.

The term *marocchino*, often applied to non-European immigrants in general, is not a new trope but, as I have noted in the case of the Calabrian worker recalling his arrival in Turin in the 1950s, it was also used of Southern immigrants. It is true that Moroccans constitute about a sixth of the non-European immigrants in the country. However, the label has been widely used for Tunisians, Algerians, Senegalese, Eritreans, Somalis, and others. *Marocchino* has become a 'marked category'. Like *meridionali*, *marocchini* are considered potentially violent, oppressive to women, involved in illicit activities, and in league with the Mafia. Like *zingari* they are considered mobile, unreliable, and dirty.

The term *marocchino* has more ancient associations too, not all of them negative. For example, the 'Mediterranean' appearance of many people from the Ligurian or the Sicilian coast is sometimes attributed to intermarriage with *i mori*, at others to their having been invaded by Moorish pirates who carried off the local women. The theme of sexual excess, often a feature of racist stereotypes and attributed also to Southern Italians, is taken up again in the story of the Moroccan troops who landed with the Allies during the last war and raped the women of a Southern village. This story has certainly been reinforced by the popular film *La ciociara* (Vittorio De Sica 1960) starring Sophia Loren and occasionally shown on television. In the North of Italy many communities celebrate annually the 'Caccia ai Saraceni' (Chasing off the Saracens) during the Carnival Processions in February. Here various Moorish invasions and temporary settlements from the ninth century are telescoped into the final defeat of the Saracens in the thirteenth century at the hands of the Christian armies. Local youths dress up as Christian and Saracen soldiers and parade in the Carnival procession. In the Central and Southern regions, village rituals evoke the routing of the noble but unruly invader by an image of the Madonna carried through the streets. These rituals, according to Clara Gallini, became more frequent when these areas were overrun by Piedmontese armies during Italian Unification and have been revived recently. It is as if they symbolized the redefinition of the community against an outside threat (Gallini forthcoming).

Paradoxically, the marking of some categories in a xenophobic way has left others relatively free of negative associations. 'African', although it has absorbed some connotations of 'primitiveness' from colonial literature, has remained fairly neutral. It means 'from far-off, from somewhere I've no knowledge of'. A recent study in Turin showed that many Piedmontese consider Black Africans to be agreeable. Southern Italians were also considered more *simpatici* than Piedmontese. The term *negri*, which Africans consider insulting, was used by some respondents in the questionnaire (IRES-Piemonte 1992). Its findings suggest that Africans are childlike and unthreatening because subordinate, and that African women, unlike Southern Italian, Moroccan, or Rom women, are sexually available. The traffic in Nigerian prostitutes confirms this prejudice. Muslims from West Africa are not usually identified in terms of their religion and only *marocchini* are supposed to have dangerous Muslim tendencies towards polygamy. In fact, under 2 per cent of marriages in Morocco are polygamous as against 20–30 per cent of marriages, even of Christians, in most West African countries (IRES-Piemonte 1991). It is as if people felt threatened by the physical and cultural affinities between Moroccans and Italians and drew the boundary more sharply by referring continually to Islam as if it were the mainspring of Moroccan behaviour and identity. In fact many Moroccans in Italy are lukewarm Muslims though all of them observe Ramadan. It appears from the Turin study on attitudes that most (74 per cent) Piedmontese are not worried by the spread of Islam although about a third of the immigrants are Muslim (IRES-Piemonte 1992: 126).

However, after a period of ecumenical experimentation by several parish priests (in Turin, one lent a parish theatre for the Senegalese Muslims to pray in), the archbishop forbade such hospitality, warning that Muslims regard their place of prayer as their territory. The Pope, while exhorting Catholics to show charity and compassion towards the immigrants, advised against intermarriage with Muslims (Carter in IRES-Piemonte 1991: 128). Probably this type of institutional characterization of the newcomers in religious terms creates a criterion of exclusion where none would otherwise exist. There are signs of religious radicalization among some Muslims, notably among Somali women. On the other hand, the sense of difference which immigrants feel may be translated in unpredictable ways into religious terms. Thus many immigrants who were Catholics in their countries of origin join the Pentecostal Church in Italy. The Pentecostal church in Turin is frequented by a large number of Southern Italian immigrants and by recent immigrants from a variety of non-European countries—the Philippines, Ivory Coast, Eritrea, etc. It is an inclusive minority church which, through the warmth of its personal relationships and its inspirational practice, counters the sense of exclusion which immigrants may experience among the Northern Catholic majority.

Official Initiatives as Agents of Ethnicization

The State, like the Church, may give salience to categories which might otherwise remain socially and politically insignificant. The effect of Fascist anti-Semitic legislation is a case in point. Primo Levi wrote that he had never particularly thought of himself as Jewish but that the consequences for him and others of the Fascist legislation had forced him to assume an ethnic identity, had 'burned the star indelibly onto him'.

State societies by their very habit of compiling 'statistics'—the registers of states—tend to define categories of persons by their relationship to the state and to treat them differently; to describe some of them as deviant, as non-citizens, or as less deserving of state benefits than others (Carter 1992: 27–57). Recent attempts by local authorities, against Lega Nord and right-wing opposition, to confer civil, not to say political, rights on immigrants, tend to create 'ethnicity' by using their own selective criteria.

A first attempt by the Regional authority in Piedmont to create an advisory body composed of the representatives of immigrant associations failed miserably because few of the immigrants' associations had acquired the legal status needed to send representatives. A second attempt by the deputy-mayor of Turin to form an Immigration Committee to advise the town council took the form of identifying twenty-five 'communities' which would have the right to participate in such a committee and help decide on the allocation of resources for immigrants. Preliminary meetings with the so-called communities ended in chaos. Most of the leaders who had been working for years to get immigrants to make common cause felt that they would be best served by candidates of any nationality who could be trusted to act impartially towards people from all areas of origin and negotiate effectively with the Italian authorities. Others claimed to represent religious tendencies (Muslims) with which many of their so-called 'representees' could not identify. The twenty-five groups (which included English and French residents) could not be considered 'ethnic communities' and left a great number of immigrants unrepresented (IRES-Piemonte 1994: 244).

Government passivity in the face of large-scale immigration resulted in the exclusion of many groups, such as nomads, from state services and legislative protection. The skills of highly qualified immigrants have not been tapped in Italy, as they have in other European countries, because, without Italian citizenship, immigrants are not considered eligible for employment in the state and parastate sector, which covers many jobs. So immigrants 'do jobs Italians don't want to do'. This is a definition of social hierarchy which approaches that of apartheid, although it is often quoted to show that immigrants do not take jobs away from Italians.

Conclusions

Italian reactions to the new immigration are similar in many ways to those of other European populations, but in other ways they can only be understood in relation to Italian history and social organization. Over the past couple of centuries, Italy has frequently been overrun by foreign armies, and its different regions by those of other regions. The social boundaries set up against foreigners are highly structured, but in some cases they resemble those erected between Italians depending on their region of provenance or political alignments. The reactions to migrants from the South of the world are determined less by real knowledge or interaction with them than by representations generated by the experience of Italian migration abroad and at home, by Fascist mythology and colonial wars, and by a series of more ancient stereotypes such as *marocchino*, *zingaro*, *ebreo*, *africano* which are not descriptive but classificatory, indicating various kinds of social exclusion. The social and political fragmentation of Italian society, the authoritarian and bureaucratic tendencies of state institutions, the widespread corruption in many spheres of life create a situation in which many Italians feel that their rights as citizens are anything but assured. The arrival of non-European immigrants is felt as threatening, and the racist reactions against them have thrown into relief certain categories of Italian citizens who feel increasingly vulnerable and exposed. On the other hand, there has been a vast voluntary effort to offer practical help to immigrants in the name of 'anti-racism' and civil rights. And for some Italians the arrival of immigrants, many of them enterprising and creative, from other parts of the world, has been like a breath of fresh air.

Further Reading

There is not very much in English on the new immigration but there is a good deal in Italian. For an introduction to the contemporary political debate on nationhood and citizenship I would suggest G. E. Rusconi, *Se cessiamo di essere una nazione* (Bologna, 1993) and G. Zincone, *Uno schermo contro il razzismo. Per una politica dei diritti utili* (Rome, 1994).

On Italian emigration to the USA see H. S. Nelli, *From Emigrants to Ethnics* (Oxford, 1983), which has a useful bibliography. On internal migration in the period of the economic miracle see G. Fofi, *L'immigrazione meridionale a Torino* (Milan, 1964). On Jews in Italy see A. Milano *Storia degli ebrei in Italia* (Turin, 1992); on nomads, L. Piasere, *Popoli delle discariche* (Rome, 1991).

The three volumes published in Turin for IRES-Piemonte, the Piedmontese Institute for Social and Economic Research, constitute a well-documented local case study. Their short titles are *Uguali e diversi* (1991), which presents an immigrants' analysis, *Rumore* (1992), which presents research on Piedmontese attitudes to the new immigration, and *Le chiavi delle città* (1994), which compares the policies of the local authorities of Turin and Lyons, and their attempts to secure civil and social rights for the immigrants. L. Balbo and L. Manconi, *I razzismi reali* (Milan, 1992) is an analysis of Italian racism in the 1980s and 1990s.

References

ALBERA, D. (1989), 'L'immagine dell'emigrazione biellese', in Rosoli *et al.* (1989), iv. 251–327.

ANDERSON, B. (1983), *Imagined Communities: Reflections on the Origin and Spread of Nationalism* (New York).

ASCOLI, U., and CATANZARO, R. (1987) (eds.), *La società italiana degli anni ottanta* (Bari).

BRAVO, A., and JALLA, D. (1994) (eds.), *Una misura onesta. Gli scritti di memoria della deportazione dall'Italia, 1944–1993* (Milan).

CARTER, D. M. (1992), 'Invisible Cities: Touba Turin: Senegalese Transnational Migrants in Northern Italy', Ph.D. thesis (University of Chicago).

CAVALLIERI, M. (1994), 'L'eterno pregiudizio, "ebrei, avari e atei"', *La Repubblica*, 10 Dec.

DEL BOCA, A. (1992), *Gli italiani in Africa Orientale. La conquista dell'impero* (Bari).

—— (1993), *Una sconfitta dell'intelligenza. Italia e Somalia* (Bari).

FOFI, G. (1964), *L'immigrazione meridionale a Torino* (Milan).

FRANDINO, B. (1994), 'Così sistemerò Porta Palazzo', *La Repubblica*, 30 Apr.

FUBINI, E. (1993), 'Dalla diaspora all'olocausto. Questioni di storia ebraica', *Sisifo: Contro il pregiudizio*, Quaderno 1, Oct.

FUCCILLO, M. (1994), 'Picchiatori e "figli di mamma"', *La Repubblica*, 8 June.

GALLINI, C. (forthcoming), 'L'oriente nella cultura popolare e di massa', in *Atti del Convegno L'Altro. Immagine e realtà: incontro con la sociologia dei paesi arabi*, Department of Sociology, University of Milan.

GLUCKMAN, M. (1972) (ed.), *The Allocation of Moral Responsibility* (Manchester).

IRES-Piemonte (1991): Istituto di Ricerche Economico-Sociali del Piemonte, *Uguali e diversi. Il mondo culturale, la rete di rapporti, il lavoro degli immigrati non-europei a Torino* (Turin).

—— (1992), *Rumore. Atteggiamenti verso gli immigrati stranieri* (Turin).

—— (1994), *Le chiavi della città. Politiche per gli immigrati a Torino e a Lione* (Turin).

ISTAT (1993a), Istituto Centrale di Statistica, *La presenza straniera in Italia. Una prima analisi dei dati censuari* (Rome).

—— (1993b), *Gli stranieri in Italia. Fonti statistiche, Note e Relazioni*, iv (Rome).

MILANO, A. (1992), *Storia degli ebrei in Italia* (Turin; 1st edn. 1963).

NELLI, H. S. (1983), *From Immigrants to Ethnics: The Italian Americans* (Oxford).

OKELY, J. (1983), *The Traveller-Gypsies* (Cambridge).

OLIVERO, F. (1990), 'Breve nota di aggiornamento della situazione degli stranieri extracomunitari a Torino', Ufficio Stranieri e Nomadi, Comune di Torino (mimeograph).

PETERS, E. (1972), 'The Meaning of Moral Ambiguity', in Gluckman (1972).

PIASERE, L. (1989), 'L' "unica cosa umana" degli zingari. Lo schifo nelle relazioni interetniche', in *Problemi del Socialismo*, NS 2, May–Aug. (special issue entitled *Razzismi*): 97–130.

—— (1991), *Popoli delle discariche. Saggi di antropologia zingara* (Rome).

REGINATO, M. (1990), *La presenza straniera in Italia. Il caso del Piemonte* (Milan).

ROSOLI, G. et al. (1989), *Identità e integrazione. Famiglie, percorsi ed immagini di sè nell'emigrazione biellese. Biellesi nel mondo*, iv; Fondazione Sella (Milan).

RUSCONI, G. E. (1993), *Se cessiamo di essere una nazione. Tra etnodemocrazie regionali e cittadinanza europea* (Bologna).

SAID, E. W. (1978), *Orientalism: Western Conceptions of the Orient* (London, 1991).

SIBILLA, P. (1980), *Una comunità walser delle alpi. Strutture tradizionali e processi culturali* (Florence).

VIRCIGLIO, G. (1991), *Milocca al Nord. Una comunità di immigrati siciliani ad Asti* (Milan).

ZINCONE, G. (1994), *Uno schermo contro il razzismo. Per una politica dei diritti utili* (Rome).

Two Images of Catholicism

JEFF PRATT

1. The Christian Vote

Figure 15, a poster from the Cold War period—it was used by Christian Democracy (DC) in the general election campaign of 1953—illustrates some of the ways in which Catholic political identity was defined at the time. It shows a young family protected by the sword of Christian votes from the evil serpents of divorce and free love—among the values allegedly upheld by the Communist Party, which had stood in the 1948 general election on a joint slate with the Socialist Party (with the name Fronte Popolare) but which ran in 1953 as a separate party.

With the return of democracy after the Second World War, the Catholic Church had become heavily involved in electoral politics, through the actions of the clergy and those of Church-sponsored lay organizations like the Civic Committees. The main priority was to consolidate support for Christian Democracy as a block against the forces of the left. Catholic unity became a key term in this political discourse, where 'Catholic' increasingly came to mean not a general religious identity, shared by the vast majority of Italians, but a specific political commitment to the DC. In the polarized environment of the Cold War, both sides defined themselves in opposition to each other, and the ideological connections made between Catholicism and anti-communism are particularly striking. The Catholic Church is both the creator and the defender of the family, and this becomes a key theme in the ideological battle of the period. More attention is given to the threat posed by Communism to the family than to any other aspect, real or imagined, of the left's political programme. Family life and values become the crucial ideological terrain on which the opposition between Catholicism and Communism is established.

Fig. 15

Posters from the Cold War period vary a good deal stylistically, from the scatological to the eschatological. The majority contain a very dramatic content, to the effect that Italy must choose between the forces of good and evil in this moment of apocalyptic crisis. This is achieved partly by drawing on images from the Book of Revelation which deal with the final separation of good and evil—the sword and the serpents, or, in other posters, the Archangel Michael, the City of God, and various bestial monsters. Few of these posters demonstrate any great aesthetic qualities but they were part of a very effective ideological campaign and are remembered very clearly by Italians who were politically active in that period. Although the apocalyptic aspect has disappeared from mainstream Catholic political culture, the status of the family (and of the legitimacy of divorce and abortion) have continued to be a thorny issue in Church–State relations through the post-war period.

2. Crossing the Threshold

In Figure 16, a snapshot taken in Tuscany in 1980, a mother and her son emerge from church after he has received First Communion. This ritual marks a change in the spiritual status of children. They leave the period of innocence and, after instruction in Christian doctrine (the Catechism), they become conscious of sin, and become actively involved in the sacraments of the Church. Generally, all the children of the parish take First Communion as a cohort at the age of 9 or 10. The preferred day is Pentecost, which commemorates the descent of the Holy Spirit. The white garments which children normally wear on this occasion are a kind of miniature wedding dress and evoke a range of meanings in popular culture: they represent the union of the child with the Church, mark the passage to a new social and spiritual status, and prefigure eventual marriage. Italian parents often talk of this as a particularly joyful moment in the life of the child and the family—the miniature wedding dress anticipates the achievement of social maturity and responsibility, without this being clouded by the ambivalence of an actual wedding, which for parents marks the breakup of the family unit. First Communion is associated with family achievement and the virtues of childhood, sometimes in a rather romanticized form.

Throughout Italy over the last thirty years this event has gained in prominence, not just in the spiritual preparation (*la dottrina*) of the child, but in the elaborate and increasingly costly celebrations which surround it. Kin and neighbours will give the child presents, including jewellery, which will be set out in the home for inspection. After the Mass, there will often be a banquet for guests in a restaurant, and a series of meals (*merende*) in the home for others. A photographic record is kept throughout—from the moment when the child first receives the wafer to the cutting of the cake in the restaurant—and in many Italian homes these images of children in their finery are prominently displayed.

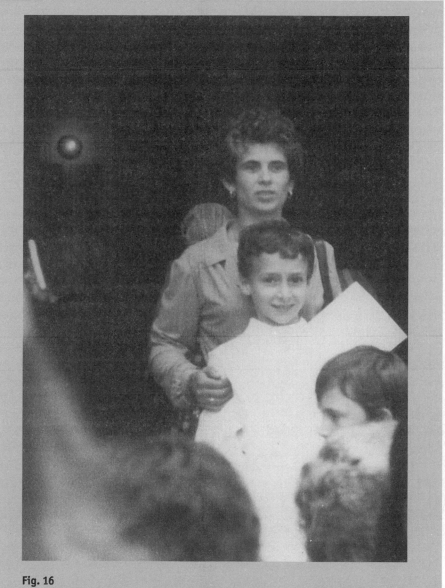

Fig. 16

Media

Introduction

PEPPINO ORTOLEVA maps the development of the media system as a whole, examining its spatial dimensions, with particular reference to the role of Milan, Turin, Rome, and Naples, as well as changes over time. Robert Lumley takes up the debate about the historical peculiarities of Italian newspapers, such as their marked regionalism, lack of a mass readership, and dependence on the political class. He situates them in the multimedia and political landscape of the 1990s. Christopher Wagstaff discusses different approaches to the analysis of cinema in Italy, from readings of particular films to studies that focus on the film industry, identifying distinctively Italian features like particular genres while considering the implications of the fact that the majority of films shown in Italy have been American imports. Television, which was dubbed the 'cinema of the poor' in its early years, initially had a low status in the cultural hierarchy, as Elena Dagrada's account of the relation between the medium and television critics shows. Indeed there are striking parallels between how the medium was judged (first in terms of 'higher' cultural forms such as theatre or literature and only later in terms of its specifics as text and production system) and how film had been treated by intellectuals at an earlier stage. By contrast, literary writing in Italy is a relatively minority medium whose practitioners enjoy a high cultural status, but whose problem is sometimes held to be that it lacks relevance. Ann Hallamore Caesar argues, however, with particular reference to women authors who have so often been excluded from the 'canon', that post-war literature has been a very important terrain for the exploration of new identities, of memory, and of selfhood.

10

A Geography of the Media since 1945

PEPPINO
ORTOLEVA

IN the study of communications a geographical or spatial approach is as indispensable as a precise historical periodization, yet it remains one of the least explored branches of communications research (for partial exceptions, dealing, however, mainly with telecommunications, see Bakis 1983; Robins and Torchi 1993; on the Italian case see Grossi 1994). It may be suggested that the media not so much regulate or direct social relations as give shape to them. One might even go further and say that the media are one of the channels—if not the major one—through which the shape of society is made visible. The way the media are organized not only has a profound effect on the way a nation perceives its own geography, how it defines its own centres and its periphery, and establishes a division of tasks between cities and regions; it also contributes to defining something that is at once a fundamental and an intangible part of the modern world: national identity.

Media and Sense of Place

A common language, common traditions (a common culture), and a common territory are at the very basis of the modern idea of nation. All the classic definitions of the concept, from the nineteenth-century liberals to Stalin, link together these three elements (Hobsbawm 1990). As Harold Adams Innis (1951) demonstrated, the principle of a common language presupposes its use by the press and as a result the standardization of its rules. In Italy, the thesis formulated thirty-five years ago by Tullio De Mauro (1961) that radio and television have been more instrumental than the press in the development of a shared national language has become a commonplace. The principle of common traditions is linked to the late eighteenth-century evolution of the concept of 'culture', which ceased to signify a process of individual formation and 'cultivation' and came instead to designate a body of knowledge whose possession goes beyond the individual (see the entry on 'Culture' in Williams 1976). The principle of common territory presupposes, as Eric Hobsbawm has reminded us (1990), a level of technological development which, through the use of modern means of transportation and ever more rapid means of communication, allows this territory to be held together. This is not to say that the organization of communications is in itself the factor which determines national identities, but that all aspects of modern national identities, and hence of modern subnational and supranational identities too, find expression also in the communications structure.

In the world that emerged from the political revolutions of France and America at the end of the eighteenth century, changes in the means of communication contributed to a modification in the content of the shared discourse, enriching or limiting those common assets that made up the shared 'culture' of a people (in national or local terms). This is perhaps even more true of those nations which were formed relatively 'late' in comparison to the model represented by Western Europe in the nineteenth and twentieth centuries: of these 'new nations', Italy is one of the few that may be considered to have been relatively successful. In all of these countries, the nation-state developed at the same time as a modern communications system, and consequently their respective histories have been more intertwined than in other countries. There is a further aspect which is just as important, although it is more often overlooked: within nations like Italy the media system contributes also to defining the areas into which each country is divided. In today's world, one of the prerequisites for 'region' status is to form a catchment area for certain media. To put it another way, the importance of the media in the definition of national identity lies not simply in their *content*, in how they perpetuate or modify representations and stereotypes, 'mental maps', and shared values, but also, and perhaps above all, in their *structure*. Yet most of the research on this subject tends instead to concentrate above all, if not exclusively, on the content aspect. This is the main shortcoming, for example, of the otherwise very useful study by Giorgio Grossi (1994).

A remark made by Walter Benjamin in his essay on Nikolai Leskov is worth taking up in this context. Commenting on the decline of ancient narrative formulas and the rise of the modern information myth, Benjamin wrote: 'Villemessant, the founder of *Le Figaro*, characterizes the nature of information in a famous formulation. "To my readers," he used to say, "an attic fire in the Latin Quarter is more important than a revolution in Madrid." . . . Information . . . lays claim to prompt verifiability. The prime requirement is that it appear "understandable in itself" ' (Benjamin 1936: 88–9). Captivated by Villemessant's formulation, Benjamin seemed to believe that the secret of modern information lay in its greater localization as compared to the more uncertain, fantastic, temporally deferred 'narrative' characteristic of oral and traditional societies: what the newspaper purchasers sought was information that corresponded to their identity as Parisians. It is actually just as legitimate to assert the opposite. The fire in the Latin Quarter was of interest to readers of Le Figaro precisely because it was a piece of information they shared with the other readers of Le Figaro: their identity as Parisians derived at least in part from their identity as readers of that newspaper.

If this observation is correct, we can say that the development of modern media determines a geography of communications which *adapts* to the map of existing communities but which, at the same time, continually *reshapes* it. The media contribute to the maintenance of pre-existing social arrangements but they also, more or less explicitly, define their boundaries and the direction in which they change. Thus the study of the geographical organization of the media, seen from this perspective, links together a sociocultural analysis of identities with a geographical study in the classic sense, that is to say a study of proximities and distances, boundaries and connections.

A special branch of studies has grown up in recent years which exemplifies this link. It pays particular attention to the development and the characteristics of networks: technical (Gras 1992), electrical (Hughes 1983), long-distance communications (Fischer 1993). In Italian, the terms *rete* and *reticolo* (modelled on the English 'network') have been used for several years now in the human sciences, particularly in anthropology, to evoke (with a metaphor as suggestive as it is vague) the complex system of social relations found in traditional communities or in contemporary egalitarian societies. Only recently have social scientists come to realize that, just when they were investigating the nature of networks as abstract relation systems, other, concrete networks made up of wires, cables, and relay stations were being strung across the globe, to become not just an auxiliary to the social relations system but an indispensable element of living in society. The concept of the network has thus become the point where a sociocultural view of technology and the world of objects meets a materialist view of social relations. The network presents itself as the objective basis of relationships between people, as well as the mirror of the idea that society has of itself. This is as true of physical transport networks as it is of networks over the air and telecommunications channels.

This subject has particular significance for Italy. Throughout its history as a unified nation, Italy has had episodes of decentralized enterprise as well as of strong unification of its networks imposed 'from above'. An early example is the railway system, built in a fragmentary way but nationalized (1905) in accordance with a fundamental policy of the government led by Giovanni Giolitti. In the

1920s and 1930s, Fascist policy on the radio networks and the telephone system bore the hallmarks of a peculiar strategy whereby although both were centralized and state-owned they also had a dual nature, both in geographical terms (they were controlled from a decentralized headquarters in Turin), and in institutional terms (mixed ownership). From the point of view of the geography of communications, the moment of greatest centralism in the history of Italy in the twentieth century came with the post-1945 governments of the centre and centre-left, which ran the television and telephone monopolies reasonably efficiently and paid close attention to the unity of the country. It is worth recalling here that even more important than the high degree of saturation reached by the television system was the fact that Italy was the second country in Europe after the Netherlands to adopt the direct dialling telephone system.

The international crisis of the mass media system, the first symptoms of which could be seen during the 1970s, produced a new wave of decentralization, particularly in radio and television, at exactly the same time as tendencies towards localism, which seemed to have vanished, began to reappear (on the re-emergence of localism, particularly in relation to the political phenomenon of the growth of the Lega Nord, see Rusconi 1993; De Luna 1993; and, in this volume, Chapter 6—Parker, 'Political Identities'). It is worth noting, however, that while the *political* phenomenon of localism continued to grow during the 1980s, becoming one of the main signs if not the main sign of the growing rift between society and the party system, the *communicative* phenomenon of localism was to a great extent absorbed, relegated to folklore, or completely forgotten. In practice the national dimension of communication prevailed, favoured by the emergence in the 1980s of the RAI–Fininvest duopoly (see Dagrada, 'Television and its Critics', Chapter 13 below) but also perhaps by the long-term effect of the mass state school system. There may be more than symbolic value in the fact that it was Berlusconi, the man whose very name stood for this duopoly, who was to 'domesticate' localism in a political sense also, recycling it as part of a wholly national and centralist policy in his 1994 election campaign.

Three Types of Media Geography

The term 'media geography' has three different meanings, corresponding to the main ways in which the spatial organization of a country's media system may be examined. First, there is a *geography of networks*, or of distribution. This allows us to see how information moves around the country, and the way in which near and distant, hierarchical or equal relations come to be established between different areas. Secondly, there is a *geography of content*. This deals with the attention given to different areas and local 'identities', and allows us to understand the extent to which each identity is considered part of the nation's overall unity and, conversely, to what extent it is marginalized or excluded. It allows us, therefore, to understand the relationships of inclusiveness and exclusiveness between the national and the local. Thirdly, there is a *geography of production*. This enables us to see which are the most active centres of the media system and which instead are marginalized, allowing us to identify the underlying power relations.

How are these three geographies related to one another? The same characteristics are not shared by all countries. In some (the classic, most obvious example is that of France), the three seem largely to coincide: Paris is the absolute centre of the geography of the network, and indeed for many years it has even enjoyed networks of its own such as the pneumatic post; it is the hub of the publishing, television, and cinema industries; and it is the city that is talked about, the object of unrivalled attention, despite frequent revivals of localism and dialect. By contrast, other countries display forms of *polycentrism*: in the USA, for instance, there is a clear-cut division of roles, with the 'traditional' publishing industry being concentrated mainly in New York and on the East Coast, the cinema industry centring on the West Coast, and the South and the urban culture of certain minorities continuing to play an important role as treasure houses of ideas and styles. Italy is probably nearer the American model than the French one. A close look at the essential characteristics of this geography might also help us see how far it conforms to other aspects of the national reality.

Italy's Media Geography

In the first half of the twentieth century, the media industry in Italy was organized in a distinctive fashion which might be defined as not so much decentralized as polycentric. Its characteristic was a clear-cut and explicit division of tasks among different places in the peninsula: a type of organization which paradoxically probably contributed greatly to the cultural unity of the nation.

Milan and the Publishing Industry

The publishing industry—this means above all book and magazine publishing (for a discussion of the latter sector, see Lombardo and Pignatel 1975) since newspaper publishing is by its very nature organized on a wider scale, even though this is less true of Italy—had for a number of years been concentrating in one, maybe two national centres, while at the same time maintaining a widespread presence in almost all of the major cities. The principal centre was (and remains) Milan, capital of Italian publishing since the early nineteenth century (see Berengo 1980). Milan is the headquarters not only of some of the major book publishers, but of almost all of the major periodicals, and therefore the strategic point of synergy (commercial interdependency and mutual reinforcement) between the two sectors. The city has been home not just to the head offices of the publishing firms Rizzoli, Mondadori, and Garzanti, but also to the main distribution agencies. It is thus the nerve centre of the publishing network. Its central role in publishing was one reason why, from the beginning of the century, Milan became the national capital of advertising (see Cesarani 1986). For as long as restrictions on commercial television advertising were in place—in other words, up till the end of the RAI's national television monopoly in the late 1970s—the main vehicle for advertising in the country continued to be the printed page. Milan was thus the logical choice for US advertising agencies setting up offices in Italy.

Immediately after the Second World War, almost all the other major cities in the country boasted (and still boast) a publishing house whose links with the local intelligentsia and often with the local university gave it national relevance, at least as far as the publishing of non-fiction was concerned. Rome occupied a strangely secondary position, with low-profile university presses and the isolated, though powerful, institution of the Istituto dell'Enciclopedia Italiana (see Turi 1980). During this period, two other cities could aspire to the role of second national publishing centre, but both of them had serious weaknesses: the first, Florence, relied on a great tradition and on a number of prestigious publishers, but around the end of the 1950s, at the latest, it began to decline; the second, Turin, counted several very important publishers (from UTET to Einaudi and SEI) but suffered from a malady characteristic of the pre-Unification period, namely an almost total lack of communication between the different centres of influence in the city.

During the 1960s and 1970s the economic importance, if not the prestige, of Milanese publishing grew to a point where the Italian publishing industry was a largely monocentric system. At the beginning of the 1990s, all the major Italian magazines were based in Milan, with the exceptions of *L'Espresso* and the titles published by Edizioni Paoline in Alba, Piedmont. An even more remarkable fact emerged from a study carried out in 1983 of journalists employed in the periodicals sector who were working in Milan (i.e. the majority of journalists working in the sector nationally): almost 70 per cent were found to have been born in Lombardy (see Lombardo and Pignatel 1975, elaborating data from a survey by M. G. Cucco and A. Giobbio). However, Milan's pivotal role in the publishing sector is countered by its obvious and lasting weakness as far as the other main form of mass communication is concerned: until the advent of private television stations, Milan played a marginal role in film production.

Rome and Audiovisual Media

Film production also began polycentrically, with a slight bias if anything towards the north-west of the country, but it subsequently centred increasingly in Rome. With the creation first of the Istituto LUCE (1925) and then of Cinecittà (opened in 1937), Rome became the absolute capital of Italian film production, and all attempts to establish alternative centres in other parts of the country failed. The cinema industry was in fact the first of the national cultural industries to have its production capital based in the political capital.

From the second half of the 1950s, Rome's predominance extended, without meeting particular resistance, to the second great audiovisual sector, television. Television broadcasting had started life in Rome, but had become based in Turin during the years of radio (see Papa 1978; Monteleone 1993; Ortoleva 1994). However, the Christian Democrat management of the RAI preferred to concentrate the company, and especially the creative and production side of its operations, increasingly in Rome, leaving Turin with a mainly administrative role. Television was a second audiovisual industry which functioned at first in a parallel, indeed, quite separate way from the film industry, and which slowly became increasingly integrated with it in a relationship of interdependency and exchange.

Milan had a minor though not unimportant role to play in the country's audiovisual system in the production of advertising. This encouraged the local recruitment of certain specialized skills, for example in the animation sector. It remained subordinate, however, not least because for a long time the production of advertisements was considered to be a task firmly in the bread-and-butter category, a way for professionals in the film business to make a quick buck: directors, set-designers, directors of photography would go to Milan to earn some money but continued to think of Rome as the real headquarters of their work. This situation changed in a significant way only after the arrival, well into the 1980s, of private television stations.

Turin and the Networks

It is said that Mussolini disliked Turin, a city which on more than one occasion manifested coldness if not hostility towards him. It cannot, however, be denied that during the Fascist period Turin found, alongside its own industrial growth, a new and special role as capital of the country's networks. The choice of Turin as capital of the telephone network (it was the headquarters of STET (Società Torinese di Elettricità e Telefonia), the holding company which controlled the country's telephone system) as well as nerve centre of the radio network was probably made on technocratic grounds. Both networks demanded a strong engineering and management base which it seemed 'natural' to seek in the city which was home to both the Politecnico and the Istituto Elettrotecnico Nazionale, as well as Fiat (founded in 1899): by choosing Turin as the headquarters, the Fascist regime showed that it placed the efficient working of the two organizations above their direct integration with the ruling party.

In the post-war years, Turin's position was progressively weakened, with the effective transfer to Rome of the heart of the RAI and then with the creation of a single telephone company which was also progressively 'Romanized'. While this is not the place to air the complaints of Piedmontese localism, it is interesting to note that, deliberately or not, the national network system had previously had a sort of built-in corrective against centralizing tendencies, consisting of a separation between what I have called the 'geography of networks' and the 'geography of

Fig. 17 *The festa di Piedigrotta*, held annually in Naples on 8 September, became the focus of a massive popularization of the Neapolitan song both in Italy and internationally which reached its peak in the first half of the twentieth century. A large number of professional intermediaries became involved, from impresarios to sheet music publishers and foreign record companies. The iconography of the city—Vesuvius, the Bay of Naples, the funicular—was an important part of a largely reinvented local tradition. The decline in the 1950s of Neapolitan song, and of Naples as a centre of popular culture in Italy, was widely attributed to the rise of more 'modern' cultural forms and patterns of consumption associated with the North and Centre, most notably television.

production'. This corrective has now been lost as a result of certain choices that have contributed, among other things, to the commingling of the boards of directors of the RAI and the Turin-based telephone company SIP (since 1994, Telecom Italia) with the political élites.

Naples and Popular Mass Culture

The picture that has been drawn so far is of the country's cultural and communications industries firmly rooted in Central and Northern Italy, in particular on the Rome–Milan axis. Until the 1960s, however, a city in the South—Naples—played a role as important as that of Rome or Milan in the country's mass communications. The role of Naples was real, but more importantly it was symbolic. It meant more in terms of 'the geography of content' than of the geography of production.

From the beginning of the century until the 1960s, the city, which was already the home of important publishing houses and cultural centres, of a great opera house, and the greatest university in Southern Italy, played a vital role in the field of popular mass culture. It was the national centre of popular music (see Borgna 1984; in fact for many years it boasted its very own festival of popular music, comparable in ambition and prestige to that of San Remo), while as a national centre of live variety theatre it was on a par with Rome and Milan. Its dialect was unique in that it was recognized as having a truly national function: with the exception of Florentine, it was the only dialect which could safely be assumed to be understood from one end of the peninsula to the other.

The question of how the former Bourbon capital came to assume this particular role is too complex to be examined in detail here, but briefly Naples may be said to combine two important characteristics. On the one hand, it was an ancient and great city in which an urban mass culture had been forming from the days of Bourbon rule, before Unification, in a way that would not have been possible, at least before the end of the nineteenth century, in other major Italian cities. On the other hand, it was the major city of the South, a treasure house for a vast repertoire of traditions and skills that were valuable for the entire country.

It could be said, without forcing the analogy too much, that for a long time Naples was to Italian popular culture what the New Orleans–Nashville axis is to US mass culture: a hotbed of talent, a centre both of tradition and experiment, and a symbol of the spontaneous and popular roots of a mass culture that is continually threatening, as a result of industrialization, to turn into something purely mechanical and purely commercial. Interestingly, Neapolitan popular culture has been caught between contrary impulses throughout the twentieth century: on the one hand the tendency to separate from its local context and take on a national role (with the conventionalization of its dialect, the national adoption of non-Neapolitan actors and singers), and on the other a tendency to 'rediscover its roots', a typical embodiment of which may be seen in Raffaele Viviani before the war and later, partly, in the actor and playwright Eduardo De Filippo (1900–84).

The progressive loss of a national role during the 1970s gave a fresh impetus to the return to roots, the results of which may be seen in song-writing, comedy, and the cinema.

The loss, however, has been a real one: from the 1970s onwards, Naples has had a relatively secondary role in Italian popular music and cinema, with an output not much greater than cities like Turin or Bari; its dialect is no longer understood by everybody, one reason being that an authentic Italian vernacular does now exist, and as a result all dialects, including Neapolitan, are being driven back to their local roots (see Poggi Salani 1993).

The Dynamics of the Media System

Having described some of the tendencies of the different regional centres, let us now try to get an overall view of the changes that have come about in the national geography of the media during the period since 1945.

Multiple Capitals (1945–1957)

In a first phase, which lasted up to 1957, the polycentric system was at the height of its powers, just at the time that Italy, with its rapid industrialization, was experiencing the most dynamic unification ever of its national culture. In this period of basically peaceful sharing of roles, those tensions that did arise regarded above all the newly emerging medium of television, whose destiny of pre-eminence was obvious from the start. There was a battle between Rome and Turin for control of the RAI: until the late 1960s this would continue to influence the wrangles between those who identified with the interests of the RAI as a company and those who wanted to control it politically. And within Rome itself there was also a battle between the Rome of the cinema and the Rome of the RAI. The move towards cultural unification prevailed, however, and it was radio, television, and cinema (see Sorlin 1991) which brought it about.

Towards Bipolarism (1958–1973)

A 'minor' event provides the symbolic beginning of the next phase: the triumphal success of Domenico Modugno's 'Nel blu dipinto di blu' (also known as 'Volare'), the hit of the the 1958 San Remo Festival, seems emblematic of the victory of the 'Italian' over the Neapolitan song. It is worth recalling that for a long time Modugno had himself wavered between writing his lyrics in Italian and writing them in Neapolitan, which was not his native dialect (he came from Bari) but which he, like other song-writers of his generation, considered to be the language of song by definition. Naples's role in a national context was diminishing and would decline from this point onwards, while the popularity of transnational music and subsequently of rock was growing (see Portelli 1985; Filippa 'Popular Song', Chapter 19 in this volume). Physical geography ceased to be as important a factor as generational geography where popular music was concerned. Turin too began to play a more minor role as the early phase of the history of the networks neared its conclusion and the demand grew for bureaucrats and administrators rather than engineers.

On both a concrete and an ideological level, 1968 was an era of great geographical and cultural pluralism, which witnessed the emergence of a new interest in local identities, dialects, and hybrid languages (see Ortoleva 1988). Yet it is also the case that part of the agenda of the New Left was a fresh move in the direction of cultural nationalization with an accelerated development of centralistic organizations (Bobbio 1988). By the beginning of the 1970s, Italy was left with only two communication capitals: Rome and Milan. Excluded from playing any major role were both the South, which increasingly became above all an *object* of narration in tones ranging from the folkloristic to the concerned (see Buonanno 1991), and the 'thousand cities' of the so-called Third Italy of the Centre and North-East (Bagnasco 1977). This was a mark—perhaps the most obvious mark—of the extent to which the media system had grown out of synchrony with society as a whole.

The Contradictions of a Centralized and Bipolar System (1974–1995)

In the two decades that followed, the geography of the Italian media was the site of two major contradictions. In the first place, while the tendency towards centralization became established and was reinforced, excluding or marginalizing those centres which had once been lively and productive, there was at the same time a frequently felt need to give new expression by new means to local cultures. This contradiction was felt not so much and not so keenly by television as by the radio stations which had come into existence after the effective liberalization of the airwaves in 1975; it also made itself felt in the field of popular music, where increasing subordination to big national and international centres of production had not extinguished the need to rehabilitate regional and often forgotten traditions. Thus it was that in the 1980s the popular culture of Naples fulfilled a curious destiny: having almost totally lost any national standing, it recovered not only its roots, so to speak, but also and above all its relationship with the local reality. It is interesting to note that on this count, the 'Third Italy' has decidedly less to offer: on the one hand *liscio*, a musical and dance form typical of the central Adriatic, and on the other the revival of local fairs and village festivals.

Overall, however, the national dimension has prevailed in the last twenty years. This is proved by what has happened to television, corner-stone of the whole system: despite a strong ideological move in favour of community-based television, a move supported in the 1970s by certain sections of the left and in subsequent years by the emergent and mainly Northern-based localist political forces, and despite the attempt by the Constitutional Court to promote, by strictly legal means, the formation of local broadcasting stations, attempts to provide local information and a service to the community have remained, in the history of private broadcasting in Italy, on a decidedly minority footing. The July 1976 Ruling of the Constitutional Court which ended state monopoly was explicit in restricting the right of private broadcasting to *local* television stations only. This restriction was at first side-stepped by the simultaneous broadcasting of pre-recorded programmes on videocassette. Subsequently, the 'Berlusconi Decree' (December 1984; converted into a law in February 1985) and the 'Mammì Law' (the Broadcasting Act of 1990) gave the go-ahead to television broadcasting by private networks on a national scale. On this point, there is a very clear difference between television and radio (see Fenati 1993 and Menduni 1994 for an illuminating discussion). Further confirmation of the same trend is found in newspaper publishing. Partly because of the technical breakthrough of teletransmission, by which entire newspapers could be sent down a telephone line from one city to another to be printed and distributed there, many national newspapers began in the 1970s to produce 'local' editions for different regions of the country, while at the same time giving their traditional local 'base' an increasingly subordinate role. In 1976, the first truly 'national' newspaper—*La Repubblica*—was founded. It was characterized initially by total detachment from any local base whatsoever (though significantly there was an experiment—later to be abandoned—with a page entitled 'Le capitali' which carried news stories from both Rome and Milan), and in a subsequent phase by a number of local editions which were identical in every detail except for the insert of local news pages.

It is within this framework of a high degree of 'nationalization' of the system that the second, and perhaps most profound, contradiction is found. In the geography of the media in the inter-war years outlined above, Rome and Milan were the two main capitals of the system but the principal roles were shared out between them. In the course of the 1970s and 1980s, as the pre-eminence of *both* cities increased, differentiation decreased and forms of direct competition emerged. In the audiovisual field, particularly in broadcasting, there was pressure (notably from the Socialist Party) to 'decentralize' the RAI. One important result of this, had it happened, would have been the creation of a second, Milan-based network. But the best indication of how things were changing was the emergence of the Fininvest monopoly in the field of private broadcasting. Since the mid-1980s there have been two and only two television capitals in Italy—Rome and Milan. Competition between the RAI and Fininvest has also come to mean competition between a national television of the Centre and one of the North. In journalism, *La Repubblica* has been the first indication of Rome's ability to play a national role. True, it is an isolated case, but it has been so successful that it constitutes a remarkable precedent.

The present situation of media geography in Italy provides much material for reflection. Such a centralized media system risks losing touch with a country which in the last decades has seen, if anything, an increase in localism, just at a time when it has become increasingly difficult to draw the media's attention to events taking place outside the two capitals. Moreover, a media system characterized by two centres that are equal and in competition with each other is probably more liable to be conditioned by favouritism and lobbying than one that is genuinely polycentric.

Further Reading

There are few general histories of the media in Italy. A good overview is provided by D. Forgacs, *Italian Culture in the Industrial Era, 1880–1980: Cultural Industries, Politics and the Public* (Manchester, 1990), also available in a revised Italian version as *L'industrializzazione della cultura italiana, 1880–1990* (Bologna, 1993). On the history of broadcasting, see F. Monteleone, *Storia della radio e della televisione in Italia* (Venice, 1993). On the press, see the seven-volume *Storia della stampa italiana*, edited by V. Castronovo and N. Tranfaglia (Rome and Bari, 1976–94).

On the development of 'industrial' forms of communication in pre-industrial areas of Italy, the work of Italian sociologists of the 1950s and 1960s remains more perceptive and open than that of their successors. See L. De Rita, *I contadini e la televisione* (Bologna, 1963) and S. Acquaviva and G. Eisner, *La montagna del sole* (Turin, 1984). See also the works cited by D. Forgacs in *Italian Culture in the Industrial Era* and S. Lanaro in *Storia dell'Italia repubblicana* (Venice, 1992).

On a geographical approach to the media there is a certain amount of work dealing with telecommunications—see for example H. Bakis, *Géographie des télécommunications* (Paris, 1983). On the geography of the media as such, see K. Robins and A. Torchi, *Geografie dei media* (Bologna, 1993). On the Italian case see G. Grossi, *Italia Italie. Immagine e identità del bel paese nell'attualità televisiva* (Rome, 1994).

References

Bagnasco, A. (1977), *Tre Italie. La problematica territoriale dello sviluppo italiano* (Bologna).

Bakis, H. (1983), *Géographie des télécommunications* (Paris).

Benjamin, W. (1936), 'The Storyteller: Reflections on the Work of Nikolai Leskov', in *Illuminations*, ed. H. Arendt, trans. H. Zohn (London, 1970), 83–109.

Berengo, M. (1980), *Editori e librai nella Milano della Restaurazione* (Turin).

Bobbio, L. (1988), *Storia di Lotta Continua* (Milan).

Borgna, G. (1984), *Storia della canzone italiana* (Rome and Bari).

Buonanno, M. (1991) (ed.), *Il reale e l'immaginario* (Rome).

Cesarani, G. P. (1986), *Storia della pubblicità in Italia* (Rome and Bari).

De Luna, G. (1993) (ed.), *Figli di un benessere minore. La Lega 1979–1993* (Florence).

De Mauro, T. (1961), *Storia linguistica dell'Italia unita* (Bari).

Fenati, B. (1993), *Fare radio negli anni Novanta* (Rome).

Fischer, C. (1993), *America Calling: A Social History of the Telephone, 1876–1940* (Berkeley).

Gras, A. (1992), *Grandeur et dépendance. Sociologie des grands systèmes techniques* (Paris).

Grossi, G. (1994), *Italia Italie. Immagine e identità del bel paese nell'attualità televisiva* (Rome).

Hobsbawm, E. J. (1990), *Nations and Nationalism since 1780: Programme, Myth, Reality* (Cambridge).

Hughes, T. (1983), *Networks of Power: The Electrification of Western Societies* (Baltimore).

Innis, H. A. (1951), *The Bias of Communication* (Toronto).

Lombardo, M., and Pignatel, F. (1975), *La stampa periodica in Italia. Mezzo secolo di riviste illustrate* (Rome).

Menduni, E. (1994), *La radio nell'era della televisione* (Bologna).

MONTELEONE, F. (1993), *Storia della radio e della televisione in Italia* (Venice).

ORTOLEVA, P. (1988), *Saggio sui movimenti del 1968 in Europa e in America* (Rome).

—— (1994), *Torino e la radio. Nascita di un mezzo di comunicazione di massa* (Milan).

PAPA, A. (1978), *Storia politica della radio in Italia* (Naples).

POGGI SALANI, M. T. (1993), 'Una tardiva unificazione linguistica: i riflessi sull'oggi', in Soldani and Turi 1993, ii. 211–47.

PORTELLI, A. (1985), 'L'orsacchiotto e la tigre di carta. Il rock and roll arriva in Italia, *Quaderni Storici*, 58/1 (April): 135–47.

RUSCONI, G. E. (1993), *Se cessiamo di essere una nazione* (Bologna).

SOLDANI, S., and TURI, G. (1993) (eds.), *Fare gli italiani. Scuola e cultura nell'Italia contemporanea*, 2 vols. (Bologna).

SORLIN, P. (1991), *European Cinemas, European Societies 1939–1990* (London).

TURI, G. (1980), *Il fascismo e il consenso degli intellettuali* (Bologna).

WILLIAMS, R. (1976), *Keywords: A Vocabulary of Culture and Society* (London).

11

Peculiarities of the Italian Newspaper

ROBERT
LUMLEY

NEWSPAPERS are, by nature, industrial products. Originating
(as dailies) in the eighteenth century, and establishing mass
readerships in the late nineteenth and early twentieth century,
they were part of the process of industrialization, urbanization,
and the making of nation-states that transformed first Europe
and then the rest of the world (Anderson 1991; Smith 1991). Newspapers were important vehicles in spreading the commercial
information necessary to the operation of free markets and the
political information needed for the operation of democracies.
Their production, using the latest technologies, such as the tele-
graph, and distribution, via newly created rail networks, made
them into the embodiments of a new civilization. In the liberal
imagination, moreover, the free press represented the forces of
enlightenment, progress, science, economic improvement, and
political liberty (Hobsbawm 1977).

The press in the late twentieth century is no longer associated
with the vanguard of progress. It is now considered an older
medium in technological terms, and its commercial and political functions have diminished. However, many of the ideals
first promoted in newspapers, such as freedom of opinion
and debate, remain important as models of how things should
be done. Indeed, in the Italian case, the measurement of existing newspapers against a 'superior' (usually Anglo-American)
model has been a recurrent theme in discussion, the peculiarities

of the Italian press being seen as a symptom or mirror of an unhappy national condition.

The peculiarities that are usually mentioned can be encapsulated in three questions: first, why is the Italian press *not truly national*?; secondly, why does *only a small percentage of the population read newspapers* in Italy?; and, thirdly, why is the Italian press *not independent*? Each of these questions is polemical and belongs to a debate that has lasted several decades. Together, therefore, they provide an excellent starting-point for a description and analysis of the place of the newspaper in Italian culture and society.

The first question concerns the predominance of regional and pluri-regional newspapers in Italy and the fact that there is no equivalent of *Le Monde* or *The Times*. Why in Italy, it is asked, is there no paper with a genuinely national readership whose authority within the country is the basis for an international reputation?

Il Corriere della Sera has long aspired to this role. Founded in 1876 by a family of textile magnates, it established itself in the economic boom of the early twentieth century, attaining, under the editorship of Luigi Albertini, daily sales of 300,000 copies. However, *Il Corriere* has always kept its headquarters in Milan, and its circulation has been concentrated in Lombardy, which in 1971 accounted for 66 per cent of the total. Giovanni Spadolini recalls that when he was editor he felt the Milanese patriotism of the Crespi family: 'I went to Rome six or seven times a year; more frequently than Albertini, who went three of four times a year. And every time I went, I provoked a sense of irritation in the Crespis, who did not want the editor of their newspaper contaminated by the capital' (quoted in Porter 1983: 121). Change of ownership and a more national orientation have helped *Il Corriere della Sera* to re-establish itself as the leading paper in terms of sales (with a circulation of 778,000 in the first quarter of 1994) and reputation, but the regional bias remains.

For *La Stampa*, the problem is even more serious. Based in Turin and with a circulation of over 400,000 in 1990, its readership has been declining. Furthermore, the vast majority of readers live in Piedmont, and the identity of the paper is bound up with this region and with the Piedmontese owners, the Agnelli family, who also have a controlling interest in the Fiat motor company. Symptomatically, an attempt by *La Stampa* to hive off the pages of *cronaca cittadina* or 'city news' met with a wave of protest and had to be abandoned.

There is a regional press that does not have national distribution. In Central Italy *Il Resto del Carlino* has a circulation (number of papers actually sold) of about 230,000 in Bologna and the surrounding region in 1993, while *La Nazione* (with around 200,000 in 1993) is bought mainly in Tuscany. In Campania there is *Il Mattino* (circulation of 150,000 in 1993) based in Naples, and in Puglia there is *La Gazzetta del Mezzogiorno* (79,000).

Apart from these pluri-regional or regional papers, each city or major town often has its own daily paper that is also distributed in the surrounding province. For example, Verona has *L'Arena* (54,000 in 1993), while Bergamo has two papers,

L'Eco di Bergamo (60,000), and *Bergamo Oggi*, which together in 1983 accounted for 42 per cent of sales in the province as against the 14 per cent of the *Gazzetta dello Sport* and the 12 per cent of the *Corriere della Sera*. Most of these papers cover the international and national news thanks to the use of news agencies and perhaps a Rome correspondent. Otherwise, the bulk of the pages consist of local news produced by staff reporters. Finally, there is a smaller provincial press which comes out once or twice a week and which is exclusively local, covering such things as cattle prices.

The papers which, at least until recently, had the best claim to be national, in that their circulation was evenly spread over the peninsula, were probably *L'Unità*, the organ of the former Communist Party (now the Democratic Party of the Left), and *L'Osservatore Romano*, the official daily paper of the Vatican. Otherwise the paper with the most convincing national profile is *La Repubblica*, which had a circulation of 699,000 in 1990. Launched in 1976 and based in Rome, it did not have the disadvantages of age of *Il Corriere della Sera* or *La Stampa*: it was not associated with a particular region or city, nor did it have an older generation of readers bent on preserving tradition. *La Repubblica* identified a younger generation with new sets of cultural and political demands as its potential readership. According to its editor, Eugenio Scalfari, 'half of our readers belong to the education world (teachers and students), large groups to the professions, private sector, and management. Industrial workers form 10 per cent of the total, while the percentage of women (23 per cent) is the highest of any newspaper. The average age is just over 30' (quoted in Murialdi 1983: 613). Its adoption of tabloid format and new graphics underlined its youthful image. From 1984 it decentralized its production, taking advantage of the new technologies in order to produce regional editions, enabling readers in Milan, Rome, Turin, Bologna, Florence, or Naples to read the same paper but with an insert of several pages with information (political, cultural, sporting, etc.) on their own city and region (Altino 1988).

Whether *La Repubblica* now qualifies as *the* national newspaper is a moot point, however, as its sales have slipped back from its peak when it overtook *Il Corriere della Sera*. What is clear is that, historically, the Italian press has a strong regional character and that this continues to be the case.

This regionalism derives, in part, from Italy's lack of a historical metropolitan capital comparable to London, Paris, Berlin, or Tokyo from whose central position the rest of the country could be dominated. Whereas Rome is the political capital and seat of government, Milan is the economic and cultural capital. While many party papers have been based in Rome (*Il Secolo d'Italia*, *L'Unità*, *La Voce Repubblicana*, and so on), there are more major daily papers based in Milan (*Il Corriere della Sera*, *Il Giornale*, *L'Indipendente*), including the financial press (*Il Sole–24 Ore*), and nearly all the new papers founded since the foundation of *Il Giorno* in 1956 have their headquarters there.

Put in a way that stresses positive attributes rather than lacks or inadequacies, Italy can be seen as a country of multiple urban centres which have not only maintained their identities but which are currently reclaiming their distinctive traditions in the name of a greater degree of self-government (Putnam *et al.* 1993). *Il Resto del Carlino*, for instance, interprets this spirit with its column written in dialect, its campaigns over Bologna's heritage, and coverage of business initiatives, notably the Fiera, the city's trade fair. If regions become more powerful as centres of government, taxation, and economic activity, then the *raison d'être* of this kind of press is enhanced.

The vigour of the regional and provincial press is, however, a feature of Northern and Central Italy. This is partly explicable in economic terms: the flourishing small businesses of the 'Third Italy' (Bagnasco and Trigilia 1984) have needed advertising outlets, and the expansion of this sector was exploited in the 1980s by Carlo Caracciolo, who added a chain of local tabloid dailies, like *Il Mattino di Padova* and *Il Tirreno* of Livorno, to his holdings in *L'Espresso* and *La Repubblica* (Grandinetti 1992: 62, 97). But the strength of local identities has also been an important factor, and something that the Catholic Church had long cultivated, celebrating the values of family and community in a multitude of small publications (Allum 1990: 85; Antonelli 1983; Nanni 1986). It was this localism, which distinguished itself from the national and state-building vocation of the Socialist and Communist Parties, that provided the cultural matrix of *leghismo* (Diamanti 1993). In the South and Islands the situation is very different. Of the 104 daily papers listed in the *Repertorio della stampa quotidiana in Italia* for 1991, only about nineteen were published in these regions. Within the South, Puglia is relatively well-served whereas Calabria is poor in newsprint.

The question about the national press has a spatial dimension. What geographical area is represented through the press? Does 'Italy' exist in print? But the spatial metaphor also concerns the rootedness of newspapers in Italian society, and this raises the second set of questions. Just how deeply implanted are *Il Corriere della Sera* or *La Repubblica* in the national life if they are only read by a small minority? Why are there no papers that are popular in format and readership?

The figures are striking. Between 1915 and 1980 the readership of the daily press remained constant at around 5 million (Forgacs 1990: 33). Comparative statistics for different countries for the early 1950s put Italy well behind the leading industrialized countries, such as the USA, the United Kingdom, France, and Germany, though ahead of Mediterranean countries like Spain and Greece (see Table 11.1). A survey of 1956 found that 64.5 per cent of the population never read anything at all. And while the situation improved, notably during the 1980s, so that by 1990 some 6.5 million Italians were buying a daily paper, the readership pattern was still regionally skewed. Whereas the ratio was one paper per 6.6 inhabitants in the North (7.4 in the Centre), it stood at one per 16 inhabitants in the South (Olmi 1992: 96). Comparative statistics show Italy as a nation falling behind other countries in newspaper readership (see Table 11.2).

The situation for the earlier period is easier to understand. Outside the main cities, Italy was predominantly a country of peasant cultivators. There were high

Table 11.1. Number and circulation of daily newspapers in Italy and five other countries, 1952

Country	No. daily newspapers	Est. circulation in number of copies	
		Total (millions)	Per 1,000 inhabitants
UK	122	31.0	615
USA	1,865	55.4	353
France	151	10.2	240
Spain	106	5.5	196
Italy	107	5.0	107
Greece	68	0.5	71

Source: UNESCO, Basic Facts and Figures (Paris, 1954), 61–3.

Table 11.2. Circulation of daily newspapers in twenty-six industrialized countries, 1972 and 1965 (copies per 1,000 inhabitants)

Country	1972 (in rank order)	1965 circulation	1965 rank order
Japan	529	451	3
Sweden	512	505	1
Iceland	439	435	4
Great Britain	437	479	2
GDR	425	400	5
Norway	391	384	7
Switzerland	390	376	8
New Zealand	367	399	6
Denmark	364	347	10
USSR	333	264	16
FRG	330	326	11
Austria	328	249	17
Australia	321	373	9
USA	314	310	13
Low Countries	307	293	14
Czechoslovakia	280	280	15
Uruguay	269	314	12
Canada	234	227	20
France	233	248	18
Ireland	233	246	19
Poland	231	167	21
Mexico	200	116	25
Israel	183	143	24
Argentina	180	148	23
Romania	173	157	22
Italy	142	113	26

Source: UNESCO, World Communication: A 200 Country Survey of Press, Radio and Television (Paris, 1975).

rates of illiteracy, especially in the South and country areas. Dialect was prevalent in everyday communication for 82 per cent of the population in 1956 (De Mauro 1979: 420). Urbanization was still limited, with 79 per cent of the population living in places with fewer than 20,000 inhabitants, and the communication system (post, roads) slow and often inadequate. There was also considerable poverty. Italy, in other words, was simultaneously an advanced industrialized nation, producing cars and typewriters of the highest quality, and an 'underdeveloped' one.

The situation is more difficult to understand for the period after the introduction of schooling to the age of 14. By 1968 some 19 million Italians (excluding those under 15, the illiterate and semi-literate, and the unemployed) *could* read a daily newspaper but chose not to.

Various explanations have been offered. Some, like those of Tullio De Mauro (1979) and Maurizio Dardano (1986), focus on problems of language, looking at the way many Italians did not feel at home with the national language even if they could speak it, and at how newspapers made no attempt to make themselves more accessible. The opacity and abstractness of bureaucratic and political discourses were said to be reproduced by journalists who should have been translating these sectoral languages into a journalistic prose comprehensible to the widest number of people. Others, like Paolo Murialdi, point to the vested interests that prevented publishers from launching popular papers back in the 1950s when weekly magazines proved that a wider readership could be reached. Because they were protected by the state they had less need to expand their market (Murialdi 1986: 185).When an attempt was eventually made to emulate the *Daily Mirror* with *L'Occhio* in 1979, it was poorly executed and quickly ended in failure (Varvello 1986). Finally, there is feminist analysis according to which low readership is related to the traditional exclusion of women from public life in Italy; as Milly Buonanno has argued, newspaper readers are predominantly male with women constituting 70 per cent of the category 'non-readers' in a 1980 survey (Buonanno 1982).

It still remains an open question as to whether a popular paper, the equivalent of the *Bild-Zeitung* or the *Sun*, could be successfully launched in Italy. There might be a market for some form of popular daily, and reports in April–May 1994 certainly suggested that the Fininvest group was exploring the idea. However, the press in Italy is structured so that the division between 'quality'/broadsheet and 'popular'/tabloid papers along British lines is unlikely to develop. First, because a regional and local identity and its newspaper representation cuts across the divisions of social class. Secondly, because 'popular' areas of reporting, such as crime and sports, are covered by the Italian press in a different way. And, thirdly, because of the prior existence of weekly magazines with large readerships.

Sport, which in Italy means football above all, is massively covered in the press, with regional and local publications giving special attention to their teams (Carcano and Merlo 1984). There are also three daily sports papers—*Il Corriere dello Sport* and *La Gazzetta dello Sport*, whose Monday editions (following the Sunday matches) respectively sold 511,000 and 809,000 in 1990, and *Tuttosport*, based in Turin. In the

1950s there were actually four such papers. Moreover, it is important to underline that football in Italy is popular in the sense that it is followed with equal enthusiasm by all social classes, whereas in the British case it is popular in a sense that tends to exclude the upper classes (Dal Lago 1990). As for crime stories, these constitute the backbone of local news, whether in *Il Corriere della Sera* or *L'Arena di Verona*, and local news, in the words of an old manual, is the 'quintessence of a paper, it is what affects the reader directly, the life of the city where he lives' (Mottana 1960: 78). Moreover, crime stories, usually murders, are covered by the national television news even when the individuals involved are not famous.

By looking at these two genres, crime and sports reporting, it is possible to identify elements of what elsewhere would be called 'popular journalism': the focus on the personal and 'human interest' story; the aim (characteristic of melodrama) to elicit emotional responses, whether of disgust, amazement, or exhilaration; the deployment of idioms and expressions of everyday language; the use of graphics and layout (shouting headlines; bold typefaces) for maximum impact. It has even been suggested by sociologists of journalism that the hard-and-fast distinction between 'high' and 'low', 'quality' and 'popular', is too simplistic, and that the story-telling mode, which is especially evident in crime reporting, 'unites journalism and popular culture' (Dahlgren and Sparks 1992: 14). In the Italian case, there is no 'popular' (mass-circulation) press as such, but elements of that kind of journalism are found in different formats, especially given the 'omnibus' nature of papers such as *Il Corriere della Sera* and *La Repubblica* and their strategy of reaching out beyond an élite readership. It has even been suggested by Giorgio Bocca that, since the development of colour supplements and new promotional campaigns in the late 1980s, the popular element that used to take the form of the local pages is now expressed in the language and taste of all parts of newspapers, making them print equivalents of television (Bocca 1989: 30).

The third reason why it has proved difficult to launch a mass-circulation daily paper in Italy concerns the role of the weekly magazine. The magazine has been widely seen as the success story of the Italian press when it comes to winning new readers. In a process similar to the German experience earlier in the century, magazines became national publications with a mass circulation at a time when newspapers were more regional in character. The *Guardian* correspondent in Italy, Sylvia Sprigge, noted in 1952 that 'while the dailies witness their sales falling, the new and ever more numerous weeklies may take their place. They are the cinema of the poor, and familes regularly get one or two a week' (quoted Lombardo and Pignatel 1985: 54). This was a trend that was already being established before the war (the mass-selling *Famiglia cristiana*, for example, was founded in 1931), but the arrival of *Epoca*, *Gente*, *Oggi*, and others, which looked to the American *Look* and *Life* and the French *Paris Match* as models, marked a new development. They showed themselves more accessible than newspapers on a number of counts: their language ('simplified and full of stereotypes'); their abundant use of photographs and graphics comprehensible to those with limited reading skills; and their content—stories about the private lives of Hollywood stars rather than about politics (Lombardo and Pignatel 1985: 55). (It is significant perhaps that Italian newspapers, unlike the magazines, have paid relatively little attention to the quality of their newsphotos, which even in the 1990s remains low on picture-definition and picture-values.) Commentators did note that the dailies began in the 1980s to take on some of the characteristics of the weeklies ('*settimanalizzazione*'), particularly in their coverage of 'lifestyle' matters, such as fashion and health (Murialdi 1988). This also coincided with the growing numbers and growing influence of women journalists; in 1992 women constituted 34 per cent of the profession in Milan, mostly working in the magazine sector, and 50 per cent of new trainees (Mafai 1993: 292). There is no doubt that major changes are taking place *within* the existing newspapers, notably the growth of a female readership and a journalism that addresses itself to this constituency. However, the weeklies have provided a stimulus, without ceding their position and without prompting the creation of a popular picture-led daily paper.

If sports papers and weekly magazines are included, then Italians are, despite convictions to the contrary, a nation of readers (Cesareo 1994: 584). They are not, however, a nation of newspaper readers comparable to those formed in the nineteenth century when the spread of literacy and the emergence of a popular press went hand in hand in certain countries like Britain (Williams 1961; Smith 1991). In Italy this was not the case, and only an élite readership was formed. In the second half of the twentieth century, when the majority of Italians became literate, the newspaper had ceased to have a monopoly of information, thanks to radio and (more importantly) television. Furthermore, when television massively increased its presence in national life as a result of commercial development in the 1980s, it seized the mass advertising market that would in other circumstances have been the natural money-spinner for a popular daily; in fact, the Italian situation, in which total newspaper advertising revenue is less (about half) than that of television, is a total anomaly with respect to the European pattern (Mosconi 1992: 80–4). Ultimately, it could be said, television in Italy has occupied the entire space that in some other countries is shared with the popular press.

The third question, 'why is the Italian press not independent?', refers to the relationship between newspapers and centres of power. It is frequently argued that the Italian case is anomalous because the press is not a properly autonomous force (Murialdi 1983; Bechelloni 1980).

For analytic purposes, this question can be treated in terms of factors external to journalism that have created forms of dependence, and those internal to journalism. In turn, the external factors can be subdivided into political institutions and political parties on the one hand, and economic groups and forces on the other.

The relationship between newspapers and politics in Italy goes back to the time of Unification, but for the contemporary period a crucial moment was the formation of a party press in the late nineteenth century, notably the Italian Socialist

Party's *Avanti!* Since then every political organization from the Anarchists (*L'Umanità Nuova*) to the Neo-Fascists (*Il Secolo d'Italia*) and Republicans (*La Voce Italiana*) have or have had their daily paper. An extensive Catholic press, more locally based in its reporting and circulation, also emerged about a century ago when a Catholic subculture developed particularly in the north-east, and in 1960 an estimated 76 per cent of newspapers were controlled by the Church and Christian Democrats (Murialdi 1978: 245).

There are big differences between the papers of the 'party press'. Above all, they differ in their political orientations. The same event will tend to be reported and interpreted in very different ways. This was especially the case at the height of the Cold War. The death of Stalin, for example, was deeply mourned by the Communist press, in whose eyes the Soviet leader was a father-figure and an immortal hero, whereas *L'Osservatore Romano* took the opportunity of reminding readers of the nature of human mortality and the persecution suffered by the Catholic Church in the East (Lumley 1995). This political polarization should not, however, prevent us from noting some of the features common to a press subject to a party or an institution. On many counts the Vatican and the leadership of the Soviet Union belonged to different worlds. Yet, as *The Economist* observed about the Vatican newspaper, even *Pravda* seemed positively to bristle with gossip by comparison with *L'Osservatore Romano*. Of the latter Pope Paul VI, son of a Brescia newspaper editor, said it reported on meetings before they have actually met—'to make sure that nothing untoward leaks out' (Hebblethwaite 1986: 181). The newspaper that is the official organ of a party or church will tend to require respect for orthodoxy and censorship of heretical or dissident views. Its principal purpose is to form as well as inform opinion within its ranks. Its criteria of news-values are liable to be directly subordinate to political considerations. Similarly, extra-journalistic criteria help determine the appointment of journalists, who in turn usually pursue a career within the framework of the organization rather than pursuing a career in journalism *per se*. Hence the number of politicians in Italy that have, at least in the past, been members of the profession thanks to writing in the party publication; hence the lack of movement between party and commercial papers, such as *Il Corriere della Sera* or *La Stampa*. The official organ is characterized by its institutional function of organizing consensus within a determinate area of opinion. Homogeneity or containment of opinion within certain limits is likely to be a goal, especially in the face of factionalism and in-fighting. It is a press that is protected from the market in that it does not depend financially on sales and advertising. Often circulation is undertaken by the organization itself, whether it is through parishes or party branches.

Party newspapers used to be a notable feature of the Italian press and one of the aspects that distinguished it from the structure of the press in North America or the United Kingdom. However, party papers have declined in importance, as the subcultures to which their readers have belonged have retreated. The full consequences of this cultural sea change for the press would have made themselves felt earlier had it not been for state subsidies and protection granted in the mid-1970s. Since the fall of the Berlin Wall and the ensuing crisis of the political system in Italy (Gundle and Parker 1995) these defences have been removed. The Tangentopoli scandals meant that sources of funding dried up, while the credibility of leading parties, notably the Christian Democrats and Socialists, was fatally undermined. A measure of the change in circumstances is provided by *L'Unità*: in 1952, the year before Stalin's death, it had a circulation of 500,000 and special editions in Rome, Milan, Turin, Genoa, and Naples (Porter 1983: 112; Bechelloni and Buonanno 1981). Party members would sell the paper, and its pages formed part of the urban landscape. By 1992 it was a shadow of its former self, and had a circulation of a mere 124,000. In many respects, *L'Unità* has probably become a better newspaper—more open to a diversity of opinion, less constrained by a certain official language, readier to laugh at itself. The story of the satire pages (first 'Tango' and then 'Cuore') gives an insight into the new relationship between party and paper in which journalists have more freedom to criticize and even to be irreverent about the leadership (Chiesa 1990: 282–308; Lumley forthcoming). Yet the new *L'Unità* is very much a 'second paper'—the newspaper of opinion and commentary that supplements the paper that carries the news—and one whose influence is radically diminished.

The press tied to the Church has also undergone a decline. The 'Catholic world' too has experienced processes of fragmentation and the demise of its subculture (Allum 1990). But the relative strength and influence of Catholic organizations, a local orientation, and a close relationship to business (it never suffered the boycott on advertising hitting left publications) has made the Catholic press more durable than the publications of the subculture associated with the PCI (Antonelli 1983).

If the party press was significant for channelling opinion *within* the parties themselves, more important for influencing wider public opinion (albeit that represented by newspaper readers) has been the commercial press in the form of papers such as *Il Corriere della Sera* or *Il Mattino*. Particularly in times of sudden change when readers are looking for guidance and when political figures are seeking to construct new alliances and to win support, these newspapers have played a notable political role. Indeed it is argued by Mauro Calise that the press played a crucial role in defining issues and setting agendas at the time of the 1993 referendum on electoral reform, becoming a quasi-independent political force:

The new development can be seen as the natural outcome of transformations in the communications circuit of Italian politics which were increasingly separated from the political parties. Instead, a direct, unmediated relationship was established between newspapers and voters with the papers turning into independent 'parties'. (Calise 1994: 125)

During the 1994 election campaign papers such as *Il Corriere* and *La Stampa* were clearly sympathetic to the Progressive Alliance and highly critical of Berlusconi and his allies. This situation can be contrasted with that pertaining during the heyday of the First Republic, when newspapers acted as a medium through which politicians spoke to one another in a coded language impenetrable to those out-side the charmed circle. In the words of a celebrated article by Enzo Forcella:

A political journalist in our country can count on around 1,500 readers—ministers and under-secretaries (all of them), members of parliament (some of them), party leaders, trade union officials, high prelates, and some industrialists who want to be informed. The rest do not count, even though the paper sells 300,000 copies. . . . The whole system is based on the rapport between the political journalist and this group of privileged readers. If we lose sight of this factor, we cannot understand the most characteristic aspect of our political journalism, perhaps of Italian politics in general—the feeling of talk within the family, with protagonists who have known each other since childhood. (Quoted in Porter 1983: 10)

This close relationship between journalism and *partitocrazia* is related to the way politicians have become journalists and vice versa. The career of Giovanni Spadolini is emblematic; editor of *Il Corriere della Sera*, he became leader of the Partito Repubblicano and then prime minister.

Political interference and efforts to condition the press in Italy are perhaps especially associated with the Fascist period. And when in the early 1970s a jour-nalist was imprisoned on political grounds, the charges of anti-State encitement were straight out of the Rocco Penal Code (Murialdi 1978: 530). The infiltration of the press by secret service agents and covert funding were just two of the forms of political instrumentalization that were commonly adopted during the Cold War. Yet the continuities with Fascism also appeared in measures designed to protect newspapers; for example, the state subsidies instituted in 1974 bailed out an industry in economic difficulties, while the ceiling on public television adver-tising regulated competition in favour of the older medium. Particularly signifi-cant was the vote by political parties and the journalists' trade union in 1944 for the maintenance of the *albo dei giornalisti*, a piece of corporativist legislation that limited access to the profession to those admitted via examination to the *albo* or list. Together with a law passed in 1963 which made journalism into a profession equivalent in statute to the law or medicine, this created a situation described, with a note of horror, by an American scholar: 'From the moment he steps into the examining room for the final test of his professional competence . . . the jour-nalist is tied to civil authority at almost every turn. Government defines the pro-fession; government gives its corporate decisions the force of law; government protects the people in it from outside competition' (Porter 1983: 71–2). His sen-timents are echoed by Paolo Murialdi, a campaigner against such legislation, who has argued that the 'the vast majority of the political class and the journalist class' in Italy has resisted the idea that a broadly liberal press is the one best suited to a market economy (Murialdi 1986: 179).

Subservience to government was certainly considered a characteristic of most of the Italian press in the period between 1947 and the early 1970s, though such a description oversimplifies the relationship; Piero Ottone writes: 'Until yesterday newspapers were class-based, and most of them were in the hands of the bour-geoisie. Readers saw them as a line of defence protecting a form of society in which they believed' (Ottone 1987: 80). The majority of influential newspapers were, and are, controlled by companies, not by parties or government. Through newspapers, generations of entrepreneurs in Italy have sought to exercise their influence. The Agnelli family is but one instance (Castronovo 1977). Behind virtually every paper there is a controlling group whose interests lie outside publishing. *Il Resto del Carlino* and *La Nazione*, for example, were bought up in 1966 by Attilio Monti, head of a petroleum and sugar group which still owns them (Murialdi 1983: 201). The newspaper, for these companies, is not so much a financial investment in which profitability is the criterion of success (often losses are sustained over several years) as a voice in public affairs. In the narrowest sense, this can entail trying to influence policy- and decision-making that directly affect a company's position (tariff control, for example). Certainly *Il Sole–24 Ore*, which is the mouthpiece of the Confindustria, the industrialists' organization, speaks up for business interests. In a broader perspective, it means orienting public opinion in a given direction (for instance, in relation to ecological issues). In the words of the industrialist Raul Gardini, 'I'll buy papers, concern myself with papers, talk to journalists, because it is in my interests to prepare public opinion for paying the price for clean air and a non-polluting agriculture' (quoted in Bocca 1989: 22).

Newspapers are, in a general sense, subject to the interests of their owners. Yet exactly what this implies in practice is not so easy to establish. Perhaps in moments of crisis and conflict resulting from a take-over or the sacking of an editor, the role of owners is thrown into relief; cases include the sacking of the editor of *L'Indipendente* within a few months of its launch in November 1991 as a paper that really would be *independent* with respect to its economic backers and to the political world. The new editor quickly turned it into a pro-Lega Lombarda publication. Then there was the clash between Paolo Berlusconi (brother of Silvio) and Indro Montanelli, founding editor of *Il Giornale*, which ended in the latter's resignation from the paper in February 1994 after his refusal to endorse Forza Italia. Montanelli went on to found *La Voce* with the aim of guaranteeing independence by making readers into shareholders, thereby forestalling the concentration of ownership that was seen as inimical to journalistic freedom.

Constraints on newspaper independence appear as 'external' precisely at such moments of conflict, though the owners are never in fact 'on the outside', thanks to daily telephone calls, regular meetings, and so on. In the normal course of things, and especially since the mid-1970s when a more hands-off approach was adopted by most owners in response to journalists' campaigns for greater control of their work situation, journalists rarely find themselves openly censored or told what to think. Instead, it is claimed that threats to independence are now covert, not overt, and that the external pressures have changed and have become internalized by journalists. Alberto Papuzzi, returning to journalism in the early 1980s after a period of absence, noted the changed environment: 'Journalists now saw themselves as cogs in a gigantic machine—the mass media industry. An industry that produces news but also communication, advertising, propaganda, entertainment.

The journalist had become a terminal in an economy of information based on scale' (Papuzzi 1993: p. xxiv).

The infernal incarnation of this new development is television, while its heavenly embodiment is computer technology. The computer terminal can bring advantages: direct inputting by the journalist and therefore greater control over what gets printed; access to massive data banks; speed of communication and transcription with use of the modem. But there are also dangers; not least, that articles can be put together entirely in the office using information from agencies and other sources, such as press releases. As a consequence, the number and importance of sub-editors increases at the expense of the traditional on-the-spot reporter, diminishing the role of the person traditionally seen as the linchpin of the profession.

Both the new technologies and television are said to have negative consequences for print journalism in that it is claimed they undermine the relationship between representation and reality which the press has traditionally mediated in the name of the reader. That is to say, reporting has increasingly become a second-hand activity in which the media cross-reference one another to the point that sources are ever more distant from the events they purport to describe. The referent is displaced as words refer to other words and no longer to an external reality. The effects of television on the press are described as uniformly deleterious. It is not just that television puts a premium on entertainment values (i.e. making news into a spectacle for consumption) or that it privileges visuals so that a story is not reported unless accompanied by pictures; nor just that television has overtaken the press in speed of reporting, establishing itself as the chief source of news for the majority of Italians. As Alberto Papuzzi has observed, the problem is that the press in Italy has allowed television to set its agendas so that anything in the *telegiornale* has to be covered in the morning edition (Papuzzi 1994). It has also tried to become more 'entertaining', symptomatically giving extensive coverage to television personalities and 'events' (Lumley 1995). Instead of pursuing what distinguishes their work from that of broadcasters, journalists from the editors down have tended to internalize the values of a 'television culture' at the expense of their own independence. The decline of serious investigative journalism is symptomatic of a wider cultural change in the world of journalism (Agostini 1988).

The question of newspaper independence and freedom has therefore been fundamentally revised in the context of wider cultural and technological changes. The newspaper is simply not the voice in public affairs that it once was; the era in which the editor of *Il Corriere della Sera* became prime minister has been replaced by one in which a television mogul can become prime minister.

In conclusion, one might want to question some of the questions that have been asked. They all presuppose a 'normal' course of development (that of the first industrialized nations) and an ideal in which newspapers are representatives of national public opinion and embodiments of free speech. This perspective is not, however, the invention of foreign commentators. It is a topos of debates about the press within Italy and consonant with the general propensity to what has been called 'triumphalism turned upside down'—'We cannot be the first? All right then, we will be the last!' (Fruttero and Lucentini 1994). When Table 11.2 was reproduced in an Italian study it drew attention to the fact that Italy was at the bottom of the league table of international newspaper readership. Anyone who has had discussions with Italian journalists will quickly find them comparing their press unfavourably with that of other countries. Yet just that fact might alert one to the presence of a critical, open-minded, and non-nationalist approach that does not fit the negative picture being drawn.

The point here is not to engage in a moral discourse. If Italians are not a nation of newspaper readers comparable to the Germans or the British, or if Italians want to read a lot about sport, it does not follow that they are culturally backward or in danger of slipping off the map of Europe. Instead, I want to make two observations.

The first is to note that several of the distinguishing features of Italian newspapers have been disappearing. The demise of the party press has already been mentioned, but this is symptomatic of a bigger change, namely the declining importance of the institutional/political as opposed to the market context in which the press operates. The consequences have not always been welcomed. But anxieties about the influence of advertising (in encouraging the dailies to imitate the weeklies), about the decline of standards (the eclipse of the journalist by the generic media professional), or about opinion polls and market research (typical features of private-sector television) indicate the depth of the transformations under way. And if the new situation threatens the role of the critical and independent-minded journalist, it is bizarre to follow Giorgio Bocca nostalgically into the 'grave-yard of newspaper genres' to lament the passing of phenomena such as the *pastone romano*, the traditional round-up of political gossip at the Chamber of Deputies (Bocca 1989). Some of the changes, such as the greater proportion of women in journalism and the greater attention to social rather than narrowly political themes, are positive. Even the dominance of television (a development not restricted to Italy, though marked by the acute crisis of the public service model in this country) offers new possibilities. For instance, newspapers are freer to focus on commentary and analysis of news that has already been delivered by the other media.

The second observation concerns the assumption that somehow a truly independent national press exists elsewhere. The assumption has its uses, providing a stick with which to beat benighted opponents, but it frequently forestalls a proper comparative analysis (see Michael Eve's Chapter 2 in this volume). On the one hand, too much authority is accredited to publications like *The Times* on account of their status, giving rise to the habit of servilely quoting the foreign press every time there is a political crisis; on the other, the merits of the Italian press are overlooked. The Italian press has not, to date, been responsible for a Watergate. However, it has played a creditable role in withstanding authoritarian manœuvres (for example, the strategy of tension following the Piazza Fontana bombing of 1969), and was remarkable for its independent positions before, during, and after the March 1994 elections. It is significant at a time when the control of television is deemed so important for influencing public opinion that it should be the press in Italy that has stood up for freedom of speech.

Further Reading

There is little available in English on newspapers and journalism in Italy. William E. Porter's *The Italian Journalist* (Ann Arbor, 1983) provides a useful account in the light of the situation in the USA. For an anthology of texts in Italian but with introduction and notes in English, see Robert Lumley, *Italian Journalism: A Critical Anthology* (Manchester, 1996).

Leading Italian journalists are prolific book-writers and many of their articles are published in collections. Giorgio Bocca is outstanding in this respect and is worth serious attention; his *La scoperta dell'Italia* (Bari, 1963) was among his first 'journeys' through Italy; *L'inferno. Profondo sud, male oscuro* (Milan, 1992) is an extended (and much criticized) report on the 'Southern question'; *Il provinciale* (Milan, 1991) is Bocca's autobiography. Contemporary commentaries by journalists on the Italian press tend to be polemical; a classic case is G. P. Pansa, *Carte false* (Milan, 1988). An exception is Alberto Papuzzi's *Manuale del giornalista* (Rome, 1993), a balanced and informative critique of the state of Italian journalism. For a discussion of the role of female as well as male journalists, see 'Le giornaliste in Italia: molta visibilità, poco potere', in *Problemi dell'informazione* (Sept. 1993), 271–95; also Milly Buonanno, *L'elite senza sapere* (Naples, 1988). For an analysis of investigative journalism, see Angelo Agostini, *Dentro la notizia* (Milan, 1988).

The language of Italian journalism has been analysed by scholars of linguistics; the authoritative study, Maurizio Dardano, *Il linguaggio dei giornali italiani* (Bari, 1986), is rather dated in its examples but has a useful appendix on Anglicisms; otherwise there is Mario Medici and Domenico Proietti (eds.), *Il linguaggio del giornalismo* (Milan, 1992); Paolo Murialdi's *Come si legge un giornale* (Bari, 1986) remains useful. For a guide to terminology, Carlo De Martino and Fabio Bonifacci, *Dizionario pratico di giornalismo* (Milan, 1990). For a satirical look at how journalism has evolved, see Michele Serra's writings, notably *Visti da lontano* (Milan, 1987), and *Il nuovo che avanza* (Milan, 1989). The best source of up-to-date information and analysis is the quarterly media journal *Problemi dell'informazione*, while details of circulation figures and news about the newspaper industry can be found in the monthly review *Prima comunicazione*.

The most accessible history of the Italian press is Paolo Murialdi, *Storia del giornalismo italiano* (Turin, 1986). The most comprehensive, on the other hand, is V. Castronovo and N. Tranfaglia (eds.), *Storia della stampa italiana* in seven volumes (Bari, 1976–94). Often more interesting than the general histories are the studies of particular periods or genres; on the role of columnists, see Mario Isnenghi, 'Il grande opinionista da Albertini a Bocca', in S. Soldani and G. Turi (eds.), *Fare gli italiani. Scuola e cultura nell'Italia contemporanea*, ii. (Bologna, 1993); on satire and cartoons, see, Adolfo Chiesa, *La satira politica in Italia* (Bari, 1990), and R. Lumley, 'The Last Laugh', in L. Cheles and L. Sponza (eds.), *The Art of Persuasion: Political Communication in Italy 1945–1995* (Manchester, forthcoming). For a comparative perspective on 'popular' forms of journalism, see P. Dahlgren and C. Sparks, *Journalism and Popular Culture* (London, 1992).

The history of the press and of journalism must, of course, be put in the context of broader historical events and processes. For a political and social history, see Paul Ginsborg, *A History of Contemporary Italy* (London, 1990); for cultural developments, see David Forgacs, *Italian Culture in the Industrial Era* (Manchester, 1990), and Zygmunt Baranski and Robert Lumley (eds.), *Culture and Conflict in Postwar Italy* (London, 1990); for the crisis of the First Republic, see Stephen Gundle and Simon Parker (eds.), *The New Italian Republic: From the Fall of the Berlin Wall to Berlusconi* (London, 1996).

References

AGOSTINI, A. (1988), *Dentro la notizia* (Milan).

ALLUM, P. (1990), 'Uniformity Undone: Catholic Culture in Postwar Italy' in Z. G. Baranski and R. Lumley (eds.), *Culture and Conflict in Postwar Italy* (London), 79–96.

ALTINO, T. (1988), 'L'esperienza di "La Repubblica" con le tecnologie avanzate', *Problemi dell'informazione*, 12: 569–83.

ANDERSON, B. (1991), *Imagined Communities: Reflections on the Origin and Spread of Nationalism* (London).

ANTONELLI, Q. (1983), 'Il fenomeno della stampa diocesana', *Problemi dell'informazione*, 8: 575–604.

BAGNASCO, A., and TRIGILIA, C. (1984) (eds.), *Società e politica nelle aree di piccola impresa* (Venice).

BECHELLONI, G. (1980), 'The Journalist as Political Client', in Smith (1980).

—— and BUONANNO, M. (1981), 'Un quotidiano di partito sui generis: "L'Unità"', *Problemi dell'informazione*, 6: 219–42.

BOCCA, G. (1989), *Il padrone in redazione* (Milan).

BOLLATI, G. (1983), *L'italiano. Il carattere nazionale come storia e come invenzione* (Turin).

BUONANNO, M. (1982), 'Aumentano le lettrici dei quotidiani. Ovvero: perché si legge poco in Italia', *Problemi dell'informazione*, 7: 563–5.

CALISE, M. (1994), *Dopo la partitocrazia* (Turin).

CARCANO, G., and MERLO, A. M. (1984), 'Il grande parco dei divertimenti: indagine sul boom dei quotidiani sportivi', *Problemi dell'informazione*, 9: 391–425.

CASTRONOVO, V. (1977), *Giovanni Agnelli* (Turin).

CESAREO, G. (1994), 'Giornali e giornalisti: informazione e scambio politico' in Ginsborg (1994).

CHIESA, A. (1990), *La satira politica in Italia* (Bari).

DAHLGREN, P., and SPARKS, C. (1992) (eds.), *Journalism and Popular Culture* (London).

DAL LAGO, A. (1990), *Descrizione di una battaglia. Rituali del calcio* (Bologna).

DARDANO, M. (1986), *Il linguaggio dei giornali* (Bari).

DE MAURO, T. (1979), 'L'italiano dei non lettori', *Problemi dell'informazione*, 3: 419–31.

DIAMANTI, I. (1993), *La Lega. Geografia, storia e sociologia di un nuovo soggetto politico* (Rome).

FORGACS, D. (1990), *Italian Culture in the Industrial Era, 1880–1980: Cultural Industries, Politics and the Public* (Manchester).

FRUTTERO, C., and LUCENTINI, F. (1994), 'I nuovi primati italiani', *La Stampa*, 4 May.

GINSBORG, P. (1994) (ed.), *Stato dell'Italia* (Milan).

GRANDINETTI, M. (1992), *I quotidiani in Italia, 1943–91* (Milan).

GUNDLE, S., and PARKER, S. (1996) (eds.), *The New Italian Republic: From the Fall of the Berlin Wall to Berlusconi* (London).

HEBBLETHWAITE, P. (1986), *In the Vatican* (London).

HOBSBAWM, E. J. (1977), *The Age of Capital* (London).

LOMBARDO, M., and PIGNATEL, F. (1985), *La stampa periodica in Italia* (Rome).

LUMLEY, R. (1996), *Italian Journalism: A Critical Anthology* (Manchester).

—— (forthcoming), 'The Last Laugh: Political Satire in Italy, 1968–94', in L. Cheles and L. Sponza (eds.), *The Art of Persuasion: Political Communication in Italy 1945–1995* (Manchester).

MAFAI, M. (1993), 'Creativi o organizzativi?', *Problemi dell'informazione*, 18: 291–5.

MOSCONI, F. (1992), 'Multimedialità e oligopolio', *Problemi dell'informazione*, 17: 73–103.

MOTTANA, G. (1960), *Il giornalismo e la sua tecnica* (Milan).

MURIALDI, P. (1978), *La stampa italiana del dopoguerra, 1943–72* (Bari).

—— (1983), 'Contributo alla storia di "Repubblica", il quotidiano diverso', *Problemi dell'informazione*, 8: 605–17.

—— (1986), *Storia del giornalismo italiano* (Turin).

—— (1988), 'I quotidiani italiani e gli effetti del mercato', *Problemi dell'informazione*, 13: 39–46.

Nanni, G. (1986), 'Quotidiani e società nella provincia di Bergamo', *Problemi dell'informazione*, 11: 101.

Olmi, M. (1992), *Il giornalismo in Italia* (Rome).

Ottone, P. (1987), *Il buon giornale* (Milan).

Papuzzi, A. (1993), *Manuale del giornalista* (Rome).

—— (1994), Interview with the author.

Porter, W. (1983), *The Italian Journalist* (Ann Arbor).

Putnam, R., Nanetti, R., and Leonardi, R. (1993), *Making Democracy Work: Civic Traditions in Modern Italy* (Princeton).

Smith, A. D. (1979), *The Newspaper: An International History* (London).

—— (1980) (ed.), *Newspapers and Democracy* (Cambridge, Mass.).

—— (1991), *National Identity* (London).

Varvello, M. (1986), '"L'Occhio": indagine su un fallimento', *Problemi dell'informazione*, 11: 267–88.

Williams, R. (1961), *The Long Revolution* (London).

Wolf, M. (1994), 'Mass media: tra bulimia e anoressia', in Ginsborg (1994).

12

Cinema

CHRISTOPHER
WAGSTAFF

CINEMA, as we define it today, that is to say the projection of moving photographic images telling a story in public places to a ticket-buying audience, began in 1895. As with other mass media like radio, gramophone records, and television, the history of cinema has to begin by examining technological inventions and their development, and the exploitation for profit of the patents taken out by the inventors and developers (Neale 1984), and then proceed to a study of the way the new medium becomes integrated into patterns of consumption of other media, and how it develops its own forms of consumption and its own institutions (Brunetta 1993). Early Italian cinematographers built their own cameras and projectors, shot their own films in their own studios, and showed them wherever they could, at fairgrounds, in theatres, and in music halls, for example. The novelty of seeing moving images was integrated into other institutions of public entertainment. As the novelty wore off, the films had to draw an audience by developing a greater story-telling ability, by showing more interesting events happening to more subtly developed characters, who in turn had to be performed by actors who were better versed in the kind of acting that the camera, as opposed to the stage, required. Thus we find that the development of the technology, of the institutions, and of the artistic and aesthetic aspects of cinema go hand in hand.

The methods used for studying cinema are determined by the way in which the object of study is defined. The object of study can be the technological development of the medium, or the growth of forms of consumption; it can be the industrial and marketing structures that have grown up around the medium, or the evolution of the narrative conventions that have characterized films. These, though very different from one another, are all objects of study for which methods of historical enquiry are appropriate (Allen and Gomery 1985). If the object of study is the development of a film director's *œuvre* over his lifetime (for example, that of Federico Fellini), this will probably entail both historical enquiry and a labour of critical and interpretative analysis (Bondanella 1993). The discipline of 'Film Theory' sets itself the task of identifying the different ways in which cinema can be approached, and the methods that are appropriate to the different approaches: questions like what is the artistic nature of film (Andrew 1976), what is the source of a film (Caughie 1981; Grant 1986), what is the nature of the pleasure that the viewer derives from watching a film (Metz 1977; Dyer 1982), how gender is constituted in cinema (De Lauretis 1984; Penley 1988), whether or not the cinema has a language of its own (Metz 1968, 1971; Arijohn 1976), and what relationship films have with the real world that they supposedly represent (Williams 1981). (For surveys of 'Film Theory' see Monaco 1977; Bordwell and Thompson 1986; Lapsley and Westlake 1988; and Casetti 1993.)

For early Italian cinema, one of the major historical enterprises has been the retrieval of films. Fifteen years ago, it was believed that only a handful of the 2,000 films made in Italy up to 1930 were still in existence. Since then many discoveries have been made in European and particularly South American film archives, and we can now hope to be able to see several hundred Italian films made before the coming of sound. Historians working in this area deal with hard facts: what films were made, by whom, where, with what actors, and telling what stories, together with the critical response to these films excavated from newspapers of the period. Alongside them work archivists who track down copies, preserve, restore, catalogue them, and make them available to the public, with the end result that we have a list of films, containing the basic facts about them, and telling us if, and where, copies can still be found (Bernardini 1980–2; Martinelli 1980–93; Brunetta 1993). Until recently, we could say little about the first thirty-five years of Italian cinema. Now, thanks to the work of these historians and archivists, we can begin to know a lot more about that period, and the work of analysing the films and their language from a critical perspective can start in earnest.

Already one area of historical investigation presents itself, namely, the way in which this new popular form of art and entertainment developed as part of the social and cultural activity of ordinary Italians (as opposed to film makers themselves). It was not until after the Second World War that cinema in Italy completely divorced itself from the theatre and music hall, for even in the early 1940s film shows were often preceded by an *avanspettacolo*, consisting of songs and sketches by live artistes, which might even be scripted by the same group of writers who contributed to the scripts of the films. These writers were also busy working on popular weekly satirical magazines like *Marc'Aurelio*, and for radio comedy shows. When sound came to Italy after 1930, the techniques of acting proper to silent film had to be modified, and there was a wholesale importation of personnel from the theatre, while at the same time, the films themselves were very frequently made from successful stage plays. Cinema before 1945 in Italy was mainly an urban leisure pursuit, catering for the *piccola borghesia* (petty bourgeoisie), students, shop-keepers, bank employees. Some early silent films had shown greater cultural pretensions, depicting Roman history and adapting great works of literature. Indeed, films like Giovanni Pastrone's *Cabiria* (1914) were admired the world over as examples of film art. Nevertheless, the potential that the cinema, like radio, had for delivering cultural norms and experiences to an entire nation in the 1930s went unrealized, despite the earnest desires and endeavours of the Fascist government, not least because of the lack of a rural network of cinemas. As a result, Italian cinema of the 1930s has often, perhaps unjustifiably, been seen as particularly fascist, because Fascism appealed above all to the urban petty bourgeoisie (Carabba 1974; Argentieri 1979; Gili 1981; Hay 1987; Landy 1986; Redi 1979). It is among these classes that a popular culture developed, of listening to the radio, of buying gramophone records, and of reading weekly magazines. After the Second World War, the Catholic Church was instrumental in the creation of over 5,000 parish cinemas, often in rural areas, and the whole Italian film industry expanded both in production and exhibition (showing films in cinemas), so that by the late 1950s we can identify films as directed towards the more rural South, and we can find the box-office returns for Italian films coming as much from provincial and rural cinemas as from the urban ones. By that time another medium had arisen to cater for this public, namely television, which was referred to as *il cinema dei poveri* (the cinema of the poor). However, it was at first often consumed in a form that resembles in some ways the consumption of cinema: people did not watch programmes on their own sets, but saw them in bars, clubs, and cinemas. Hence, just at the moment when we are able to detect a nation-wide acculturation taking place as a result of Italian cinema reaching all classes and areas, we find the cinema being replaced by television. The smaller cinemas closed, and the circulation of Italian films in Italy through the third-run local and rural cinemas with cheap ticket prices dried up. But it was replaced by the very medium that supplanted it, television; for with the *de facto* deregulation of television in 1976 there sprang up a massive broadcasting of what we might call third-run films on commercial television channels which continues to this day.

The social history of the development of a popular mass-cultural medium, and of the way it integrated itself into the general growth of other forms of popular culture throughout the 1930s and 1940s, requires attention to a multitude of manifestations that are not strictly cinematic: the way people spent their leisure time, the publishing of fan periodicals, the cult of pin-ups, the star system, the relations between cinema and theatre, radio and sport (it was not until the end of the Second World War that the public's expenditure on cinema in Italy exceeded that on all other leisure pursuits taken together), the building and location of cinemas, forms of transport, the penetration of foreign cultural norms into Italian society (from 1916 to 1965 Italians saw mostly American films). All of these things had social consequences, and can be the object of a study that starts from the phenomenon of cinema (Ellwood and Brunetta 1991). At this point it is important to remember that an investigation of 'Italian' cinema that deals with considerations of the market and social behaviour must take account of the fact that Italian cinemas have been dominated by Hollywood imports for much of their history. If, on the other hand, we direct our attention to individual films and their meaning and value, or to film genres, we can justifiably concentrate our attention on films made in Italy by Italian film makers.

However, an example of an area of study which does not necessarily take individual films as its object is the Italian film industry and its relations with the state and with foreign film industries (Bizzarri and Solaroli 1958; Quaglietti 1980; Contaldo and Fanelli 1979; Guback 1969; Forgacs 1990; Wagstaff 1984 and forthcoming). In the period up to 1915, Italy was one of the world's major exporters of films. A few large production companies had grown up, and around them there existed a multitude of smaller companies. Italy became known as a producer of spectacular films on historical themes, and these films exported partly because of their exotic value. With the First World War, and the rapid growth and organization of the US film industry, Italian production went bankrupt and collapsed. Whereas in 1915 Italy produced 562 films, by 1930 that number had dropped to twelve. The Fascist government set about reorganizing the industry along more efficient and less wasteful lines, eventually finding itself owning studios, distribution companies, and a chain of cinemas. It put into effect measures to protect Italian films against the overwhelming competition from Hollywood by, for example, setting a quota of the number of days a year an Italian cinema had to show Italian films, and by insisting that all foreign films be dubbed into Italian. The state tried to supervise the quality of films made in Italy by offering subsidies which were dependent on a script's approval by the government body responsible (a measure that could also be used to deter unwelcome criticism of the state, or the representation of Italian life and society in an unsavoury light). The Cinecittà studios were built with state money and were taken over by the state; the Centro Sperimentale di Cinematografia, a university-level film school, was established; and the Venice Film Festival was launched as an international showcase for Italian films. In 1938 the state took over a monopoly of distribution (by which we mean the rental of films to cinemas) of foreign films in Italy, and in retaliation the eight major Hollywood distributors withdrew from the Italian market. The result was that by 1942 Italy was producing over 100 films a year.

When the Allies landed in Italy in 1943, they brought a backlog of American films into Italy, and took over film distribution in the occupied territories. In 1945 they obliged Italy to abrogate all the measures that protected Italian films against competition on the domestic market, and 'dumped' at low prices on the Italian market over 2,000 American films, while Cinecittà was used to house refugees. Gradually, throughout the late 1940s, the Italian production sector picked up. Some of the very cheaply made films of the period dealt in a remarkably realistic way with the social and political conditions of Italian life in the aftermath of the war, and these films began to find a warm response in the art cinema circuits abroad. These exports brought with them an interest in Italian films, and other more popular films followed in their wake. The Italian government found ways to restore protectionist measures to defend Italian cinema against the onslaught of Hollywood, and while this was happening American production companies found that the costs of making films in Italy were lower than in Hollywood, and began making their films there. It was also a way in which they could use their Italian earnings, which could not be transferred to the USA because of the need for stringent exchange controls to prevent a haemorrhaging of hard currency, badly needed by the Italian economy, out of the country. Italy made agreements to exchange films with other countries, and started a massive programme of co-production with other countries, notably France, which had the effect of increasing the protected area of the domestic market for Italian films. Whereas in 1946 only 13 per cent of box-office earnings in Italy went to Italian films, for which there was virtually no export market, by the 1960s Italian films were taking half of the box-office returns in Italy, and were covering half of their production costs through sales abroad. By the late 1960s Italy was making more films than Hollywood. However, when Hollywood began to concentrate its industrial structure in the 1970s, American films began to recapture the Italian market. This coincided with the deregulation of television in Italy, and with a rapid collapse of cinema attendance, with the result that soon Italy's production sector was reduced to the level it had been at the end of the 1930s, heavily dependent on subsidies, struggling unsuccessfully with a suffocating competitor, and incapable of finding export markets for its products.

The study of the industry, therefore, entails research into the economic relations between state and industry (matters of exchange control, taxation, state subsidy, investment banking), diplomatic and commercial relations between countries and the regulation of free markets, questions of state control like censorship and export permits, and matters connected with technological developments like the coming of sound, colour, and wide-screen projection (each of which gave American films a huge advantage for a while on the Italian market), quite apart from cultural considerations. Given the dominance of US imports in Italian cinemas, the history of the industry has been one in which the production sector has had peaks and troughs, but in which the distribution and exhibition sectors have steadily grown on a diet of Hollywood movies, until the fall in cinema attendances began to accelerate at the start of the 1970s. This has consequences for a 'cultural history' approach to Italian cinema, for it means that the public has for the most part been consuming the popular culture of another nation.

Accepting this, and focusing our attention now on the Italian films that have been made and viewed in the course of the industry's history, we cannot help noting how Italian cinema in this sense has generally been studied in terms of individual films identified by their title, their director, and the year of production, in terms of the *œuvre* of individual directors, or in terms of aesthetic movements like neorealism. This approach presupposes an origin for the films in the director (or, in the case of a movement, the directors) who 'made' them, and 'film theorists' refer to this approach as the 'auteur theory' (Caughie 1981). While this may be an appropriate approach to the critical and historical study of individual films or aesthetic movements, it is an inadequate way of conceptualizing the origin of films. What the audience purchases with its ticket-money is not usually an artistic experience, but a psychological service; it is paying to be made to laugh, to be moved to tears, to feel the tension and release of suspense, to indulge in romantic and erotic fantasies, to witness the playing out of unresolvable conflicts in social life, to experience for two hours the plush luxury of the movie palace, to be momentarily freed from the trials of daily life, and many other things. What the cinema industry is trying to do to get that ticket money and to make a profit from its activities of producing, distributing, and exhibiting films is to supply a homogeneous product that balances the needs and exigencies of the cinema-going public with the capacities of the industry and the motivations of the film makers. The production sector cannot draw on an unlimited supply of creative and inventive talent, nor can it afford the dangerous tactic of constantly innovating. Hence it is engaged in an activity of repetition with variation: finding stories wherever it can (from plays, novels, short stories, newspaper items, and, by no means least, from other films); reusing sets, costumes, story-plots, and, of course, performers as much as possible; and striving to produce new films that serve up once again the recipe that most succeeded in appealing to the public's taste the previous year. Films are not sold by the name and artistic reputation of the director or scriptwriter; they are marketed on the basis of the stars performing in the film and the type of story that the film tells, or the type of emotional experience it evokes in the audience. The type of story or emotional experience provoked are described with the notion of 'genre'. A film is identifiable to the public (before they see it) as, for example, a comedy starring Vittorio De Sica, or a romantic cloak and dagger (*cappa e spada*) adventure starring Amedeo Nazzari; this is what the distributor tries to persuade the cinema-owner to hire, and this is what the latter advertises (the job of a cinema poster is to make this message clear) in his glass cases and in the local newspaper. Hence the origin of the majority of films lies in what have been called the 'signifying practices' of the cinema industry: the procedures used to give stories clarity and impact, and the stereotyped situations that evoke laughter, fear, suspense, identification with the hero or heroine, and erotic satisfaction, for example.

This raises two issues for the student of Italian cinema. The first is that of the technical means used to tell stories and to make their significance immediately clear to the audience, while the second is that of identifying the succession of genres that characterize the history of Italian cinema. Films are not audio-visual recordings of reality; they are structured discourses which use a careful selection of images and sounds to convey a narrative, evoke a response, and encode a message. Silent film, of course, did not even have synchronized sound, by which we mean that the sounds produced by the actors and the environment of the story were not relayed to the audience directly. In actual fact, performances of silent films were rarely conducted in silence; they were usually accompanied by music which expressed the emotional state of the action, and often in addition by performers creating sound effects, or sometimes even reciting dialogue. Nevertheless, actors in silent cinema used a stylized gestural code to replace the channel of information later filled by synchronized sound. It was a code far removed from that to which we are accustomed in contemporary cinema, and when a film like Gustavo Serena's *Assunta Spina* (1915) used another, less stylized code, the response of viewers was to find it remarkably 'realistic'. In early silent film, the camera did not move or even swivel, so all the action in each shot had to take place within a confined space before the camera, a limitation that was overcome when *Cabiria* used a camera mounted on a trolley that moved through its complex set, making the film one of the pioneers of what is referred to as the 'tracking shot'. Dialogue in early silent cinema was shot with two characters in front of the camera talking to each other. Gradually, film makers discovered the emotional impact that close-ups could have on the audience, from which it was a logical step to film dialogue in a series of more or less close-up shots of first one speaker and then the other. With this grew up the convention of showing a character looking, followed by a shot of what he or she was looking at, taken from his or her point of view (a procedure called either 'reverse angle' or 'shot-counter shot' photography). Already from this it should be clear that narratives can be constructed either by having an evolving series of events taking place before the camera in one shot (called a technique of 'mise en scène'), or by having different fragments of the action captured in different shots which are then literally glued together one after the other (called 'montage'). A reverse-angle montage sequence can have the effect of involving the viewer emotionally in the action (because he or she is at times seeing with the eyes of one of the characters); a mise en scène procedure can be more effective for spectacular epic effects. Later, in the period before and after the Second World War, the use of mise en scène by directors like the French Jean Renoir and the Italians Vittorio De Sica and Roberto Rossellini were held up as examples of a particularly 'realist' use of cinema, as opposed to the deception involved in the use of montage effects (Bazin 1967, 1971). One can relate this to genre in a rather crude way by pointing to the extent to which comedy prefers mise en scène, while melodrama makes prolific use of reverse angle montage procedures; the audience stands outside of, and laughs at, the complicated predicaments of the protagonists of comedy, while it identifies with the intense predicaments of the protagonists of melodrama.

Photographic and lighting procedures, too, can be used for all sorts of purposes: the crudest and most obvious is to light the face of a villain from below. If we jump to the 1960s, we can point to a director like Michelangelo Antonioni who uses in one film, *Il deserto rosso* (1964), predominantly a telephoto (or long focal length) lens to bring about a flattening of foreground against background, while in his next film, *Blow-up* (1966), he makes great use of a wide-angle (or short focal length) lens to give depth to his image, and to distance his protagonist from his environment. Once sound was introduced, the distinction between films that made use of non-diegetic sound (sound that was not produced by the action being filmed: for example, background music, or a 'voice-over' commenting on the story) and films that did not (all the sound heard was produced by the action being filmed) was also used to describe the latter type of filming as being more 'realist' than the former (Weis and Belton 1985). An eminent Italian film director who should have known better once said that the older Visconti used the zoom lens (it can change from wide angle to telephoto while filming) because he was too old and disabled to move the camera around. If we tried this assertion out on *Death in Venice* (1971), we might be inclined to say that the telephoto lens was used to make it difficult for the viewer to know where he or she is placed in the environment (an index of the protagonist's disorientation), while a very accurate sense of us being exactly where the protagonist is in the setting is given us by the remarkable way the soundtrack is recorded and mixed (for example, scenes on the beach). It is essential, therefore, to study and understand the signifying practices of cinema in order to identify and interpret the procedures that are being used by film makers at any one time.

Turning now to the question of the succession of genres that characterize the history of Italian cinema, we find that one of Italy's most successful exports before the First World War was that of historical tableaux, representing great moments in Italian medieval or Renaissance history. But Italy was known most of all for its epics of ancient Rome, often based on literary works: Edward Bulwer-Lytton's *The Last Days of Pompeii* was filmed three times in Italy, in 1908, 1913, and 1926. The most famous of this genre of films is *Cabiria*, for which a prominent poet of the time, Gabriele D'Annunzio, wrote the intertitles (the written passages that explain the action or relate the words of the characters between sequences).

Italy never abandoned this genre of film, which adopted a pose of cultural dignity, and which had the virtues of being spectacular, of reinforcing nationalist notions of Italy's great past, of inviting comparisons between the politically righteous and the dissolutely opportunist, and which often combined all these assets with the emotional pull of melodrama. To justify its military expedition to Abyssinia the Fascist regime promoted heavily the production of a film called *Scipione l'Africano* (Carmine Gallone 1937) about Scipio Africanus's strategy of taking the war to Carthage in order to stop Hannibal from attacking Rome in 207 BC. After the Second World War the Italian industry's first large-scale collaboration with France in co-production was a film of this genre called *Fabiola* (1946), directed by the grand old man of Italian cinema, Alessandro Blasetti, costing far more than several conventional films put together, and drawing on the talents and expertise of scholars, historians, and literary figures. Lux Film, Italy's major production company, hired Kirk Douglas and Anthony Quinn to star in a prestige version of Homer's *Odyssey*, called *Ulisse*, directed by another of Italy's veteran directors, Mario Camerini, in 1953. The genre denoted high purpose and cultural prestige, and was aimed at the international market. Meanwhile, samples of the genre with fewer cultural pretensions were being made all the time, some being even comic slapstick parodies (Elley 1984). However, in 1957 something extraordinary happened. The director Pietro Francisci, in collaboration with the scriptwriter Ennio De Concini, concocted a slightly tongue-in-cheek adventure-story version of Apollonius Rhodius's *Argonautica*, using an American Mr Universe, Steve Reeves, as the protagonist, and aimed at a popular audience. *Le fatiche di Ercole* (*The Labors of Hercules*, 1957) was an enormous success, as was its sequel, *Ercole e la regina di Lidia* (1958), and particularly in what is called the 'depth' of the domestic market, cinemas in provincial towns and rural areas, and in the South of Italy. An American distributor bought it, spent several million dollars promoting it, and it was a huge success in the USA, ending up on television there. The Italian industry needed at that moment to expand production, and imitation and repetition offered a way of achieving this in the absence of a large pool of untapped creative talent waiting to be exploited. In the next ten years some 300 films of this type (referred to as *peplum* films after a classical garment often worn by the characters) were produced, distributed in Italy, and very successfully exported abroad. In 1964, while a moderately expensive Italian western called *Le pistole non discutono* was being shot in Spain (a few westerns were made in the early 1960s without much success), Sergio Leone persuaded the backers to put up a small sum, and allow him to use the sets to film a western based almost literally on a Japanese Samurai film by Akiro Kurosawa called *Yojimbo*. His film, *Per un pugno di dollari* (*A Fistful of Dollars*, 1964), starred a young American actor, Clint Eastwood, cost 200 million lire to make, and netted over fifteen times that amount world-wide (some of it had to go to Kurosawa for plagiarism). It launched another bandwagon, onto which the Italian industry leaped gladly, now that the *peplum* was beginning to lose its appeal (Wagstaff 1992*a*; Della Fornace 1983; Frayling 1981; Staig and Williams 1975). In twelve years Italy produced some 450 spaghetti westerns. These two genres were only the most famous examples of a phenomenon that in Italy is called the *filone*, films that repeat a formula; there were hundreds of James Bond spin-offs, of pseudo-documentaries that scoured the night-life of the world for striptease and the like, and of other *filoni*.

These *filoni* offer an interesting case study for the student approaching cinema from the perspective of cultural history, because they are a manifestation of a truly popular cinema (in many of the senses that the term 'popular' can be given), at a time when Italian cinema was being received by all sectors of the Italian population, and their reception in different parts of the country (erotic and spy formulas did well in the North, comic and *peplum* formulas did well in the South) can be interpreted as a measure of the acculturation of a rapidly developing society (Spinazzola 1974). They are also an example of the procedures of the industry being at the source of the films rather than the creative artistic personalities of individual directors (though here, too, variations from one individual example of a *filone* to another can be read to reveal an authorial hand somewhere in the process).

One cannot help being struck by the extent to which comedy has always been a staple of Italian cinema, as it has of most nations' cinema (Savio 1975; Gili 1983; Grande 1986; Bernardi 1985; Bolzoni 1986). Early silent comedies were of the slapstick variety, making use of acrobatic stars, involving chases, fights, falls, clumsiness, and all the paraphernalia of clowning. Between 1909 and 1911, some sixty-nine films of about ten minutes' length featured one such comic, André Deed, called in the films 'Cretinetti' (translated at the time into the English 'Foolshead'), produced by Itala Film of Turin, copies of a number of which are held by the British National Film Archive (Robinson 1986).

In the 1930s there was a flowering of comedy films in Italy (as there was in many countries, including the USA). Because the making of these films coincided with the political regime of the Fascist Party, they have generally been dismissed by Italian historians (particularly those on the left) as a device to distract the public from political and social matters, and as failing to represent anything of the reality of Italy at the time except the desire for escapism of the petty bourgeoisie. Certainly, the films can be read for the purpose of gathering evidence of the compliance of the populace in the values of Fascism. However, they are the products of the machinery of genre, and comedy has a long history, going back to ancient Greece, in which maidens have tried to marry above their station, goals have been reached by deception, and mistaken identities have created untold chaos. It would not be an exaggeration to say that two formulas dominate in comedies of the 1930s: the Cinderella theme, and that of the *Taming of the Shrew*. The comedies were at first based frequently on Austro-Hungarian stage comedies, and were of the kind where a series of errors is compounded until a tangled knot is tied, causing extreme anxiety in the protagonists, from which the audience derives great pleasure, whereupon the knot is summarily and swiftly untied at the end. This type of comedy is referred to as *commedia brillante*, and gradually gave way to *commedia sentimentale*, in which the audience shares the anxiety of the protagonists, and derives pleasure in the second half of the film as the knot is progressively and laboriously untied. A director who straddled the two varieties, and whose films can represent the very best of Italian cinema in this period, is Mario Camerini, with his famous tetralogy of *Gli uomini che mascalzoni!* (1932), *Darò un milione* (1935), *Il signor Max* (1937), and *Grandi magazzini* (1939) (see Germani 1980; Farassino 1992). *Commedia sentimentale* leads easily into melodrama, which became one of the most successful genres in Italy soon after the War, reaching all levels of the market and all areas of the country (the 'depths') with the series of films directed by Raffaello Matarazzo, beginning with *Catene* in 1949, and launching the phenomenon of *filoni* with one called in Italy *strappalacrime* (tear-jerker).

Comedy relies heavily on the talents of actors, and Italian comedy of the 1930s leaned heavily on actors recruited from the stage, eventually building up a stable of consummate character actors most of whose names are unknown outside Italy. The most famous of all, Vittorio De Sica, began at the end of the period directing his own *commedie sentimentali*, and then, when the war was over, directed some of the finest neorealist films, after which he returned to acting in and directing comedies. But before coming to neorealism's complicated relations with comedy, we should identify the type of comedy that is built around a comic actor of a certain kind, the clown. There were two that stood out in Italy in the period 1935–55, Erminio Macario and Totò, both of whose films were among those which reached into what we have called the 'depths' of the market, representing a truly popular national cultural phenomenon: Macario was the little man lost in a world too complex for him to understand; Totò was the Neapolitan clown turning the world upside down in the anarchic expression of his vitality, and his appeal in the South was enormous.

While the battered Italian cinema industry proceeded with its genres as best it could at the end of the Second World War, an aesthetic movement of film makers grew up in a disorganized way, responding to calls made by intellectuals before the war for a cinema that would be truly Italian, that would shun escapism, that would exploit cinematography's capacity for representing man in his real environment, and that would make known to all Italians the conditions of life experienced by people in all parts of the nation (Armes 1971; Overbey 1978). Financial constraints meant that films had to be made cheaply, with little equipment, outside studios, and without stars. The films that resulted were called 'neorealist' (Wagstaff 1989). There are two theories about realism in Italian cinema. The first is expressed by Lino Miccichè (1975), according to which there has always been a thread of realism running through the history of Italian film-making, going back to the famous (but lost) *Sperduti nel buio* of Nino Martoglio made in Naples in 1914, and films like the *Assunta Spina* (also made in Naples) that I have already mentioned, and running clandestinely through the *cinema di regime* of the 1930s, bursting out in 1945 with the liberation of Italy from totalitarianism and occupation; quoting Miccichè, we could call it the theory of the 'filo rosso della realtà' (the red thread of reality). The other theory, expressed by Alberto Farassino (1989), points out that Italian cinema has always been a cinema of genre, no less during the post-war period than in any other. However, a concern with the representation of a material, historical Italian reality was added to this cinema of genre after 1945, and contaminated all the genres: to Miccichè's *filo rosso* he prefers the notion of a *palude*, a swamp that engulfs and drenches all film-making of the time, so that we find what we might call a neorealist atmosphere in everything from heroic adventure to melodrama, to slapstick comedy. A fine case in point is a film made in 1946 by the leading director of opera films in Italy, Carmine Gallone (whose career goes back to the silent era), called *Davanti a lui tremava tutta Roma*. It is a film of Puccini's *Tosca*, in which the story of the opera is told by means of a 'contamination' with a story of partisan resistance to the Germans.

If the notion of fidelity to reality, implicit in the term 'realism', is to have any weight, it must also imply the avoidance of the conventional manipulation of audience response proper to the machinery of genre. There were neorealist films that successfully avoided the temptations of genre, films like Visconti's *La terra trema* (1948), De Sica's *Umberto D.* (1952), Rossellini's *Paisà* (1946), and his later films like *Stromboli* (1948), *Europa '51* (1952) and *Viaggio in Italia* (1954), none of which had much success at the box-office (with the exception of *Paisà*). However, if we look at the commercially successful neorealist films, Rossellini's *Roma città aperta* (1945), Zampa's *Vivere in pace* (1947), De Santis's *Riso amaro* (1948), or Germi's *In nome della legge* (1949) and *Il cammino della speranza* (1950), we see very clearly the depiction of a contemporary social reality contaminated with the machinery of genre and its stereotyped characters: comedy, melodrama, thriller, and, in the case of the last two, the American western. These contaminations were a deliberate strategy adopted by the film makers (and in particular by the production company Lux Film) to create a popular cultural product that could both entertain and inform the public (Farassino and Sanguineti 1984). The conclusion to be drawn, for the purposes of the study of Italian cinema, is that no amount of appeal to notions of fidelity to reality will explain the artistic achievement of a neorealist film like De Sica's *Ladri di biciclette* (1948), which has to be studied with all the formal and technical tools available to the film analyst (see the analysis on pp. 262–7 below, and Wagstaff 1992*b*).

Neorealism's depiction of the ordinary, everyday life of typical Italians owed a lot to the narrative strategies accumulated in the 1930s and 1940s for comedy films (the genre that most often used this type of social setting), and it is no surprise to find that in the search for wider audiences, neorealist film makers soon found themselves (in the 1950s and 1960s) back in the realm of comedy, which is the route that led to the phenomenon of the *commedia all'italiana*, a satirical and affectionate portrayal of the foibles of stereotyped Italian figures like Latin lovers, insatiable women, possessive mothers, pretentious layabouts, etc. (D'Amico 1985; Aprà and Pistagnesi 1986).

At the same time, however, Italian cinema was building for itself an international reputation for 'art cinema', films whose origins lay in the ideas and artistic creativity of their directors, and which were viewed by sophisticated, middle-class audiences in Italy, in the 'art cinemas' of the major cities of the world, at film festivals, in universities, and in film clubs and societies. Neorealist films created this reputation, and it was reinforced by the films of Federico Fellini (coming from a background drawing caricatures and writing scripts and gags for all forms of popular entertainment from 1939 onwards) and Michelangelo Antonioni (coming from a background of film criticism in the early 1940s, of scriptwriting for neorealists, and of documentary film-making). Just as these two directors were hitting their peak 'middle periods' in the 1960s, a new generation of film makers emerged, with a variety of backgrounds: Pasolini from left-wing literary circles, Rosi from a neorealist background working with Visconti, Bertolucci from poetry, from Pasolini, and from the French *nouvelle vague*, Olmi from documentary film-making, and others like Petri and Bellocchio. 'Authors' like these directors provided the fodder for the film criticism that most people think of when they talk about the study of Italian cinema, and the various methods of approaching films defined as the products of 'authors' (rather than of the signifying practices and working methods of the cinema industry) can be found in the many monographs that have been written on the work of these directors (Bondanella 1983, 1992; Kezich 1987; Marcus 1987; Chatman 1985; Rifkin 1983; Cuccu 1973; Bernardi 1978; Casetti 1976; Wagstaff 1982; Kline 1987; Kolker 1985; Armes 1971; Brunette 1988; Nowell-Smith 1973; Bencivenni 1982; Miccické 1990).

The vigour of the Italian authorial art cinema in the 1960s, relying on the work both of established figures like Michelangelo Antonioni and Luchino Visconti and of a new and younger generation of people like Bernardo Bertolucci, Marco Bellocchio, Pier Paolo Pasolini, Elio Petri, Liliana Cavani, Marco Ferreri, Ermanno Olmi, Lina Wertmüller, and the brothers Paolo and Vittorio Taviani, depended on the general vigour of the Italian production sector, particularly at the popular level, supported by ticket sales of 700 million a year and plentiful American investment in production. In the mid–1970s American finance was withdrawn and the reorganization of distribution led to rapid falls in ticket sales. The successful *filoni* (typical is the case of the spaghetti western) began to dry up, television replaced routine cinema-going, and with this contraction of the 'base', higher-quality film production became starved of finance. Between 1950 and 1969, Antonioni directed twelve feature films (if we count two episodes in portmanteau films as one); between 1970 and 1990 he directed four (two of which were made for television, one in high-definition video and one a documentary in 16 millimetre, leaving just *The Passenger*—also known as *Professione Reporter*—1975, and *Identificazione di una donna*, 1982, as regularly produced 35 millimetre films for theatrical release). The Italian state television broadcasting network, RAI, entered production in the 1970s, financing important art films by younger directors (Liliana Cavani, Bernardo Bertolucci, Ermanno Olmi, Jean Marie Straub, Marco Leto, Gianni Amico, Paolo and Vittorio Taviani, Florestano Vancini, and Nelo Risi), and parliamentary legislation made available subsidies for the productions of new directors in Clause 28 of the law regulating the cinema (many of the films made under this *articolo ventotto* never received distribution). From an annual output of up to 300 films in the late 1960s and ticket sales of over 700 million, more than half of them to Italian films, annual production is currently around 100 films and ticket sales just over 100 million, with 80 per cent of the money going to US films. State and private television stations broadcast between 5,000 and 10,000 films annually. Films get their receipts now about equally from theatrical distribution, videocassette sales, and the sale of television rights. Private television now plays a major role in film production and distribution, with Silvio Berlusconi's Fininvest company (which owns the three major private networks, as well as pay-TV channels) in combination with the Cecchi Gori group together forming the distribution company Penta Film, which distributes roughly 25 per cent of films in Italy. Cinemas themselves are organized into cartels or consortia. This industrial configuration limits the outlet for art films, resulting in a situation in which Italy's quality cinema has increasingly taken on what critics refer to as a 'minimalist' character: these films are small-scale, intimate, and provincial, offering few attractions to an international audience. Directors, therefore, have great difficulty in achieving the kind of box-office success that would launch them, and exceptions like Gianni Amelio, Giuseppe Tornatore, and Gabriele Salvatores either make compromises on the level of artistic commitment, or else produce minimalist works. If we take the genre of comedy, we find at the top the sophisticated satire of someone who is perhaps the most important 'author' filming in Italy at present, Nanni Moretti, and then a gradual slide down the scale of quality from Massimo Troisi, through Carlo Verdone, to the films featuring Paolo Villaggio ('Fantozzi'), Renato Pozzetto, and finally to the smutty slapstick of films featuring Lino Banfi.

One alternative to the films of the minimalists and the popular comedies is the *film medio*, the middle-quality film of adventure, crime, or romance, directed by a respected new or established director, and only occasionally getting distribution abroad (a recent example is Ricky Tognazzi's *La scorta*, 1993). Another alternative has been the gradual development of the 'quality' international film, financed multinationally together with television, using international stars and a big production budget to attract the older and more sophisticated international public. Established directors are part of the 'package', and an outstanding early case might be Visconti's *Il Gattopardo* (*The Leopard*, 1962), while other representatives of the type might be Bertolucci's *Novecento* (*1900*, 1976), and recent films by Francesco Rosi and by the Taviani brothers. A serious approach to this type of film requires a delicate balancing act in which the analyst gives equal weight to industrial and marketing considerations on the one hand, and to the thematic and stylistic concerns of the director on the other. These films often thwart the critic's and historian's desire to have a body of films whose artistic quality is universally accepted. Whereas there are no real arguments about the artistic quality and cultural importance of Francesco Rosi's *Salvatore Giuliano* (1961) or Bertolucci's *Strategia del ragno* (1970), there is no such unanimity about Rosi's *Cronaca di una morte annunciata* (1985) or Bertolucci's *Little Buddha* (1993). Current Italian cinema is no longer, therefore, a proper object of the purely 'authorial' approach to film study that has so characterized the treatment of Italian cinema of the period between the late 1940s and the early 1970s.

Further Reading

There is no shortage of manuals to help the student approach the study of film, and a good starting-place is James Monaco's *How to Read a Film* (New York, 1977). Steven Neale, in *Cinema and Technology: Image, Sound, Colour* (Basingstoke and London, 1984), gives a good introduction to the early history of the technology. Two good surveys of film theory, one in English and one in Italian, are to be found respectively in R. Lapsley and M. Westlake, *Film Theory: An Introduction* (Manchester, 1988), and Francesco Casetti, *Teorie del cinema* (Milan, 1993), while a stimulating illustration of various theories in action is to be found in Bill Nichols, *Movies and Methods* (2 vols.; Berkeley, 1976 and 1985). The best history of Italian cinema is Gian Piero Brunetta, *Storia del cinema italiano* (4 vols.; Rome, 1993), which has a wealth of bibliographical information. In English, the best available are Pierre Leprohon, *The Italian Cinema* (London, 1972), and for the post-war period Peter Bondanella, *Italian Cinema from Neorealism to the Present* (New York, 1983), while there is an interesting first-hand account in Vernon Jarratt's *Italian Cinema* (London, 1951). The publishers Gremese (Rome) are issuing a *Dizionario del cinema italiano. I film*, giving complete filmographic details of all Italian films made from 1930 to the present, of which volumes i–iii have already been published, covering 1930–69. For the silent period, Vittorio Martinelli's volumes in the *Cinema muto italiano* series, continually being published in Rome by the Centro Sperimentale di Cinematografia, give the most complete details for the years so far covered, while a complete but less detailed filmography is to be found in Aldo Bernardini's *Archivio del cinema italiano*, whose four volumes cover the period from 1905 to 1990; they are published by, and available only from, ANICA (Associazione Nazionale Industrie Cinematografiche e Audiovisive) in Rome. For the politics and economics of the industry, the best starting-place is the late Lorenzo Quaglietti's *Storia economico-politica del cinema italiano 1945–1980* (Rome, 1980), while a source in English is Christopher Wagstaff, 'The Italian Cinema during the Fascist Regime', *Italianist*, 4 (1984), 160–74, and 'Italy in the Post-War Italian Cinema Market', in C. Duggan and C. Wagstaff (eds.), *Italy in the Cold War: Politics, Culture and Society 1948–1958* (Oxford, forthcoming).

References

ALLEN, R., and GOMERY, D. (1985), *Film History: Theory and Practice* (New York).

ANDREW, J. D. (1976), *Major Film Theories* (New York).

APRÀ, A. (1976), *Neorealismo d'appendice* (Florence).

—— and PISTAGNESI, P. (1986), *Comedy Italian Style 1950–1980* (Turin).

ARGENTIERI, M. (1979), *L'occhio del regime. Informazione e propaganda nel cinema del fascismo* (Florence).

ARIJON, D. (1976), *Grammar of the Film Language* (London).

ARMES, R. (1971), *Patterns of Realism* (London).

BAZIN, A. (1967, 1971), *What Is Cinema?*, 2 vols. (Berkeley).

BENCIVENNI, A. (1982), *Visconti* (Florence).

BERNARDI, S. (1978), *Marco Bellocchio* (Florence).

—— (1985), *Si fa per ridere… ma è una cosa seria* (Florence).

BERNARDINI, A. (1980–2), *Cinema muto italiano*, 3 vols. (Bari).

BIZZARRI, L., and SOLAROLI, L. (1958), *L'industria cinematografica italiana* (Florence).

BOLZONI, F. (1986), *La barca dei comici* (Rome).

BONDANELLA, P. (1983), *Italian Cinema from Neorealism to the Present* (New York).

—— (1992), *The Cinema of Federico Fellini* (Princeton).

BORDWELL, D., and THOMPSON, K. (1986), *Film Art: An Introduction*, 2nd edn. (New York).

BRUNETTA, G. P. (1993), *Storia del cinema italiano*, 4 vols. (Rome).

BRUNETTE, P. (1988), *Roberto Rossellini* (New York).

CARABBA, L. (1974), *Il cinema del ventennio nero* (Florence).

CASETTI, F. (1976), *Bertolucci* (Florence).

—— (1993), *Teorie del cinema 1945–1990* (Milan).

CAUGHIE, J. (1981) (ed.), *Theories of Authorship* (London).

CHATMAN, S. (1985), *Antonioni, or the Surface of the World* (Berkeley).

CONTALDO, F., and FANELLI, F. (1979), *L'affare cinema. Multinazionali, produttori e politici nella crisi del cinema italiano* (Milan).

CUCCU, L. (1973), *La visione come problema, forme e svolgimento del cinema di Antonioni* (Rome).

D'AMICO, M. (1985), *La commedia all'italiana* (Milan).

DE LAURETIS, T. (1984), *Alice Doesn't: Feminism, Semiotics, Cinema* (Basingstoke and London).

DELLA FORNACE, L. (1983), *Il labirinto cinematografico* (Rome).

DYER, R. (1979; revised edn. 1982), *Stars* (London).

ELLEY, D. (1984), *The Epic Film* (London).

ELLWOOD, D. W., and BRUNETTA, G. P. (1991) (eds.), *Hollywood in Europa. Industria, politica, pubblico del cinema 1945–1960* (Florence).

FARASSINO, A. (1989) (ed.), *Neorealismo. Cinema italiano 1945–1949* (Turin).

—— (1992) (ed.), *Mario Camerini* (Locarno).

—— and SANGUINETI, T. (1984), *Lux Film: Esthétique et système d'un studio italien* (Locarno).

FORGACS, D. (1990), *Italian Culture in the Industrial Era 1880–1980: Cultural Industries, Politics and the Public* (Manchester).

FRAYLING, C. (1981), *Spaghetti Westerns* (London).

GERMANI, S. (1980), *Camerini* (Florence).

GILI, J. A. (1981), *Stato fascista e cinematografia* (Rome).

—— (1983), *La Comédie italienne* (Paris).

GRANDE, M. (1986), *Abiti nuziali e biglietti in banca. La società della commedia nel cinema italiano* (Rome).

GRANT, K. (1986), *Film Genre Reader* (Austin, Tex.).

GUBACK, T. H. (1969), *The International Film Industry: Western Europe and America since 1945* (Bloomington).

HAY, J. (1987), *Popular Film Culture in Fascist Italy* (Bloomingon, Ind.).

KEZICH, T. (1987), *Fellini* (Milan).

KLINE, T. J. (1987), *Bertolucci's Dream Loom: A Psychoanalytical Study of Cinema* (Amherst, Mass.).

KOLKER, R. P. (1985), *Bernardo Bertolucci* (London).

LANDY, M. (1986), *Fascism in Film: The Italian Commercial Cinema 1931–1943* (Princeton).

LAPSLEY, R., and WESTLAKE, M. (1988), *Film Theory: An Introduction* (Manchester).

MARCUS, M. (1987), *Italian Film in the Light of Neorealism* (Princeton).

MARTINELLI, V. (1980–93), *Cinema muto italiano*, 13 vols. (Rome).

METZ, C. (1968), *Essais sur la signification au cinéma* (Paris).

—— (1971), *Langage et cinéma* (Paris).

—— (1977), *Le Signifiant imaginaire* (Paris).

MICCICHÉ, L. (1975) (ed.), *Il neorealismo cinematografico italiano* (Venice).

—— (1990), *Visconti* (Venice).

MONACO, J. (1977), *How to Read a Film* (New York).

NEALE, S. (1984), *Cinema and Technology: Image, Sound, Colour* (Basingstoke and London).

NOWELL-SMITH, G. (1973), *Luchino Visconti* (London).

OVERBEY, D. (1978) (ed.), *Springtime in Italy: A Reader on Neo-Realism* (London).

PENLEY, C. (1988) (ed.), *Feminism and Film Theory* (London).

QUAGLIETTI, L. (1980), *Storia economico-politica del cinema italiano 1945–1980* (Rome).

REDI, R. (1979) (ed.), *Il cinema italiano sotto il fascismo* (Venice).

RIFKIN, N. (1983), *Antonioni's Visual Language* (Ann Arbor).

ROBINSON, D. (1986), 'The Italian Comedy', *Sight and Sound*, 55/2 (Spring): 105–12.

SAVIO, F. (1975), *Ma l'amore no* (Milan).

SPINAZZOLA, V. (1974), *Cinema e pubblico* (Milan).

STAIG, L., and WILLIAMS, T. (1975), *Italian Western: The Opera of Violence* (London).

WEIS, E., and BELTON, J. (1985), *Film Sound: Theory and Practice* (New York).

WILLIAMS, C. (1981) (ed.), *Realism and the Cinema* (London).

WAGSTAFF, C. (1982), 'Forty-Seven Shots of Bertolucci's "Il conformista"', *Italianist*, 2: 76–101.

—— (1984), 'The Italian Cinema during the Fascist Regime', *Italianist*, 4: 160–74.

—— (1989), 'The Place of Neorealism in the Italian Cinema from 1945–1954', in N. Hewitt (ed.), *The Culture of Reconstruction* (Basingstoke and London), 67–87.

—— (1992a), 'A Forkful of Westerns: Industry, Audiences and the Italian Western', in R. Dyer and G. Vincendeau (eds.), *Popular European Cinema* (London), 244–61.

—— (1992b), 'Comic Positions', in *Sight and Sound*, 2/7 (Nov.): 25–7.

—— (forthcoming), 'Italy in the Post-War Italian Cinema Market', in C. Duggan and C. Wagstaff (eds.), *Italy in the Cold War: Politics, Culture and Society 1948–1958* (Oxford).

Television and its Critics:
A Parallel History

ELENA
DAGRADA

WHEN the first Italian nation-wide television network was established by the the RAI (Radio Audizioni Italia) in January 1954, the press, both newspapers and magazines, attributed considerable importance to the event. The features which attracted most attention were the curiosity value of the new medium from a technological point of view and its cultural potential. The first experimental transmissions, which the RAI carried out in a few selected areas during the previous year, had already prompted some reflections in specialist journals, particularly film magazines. This sudden appearance of television in the print media is symptomatic of the lasting and parallel development of the history of television and its history in the press. It was the first sign of the interdependence between the two media, and their shared development. This parallel history is the subject of this chapter.

If one writes a history of Italian television criticism one is also writing a historical account of Italian television and its complex relationship with intellectuals. At first there was a complete rejection on the part of critics whose cultural background was predominantly literary and who were reluctant to get involved with an audio-visual medium, especially such a popular one. As time passed, however, the relationship began to change and became one of gradual acceptance. More recently it has even involved forms of courtship and mutual admiration.

This parallel history of television and television criticism can be divided into three stages, which coincide with the three principal stages in the institutional development of Italian television. In the first stage, from 1954 to the first half of the 1970s, television was a state monopoly. In the second, from 1975 to the early 1980s, television broadcasting operated in a legislative vacuum which favoured the rise of private broadcasting, at first chaotically, then structured and controlled by the more important media groups. The third stage, from the rest of the 1980s to the early 1990s, saw the establishment of the so-called 'mixed system'—the RAI–Fininvest duopoly—which has been threatened by subsequent developments in Italian politics.

The Years of RAI Monopoly and Censorship: 1954–1975

The monopolistic position of the RAI in Italian broadcasting was a continuation of that of the EIAR (Ente Italiano per le Audizioni Radiofoniche) which had changed its name to RAI by legislative decree on 26 October 1944. The EIAR had been granted a monopoly over radio broadcasting under Fascism, and after the latter's fall and the establishment of the Republic, the Christian Democrats maintained state control over the organization. In 1951 the government granted the RAI a monopoly of radio and of future television broadcasting services until 15 December 1972. In the years of this monopoly, television reflected the ideas of the political majority, and became in its hands an instrument for controlling public opinion. It was required, along the lines laid down for the BBC by Lord Reith in the 1920s, not only to inform and entertain but also to educate. The DC-led governments thus favoured a model which was essentially an instrument for holding power.

This model was to be favoured also by television critics, although initially television journalism was simply a matter of reporting the novelty aspects of the medium. The first impetus came from the extremely popular quiz show *Lascia o raddoppia?* which started in November 1955, and was on the whole disdainfully ignored by the intellectuals. The newspapers would give an account of the programme for those who were unable to see it, since very few people owned their own set and some areas could not yet receive transmissions. Despite this, the quiz show became part of the national culture, and most of the daily newspapers, in order to convey the programme to everyone and compete with their rivals, devoted whole pages to it. It was taken down in shorthand and then transcribed in full. These pages were gradually enhanced with snippets of news, gossip, estimated viewing figures, and finally critical comments. Newspapers of the time called this *cronaca televisiva* ('news about television').

It was during this period that the Italian daily newspapers began publishing the television programme schedules (Iozzia 1982), an innovation which helped boost their circulation. The first was *Il Giorno*, which from its first issue (21 April 1956) had a television page with a column for criticism; other newspapers soon followed suit (Bellotto 1960). Critics began to review everything, even though at that time scheduling was devised to concentrate viewing on a small number of prominent programmes. This trend was symptomatic. Television criticism, unlike literary criticism or art criticism, came into existence at the same time as television itself. The early television critics, by educational background and vocation, would rather have written about literature, theatre, or film. They accepted the role of television critic as an expedient, and had no tradition to refer back to, apart from the other arts, in particular the performing arts. Consequently, the only course which appeared open to them was to transfer the canons and characteristics of film, theatre, and literary criticism to television criticism, and to assimilate the products of television to the objects of classical aesthetics. Programmes were reviewed one at a time, and judged on the basis of traditional evaluative criteria, in the hope that television would learn to adapt to them. Thus, throughout the 1950s, television criticism was perceived solely as the reviewing of individual programmes. The programme was considered the only significant entity, an artistic 'work' just like a novel, a play, or a film.

But it was soon realized that being a television critic was not like being a film or theatre critic. It was, for example, no longer possible to apply basic concepts like the author or the work, which needed to be adapted to the particular conditions of the new medium. It became clear that television produced entirely new genres, such as serials, quiz shows, programme information, and singing competitions, which did not conform to those of the traditional performing arts. In other words, it could be sensed that television was something inescapably innovative and different from anything critics had dealt with before. This explains why intellectuals at the time rejected television (Pinto 1977, 1979; Rositi 1971) and television criticism in general. A typical example is that of Morando Morandini, who finally moved on into film criticism in 1974. When in 1966 he bought his first television fifteen days before starting work as a television critic, he asked *Il Giorno* to pay 50 per cent of the cost as expenses, as he considered television to be detrimental to the upbringing of his three children.

This rejection was not limited to just one political position but involved conservatives, Communists, Catholics, and others in equal measure. It was more a matter of élite culture rejecting popular culture, either because (in the case of left intellectuals) it saw television as a diabolic invention of the corrupt capitalist West or because (Catholic and conservative intellectuals) television threatened to undermine traditional religious and ethical values. Those with literary or theatrical backgrounds still had difficulty in coming to terms with the cinema, so it is hardly surprising that they saw television as the bearer of a massified culture, a commodification of art, and as lowering the status of the intellectuals who wrote about it. As for those whose background was in film, they hid their fears that television might eventually replace cinema by listing the reasons why the new medium could never be a true art (Pandolfi 1953). A contradictory situation thus arose. On the one hand it was stated that television could never be an art form, and on the other, it was demanded that it should become one, so that one could produce it, watch it, and criticize it.

This trend accelerated during the 1960s. Under the direction of Ettore Bernabei, ex-editor of the Christian Democrat newspaper *Il Popolo* and controller of the RAI from January 1961 to September 1974, state television perfected its educative model. A second channel, RAI 2, was launched in November 1961, and broadcasting hours were increased with informational, cultural, and school programmes. As the number of programmes to be reviewed increased, so did the number of critics, who were often specialized in particular genres. The criteria adopted by these critics were as educative as the television they were called upon to judge. Their concern about the negative consequences of an 'incorrect' use of the television led to a great deal of energy being put into discussing its more 'appropriate' use. Leading intellectuals, including Gianfranco Bettetini and Umberto Eco, were mobilized for this purpose (Bellotto *et al.* 1973).

Intellectuals and critics of all ideological persuasions were thus in agreement over their assumed educational remit. But they soon divided over how to interpret this remit. Two opposing tendencies emerged. On the one hand were the reviewers, who aligned themselves with the television authorities and were duly represented in the most prestigious and high-circulation newspapers based in Milan, such as *Il Corriere della Sera*. On the other hand were the 'structural' critics, who were severely critical of the television authorities, and were mainly centred in Rome, where the more important papers of the opposition were based, such as *L'Unità* and *Paese Sera*. The reviewers used a model based on traditional stylistic and textual criticism, giving priority to the concepts of author and work of art. The structural critics (notably Giovanni Cesareo, *L'Unità* critic from 1961 to 1975) criticized the structure and organization of television as a whole. They sought to develop an innovative and materialist model, giving priority to the programme planners and the concept of the programme schedule (*palinsesto*). There was thus a choice between two educative approaches: one which educated the television medium so that it could be used to raise the cultural standards of the viewers, and one which also educated the public so that they would not have to watch each programme passively.

A good example of these two contrasting types of television criticism can be seen in the treatment of *I promessi sposi* (1966–7), the serial adapted from Alessandro Manzoni's novel and directed by Sandro Bolchi. The structural critics analysed the work by investigating the role of the complex process of planning, scheduling, production, and broadcasting, that is to say the principal stages between choosing Manzoni's novel and placing the new programme in the Italian television schedules, while making comparisons between Bolchi's adaptation and previous ones (Bellotto 1967). The reviewers, on the other hand, concentrated their attention solely on the aesthetic quality of the adaptation and on Bolchi and his co-writer, the novelist Riccardo Bacchelli, as scriptwriters or artists.

Despite these differences of approach, the idea of television as an educative medium affected critics on both sides of the divide during this first stage and led them to share a bias against the more popular genres and light entertainment, and therefore against the tastes of the general public. They tended to see the loftier genres as being closer to the distinctive nature of television. Just as film critics in the 1910s and 1920s had developed a myth of the distinctive nature of cinema, so early television critics wanted to identify some property which differentiated television from other performance arts, as the best way to legitimize its cultural existence and demonstrate that theirs was a useful intellectual task and a high-brow activity. This was true both of the structural critics, who believed it was the particular organization of the new medium which made it radical, and the review-ers, who wished to legitimize their stylistic approach by assessing how television's particular requirements (the small screen, real time, live programmes, etc.) were best suited to specific genres. They became involved in lengthy debates over how a play shown on television differed from the same play on film or in the theatre. These questions were of interest to television producers and media scholars as well as critics. Television terminology and television criticism were in fact influ-encing each other a great deal and evolving at the same rate (Bellotto and Bettetini 1985). After the temporary illusion that live programmes represented the long sought-after distinctiveness, television critics finally agreed that the only true dis-tinctiveness of the medium lay in the limitations to which it appeared to be con-demned: namely its ability to cover everything and be everywhere (Micciché 1971), and the delayed publication of criticism in relation to the transmission of pro-grammes. This delay meant it was impossible to influence the viewer's choice beforehand, and therefore to perform any kind of educational role.

The solution to this problem was almost obvious. If critics could not intervene *beforehand*, they would have to help the public reflect about programmes *after-wards*. In this way they would help viewers analyse programmes they would see in the future, and provide them with the wherewithal to assess programmes bet-ter on their own, independently of the critic's subsequent judgement. Almost all critics shared this view, despite the many differences between them, since they were all confident in their educational remit. And this applied not only to Italy (Tardy 1966).

At the same time it was realized that a distinctive feature of the television medium was that programmes could be modified and improved even during their production, which is not the case with a novel or a film. Most television pro-grammes are part of a series of regular transmissions, even when they are live. Consequently, far from judging them solely after the event, the television critic can influence the development of the programmes and the overall quality of the series and its content. Although television critics are at a disadvantage compared with other kinds of critics as far as guiding the public is concerned, they are able to regain quite a bit of ground when it comes to influencing programmes.

At the same time as critics made these theoretical considerations, television tech-nology was advancing. Programmes began to be shown that had been previously

Fig. 18 Dario Fo and Franca Rame on the RAI Saturday night television show *Canzonissima* in 1962. The show, which had started in 1958 and centred on a song contest, was also a vehicle for the draw of the Lotteria di Capadanno, and served as a launchpad for several television personalities, including Pippo Baudo, Raffaella Carrà, Corrado, and Walter Chiari. Fo and Rame had been invited to host the show by the RAI, but their satires on bureaucracy, the police, factory work and the economic miracle produced such hostile reactions in the press and even in Parliament that their scripts were censored. After seven weeks they walked out over a case of last-minute censorship.

made on film or recorded on videotape. October 1959 saw the introduction of the Ampex videotape recorder, and its use became almost standard from 1962. In part this was because of an episode in that year involving the playwright and actor Dario Fo, who with his wife Franca Rame appeared regularly in the popular Saturday night variety show *Canzonissima*. Shortly before the programme went on the air, the RAI management demanded that one of their sketches, a political satire on safety in building sites, be replaced, even though it had already been examined and approved, because it coincided with a union dispute in the building industry. Fo and Rame walked out while the programme was on the air, revealing a clear case of censorship and causing a scandal, all of which received much coverage in the press.

The RAI was in fact regulated by a powerful system of internal censorship during its period of monopoly. Programmes were controlled by a group of censors who had various links with the government parties, and a self-regulatory code was drawn up by Filiberto Guala, the managing director appointed by the Christian Democrats, who later became a Trappist monk. The Fo and Rame episode made it clear that prerecording would make censorship easier and prevent undesirable scandals. With prerecording the risks and restrictions of live programming disappear.

With the introduction of prerecorded programmes, television critics found themselves dealing with the RAI through its Press Office. When Paolo Valmarana was appointed Press Office chief from 1961 to 1967, previews (*anteprime*) became the norm. However, previews soon proved to be a double-edged sword. If critics write only previews, they have the advantage of viewing programmes before they are broadcast but they are restricted to seeing what the Press Office wants them to see. The programmes selected for this service were generally dramas, whose popularity was ensured by their being scheduled for prime-time transmission and by the abundance of information and publicity material which the RAI Press Office supplied to the newspapers. In other words, for the RAI the preview soon took on the characteristics of a promotional campaign. Although it was supposed to assist the critics, it did not always enable them to publish their pieces before the programme was broadcast. If the preview took place in the morning and the programme went on the air the same evening, the only advantage for the critics was that they could write their piece in a more relaxed manner during the afternoon. They would still hand it in the same evening the programme was broadcast, and it would appear in the newspaper the day after.

This situation naturally provoked considerable irritation amongst the critics. Seen from the inside, from the point of view of the RAI, the Press Office was a company service, which publicized exactly what the company wanted to publicize, and avoided unwanted publicity. It was designed as an instrument for creating and maintaining an image. This was very much the case when Gian Paolo Cresci was Press Office manager in 1969–75, that is to say from immediately after the events of 1968 until the reform of the RAI's monopoly. Seen from the outside, the implications of the Press Office were very different. Television critics saw the

RAI as a public service, not a public enterprise. They therefore felt that its Press Office should put itself at the service of the press, equitably assisting journalists to carry out their work in the best possible manner. The critics thus asked for a correct and balanced information service, one which was not restricted to showing previews of the most important programmes but which also showed the minor and often marginalized ones. They also wanted to be able to publish their articles on the same day as the programmes went on the air, and not just to be able to see them beforehand.

This battle was fought with equal determination both by the principal critics working for the opposition press and by a number of critics in the Catholic camp. In 1972 the Italian Association of Television and Radio Critics (Associazione Italiana Critici Radio e Televisione—AICRET) was set up. Among its aims was that of increasing critics' contractual power in dealing with the RAI's Press Office. However, Mino Doletti, the television critic for the conservative newspaper *Il Tempo* and loyal ally of Cresci's management, was elected chairman of AICRET, leading to many resignations. The campaign was abandoned, and the practice of reviewing programmes before they went on the air, which was by now quite feasible, was never to be established. Ironically, the struggle for the right to preview was given up just when the final triumph of serialization and the use of videocassettes had made preview criticism a real possibility. But a revolution was being prepared for Italian television which was to produce a profound change in criticism, and by which the educational remit was to become outmoded: the advent of private broadcasting following the end of the RAI's monopoly, and the establishment of the private networks.

The Breakup of Monopoly: 1975 to the Early 1980s

The revolution which swept through Italian television in the mid-1970s was partly the product of the battle waged by the more active television critics against the RAI and its Press Office. But there were at least two more significant causes: the institutional changes favoured by the expiry of the RAI's monopoly in 1972, which was followed by a liberalization of the airwaves and the creation of private television stations, and the economic changes of the 1970s which among other things created a solid alliance between the press and television. These events marked the commencement of the second stage of television criticism, which saw an immediate increase in press coverage, but in new forms no longer linked to previous cultural traditions. The end of the old television criticism coincided with the birth of a completely new type of press treatment of television—one that was mainly informative, promotional, and divided into various sectors.

The institutional changes stemmed from expiry of the RAI's legal monopoly—an opportunity many people had been waiting for to introduce a reform of the public service. On the one hand were private entrepreneurs who pressed for the abolition of the monopoly with *laissez-faire* arguments based on their own financial self-interest. On the other were leftists, including those who wanted to reject advertising altogether, both to avoid constraints on programme-makers and to avert the risks of diseducation for the viewing public (*their* educational remit had not yet run out!) Many took up impossible positions, like trying to hold back the advent of private broadcasting.

Meanwhile, after many delays, Law 103 of 14 April 1975 brought into force 'New regulations concerning radio and television broadcasting'. The law, which was a compromise between the parties, reconfirmed the RAI's monopoly. However, it transferred control of the RAI from the executive (i.e. the government) to parliament, and replaced a monopoly under the hegemony of the Christian Democrats with a monopoly shared out between networks and news programmes, each subordinate to a different political party. This was the beginning of *lottizzazione* or 'parcelling out', the dividing up of television broadcasting between the major competing political parties (RAI 1 to the Christian Democrats, RAI 2 to the Socialists, and from its inception in 1979 RAI 3, a third channel with a regional remit, to the Communists, with the exception of local news). This was not a truly pluralistic television committed to debate and mutual progress. Rather, *lottizzazione* was an effect of the continued organization of television in a centralized and hierarchical manner, as an instrument needing to be regulated in order to control public opinion.

Law 103 did not offer any openings for the private sector in the Italian radio and television broadcasting system; however, the whole broadcasting picture had changed in the meantime, and in the absence of a regulatory framework for audiovisual media, the private sector developed notwithstanding. Initially this occurred in an anarchic manner between 1974 and 1979, an era in which local private television stations proliferated, and various regulatory proposals were put forward. Between 1979 and the early 1980s, private broadcasting was gradually concentrated in publishing groups which subsequently came under the control of Silvio Berlusconi, who had set up his first cable television station, Telemilano, as early as 1974. Just one year after Law 103, the Constitutional Court decided to liberalize local radio and television broadcasting over the air (Ruling 202 of July 1976), thus filling a gap in the law and making up for a failure to deal with the question of private broadcasting by the movement for the internal reform of the RAI, which included the structural critics.

As for the economic changes of the 1970s, television critics remained in the background, mere powerless witnesses. This was a critical period for the entertainment industry, particularly the cinema, which was going through the most difficult phase in its history. The austerity caused by the oil crisis, which led to the early closing of many places of entertainment, also induced Italians to save by staying at home to watch television. After 1974, the amount spent on public entertainments (i.e. outside the home) fell continuously, and in 1978 an important milestone was passed: television, with just the RAI licence fee, started to earn more revenue than the cinema. This situation was repeated the following year, even though the licence fee was not increased (Iozzia 1982). Thus the crisis and restructuring in the entertainment industry generated a new framework in which the main player was clearly television. It is not that the consumption of entertainment fell overall; rather that it was distributed in a different manner. This period witnessed the defeat of the public place of entertainment by home-based entertainment, which had the not inconsiderable advantage of being spread around the entire country with fewer inequalities. Television became the most fertile ground for advertising investments. Private broadcasters sprang up everywhere, initially at a local level, and they proved to be a wonderful opportunity for the building of new financial empires. The number of channels multiplied. Television in Italy no longer meant just the RAI.

All this constituted a revolution for Italian television critics. The questions which had been debated a few years before were suddenly all outdated: the distinctive nature of television, the educational remit, and so forth. As though this were not enough, the increased importance of television had created a new situation of mutual fascination between the press and television. The press was interested in television because it was at the centre of power. Television was interested in the press because of its decisive role in organizing the intelligentsia around the question of reforming the RAI (for example, it was Eugenio Scalfari in *L'Espresso* who wrote in favour of abolition of the monopoly). Thus links between television management and newspaper management became much closer, further stimulated by an economic factor: advertising. These links soon became entrepreneurial, as financial empires were gradually built around the control of different media, and immediately led to a change in the way newspapers viewed television critics. Up to that time, the newspapers had entrusted the discussion of television to the critics, but the latter now lost their privileged role. This was partly due to the dizzying growth in viewing figures which compelled the newspapers to devote more coverage to news and information about programmes. In other words, the increased interest in television affected journalism, which took on a more informative and promotional role, and the critic had to come to terms with an unexpected situation.

The most immediate consequence was the exodus of almost the entire old guard of television critics, especially those who had been most involved in the reform campaign. Newspaper editors were no longer interested in the intellectual with a solid experience of culture and politics. Conditions now existed for the creation of new types of professionals, who dealt exclusively with questions concerning television institutions, or the promotion of programmes. This was the triumph of specialization which had been so contested by the structural critics. Much more was being written about television, but in a different way and on different pages. There was much more news about the politics of broadcasting, and more discussion about the fundamental problems of the mass media, but not on the television page, and not necessarily written by the television critic. More was written about entertainment in general, but in new ways, more in keeping with the increased public interest in television.

The old television criticism columns thus disappeared with the arrival of the new-style presentation of programmes. In their place was informative journalism at the service of the reader. There was more news, and it was more accurate, more lively, and, above all, in advance of the programmes. Dramatic aspects of programmes were discussed, along with their characters, actors, and producers: in a word, their 'stars'. The interview became the dominant journalistic format. The critic was completely replaced by the 'previewer', who presented what was to be shown and had a delicate role. Professional ethics suggest that previewers should be neutral; in reality they were more or less openly promotional. A television programme is a mass product, and it is both questionable and risky to present it in a bad light or discourage the public from watching it outside the context of television criticism. It could put readers off and damage the newspaper. Journalists therefore tended to avoid entering into the merits of particular programmes and to deal with them all in the same neutral but stimulating tone. Their articles thus became a form of free advertising. (On changing relations between the press and television since the 1980s, see also Lumley, 'Peculiarities of the Italian Newspaper', Chapter 11 in this volume.)

Thus, at the threshold of the duopoly, made up of the publicly owned RAI with its three channels and Silvio Berlusconi's privately owned Fininvest, also with three nation-wide channels (Canale 5, Italia 1, and Retequattro), television criticism appeared to be finished and lacking any further purpose. But out of its ashes a third stage was to be born, undoubtedly the most assertive and gratifying yet.

The Era of Duopoly

Faced with the innovations in Italian television, the intellectuals changed tack, and for the first time approached television with a little less contempt. After the initial culture shock produced by an object so distant from the traditional parameters of humanist culture, a new generation of intellectuals countered with an unprecedented readiness to investigate the new reality. Instead of proposing alternative models for television, as in the past, they began to perceive a need to accept the existing model in a dynamic way. The old approach of projecting all one's cultural ideals onto television at any cost was replaced by a more detached and investigative approach, affected by the immense power which television was increasingly being shown to command. Television, in a word, became fashionable, along with light entertainment and everything else which had once been so despised. This was a real cultural transformation.

In this way, after the crisis which followed the reform, the birth of promotional journalism, and the disappearance of the traditional columns, television criticism began to make a slow but unmistakable recovery in the 1980s. It is symptomatic that this occurred at the same time as the establishment of the duopoly. The duopoly did not fundamentally alter the relationship between television and politics that had prevailed with the *lottizzazione* of the RAI in the late 1970s. The PSI, which was allied to Berlusconi, developed the idea of the 'mixed system', the recognition of a coexistence of public and private networks, as an alternative to the numerous plans 'to reform the reform' of the RAI's public monopoly. The success of the mixed-system policy was assisted by the fact that the prime minister in the coalition government from 1983 to 1987 was a Socialist, Bettino Craxi. The decree of 6 December 1984 concerning 'Urgent measures for radio and television broadcasting' (nicknamed the Berlusconi Decree), converted into law on 4 February 1985, officially recognized the existence of private television stations, national as well as local. Television changed radically. It was perceived no longer as an educative instrument but as an integral part of the cultural industry, which could be run as a competitive business, thus leading, amongst other things, to market segmentation.

At the same time, television criticism became involved in the market segmentation of its readership, who were no longer seen as a general public which needed to be educated. The first sign of this transformation came in November 1979 when *Il Corriere della Sera* introduced a column of television criticism by the author Alberto Bevilacqua. Bevilacqua had himself proposed this twice-weekly column to the newspaper, because he believed that television had supplanted everything, including the cinema, which was by then being produced by television, and that it therefore merited proper critical attention. Bevilacqua was a completely different creature from the previous generation of television critics. First, he was an established cultural figure, a novelist and film director. Moreover, he *chose* to be a television critic; he was not accepting the position out of expediency, as so many of his predecessors had. He was not obliged to practise the profession to make a living, while harbouring frustrated ambitions to be a film, theatre or literary critic. He already had a profession, and prestige too. When he joined the ranks of the television critics, he symbolized the two most important changes to television criticism which occurred during the 1980s: choice and the prestige byline.

On 5 December 1985, the Italian newspapers published for the first time the electronically metered audience figures produced by Auditel. These figures immediately became gospel when it came to signing contracts, launching programmes, and axing others. Contrary to expectations, however, Auditel did not supplant the critic. Rather, it sanctioned the definitive division of labour between critics and reporters. Auditel has the task of recording numbers of viewers, and these are partly boosted by promotional items and stories about television in the press. The critic is left with the less dramatic task of considering and analysing the enjoyment (or at any rate his or her enjoyment) produced by particular programmes. As these critics are now established figures like Beniamino Placido of *La Repubblica*, often from academic circles, criticism has become prestigious. It is an abstract power, no doubt, but by no means a negligible one.

As it made its comeback, television criticism also made a leap forward. The appearance of a name like Placido's in particular confirmed and consolidated the trend towards prestigious columnists which had started with Bevilacqua. Placido is a cultured individual of many parts: as well as being a writer and scholar he has produced and taken part in several television arts programmes. This last fact points to another aspect of the 1980s, a trend which went in the opposite direction to that of the preceding generation, when many critics had left their columns in order to work for the RAI. Placido did the opposite, and he explicitly stated this in his first column, when he undertook not to produce any more television while he was still writing criticism (Placido 1985). This was an important event. From Placido's privileged vantage point, the programme often became a pretext for seemingly personal digressions, but these always led back to reflections on the nature of television, perceived as an all-embracing social phenomenon which affects the total experience of its viewers.

In other words, with the demise of a single and centralized broadcasting body, as the RAI had been in the days of its monopoly, any attempt at an equally absolute and monolithic television criticism had become obsolete. The serial nature of programmes imposed an equally fragmentary and serial style upon the television critic, who could write about everything from advertisements to announcers. The replacement of the old-style vertical and educative television by a system which was more interactive between the organization and the viewer produced a similar break with the old educative criticism, which was in turn replaced by a more interactive form of criticism. But it was not interactive with the viewing public, towards whom the educative attitude had disappeared (except where simulated as a rhetorical device). Now the critics' real interlocutors had become their own social group—the intellectuals, especially those who worked in television.

The long and fruitless debates over such questions as the delay in reviews suddenly lost all relevance. This was not just because over the years television had relegated the press to the role of commentator; nor was it just because the serial nature of programmes gave the critic greater freedom as each programme was part of a continuing series. The principal reason was that the object of television criticism had now become *television* itself, which the critic watched at home at the same time as the public, switching channels with the remote control just like any other viewer. Thus a critic could refer to a programme some two or three days after it was shown, or write a weekly or twice-weekly column for a daily newspaper. He or she was no longer in a hurry. Promptness was now the concern of promotional news, or of the Auditel audience figures, anxiously awaited by producers and managers in the television industry.

The press offices no longer treated the critics as their most important contacts, and the battles fought in the 1970s between critics and press offices now became inconceivable. This may certainly have been due in part to a mutual respect for each other's independence, but it was also because the press offices were now talking to the reporters and journalists who gave out information on programmes and followed the promotion with interviews and news in advance. These were the people who crowded the press conferences, and received information packs and videocassettes at their places of work.

This division of labour between critic and reporter increasingly became a physical distinction. The victory of specialization, so opposed by the structural critics, was transformed into a sectoral division between the journalistic genres dealing with television, and led to the inevitable predominance of the informative over the critical. The critic and the reporter might be working together elbow to elbow, but each one becomes more and more entrenched in his or her own space. For the critic this is almost always a clearly defined and limited space in the graphic layout, in which the critic encloses his or her own subjective and evaluative arguments, as opposed to the anonymous information which surrounds it. A critic can even write in verse (Placido 1990, 1991), but he or she is always more than a decorative element for the newspaper. A prestigious critic confers prestige on the newspaper, and on the stations and networks which he or she praises.

By the beginning of the 1990s, then, television criticism had definitively ceased to be considered a second-rate profession, and was now a sought-after genre. It is a literary and personalized journalistic genre, performed by distinguished journalists, academics, and writers. It is a genre with new rules, a new rhetoric, new readers (intellectuals working in television), and above all a new television about which to write.

Currently, this new television and the critics who write about it are going through further transformations which inevitably mark the end of the third stage as it has been analysed here. As far as television is concerned, the most unsettling event was Silvio Berlusconi's entrance into political life in January 1994, which provoked a fierce debate over the need for anti-trust regulation, as well as the urgent need to reform the law concerning television broadcasting through the airwaves (the Mammì Law of 1990) in order amongst other things officially to recognize private television's right to live programming and the subsequent obligation on Fininvest to produce news programmes. Thus, the parallel development of television and television criticism, which began with the advent of television in the early 1950s, is still continuing and is probably about to enter a fourth stage.

Further Reading

There is a limited amount of material in English on the history of Italian television. Its development up to the 1980s is outlined by David Forgacs in *Italian Culture in the Industrial Era, 1880–1980: Cultural Industries, Politics and the Public* (Manchester, 1990), with particular emphasis in chapter 8 on the rise of private broadcasting after 1976. A section of the volume edited by Zygmunt Baranski and Robert Lumley, *Culture and Conflict in Postwar Italy* (Basingstoke and London, 1990) is devoted to Italian television in the late 1970s and 1980s (chapters by Umberto Eco, Giuseppe Richeri, Philip Schlesinger, Mauro Wolf, Christopher Wagstaff, and Lidia Curti).

There is also a section on Italy in Alessandro Silj (ed.), *The New Television in Europe* (London, 1992) (chapters by Barbara Fenati and Nora Rizzi, Antonio Pilati, and Peppino Ortoleva). See also Francesca Anania, 'Italian Public Television in the 1970s: a predictable confusion', *Historical Journal of Film, Radio and Television*, 15/3 (1995), 401–6.

A number of works in English deal with the political and economic dimensions of television. The 1975 reform of broadcasting is examined by Fabio Luca Cavazza, 'Italy: from Party Occupation to Party Partition' in A. Smith (ed.), *Television and Political Life: Studies in Six European Countries* (Basingstoke and London, 1979). The transition from public service monopoly to the 'mixed system' is discussed by Donald Sassoon, 'Political and Market Forces in Italian Broadcasting', in Raymond Kuhn (ed.), *Broadcasting and Politics in Western Europe* (London, 1985). The 1990 Broadcasting Act ('Legge Mammì') is outlined by Giuseppe Rao, 'Italy: in the throes of change', *Intermedia*, 19/2 (Mar.–Apr. 1991), 16–20. On subsequent events, see Stephen Gundle, 'RAI and Fininvest in the Year of Berlusconi', in R. S. Katz and P. Ignazi (eds.), *Italian Politics 1994: The Year of the Tycoon* (Boulder, Colorado, 1995), and Stephen Gundle and Noëlleanne O'Sullivan, 'The Media and the Political Crisis', in S. Gundle and S. Parker (eds.), *The New Italian Republic: From the Fall of the Berlin Wall to Berlusconi*, (1996).

In Italian there are two useful general works on the history of television: Aldo Grasso, *Storia della televisione italiana* (Milan, 1992) and Franco Monteleone, *Storia della radio e della televisione in Italia. Società, politica, strategie, programmi* (Venice, 1992). On programmes, see Walter Veltroni, *I programmi che hanno cambiato l'Italia* (Milan, 1994). The first decade of private broadcasting was assessed by various media specialists in *Dieci anni di televisione sotto il segno di Berlusconi*, a special issue of *Problemi dell'Informazione*, 15/4 (1990). Recommended among recent works are Gian Paolo Caprettini, *Totem e TV* (Venice, 1994), Peppino Ortoleva, *Un ventennio a colori* (Florence, 1995), and Alberto Abruzzese, *Lo splendore della TV* (Genoa, 1995).

References

BELLOTTO, A. (1960), 'La critica televisiva in Italia', *Comunità*, 85, 92–7.

—— (1967), 'Un'occasione per la critica: *I promessi sposi*', *Studi Cattolici*, 11: 70, 68–9.

—— and BETTETINI, G. (1985) (eds.), *Questioni di storia e teoria della radio e della televisione* (Milan).

—— et al. (1973), 'Criteri e funzioni della critica televisiva', in *Atti del convegno (Torino, 18–20 settembre 1972)* (Turin).

CESAREO, G. (1970), *Anatomia del potere televisivo* (Milan).

—— (1974), *La televisione sprecata* (Milan).

GAVIOLI, O. (1980), 'Meglio un servizio al lettore', *Speciale critica TV: i critici contro la critica*, *Radio TV e società*, 7: 7.

GIOVANNINI, F. (1990), 'Intellettuali e mass media negli anni Sessanta', *Democrazia e diritto*, 3–4: 153–77.

IOZZIA, G. (1982), 'Le pagine dello spettacolo', *Informazione Radio e TV*, 1–6: 3–31.

MICCICHÉ, L. (1971), 'Il recensore leonardesco', *Sipario*, 300: 17–19.

PANDOLFI, V. (1953), 'Libertà e schiavitù della televisione', *Cinema nuovo*, 2/5: 102.

PINTO, F. (1977), *Intellettuali e TV negli anni '50* (Rome).

—— (1979), 'La nascita della TV e l'ideologia del rifiuto', in G. Tinazzi (ed.), *Il cinema italiano degli anni cinquanta* (Venice), 363–72.

PLACIDO, B. (1985), 'Da oggi, cari lettori, guarderò per voi la televisione. Anche la domenica', *La Repubblica*, 14–15 Apr.

—— (1990), 'Pippo arbitro tapino fra sor Sgarbi e D'Agostino', *La Repubblica*, 16 Nov.

—— (1991), 'Arriva Milo, me ne scappo in riva al Nilo', *La Repubblica*, 28–9 July.

ROSITI, F. (1971), *Contraddizioni di cultura. Ideologie collettive e capitalismo avanzato* (Bologna).

TARDY, M. (1966), 'Sur la critique de télévision', *Communications*, 7: 40–51.

Post-War Italian Narrative: An Alternative Account

ANN HALLAMORE CAESAR

CULTURAL histories of post-war Italy have characteristically taken schools or movements as the organizing principle of modern literature, often giving short shrift to those works that resist assimilation. In his own study of modern Italian poetry, the poet and critic Franco Fortini began with a warning to readers that he was not going to follow the usual practice of championing avant-garde poets, a practice which in his view encouraged critics to draw attention only to those poetic features that appeared to anticipate future movements (1977: 3). The effect of such an approach, he argued, was a literary history built on exclusions that were as unjust as they were wrongheaded.

What Fortini saw as having been the fate of traditional poetry has been repeated in the critical reception of writing by women, which has been removed to the margins. One of the most talented twentieth-century writers, Anna Banti, remarked in an interview given in 1984 that even where individual works by women have received critical acclaim and literary prizes they still fail to win a place in the literary histories (1984: 106). The avant-garde writer and critic Christine Brooke-Rose proposed a psychoanalytic explanation for a phenomenon which is not tied to any one culture: 'In theory the canonic/non-canonic opposition applies to all writers and thus cuts across the sexual or any other opposition. In practice a canon is very much a masculine notion, a priesthood (not to be polluted), a club, a sacred male preserve.' (1992: 250) In Italy, the position of women writers has been made more difficult by their absence from the technical and formalist experimentation traditionally associated with literary avant-gardes (the most influential avant-garde movement of the post-war period—the Gruppo 63—was made up entirely of men), and by their historical reluctance to describe themselves or their work in terms of schools or movements. The list of Further Reading to this chapter refers readers to some excellent literary histories of the period; this chapter will offer an overview based on the thesis that the conventional account of post-war literature that focuses on the conflict and eventual exchange of roles between neorealism of the 1940s and 1950s and experimentalism of the 1960s and 1970s, has tended to obscure the central role in the development of the novel in Italy played by women writers over the decades since the war.

I shall begin my account with the immediate post-war period, but I first want to draw attention to aspects of the novel and its evolution which are unique to Italy. Post-war Italian narrative has been characterized by a distinctive feature. On the one hand, in a country where translations of foreign novels dominate the literary market, Italian writers have been very responsive to contemporary writing abroad, as well as being well versed in the established European canon; on the other their writing, and the literary tradition of which it is a part, has retained a marked indigenous identity. To understand the presence of this duality in the national tradition, we have to return to the novel's nineteenth-century origins, and look briefly at the way in which the problems it then faced continued to haunt Italian narrative up until the 1970s. Post-1970s writing has benefited from an enlarged reading public and a powerful cultural industry, but confidence in the large-scale ideological discourses for which the novel once acted as vehicle has gone.

In England and in France accounts of the rise of the novel describe the slow evolution of a genre over at least two centuries; historically linked to the romance, its attention was on the 'private' person and the issues were love and courtship, marriage and the family. Not so in Italy. Here the rise of the novel is associated with one book—Alessandro Manzoni's *I promessi sposi* (1825–7)—a historical novel which, unsurprisingly in the light of its solitary position, has remained an authoritative work for much of the twentieth century. Although few writers have shared Manzoni's faith in the workings of Providence in human history, the novel has established a model of how to look at social events. In the novel, a benignly omniscient narrator reveals, through the vicissitudes of a young peasant couple, the moral and political corruption practised by the Spanish occupiers of seventeenth-century Lombardy and sections of the local ruling classes.

The realists, writing in the last quarter of the nineteenth century, and, after them, the neorealists, writing in the middle of the twentieth century, shared some of Manzoni's belief in the possibility of identifying discernible patterns in history, and furthermore they shared with Manzoni the belief that writers of novels have an educational mission. But it was tempered by an uncomfortable awareness of the glaring anomaly at the heart of their project. If the novel was to exercise a didactic function, it required a broadly based readership. Like Manzoni, whose novel includes a passing, self-deprecatory reference to 'i miei venticinque lettori', they knew that they were writing for a small readership, and one which certainly did not come from the ranks of those their books were about—in 1957 it was estimated that 40 per cent of Italians had not read anything by way of a magazine, newspaper, or book in the previous year (Aspetti 1975: 67). Matters were not helped by the persistent absence of a linguistic norm which all classes could refer to. When Manzoni wrote the first draft of his novel he had combined his native Milanese with a lexicon drawn from many other regions, but then, spurred by a belief that a written language which was not rooted in a living speech community was unlikely to flourish, he rewrote the work in an educated Tuscan tempered by actual Florentine usage. More than a century later, in 1945, writers continued to face a linguistic situation where the pervasive use of dialect as a medium to talk about everyday matters by the literate and the non-literate alike meant that the written language remained peculiarly literary, more suited to pastoral life in Arcadia than peasant life in Agrigento. There was a linguistic black hole that threatened the future of the novel as a democratic literary genre. The absence of a reading public and a flexible and responsive written language were to continue to plague the novel in Italy until the 1980s, by which time urbanization and tertiary education had created a mass public, while the media, in particular television, and geographical mobility had helped forge a national language.

When realism resumed at the end of the war as the dominant aesthetic, writers focused on the years of the Resistance and the German occupation of Italy. Cesare Pavese, *La casa in collina* (1947–8), Elio Vittorini, *Uomini e no* (1945), Beppe Fenoglio, *Una questione privata* (posthumously published in 1963 with the title *Un giorno di fuoco*; the new definitive edition appeared in 1965), and Italo Calvino, *Il sentiero dei nidi di ragno* (1947) are the novels that have come for many to represent the writing of this period. Although the cultural and ideological significance of neorealism within post-war culture should not be undervalued, it was a relatively short-lived movement, undermined by three important developments in Italy's economic and cultural life as a whole. These were the shift in attitude to historical events, the war in particular; post-war economic growth, which created a climate favourable to new writing practices; and, very significantly, a change in the critical understanding of neorealism as exemplified by one of its most famous practitioners, Italo Calvino.

First of all there was the question of attitudes to the country's recent history. Whatever the private anguish or the personal loss, neorealist narratives of the 1940s and 1950s were written in the knowledge that the partisans were ultimately, collectively, history's victors, entering the national consciousness as patriots and heroes. Gradually as one moves through the 1950s a view of history as a succession of defeats rather than victories emerges, marked out by the success in Italy of

Boris Pasternak's *Dr Zhivago* and Giuseppe Tomasi di Lampedusa's *Il Gattopardo*, published by Feltrinelli respectively in 1957 (the first world publication) and 1958. There was a greater readiness to listen to the quiet inflections of the victims of war and the defeated—the Jewish communities, women, children, civilians in general. In 1962 Giorgio Bassani's *Il giardino dei Finzi-Contini* was published: it tells from within the story of what happened to the Jews in his home-town of Ferrara after the anti-Semitic legislation was introduced in 1938; among his shorter *Storie ferraresi* (1956) which address the recent past, 'Una lapide in Via Mazzini' describes the return of a concentration camp survivor who had been taken for dead by his own community. Primo Levi wrote two remarkable documentary narratives, *Se questo è un uomo* (1947) and *La tregua* (1963), which drew on his experiences of deportation and Auschwitz. They were born of what he later described in his introduction to *I sommersi e i salvati* (1986) as his deeply held belief that the victims and the persecuted must speak their 'ghastly tale'. In the preface he refers to the SS militia's practice of taunting their prisoners with the claim that, even if Germany were to lose the war, the war against the Jews will have been won because the world would either never know, or never believe, the truth of what took place in the camps. Defeat, irrespective of who won the war, comes when people listen to the victors and not the vanquished.

Narratives by women showed an equally muted response to the war. Women writers, with the single exception of Renata Viganò, whose *L'Agnese va a morire* (1949) relates the story of an uneducated peasant woman who gives her life to the Resistance, played no part in neorealism. Although women had participated in the Resistance in significant numbers—it has been estimated that at least half a million women were actively involved—one had to wait until the publication in 1977 of Bianca Guidetti Serra's two volumes of oral testimonies, *Compagne. Testimonianze di partecipazione politica femminile*, described as 'una sorta di autobiografia politica di ciascuna', to learn why women joined the Resistance, who they were, and what they did. One explanation as to why women did not contribute to stories of the Resistance is provided by the nature of the genre itself. The Resistance, as it was relived in the collective imaginary, shared many of the attributes found in the world of boys' adventure stories where life is lived, often literally, in the wild, beyond the reach of home and family. Missions have to be accomplished, dangerous open spaces crossed, enemies killed. Conventions of the genre were established very rapidly and they excluded women.

In fact, a substantial body of women's fiction was produced during the years of neorealism; in the decade from 1943 to 1953 there were publications by, among others, Elsa Morante, Gianna Manzini, Anna Maria Ortese, and Anna Banti alongside Maria Bellonci, Natalia Ginzburg, Lalla Romano, Livia De Stefani, Alba De Cespedes, and Milena Milani. Many of their narratives did not address either Fascism or the war. The overall reticence and the specific moments of textual silence in Natalia Ginzburg's autobiographical narrative of family life during the years of Fascism, persecution, and war can be seen as emblematic of her complex response to the period and her reluctance to write about it. Ginzburg, born Natalia Levi, grew up in Turin in the 1930s, the youngest daughter of Socialists; her father was an assimilated Jew, her mother a Milanese Catholic. *Lessico famigliare* (1963) is about the closed world of family life with its own idiosyncratic ways of doing things and saying things, but their Turin home is also open to friends, some of whom are well known names in the world of opposition politics and culture, who pass through, sometimes *en route* to exile. The book also encompasses the period when the author's husband Leone Ginzburg was arrested in Rome for anti-Fascist activities, incarcerated, tortured, and killed by the Germans; after his death she was left to bring up their two small children on her own (during this period she still managed to help in the clandestine production of a magazine). Only the briefest of references is made to the events leading up to her husband's capture and death. Where the much commented-on textual silence that follows the words 'la sventurata rispose' ('the unfortunate women replied') in chapter 10 of Manzoni's *I promessi sposi* is an invitation to readers to speculate on the heinous crimes committed by the nun, Natalia Ginzburg does not encourage her readers to reach with their imagination beyond the written word; she has simply exercised an authorial right to remain silent. In her earlier novel *Tutti i nostri ieri* (1952), which traces the course of history through the story of two families, although lives are irrevocably changed by events, each character remains caught up in the particularities, some may call them minutiae, of his or her own existence. When women write about Fascism and the war in terms of civilian life, the tone is inevitably more muted, but also at times more ambivalent; in Laudomia Bonanni's *Palma e sorelle* (1954) bombing raids over the city provide a welcome relief to peasants as they find that town-dwellers will pay whatever they can to rent places in the country where they might find refuge from the nightly devastation.

The second factor that contributed to the undermining of neorealism was the accelerated growth in the post-war economy that was to bring about a shift from a predominantly peasant to a neocapitalist society. 'Il mondo contadino, dopo quattordicimila anni di vita, è finito praticamente di colpo,' Pier Paolo Pasolini wrote in the 1970s, referring to the disappearance of a world that the neorealists had made their own. Between 1958 and 1963 Italy was transformed by what entered into language as the 'economic miracle'. The country became one of the world's main industrial countries at a speed, and with an intensity, unequalled anywhere else in Europe, and a largely agricultural workforce left the land to migrate, often the length of the country, to the industrial conurbations of the North where factories and service industries needed their labour. At the same time a new generation of writers, most of whom had been educated after the Fascist period, launched a confrontational attack on neorealism and its aesthetics. The neo-avant-garde, which included amongst its ranks the novelists and essayists Edoardo Sanguineti, Giorgio Manganelli, Nanni Balestrini, and Umberto Eco, like the Futurists earlier in the century, celebrated an aggressive modernity. Their name, Gruppo 63, is linked to a much publicized conference held in Palermo that year—one of several meetings where they read from their own work and discussed the work of others, in encounters that must, at times, have been painful for the participants. While they had their origins as a group in the economic miracle, their decision to disband came in response to student and industrial militancy in the late 1960s. But, far from disappearing, their experiences and contacts within the rapidly expanding cultural industry and their links with publishers meant that a number of them became highly respected figures, active in cultural programmes on television, in newspapers, and in publishing houses and, in the case of Sanguineti and Manganelli, in the universities. During their years as a movement, their public presence was assured by the publishing boom then under way; the publisher and patron Giangiacomo Feltrinelli told *L'Espresso* on 9 December 1961: 'For everyone in my trade the problem is now to sell, sell, sell. If the boom means that people are reading more and have more money to buy books, then the boom is happening.'

What drew the neo-avant-garde together was the search for a new language-based culture that responded to and interacted with the social and economic revolution about them and in particular with the development of the mass media. In the narratives of the neo-avant-garde there is no dominant ideology, indeed the novels are a critique of ideology. The narrator of Edoardo Sanguineti's *Capriccio italiano* (1963) is no more able to make sense of what is happening to him than his reader. But it is an eventful story—his pregnant wife gives birth, a marital crisis is resolved, he has a dream where he journeys through death to meet his (at this point, unborn) son—written in an anti-style, where sentences are often grammatically correct but semantically nonsensical. It is readable, following to the letter Sanguineti's own statement that a novel, at some level, is always a 'relazione intorno a un accadimento' (Barilli and Guglielmi 1976: 208). By contrast Nanni Balestrini's *Tristano* (1964) may take its name from one of the great lovers of Western culture, but the book itself is a collage of three other texts—a geography textbook, a love-story, and a technical handbook. Made up of ten chapters, each with ten paragraphs, each paragraph with thirty-four lines, it is a work that does not require a typewriter so much as scissors and a pot of glue. Balestrini became interested later on in computer-generated poetry.

The third factor in the decline of neorealism came through a writer whose own first work had become one of the best known of the Resistance narratives. Calvino's preface to *Il sentiero dei nidi di ragno*, which he added in 1964, rewrites the history of neorealism. In an anti-political and perhaps anti-communist gesture, he pulls away from history and reclaims the Resistance for story-tellers. In his essay the importance of those years lies in the sharing of experiences which created the conditions for a different kind of relationship between writer and reader—one built on common ground. This assessment is at odds with the view that neorealism is an artistic movement designed to show, and by showing to teach, people about pre-existing realities outside their own experiences. In confident mood, Calvino describes how at the end of the war everybody had a tale to tell; the partisans who had once swapped stories around the camp-fire were now replaced by women telling of their experiences as they queued for bread or travellers exchanging tales on train journeys. What he stresses is the public, communal voice of this period—'la voce anonima dell'epoca, più forte delle nostre inflessioni individuali ancora incerte'—whose authority comes from experience and whose seedbed is 'la medesima materia dell'anonimo narratore orale' (Calvino 1991: 1186). This, for Calvino, was neorealism—not a school but a cacophony of voices, with a common need to speak out. The essay echoes, in content but not in mood, Walter Benjamin's 1936 essay 'The Storyteller', which is a meditation on the social and cultural loss incurred by the decline of an oral tradition: 'The storyteller takes what he tells from experience—his own or that reported by others. And he in turn makes it the experience of those listening to the tale' (Benjamin 1973: 87). For Calvino, Resistance literature is close to the short story, a genre in Italy which, from its medieval origins in Il Novellino and the Decameron, has sought to combine the durability of the written communication with the immediacy of the spoken.

Although Calvino was briefly linked with the neo-avant-garde, it was as a sympathetic but detached observer; his interest in modernity was stimulated by what he felt it could bring to the story-telling process. His own narratives were, over the years, linked by neither genre nor subject, but by a fascination with story-telling itself—the tales, the tellers, and the listeners or readers. Gradually his writing moved from the manner of his 1950s trilogy Gli antenati, where a recognizable reality rubs shoulders with fantasy, to the self-referential world of Le cosmicomiche, where the story-teller, a constantly changing creature—one moment mollusc, another camel—with a name, Qfwfq, that looks like an error or a formula, can draw on a bottomless reservoir of experiences. Unlike us, Qfwfq has had the advantage of having been around for all the big events of the universe. Of Calvino's novels of the 1970s in which he explores the very structures of narrative, Le città invisibili creates the most delicate balance between the cerebrality of post-modernism and the creativity of fantasy. It is built around Marco Polo's descriptions to the Kubla Khan of the fabulous cities he has visited—'invisible' because they are cityscapes of the mind, born of the imagination and of memory. Calvino in his penultimate book, the best-seller Se una notte d'inverno un viaggiatore, turns the spotlight on the reader, who, addressed throughout in the second person, has the dubious pleasure of being the book's protagonist. The reader is engaged in the frustrating business of trying to piece together a series of beginnings of novels in the hope of assembling the novel which he thought he had purchased in the bookshop. This text perhaps gives us as readers the recognition we feel we deserve after all (the opening pages do remind us that we bought the book), but reward turns out not to be part of the transaction.

Se una notte d'inverno un viaggiatore was published in 1979, the same year as Umberto Eco's reflections on the role of the reader in Lector in fabula. The meteoric international success of Eco's own first novel Il nome della rosa (1980), was watched in Italy by critics mesmerized by its status as best-seller. It is a curious irony that the most visible outcome to the neo-avant-garde seems, at first sight, to have nothing to do with it. But this is a book that is highly conscious of how the cultural industry works, and makes that knowledge an implicit part of the text. Unlike many critics and writers, its author has no prejudices about popular genres, so he is able to bring a postmodern sensibility to a novel which like some of the great nineteenth-century popular novels reworks genres and motifs. The story is about a fictional series of murders that in 1327 rocked one of the most powerful monasteries of medieval Christendom. Although the mystery is eventually solved by an English Franciscan monk and former inquisitor, William of Baskerville, assisted by the Watson-like narrator, in the final struggle one of the world's great libraries goes up in flames. Artfully constructed to appeal to a wide spectrum of readers—from those who take pleasure in its philosophical and literary references and quotations (or equally do not, but are thought to gain from it—the novel is now a set text for many Italian schoolchildren) to those who enjoy an old-fashioned whodunnit (it was successful again as a film with Sean Connery in the lead role)— it traverses the cultural terrain that links avant-garde sophistication to commercial popular fiction. At the same time, as a historical novel, it is rooted in a literary tradition known to all Italians. Relatively few Italian novelists have been translated into English, even fewer have broken through the resistance to 'foreign' books, but among those who have been successful Umberto Eco and Italo Calvino dominate the field; these are writers who have to a large extent shaken the Italian soil off their boots and become part of a literary caravan that travels under the collective name of postmodernism.

The breakdown in form first seen in the neo-avant-garde and post-neo-avant-garde was accompanied on the part of those writers who continued to work with major issues by a loss of confidence in their ability to interpret the world about them on behalf of their readers, or indeed in the feasibility of their doing so. A parallel to Calvino's fragmentation of narrative structures is to be found in Elsa Morante's anti-rationalist representation of history in her war novel *La Storia* (1974). After two earlier novels, *Menzogna e sortilegio* of 1948 and *L'isola di Arturo* of 1957, in which her first-person protagonists are cut off, either psychologically or physically, from the rest of the world, she wrote this third-person narrative set during the years of war and the Nazi occupation of Rome. *La Storia* (the word can mean both 'history' and 'story') recounts the brief life of Useppe Ramundo, conceived when his mother was raped by a young German soldier from Dachau (at that time an ordinary place name without the chilling resonance it later acquired) whose regiment had stopped off in Rome on its way to North Africa. Far from shaping history, the protagonists of this novel are its submissive victims. There are no victors and, if there is any larger context to which people can turn, it is self-evidently utopian. At the opening of each chapter a summary of the main events in this 'nuclear century', followed by a brief passage, like a child's skipping chant, is used to effect the transition from the historical to the individual; at the same time it is intended to remind readers that we all live within history (Morante refers contemptuously to history as 'a scandal which has lasted for ten thousand years').

The choice of a third-person narrator in *La Storia* was as singular for Morante as was the subject matter. In common with many women writing in Italy, she rejected impersonal discourse with its implication that we can in some way stand outside the major issues of life.

Elsa Morante did not wish to be thought of as a woman writer. Others, however, defined themselves and their work in terms of gender. When in the 1970s a generation of women writers emerged whose writing took three forms—the testimony, autobiographical narratives, and fiction—one of the most noticeable features of what otherwise manifested itself in a diversity of narrative practices was their constant recourse to first-person narration. To understand the nature of this *presa di parola*, one has to contextualize what became for a while a culture industry for and by women, often conducted in separatist bookshops and publishing houses. In the early 1970s a number of women, many of them students, often with an experience of extra-parliamentary groups such as Lotta Continua or Potere Operaio, realized that neither these groups nor the PCI, the largest parliamentary party of the left, appeared to have the measure of, or indeed interest in, women's issues. It was also a decade when, as a part of the general process of modernization that the country was undergoing, social legislation began to catch up with the demands of a modern industrial state. Women, having waited until 1946 before getting the vote, had to wait a further thirty years before a full package of family reforms was introduced. In 1974 Italians disregarded the advice of the Church and the ruling Christian Democrat Party and, in a national referendum, voted in favour of divorce. Four years later a law giving women a limited right to legal abortion was brought in (on these legal changes see Passerini, 'Gender Relations', Chapter 8 of this volume). Some of the legal inequalities that lingered on were extraordinary when put in the context of the modern state. It was only in 1981 that Article 544 of the Penal Code was rescinded; it had stated that a man who had committed rape, or any associates who had participated in the act, would not have charges brought against him if he married his victim: an injustice which had played an important part in the life of the protagonist of Italy's first feminist novel, Sibilla Aleramo's *Una donna*, of 1906. It should be remembered that although feminism in Italy was part of a movement that was making itself heard throughout most of Europe and North America, there were areas of concern and forms of activity which were specific to Italy and can only be understood within that context. Narrative, an important medium for the communication of ideas in feminist practice, slipped comfortably into the educative function that I have already signalled as a principal thread in the Italian novel since Manzoni's *I promessi sposi*.

The early nineteenth century had seen an animated debate in Italy between the Classicists and Romantics over the morality of the novel as a genre, its suitability for women (along with the question of whether it was wise to let women read at all), together with a general disquiet about its appropriateness to an Italian culture which allegedly excelled in poetry and the epic. What was absent from the debate then and continued to have little importance in Italy was the question of what constitutes a novel. There is a remarkable, and refreshing, lack of concern about the definitions of narrative genres, which has continued to the present day. Even Manzoni's own preoccupation with ensuring that the reader was capable of distinguishing the fictive from the factual did not seem to have much worried his successors. There is a long history to the Italian novel's cohabitation with other disciplines. When in 1967 Calvino declared that it was time for literature to exchange its current 'marriage with separate beds' for a *ménage à trois* (in this case a relationship with philosophy and history), he was not arguing for a radical departure from customary practice, so much as for a return to the traditional novel. One finds a similar lack of inhibition over genre. Natalia Ginzburg, for example, in her foreword to *Lessico famigliare* writes 'Benché tratto dalla realtà, penso che si debba leggere come se fosse un romanzo: e cioè senza chiedergli nulla di più, né di meno di quello che un romanzo può dare' ('Although it is based on reality, I believe the book must be read as though it were a novel: and that means without asking of it either more or less than a novel can give') (Ginzburg 1986*b*: 1133).

The same openness exists in the diversity of writing practices that can be found in women's writing in the 1970s; one of the most interesting is the *testimonianza*. Born of the need to document, in one sense these books continue with the project, presented in the first instance by realism and later neorealism, of unveiling Italy's hidden face, this time by creating a space for the marginalized, excluded and hitherto silenced, to speak for themselves (although Ignazio Silone too, as early as 1930, claimed in *Fontamara* that he had simply transcribed the words spoken to him by the peasants: 'Si lasci dunque a ognuno il diritto di raccontare i fatti suoi, a modo suo' ('So let each of them have the right to tell his story, in his own way').) The emphasis is on the *parlato* (a *parlato trascritto*) but unlike Calvino's 'anonimo narratore orale' they are speaking only for themselves, of experiences that are uniquely theirs. Included in this category are the testimonies gathered by Giuliana Morandini in ...*E allora mi hanno rinchiusa* (1977) from women incarcerated in mental hospitals (Morandini sees her own work approaching truth in a way not permitted to neorealism; hers is 'una scrittura di verità, al di là di ogni pretesa ed equivoco di neorealismo'); Gabriella Parca's *Voci dal carcere femminile* (1973)—testimonies taken from women in prison; and Armanda Guiducci's *La donna non è gente* (1977)—testimonies by women peasants from different parts of Italy, where the use of dialect has meant that Guiducci has had at times to translate the material. The public's continuing desire for documentation about the realities of Italy is reflected in the fact that these testimonies were published, in paperback, by mainstream houses. The women involved in gathering these testimonies were often themselves actively experimenting with other forms of narrative. Giuliana Morandini is Triestine (like her famous fellow citizen Italo Svevo, she writes in Italian, but draws on Central European culture with a marked psychoanalytic dimension) and has become an established writer of fiction with three novels—*I cristalli di Vienna* (1978), *Caffè specchi* (1983) set in Trieste, and *Angelo a Berlino* (1987)—each of which won a literary prize. Guiducci, on the other hand, has a strong interest in anthropology and sociology, but she applies literary devices and structures to factual narrative. She describes *La mela e il serpente*—her autobiographical meditation on the rites of passage that are a part of the biological and social process of growing up female—as a *romanzo*. In *Due donne da buttare* (1976) the narrative is made up of the voices of two women—one a housewife chained to domestic routine, the other a former prostitute tied to her past.

Dacia Maraini developed another strand of documentary fiction with *Memorie di una ladra* (1972), where she draws on the extensive research she conducted in women's prisons to tell the tale through the perspective of one Teresa Numa, thief and narrator, of a resilient and enterprising life which is reminiscent of the picaresque heroine Moll Flanders. One of the strengths of the novel is its flexibility. During the 1970s women writers were not alone in exploiting the apparent ease with which the genre could combine fact and fiction, anthropology and sociology with story-telling. In his first novel after the dissolution of the neo-avant-garde Nanni Balestrini, for example, wrote in 1971 *Vogliamo tutto*, which 'presents like a novel the taped recording of the story of the life of a worker'. The voice belongs to Alfonso, just one of the thousands of migrant workers from the South who were involved in the movement at Fiat in Turin in 1969.

'Not only has personal experience tended to be excluded from the discourse of knowledge, but the realm of the personal itself has been coded as female and devalued for that reason,' the critic Barbara Johnson has remarked (1987: 43–4). As one of the most urgent projects in feminism was the need to make visible the hypocrisies inherent in the rigid division of life into private and public, it was consistent that autobiography (not as a closing up but as a marking out of the representativeness of what passes for individual experience) was an important presence in first-person narratives. Alongside the documentary fictions came the novels, often of an autobiographical or confessional nature which turn on subjects conventionally constructed as part of a female domain, but absent from the traditional narrative canon in Italy. Aside from the glaring legal inequalities, women in Italy, where the presence of the Catholic Church was still strong, had also to contend with an ideology of motherhood and the family that made itself felt much more than in Britain. Sometimes narrated in diary form, or in fragments, experience is broken up into narrative blocks echoing the disorganized unshapeliness of life. Francesca Duranti's *Piazza mia bella piazza* (1978), describes how an apparently happy marriage starts to fall apart when the wife has her manuscript accepted for publication. Carla Cerati in *Un matrimonio perfetto* (1975), Gabriella Magrini in *Lunga giovinezza* (1976), and Dacia Maraini in *Donna in guerra* (1975) show in different ways that equality cannot exist within a marriage. The endings of these novels show the first-person narrator protagonist facing an uncertain and possibly unhappy future, after having come to the realization that the apparent contentment of the past was built on a lie. But even such muted endings which postulate divorce as an alternative to the traditional heroine's destiny of marriage or death were only historically possible in Italy after 1974. It is interesting that it is the structural inequality in the home that is perceived as the problem, and not the workplace and the question of financial autonomy, such as one finds in women's narratives of the late nineteenth and early twentieth centuries. In the absence of a tradition of social and domestic novels (Lalla Romano and Natalia Ginzburg focus on family life but, as Ginzburg once remarked, there is no protagonist in the family) these novels are introducing a new subject matter into Italian narrative, while at the same time they are part of a transnational feminist literary project.

The precariousness of selfhood has been investigated from every conceivable angle in twentieth-century fiction—modernism's literary project was closely bound up with the exploration of self. In Italy writing by women has led the way. Once socially recognized and accepted patterns of behaviour have been discarded, maintaining a self-identity becomes more problematic and more self-reflexive; the self is suddenly fragile, amorphous. Identity presupposes a continuity through time which can only be sustained through memory. Women's writing has given enormous importance to memory. Where Calvino, alongside Borges, Butor, and others, celebrates the labyrinth as trope for a post-industrial age, women writers have concentrated on trying to retie the thread of memory that Ariadne handed to Theseus so he could retrace his steps back to the entrance.

In 1951, at the height of neorealism, Anna Banti's argument in favour of the historical novel suggested that it is women who are custodians of the past. For her the highest form of testimony is one where the chronicle yields to a writing practice which is guided by memory: 'la memoria che ha fatto in tempo a scegliere, che suggerisce e trasferisce il fatto crudo dall'ordine dell'avvenuto a quello del supposto. In questo caso la cronaca è sorpassata, la storia è raggiunta, il romanzo realista è già romanzo storico' ('memory which has managed to select, which suggests and transfers bare facts from the realm of what has happened to that of what might have been. In such cases, reportage gives way to history and the realist novel is a historical novel') (Banti 1961: 42). Her own post-war historical novel *Artemisia* (1947), based on the life of the sixteenth-century artist Artemisia Gentileschi, was written from memory, after a bombing raid over Florence destroyed the manuscript along with her home. Francesca Sanvitale's novels—ranging from the semi-autobiographical account of the relationship between mother and daughter in *Madre e figlia* (1980) to the recent prize-winning historical novel based on the short life of Napoleon's son, *Il figlio dell'impero* (1993)—are about remembering (and forgetting) and the contribution of these to the tension that exists between who we are and who we think we are. Writing in 1986, she denounced literature's role within the mass media, thanks to which the contemporary writer now has to work 'nella non-memoria, nella non-coscienza, nella non-vita', now that literature has lost its 'amniotic fluid'—memory and time (Sanvitale 1988: 115). For Natalia Ginzburg, who claimed she always wrote about people and places that had been impressed upon her mind, 'la memoria è amorosa e mai casuale'. Her bleak view of contemporary life, its meaninglessness, arbitrariness, and therefore overriding purposelessness is rooted in her belief that it is a society that eschews memory. As one character says of the protagonist of the epistolary novel *Caro Michele* (1973), whose death is presented as being in every way as arbitrary and as insignificant as his life: 'I ragazzi oggi non hanno memoria, e soprattutto non la coltivano' (Ginzburg 1986*a*: 195). To reject memory is to reject one's own experiences and the ability to connect self to other, life to history, present to past. The project of so much post-war writing by women writers in Italy is to salvage and make sense of experiences that otherwise will be lost, forgotten, or suppressed.

Further Reading

For an accessible overview of recent Italian literature, Giuliano Manacorda's *Letteratura italiana d'oggi 1965–1985* (Rome, 1987). Romano Luperini's volume *Il Novecento. Apparati ideologici, ceto intellettuale, sistemi formali nella letteratura italiana contemporanea* (2 vols., Turin, 1981) is an authoritative sociocultural analysis of the dominant literary movements of the twentieth century. *Letteratura e cultura dell'età presente*, ed. Vanna Gazzola Stacchini and Romano Luperini (Rome and Bari, 1980) offers a succinct and useful introduction to Italian literature from Fascism to the 1970s. Among close studies of the novel in the last two decades see Stefano Tani, *Il romanzo di ritorno* (Milan, 1990), Giuseppe Amoroso, *Narrativa italiana, 1975–1983* (Milan, 1989), Antonio Russi, *La narrativa italiana dal neosperimentalismo alla neoavanguardia* (Rome, 1983). In English *Writers and Society in Contemporary Italy*, edited by Michael Caesar and Peter Hainsworth (Leamington Spa, 1984), which focuses on the 1960s and 1970s. For the 1980s Zygmunt G. Baranski and Lino Pertile (eds.), *The New Italian Novel* (Edinburgh, 1993).

On women's writing Anna Nozzoli, *Tabù e coscienze. La condizione femminile nella letteratura italiana del Novecento* (Florence, 1978), and the interviews with women novelists by Sandra Petrignani, *Le signore della scrittura* (Varese, 1984). Santo L. Aricò (ed.), *Contemporary Women Writers in Italy: A Modern Renaissance* (Amherst, Mass., 1980), which includes biography and journalism along with fiction, Carol Lazzaro-Weis, *From Margins to Mainstream* (Pennsylvania, 1983).

References

Aspetti (1975), 'Aspetti delle letture in Italia', in *Quaderni di vita italiana*, 9 (Rome).
BANTI, A. (1961), 'Romanzo e romanzo storico', in *Opinioni* (Milan), 38–43.
—— (1984), 'La sfortuna di essere seri', in S. Petrignani, *Le signore della scrittura. Interviste* (Milan), 101–10.
BARILLI, R., and GUGLIELMI, A. (1976) (eds.), *Gruppo 63. Critica e teoria* (Milan).
BENJAMIN, W. (1973), 'The Storyteller: Reflections on the Work of Nikolai Leskov', in *Illuminations*, ed. H. Arendt, trans. H. Zohn (London; 1st edn. 1970), 83–109.
BROOKE-ROSE, C. (1992), *Stories and Things* (Cambridge).
CALVINO, I. (1991), *Romanzi e racconti*, i, ed. C. Milanini (Milan).
FORTINI, F. (1977), *I poeti del Novecento* (Rome and Bari).
GINZBURG, N. (1986*a*), *Caro Michele* (Milan).
—— (1986*b*), *Opere*, i, ed. C. Garboli (Milan).
JOHNSON, B. (1987), 'Deconstruction, Feminism and Pedagogy', in *A World of Difference* (Baltimore).
PASOLINI, P. (1975), 'L'articolo delle lucciole', in *Scritti corsari* (Milan).
SANGUINETI, E. (1976), 'Il trattamento del materiale verbale nei testi narrativi della nuova avanguardia', in Barilli and Guglielmi (1976), 203–18.
SANVITALE, F. (1988), *Mettendo a fuoco* (Rome).

Ladri di biciclette

CHRISTOPHER WAGSTAFF

André Bazin, the finest champion of De Sica's neorealist films, talks about them abolishing cinema, and confronting the audience with reality: 'If the event is sufficient unto itself without the direction having to shed any further light on it by means of camera angles, purposely chosen camera positions, it is because it has reached that perfect stage of luminosity which makes it possible for an art to unmask a nature which in the end resembles it.' I want to argue that by combining certain genre choices with cinematographic techniques (specifically, camera angles) that force the viewer to read, rather than just observe, the image, De Sica constructs a discourse and manipulates the viewer's emotions in *Ladri di biciclette* (1948).

The film is built around comic structures and gags. It abounds in slapstick and satire. In the second visit to the clairvoyant, she tells an unrequited lover that it is pointless to sow your seed in barren earth; you hoe and harvest naught. He says he cannot understand a word of what she is saying. Exasperated, she abandons the rhetoric: 'You are ugly!' (incorrectly subtitled as 'That's enough'). The man's response to this treatment is equally comic. The episode then dissolves into slapstick as Bruno jumps the queue for his father, and is set upon by a client's lapdog.

Comedy, therefore, is one of the genre conventions that gives form to the forty-five episodes (separated by dissolves) that make up the narrative. It has a further virtue. Comedy and melodrama deal with the anxieties of the characters, and offer a position from which the viewer can respond emotionally to those anxieties, either with laughter, or with anxiety followed by relief. Anxiety colours much of De Sica's cinema, and accounts for Italian critics' descriptions of it as a cinema of suffering.

Group A

The first two sequences of the film are shot in two completely different ways. In the first sequence (from which the Figure 19 shot is taken), Antonio Ricci is told about his job, and gives his wife the news. This shot typifies the way this first sequence is photographed. The camera stands well away from the couple, includes both of them together in the frame (sometimes called a 'two-shot'), one usually higher than the other (or nearer to the camera, or one standing and the other sitting). Their poses convey the stress that they are under: Antonio is swearing, and gesturing aggressively towards Maria, who wearily hauls the bucket up the stairs, rolling her eyes in exasperation. The hard angles of the building, softened by no rounded surfaces, seem to echo their postures; indeed, even the edges of masonry close to us, and distant from the centre of the image, are in quite sharp focus, which is not the most obvious way of focusing the camera for this shot. We, the viewers stand outside the couple, impassively observing their hostility. Our experience of their emotion is merely that of knowledge; we do not share it.

The shots in Figures 20 and 21 make a completely different use of cinematography. They are the two elements of what is called a reverse-angle sequence. The camera is placed between two people or groups who are talking to each other: when one person speaks, the camera photographs that person, and when the other replies, the camera reverses its angle of view (turns round 180 degrees, in other words), and photographs the second person. The effect for us, the viewers, is that we take up the position (or very nearly) of the person being spoken to. Figure 20 shows the kindly clerk smiling, and agreeing to pay a little more for the sheets than he at first offered. He is leaning towards 'us' (Maria, in fact), with his head tilted in a gesture of acquiescence. 'We' are looking at him through the counter-window, and are receiving his benevolence. Behind him is the wall of shelved linen that the poor have had to pawn and, in a later shot taken from the point of view of Antonio looking through a nearby window, we shall see his own sheets being carried higher and higher up to the very top shelf. Figure 21 is, therefore, a shot of 'us', the addressees of the clerk (at first it is of Maria only, but then Antonio leans into the frame). But by now 'we' are in the position of the clerk, being addressed by Maria.

I am exaggerating, of course, but only in order to emphasize how very differently the viewers are treated in Figures 20 and 21, from the way they are in Figure 19. In Figure 19 we observe the emotions of the characters; in Figures 20 and 21 we share their emotions. In Figure 20 the background is softly out of focus, the perpendiculars softened by being blurred and packed with the bundles of sheets. In Figure 21 the window has rounded corners, and it is out of focus, as are the figures behind the couple. Technically speaking, we would refer to Figure 19 with the term 'deep focus', and to Figures 20 and 21 with the term 'shallow focus'. What is interesting is how the two-shot and deep focus of Figure 19 force us, as viewers, to observe and judge impassively, while the reverse-angles and the shallow focus of Figures 20 and 21 draw us into an identification with the characters. De Sica is manipulating the viewer.

Fig. 19

Fig. 20

Fig. 21

Group B

Reverse-angle cinematography can do more than emotionally manipulate the viewer; it can force viewers not just to respond passively to a position or point of view upon them, but actually to read a complex point of view from the composition of the image—and that is what Group B illustrates. The shots in Figures 22 and 23 are of the restaurant to which Antonio takes his son Bruno in order to make up for the slap he has just administered. It is a scene full of comedy, and yet eloquently serious. In Figure 22 Antonio is ordering wine, and enjoying the music played by a Neapolitan group behind him (De Sica was Neapolitan, and the popular song being sung informs a young Neapolitan woman that she can give her newly born son any name she likes, but that won't change the fact that he is black). Of course, there is no way that wine is going to make Bruno feel better, and that is exactly the point: Antonio's anxiety makes him unable to do things for Bruno. Antonio is shot from a point above and to the left of Bruno's head which, in Figure 22, occupies the bottom right-hand corner of the frame. The camera reverses its angle, and we see Bruno (Figure 23). But he is shot from somewhere near Antonio's right elbow, almost at table level; and at that moment the waiter brings the wine and the glasses. The waiter's hands, the carafe, and the wine-glasses completely obscure Bruno. Figure 23 is a shot of Bruno, and yet is taken from a strangely odd position if it is to be from Antonio's point of view. To be that close to table level is to be closer to the child's point of view than to that of the father, and the 'erasure' of the child is what Bruno experiences, not the father. So the shot expresses Bruno's point of view. Nevertheless, the subordination of Bruno to the father's need to diminish his own anxiety (with alcohol: in one shot, he actually says: 'Let's get drunk') is what we read from the implications of that shot. What is in the foreground of a shot is hierarchically superior to what is in the background, and what is clearly visible is superior to what is obscured; this is the 'code' that generally operates in cinematography. De Sica is relying on this conventional code to lead us to a 'reading' of Figure 23, as well as using the camera angle to express Bruno's experience. But this shot doesn't actually take up the physical point of view of anybody.

If we were just observers, the film would simply be the story of a misfortune that befalls a working-class Italian. But as 'readers' we are required to judge the meaning of Antonio's total absorption in his quest for the bicycle. Instead of asking someone to lend him one, he falls a prey to anxiety, and becomes too obsessed to be a father to his son. His search is for the alleviation of his anxiety; when that escape is ultimately denied him, he must face the anxiety, and in the affection of his son, find it tolerable. With the failure of his attempt to steal a bicycle himself, his obsession is destroyed, short-circuited, as it were, and he is left with his son once more. As a series of observed events, the story is inconclusive. As the product of a reading of the images and sounds, it has a clear, powerful conclusion.

Fig. 22

Fig. 23

The Political Cartoon

ROBERT LUMLEY

The entry under 'vignetta' in the *Dizionario pratico di giornalismo* describes the diffusion of cartoons in the Italian press and the attendant de-fusion of their subversive charge:

Full of immediacy and intensity, the *vignetta* often accompanies the editorial line of a paper and encapsulates the main issue in brilliant and witty fashion. . . . Once the means of demystifying the powers-that-be, today the *vignetta* is in danger of losing its power to shock. Not because of the shortcomings of the cartoonists, but thanks to changes whereby in a media-dominated world what matters is publicity, good or bad.

This entry could not have been written in 1951 when Giovanni Guareschi was imprisoned for cartoons alleged to have brought dishonour on the President of the Republic. Nor during the 1960s when the media industries were still underdeveloped. It was not until the period after 1968 that there was a huge boom in visual satire, first as part of an anti-authoritarian cultural shift and then as part of the renewal of the press and expansion of the media in Italy. Many of the leading cartoonists, such as Alfredo Chiappori, started by doing work for fringe publications on the extreme left and were then offered regular slots in magazines like *Panorama*.

The classification of cartoons according to political criteria has reflected these changes, making clear demarcations increasingly difficult to draw. Although cartoonists have tended to be of left-wing sympathies, they have found lucrative jobs in mainstream publications. The founder of the satirical page of *L'Unità*, Sergio Staino, was a contributor to Fininvest's *TV Sorrisi e Canzoni* until Berlusconi's entry

Fig. 24

Fig. 25

into politics made it too invidious a contract. The Forza Italia publicists, however, operated on the principle that even satirical attacks on Berlusconi could be turned against their opponents so that the left-wing direction of satire in Italy could be deflected. During the June 1994 European elections, *Berlusconi Story*, a propaganda magazine, actually reproduced a full-page spread of anti-Berlusconi cartoons: Berlusconi was variously depicted as Big Brother and as political incompetent. The fact that the cartoonists paid so much attention to Berlusconi was interpreted as a sign of his importance, showing the publicists' intuitive understanding of the polysemic nature of all signs.

Such sophistication was not to characterize Achille Occhetto and Massimo D'Alema. These two leaders of the PDS sought legal redress for a cartoon by Giorgio Forattini in *Panorama* depicting them as prostitutes being paid off by Soviet premier Gorbachev. They are clutching copies of *L'Unità* and *Paese Sera*, papers owned by the former PCI and said to have been funded by Moscow (Figure 24). They won their case on the grounds that the cartoon had assumed the character of 'news' owing to its position on the front cover. Their response was understandable in that Forattini had for years baited the Italian Communist Party and continued to present the newly formed PDS as the old party in disguise. If Occhetto seems ineffectual and diminutive in stature in all senses, the red menace continues to lurk in the background. Tellingly, the cover of *Karaoketto*, the compilation of 200 of Forattini's cartoons on this theme, shows Occhetto as a singing puppet in the hands of the puppeteer, Stalin, and has the subtitle 'PCUS–PCI–PDS, 1973–1994'.

Forattini replied to the conviction by making it serve his purposes. He pictured himself as the defendant in front of a magistrates' bench in which the judges are none other than Stalin (*baffone* or 'moustaches' as he was known in the PCI of old), Occhetto, D'Alema, and Hitler (see Figure 25). They look down and underneath them can be read in big letters 'Magistratura Democratica', the name of the organization of progressive-minded (read PCI) judges. The caption alludes to the one thing (but are there not others?) they have in common: moustaches. It reads: 'The evolution of the moustache in political satire.' Game, set, and match to Giorgio Forattini.

An altogether more intelligent strategy is adopted by *Cuore*, a satirical weekly close to the PDS in its sympathies (though Michele Serra, the editor, wrote to Forattini at the time of the trial expressing the solidarity of one satirist towards another). *Cuore* loves to hate Forattini and has coined the expression 'Forattinate' to refer disparagingly to typical examples of his style. On one occasion, the entire contents of a compilation book, the ultimate form of parasitic production, was reduced to one page of *Cuore* and offered free to its readers. On another occasion, in the wake of Fellini's death, a competition called for them to 'Choose your own Forattini', presenting some examples of 'One Master remembering another Master' (see Figure 26). But readers are asked to be inventive and subtle in the manner of their hero: 'Readers may offer variations. For example: movie camera abandoned

UN MAESTRO RICORDA UN MAESTRO

n quale vignetta la matita più caustica e impreve-ile d'Italia saluterà Federico Fellini? Cuore indice concorso a premi tra i lettori proponendo tre pos-il disegni del nuovo testimonial Lavazza. Tra anti indovineranno, verrà estratto il fortunato vincitore del corso completo "Da grafico a miliarda-rio in dodici lezioni" della Fratelli Fabbri. Oltre a quelle da noi suggerite qui sopra, i lettori possono indicare altre possibili varianti. Ad esempio: cine-presa abbandonata sulla spiaggia, mare, gabbiani; ciak, megafono da regista sulla spiaggia, gabbioni, sciarpa bianca, mare; mare, naso da clown su Anita Ekberg sulla spiaggia, gabbiani; statuetta dell'Oscar che piange riversa sulla spiaggia, mare, gabbiani; cappello nero ondeggiante sul mare, altri gabbiani.

Fig. 26

on the beach, sea, gulls; clapperboard, director's megaphone on the beach, gulls, white scarf, sea; sea, clown's nose on Anita Ekberg on the beach, gulls; Oscar statuette with tear upturned on beach; sea, gulls.' The implication, of course, is that Forattini is like one of those party bores who is always repeating the same anecdotes, the victim of his own stereotypes and poverty of imagination. A far crueller sentence than any magistrate could impose.

Culture and Society

Introduction

DAVID FORGACS examines the cultural transformations of the post-1945 period from the point of view of consumption, drawing on some of the theoretical approaches developed in recent sociology and anthropology. He relates the purchase and use of cultural products to the social context in which they become meaningful as indicators of taste and social distinction. The chapter by Franco Bianchini, Massimo Torrigiani, and Rinella Cere deals with the cultural policies pursued 'from above', by central and local governments. The overall picture that emerges (with the exception of the initiatives of isolated local administrators in 1975–9) is of politicians acting with a traditional idea of what constitutes culture in ways which failed to address new publics and emergent tastes, while allowing a rich heritage to fall into disrepair. For Stephen Gundle, it is the star system that affords a unique vantage point for surveying key role models in the development of consumer ideologies and behaviour from the 1950s to the 1980s. He argues that distinctively Italian forms of stardom can be identified through a careful analysis of why certain stars gained prominence. Marcella Filippa shows how popular music and musicians offer a point of entry for analysing wider social processes. She takes examples from three different moments in musical history—the mixed reception of jazz in the 1930s and 1940s, the cult of singer Fred Buscaglione in the 1950s, and Italian posse and rap since the late 1980s. Her particular emphasis is on resistance to dominant ideas in society, especially by the young.

Cultural Consumption, 1940s to 1990s

DAVID FORGACS

CONSUMPTION has become a prominent subject over the last few years in cultural and media studies, as well as in a number of other disciplines, from social and economic history to social anthropology. In all cases this development has stemmed from dissatisfaction with earlier approaches which had either concentrated on production or had looked at consumers as more or less passive recipients, as 'the market', 'the public', or, in the case of cultural production, 'the audience'. The new interest in consumption has been linked in turn to a growing attention to people as subjects playing an active part in making their social environments and no longer as a passive collectivity to be observed, quantified, and classified.

The term *cultural consumption* may be used not only for products that are 'cultural' in the narrow sense of the word (paintings, music, television programmes, etc.) but also more broadly for the consumption of symbols or meanings of the most diverse kinds. As Jean Baudrillard argued in an essay written in 1968, every act of consuming an advertised product involves the consumption of a *sign* or meaning along with the product. 'If we consume the product as product, we consume its meaning as advertising' (1988: 10). For instance, when I buy and drink a Coca Cola I assimilate with the physical object a bit of the image or lifestyle represented in its advertising. The act of consuming this image, for myself or for display to others, may well be more important than the satisfaction of my immediate physical wants, for which many other products would do just as well.

Since Baudrillard's early work, various writers on cultural consumption have argued that to consume these products is not to succumb passively to their advertising image (Bourdieu 1979; Certeau 1980; Miller 1987). Rather, it is to *appropriate* them, to enact what the social anthropologist Alfred Gell has called the 'incorporation of consumer goods into the definition of the social self' (1986: 112). This does not mean that acts of consumption are free of all social constraints. People's cultural choices are shaped by many economic and ideological determinants—for instance the amount of disposable income they have, what sort of area they live in, their level of education, social pressures to be like others. Michel de Certeau remarked pointedly, with reference to the research he and his colleagues conducted in Lyons in the 1970s, that in acts of cultural consumption the same person can be at one and the same time dominated *and* an appropriator of meanings. As he put it, 'the immigrant worker, seated in front of the television pictures, does not have the same amount of space in which to criticize or create as the French middle manager' (1980: p. xliii).

The narrower and broader senses of the term 'cultural consumption' are linked to one another in that both involve the display of *taste*. Another influential writer on cultural consumption, Pierre Bourdieu, has argued that 'taste in the sense of "the faculty of immediately and intuitively judging aesthetic values" is inseparable from taste in the sense of the capacity to discern the flavours of foods which implies a preference for some of them' (1988: 99). In each case the consumer expresses a 'disposition' or preference for one object rather than another and appropriates that object, or a part of it, giving it a function in reproducing or extending himself or herself. For Bourdieu, one of the most important functions of cultural consumption is to mark out one's social territory, to effect *distinctions* between oneself and others. By displaying my preference for a piece of experimental avant-garde music over the Blue Danube waltz I show what kind of person I am and mark myself off from others, just as I do when I choose a designer salad rather than a cream cake off the menu. 'One only has to remove the magical barrier which makes legitimate culture into a separate universe, in order to see intelligible relationships between choices as seemingly incommensurable as preferences in music or cooking, sport or politics, literature or hairstyle.' (1988: 100)

The phenomenon of the *paninari* in the mid-1980s can be used to illustrate all these various points about cultural consumption and introduce a historical approach to it in Italy. The name was used as a self-description by young people, aged between 13 and 18, who socialized in fast food restaurants and bars (the name came from the Bar Panino in Piazzale Liberty, Milan), had a clearly defined dress code (Armani or Rifle jeans, Levi waistcoats, Moncler anoraks, Timberland shoes, Ray-Ban sunglasses, ponytails for the girls), went around on Vespas or small motorcycles, and shared an elaborate invented slang. Clearly, these teenagers were consuming a set of carefully chosen signs (food, drink, clothes, transport), appropriating and combining them in order to make a distinctive discourse of their own, and using this discourse both to define themselves and to mark off their symbolic territory against out-groups, notably their parents and their less stylish peers. They proved to be a fairly short-lasting phenomenon but they showed how far and in what direction Italy's 'consumer society' had travelled by the 1980s (see the illustration and discussion of the *paninari* in the 'Analysis' section below, pp. 344–6). Such a phenomenon would have been inconceivable in Italy twenty-five years earlier. Forty years earlier it would have been meaningless to speak of 'teenagers' at all, in the sense that this term, imported from North America in the 1950s, had of a culturally distinctive age group with its own tastes, styles, and spending money.

Recent histories of post-war Italy have tended to support the view that the watershed years in the history of consumption were those of the late 1950s boom and the economic miracle of 1958–63 (Ginsborg 1990: 239–40; Lanaro 1992: 252–63). It was at that time that wages, kept low for most of the 1950s, started to rise enough for many working-class families to afford cars, white goods like refrigerators and washing machines, meat in their daily diet, and annual holidays at the seaside or in the mountains. During the 1960s many Italian homes were internally modernized or built in a new style: the old *tinello* (kitchen diner) with wooden furniture was replaced by the *soggiorno-pranzo* modelled on the American living-room with polyurethane armchairs; the kitchen was reduced from an eating and living area to a small functional space, as had been seen in American television shows; the bathroom with tiles and mirror replaced the old lavatory out on the balcony (Lanaro 1992: 228). This view of the years of the economic miracle as a 'great transformation' is essentially correct, but it has tended to obscure three things: first, the extent to which patterns of consumption were *already changing* in the first post-war decade, or even earlier; secondly, the *nature* of the 'great transformation' itself; thirdly, the equally important transformations that have come *afterwards*, particularly since 1980. In the remainder of this chapter I shall review patterns of consumption in the post-war period and deal in turn with these three points.

Consumption up to the 1950s

It is actually quite hard to determine exactly when the 'consumer society' started to emerge in Italy. Already in a film of 1954, *Un americano a Roma*, a screwball satire on Americanization directed by Steno (pseudonym of Stefano Vanzina), one has a representation of something resembling it as well as of the new phenomenon of the 'teenager'. Alberto Sordi plays Nando Mericone, a young man living with his parents in the Trastevere district of Rome, who is enthusiastically American in his cultural consumptions and tastes, from films (westerns), dress (T-shirt, jeans, and sneakers), bedroom decorations (Betty Grable pin-ups, a baseball bat, pennants), talking (a pseudo-American babble), and eating (returning home late from the cinema, he pushes aside the spaghetti and wine his mother has left out for him and makes himself an 'American' meal of bread, mustard, jam, yogurt, and milk; this proves so disgusting he goes back to the spaghetti). This fictional film registers, even as it exaggerates and parodies it, the strong influence of American styles on consumption in Italy after the Second World War. A number of factors may explain this influence. On the 'supply side' one can point to the presence of US armed forces in the country from 1943, the aggressive marketing of American films in Italy when the Monopoly Law of 1938 (which had had the effect of drastically limiting their number) was rescinded in 1945, the American aid programme to assist Italy's post-war recovery, and the massive propaganda effort which, from 1948, accompanied both this programme and the campaign against the left (see Ellwood 1985 and Harper 1986). On the 'demand side' one can cite the rapid post-war expansion both of radio licences—from 1.6 to 5.6 million between 1945 and 1955 (ISTAT 1986: 99)—and of film audiences in smaller towns and villages that had been without cinemas before the war. In an influential article, Stephen Gundle has argued (1986: 591) that Italy was more receptive than other European countries in the 1950s to cultural imports from America because of the inherited structural disequilibria in its economy (limited industrial base, persistence of traditional agriculture) combined with a very fast rate of growth after 1951 and the absence of a strong national cultural tradition at the popular level. This weakened the potential for filtering and mediating what was imported.

One needs to go back even further than the 1940s and 1950s to trace the beginnings of American influence and the first signs of an Italian consumer culture. Hollywood films had predominated in Italian cinemas from the early 1920s to the Monopoly Law, and American comic strips and dance music had likewise circulated in the towns until an embargo in 1940–3. As for consumer culture, Victoria de Grazia has argued that it began to pervade the urban middle and lower middle classes in the 1930s, under Fascism, as department stores (*grandi magazzini*) belonging to chains like La Rinascente and the more downmarket Standa and Upim multiplied in the major cities (1992: 203) and women in particular started to be targeted through magazines as consumers of a range of products from clothes to home furnishings (1992: 226–7). There is also evidence of newer kinds of cultural consumption starting to create a differentiation between generations (and hence a 'youth culture' of a sort) in the urban working classes in the latter part of the Fascist period. The young people in Vasco Pratolini's novel *Il quartiere* (written in 1943 but set in the Santa Croce district of Florence in 1932–6) reproduce some of their parents' cultural consumptions and norms (at 15 or 16 the boys can wear long trousers and brilliantine and the girls high heels and cologne) but their sites and forms of socialization are starting to become distinct (an *espresso* coffee in the bar for the young men as opposed to their fathers' card games in the *osteria*, mixed dancing to gramophone records in a married friend's home) and they are more open to the new Fascist values (the narrator wants to volunteer for the Abyssinian War, to his father's disapproval). At the end of the novel the *quartiere* itself is

physically transformed by a rebuilding progamme. In Turin, oral accounts collected by Maurizio Gribaudi from two generations of working-class families who
had lived in the Borgo San Paolo district before 1945 show that Fascism had begun
to attract some of the younger generation in the 1930s with its modernizing
image—exemplified by its emphasis on sport and physical fitness and its rationalist
design styles. This appealed to them more than the 'old' values of socialism and
working-class community upheld by their parents (Gribaudi 1987: 152–4).

It is almost certain that cultural changes like these did not extend much beyond
the cities and larger provincial towns until after the Second World War. In the
1930s and early 1940s, when nearly half Italy's working population still earned its
living from agriculture, the nascent consumer culture was almost exclusively an
urban phenomenon and whole areas of the country, and whole social groups,
remained unaffected by it. Carlo Levi's famous memoir of his internal exile in
1935–6 in a village in the province of Matera (Basilicata), *Cristo si è fermato a Eboli*
(published in 1945), may be taken as one piece of evidence for this, even when one
removes the romanticizing and dehistoricizing filters through which the northerner
Levi sees the culture of the 'primitive' and 'timeless' Southern community (for a
good discussion of both these aspects of Levi's book, see De Martino 1955). Other
evidence is provided not only by many other narratives written in the same period
dealing with poor rural areas—Silone's *Fontamara* (1930) for Abruzzo, Alvaro's
Gente in Aspromonte (1930) for Calabria, Vittorini's *Conversazione in Sicilia* (1938–9)
for Sicily, Pavese's *Paesi tuoi* (1941) for Piedmont—but also by statistics on rates of
literacy, average school-leaving ages, and family budgets and on the supply of
cultural goods, from cinemas to radio sets to books. All show persistent variations
in the quantity and type of cultural consumption between large cities, main
provincial towns, and rural areas, and between the regions of the North and
Centre on the one hand and those of the mainland South and Islands on the
other. This highly varied social geography of cultural skills, competences, and
consumptions is just one indicator among many (others include income, diet,
average life expectancy) of the high degree of inequality between regions and
classes in Italy, an inequality which started to flatten out in the late 1950s but
which persists today.

And yet, just a few years after the end of the Second World War, signs of
cultural change were starting to be detected in many of these rural areas too. In
1952 a delegation of the Parliamentary Commission of Inquiry into Poverty visited
the province of Matera and found that, although the extreme poverty, malnutrition
and ill health described by Carlo Levi had diminished little, educational initiatives
had cut illiteracy from 40 per cent to 20 per cent since 1945 (Camera dei Deputati
1953: 230). In 1957, three sociologists conducted interviews with 200 people in
Ragusa in southern Sicily, a province which in 1952 had been selected by the same
Parliamentary Commission as one of Italy's 'depressed areas'. The sociologists
found continuity between generations in the traditional roles assigned to women
and the separation between the sexes in patterns of socialization—the young

women, like their mothers before they were married, stayed indoors or visited each others' houses to play cards or walked out in groups under the gaze of the men; the young men, like their fathers, stood watching or went to cafés or the branch headquarters of a political party to play cards or billiards. And yet they recorded the older generation in Ragusa describing the situation as one of change:

the inhabitants often point out that Ragusa has become, as far as free time is concerned, an immoral and corrupt town: 'people have more vices', 'young people have more vices', 'there is immorality and corruption', 'there is more freedom and corruption in the way people enjoy themselves'.

By contrast, 'customs were more rigid in the past', 'women and young people did not have so much freedom'. . . . A housewife admitted that there had been a change in customs among students: 'now they call each other "tu" and stop and talk if they meet.' (Anfossi, Talamo, and Indovina 1959: 164–5)

Across the Straits of Messina, the region of Calabria presented a similar picture of both continuity and transition in this period. It too was one of the poorest areas of Italy and, according to the official notions of the time, one of the most culturally 'deprived'. In the 1951 census it had the highest rate of illiteracy in the country (32 per cent of the population over the age of 6, whereas the rate in Piedmont and Lombardy was 3 per cent) and according to a survey of 1958 nearly 40 per cent of *comuni* in the region had no cinema, 30 per cent of people interviewed said they had no 'pastimes' (i.e. free-time activities) on working days, and nearly 60 per cent said they never read, never listened to the radio, never went to the cinema, and never watched television. Nevertheless, the breakdown by generations in the same survey revealed that 26 per cent of young people aged 16–25 had been to the cinema the Sunday before and 29 per cent had watched television, whereas the figures for the over 45s (called 'anziani' in the survey) were respectively 8.6 per cent and 14 per cent (SIAE 1960: p. ix). In fact, between 1952 and 1958 Calabria had among the fastest rates of growth in expenditure on cinema, sport, and radio; this growth outstripped growth both in income and in expenditure on necessities (SIAE 1960: p. iii). In relation to its own past, in other words, Calabria was changing rapidly in the 1950s.

The decade after the Second World War needs to be revalued, then, as a distinctive period in which, despite the relatively low wages and consumer spending compared with the 1960s, changes in cultural consumption were visible all over the country. In addition to radio-listening and cinema-going, both of which had their golden age in 1945–55, there was an increase in the popularity of spectator sports—particularly tour cycling and football (see Lanaro 1992: 198–9)—and a rapid growth in magazine readership. A number of new illustrated weeklies were launched after the war, including *Epoca, Gente,* and *Oggi,* as well as a wholly new type of picture magazine, the *fotoromanzo.* By 1952 the total circulation of all weekly magazines had reached 12.6 million, over three times the total circulation of the daily press (Asor Rosa 1981: 1237). One needs to see in these changes not just a series of parallel developments of separate media and related consumptions but the emergence of a new 'media system' in which a 'synergetic' relationship— in other words one of partial overlap and mutual reinforcement—obtains between different media and qualitatively new forms of consumption become visible. For example, radio coverage and cinema newsreels brought cycle races and football matches to the new rural audiences that had developed for these media after the war. Illustrated weeklies, with their photographic features on current affairs, travel, film, and fashion, were an extension of print journalism into pictures and of cinema newsreels into print, and they fed a growing curiosity for information about the wider world after the restrictions imposed in the Fascist era. *Fotoromanzi* such as *Grand Hotel* (first issue 1946) and *Bolero Film* (first issue 1947) transferred the story-telling conventions of the cinema (sequences of shots, with long shots, close-ups, and so forth) to the panel-by-panel ones of the comic strip (on *fotoromanzi* see Spinazzola 1985 and Abruzzese 1989).

In qualitative terms, one can find in this period, in interplay with these widely circulating cultural forms and signs and in spite of the repressive official Catholicism, changes in sexual attitudes and norms, a greater freedom in dress codes and language (with slightly more sexual licence and greater intimacy), increased mobility within urban areas (assisted by sales of the motor scooter: the Vespa, on the market from 1946, and the Lambretta) and a consequently increased permeability of the city centre for inhabitants of the old *quartieri popolari* and of the new high-rise blocks of the *periferia*. By the end of the 1950s, new forms of youth rebelliousness were emerging which may be linked to these processes. Simonetta Piccone Stella has suggested (1994) that the incidents of *teppismo* ('hooliganism' or juvenile delinquency) which accompanied the economic miracle were symptoms at once of the disorientation produced by the slackening of traditional ties and of the formation of a separate youth identity, particularly among young men. These acts combined expressions of powerlessness and frustration ('gratutious' vandalism) with assertions of power over victim groups (beating up homosexuals) and exhibitionist displays (noise, smashing street lamps).

The 'Great Transformation'

The media system described above and the patterns of consumption associated with it were modified in the second half of the 1950s. A central element in this process was the rise of television. Regular transmissions began in Italy on 3 January 1954 and, even though broadcasts did not cover the whole of the country before 1957 and there was only one channel until 1961, many accounts show the new medium captivating audiences from very early on. Just as with radio in its early years (regular radio transmissions had started in 1924), those who could not afford their own set and the licence fee went to the house of a friend or relative or to a public place where a set had been installed, such as the bar, restaurant, or

Fig. 27 The *fotoromanzo* developed in the late 1940s and it adapted two of the basic narrative codes of the sound film—shots and dialogue—to those of the comic strip: the panel (*tavola*) and the speech-bubble (*nuvoletta*). Some stories were actual 'reductions' of current feature films; others were made directly as photoromances, sometimes by established film directors, such as Damiano Damiani. The genre was parodied by Fellini in his film *Lo sceicco bianco* (*The White Sheik*, 1952), a comic reworking of the *Madame Bovary* plot in which a bored young bride on her honeymoon in Rome briefly lives out her infatuation with a vain star of photoromances played by Alberto Sordi.

working people's recreation centre (*dopolavoro*). A survey of February–March 1955 found that for every one person viewing in their own home, there were three viewing in the homes of friends or relatives and nine viewing in public places (Monteleone 1992: 283; for some contemporary accounts of collective viewing in rural areas, see Calamandrei (1959) for Tuscany in 1957 and Anfossi (1968) for Sardinia in 1960). An early quiz show, *Campanile sera*, used outside broadcast units for a knockout competition involving towns from all over Italy which generated enormous enthusiasm. As one former participant has described the atmosphere in Mondovì (Piedmont) in 1959: 'for weeks you thought of nothing else, as you waited and got ready for that Thursday evening with the town square bubbling over with excitement, stress, and shouting' (Beccaria 1985: 147). In other words television, which according to Tullio De Mauro (1979: 124–6) was greatly to assist the tendency towards a common Italian language and was the first cultural form in Italy to become nearly universal in its national coverage—by 1993 an estimated 99.5 per cent of families had at least one television set, with negligible variations between regions (Auditel 1993: 1)—also drew in its early years on local rivalries and traditions. In the province of Naples the most popular programmes in 1956 after the quiz show *Lascia o raddoppia?* (seen by over 600,000 adults or nearly half the resident population) were those which featured Neapolitan actors ('Lui e lei' with Nino Taranto had an audience of 500,000; nearly as many watched the 'Festival della canzone napoletana') and the most popular genres after the quiz were the revue and variety (RAI 1957).

As these examples suggest, changes in cultural consumption, such as that brought about by the advent of television, do not work by a simple displacement or eradication of the old by the new but tend to involve a series of adaptations of existing patterns and rituals. The group listening and viewing, the local enthusiasms and loyalties, were extensions of forms of collective activity that were already established in these communities. It was not a simple case of television 'pushing out' their old ways of doing things. They also incorporated television within what was familiar. A similar point may be made about the television schedules themselves, which in the early years were as much shaped by the Italian humanistic high-cultural and Catholic traditions promoted and defended by the RAI as they were influenced by US and other models of popular television (see Bettetini 1985: 14–15; Mancini 1987: 138). This is worth stressing because even before the rise of the private networks there were some very influential accounts (for instance that of Pasolini 1975: 58–9) which portrayed television as not just the symbol but one of the principal agents of the 'great transformation' in cultural consumption, as aiding the erosion of cultural differences between localities and classes and the triumph of consumerism and acquisitiveness.

The point may be extended from television consumption to cultural consumption as a whole in the years of transformation: older practices were not necessarily 'pushed out' by new ones but could continue alongside them for a long time. In the life story which Giuseppe Nigro, the Communist secretary of the Camera del

Lavoro in Melissa (Calabria), recounted to Francesco Faeta in the 1970s, one finds a complex cultural repertoire. Born in 1921, he experienced army service during the Second World War, political radicalization and militancy (his brother was one of those killed by the police in the massacre of peasant protesters at Melissa in 1949), and emigration to West Germany as a factory worker in the years of the miracle. Yet alongside his Communist values there were elements of attachment to the 'traditional' practices and beliefs of his community of origin (he practised cartomancy and believed in various kinds of magical healing), just as in the community as a whole, depopulated by emigration, certain local festivals and ways of celebrating rites of passage such as baptisms, marriages, and funerals persisted alongside motorization and television viewing (Faeta 1979: 66–84). To draw attention to such cases is not to deny that a 'great transformation' happened or that over the long term the old *civiltà contadina* has been broken up and a more urbanized and industrialized culture has taken its place. But these cases do oblige us to refine our historical understanding of how, with what forms and rhythms, the transformation took place and to recognize that notions such as 'eradication', 'displacement', and 'levelling' are inadequate as representations of this more complex process.

Within the media system itself, too, the rise of television was not simply a process of inexorable displacement of the old by the new but one in which transfers, absorptions, and readjustments were made within the system as a whole. Four examples may be used to illustrate this from the consumption end: popular stage entertainments, radio, film, and print media.

Stage entertainments like the variety theatre and the *avanspettacolo* (a short show which used to precede the screening of a film in some cinemas) were already in crisis before television came along in 1954. We know this both from statistics of their box-office receipts (these show variety audiences in Naples and some other Southern cities holding up relatively well but those in other cities declining fast) and from other kinds of evidence, such as Monicelli and Steno's film *Vita da cani* and Lattuada and Fellini's *Luci del varietà* (both released in 1950) which show travelling variety companies fallen on hard times. The decline of variety before the 1950s is probably attributable in part to cinema and then radio having already taken over some of its acts and performers (Ettore Petrolini and Totò are among the best-known examples of variety artists transferring successfully to cinema); but it may also reflect the changing consumptions and tastes of the younger generations in the cities, mentioned earlier, some of whom abandoned variety for the billiard hall, dance hall, cinema, and bar. Television, in turn, took over some of the variety acts which had become a mainstay of early 1950s radio scheduling. So it did contribute to displacing the variety theatre, but it also partially absorbed it, as cinema and radio had done before. As for live theatrical and musical performances in general, television appears to have exerted a competitive pull away from them at first, but they have subsequently regained audiences (see Table 15.1).

Radio too lost audiences to television, and never got them back, at any rate not

Table 15.1. Theatre/music and cinema ticket sales, radio and television licences, 1941–1981

	Theatre and music tickets (thousands)	Cinema tickets (thousands)	Radio only licences	Television plus radio licences
1941	16,041	423,978	1,638,317	
1946	n/a	n/a	1,850,479	
1951	19,390	696,740	3,682,588	
1956	14,768	790,152	5,862,226	366,151
1961	10,050	741,019	5,726,122	2,761,738
1966	12,527	631,957	4,196,187	6,855,298
1971	14,104	535,733	1,506,342	10,344,145
1976	19,440	454,501	647,389	12,376,612
1981	26,571	215,150	402,158	13,645,043

Source: ISTAT 1986: 99.

for the number of hours a day they had devoted to it in the early 1950s. But radio survived in the television era both because of changes in its schedules and because its functions for consumers and their modes of consuming it changed. In 1950 a typical radio-owning household had one set, located in the kitchen or the main room, which families would listen to together, for instance at mealtimes, with the mid- to late evening constituting peak listening time (advertisers' 'prime time'). The most popular genres, apart from news and music, were light entertainments like variety and revue. By 1980 all these characteristics had been taken over by television, and the times, places, and styles of radio-listening had shifted. It was now typically done in briefer snatches, in cars (so that radio's prime time became commuter 'drive time') or in other parts of the house such as bathrooms or children's bedrooms (Fenati 1994: 59; Ortoleva 1986: 319). The structure and content of radio schedules were slower to adapt, but they did so eventually (Monteleone 1994: 176–7) and from the mid-1970s they were radically revised with the advent of commercial and free radio stations (*radio libere* or *radio popolari*: 'free' in the sense both of non state-controlled and counter-cultural). Technological innovations played a part in all this, notably transistorization in the 1960s, which led to the mass availability of cheap car radios and to the portable set with earplug or headphones becoming a wearable item.

Film followed a similar pattern for different reasons. The film industry lost cinema audiences to television from the mid-1950s (see Table 15.1) as people with sets stayed at home more and went to the cinema less, but in the long term it regained audiences by selling films to the television companies. By the end of the 1970s large numbers of films, including recent ones, were being consumed on television: the buying and scheduling of recent films was, with that of imported serials, the principal arena of competition between the RAI and the private networks. In addition, the home videocassette recorder (VCR), sales of which rose rapidly in the 1980s, provided a new way of using the television set to watch films.

The home video market expanded later in Italy than in the UK but it has been boosted in the 1990s by the mushrooming of retail points for prerecorded cassettes, from supermarkets and department stores to record stores and newsstands (*edicole*). Between 1988 and 1992 the number of prerecorded videocassettes sold direct to the public in Italy rose from 744,000 to 12.4 million, while the number sold to rental outlets fell (ISTAT 1994: 150). In the end, therefore, the film companies have recouped the audiences they had lost in cinemas by selling their films to the television companies and on home video. The RAI channels alone showed 830 feature films in 1984, a sevenfold increase over 1974. By the late 1980s, with cinema audiences still declining, television and video had become the film industry's most lucrative distribution outlet for feature films (see Austin 1990).

Print media, finally, have not been displaced overall by the rise of television, despite what is sometimes believed. In Italy the total readership of books, magazines, and newspapers has increased markedly since 1954. However, television has certainly *modified* the nature of the print media—for instance the immediacy of television news has meant that newspapers, no longer able to compete in this area, have increased their in-depth news commentaries and features pages—and it has probably been responsible for the decline of some individual genres and publications. Marino Livolsi has suggested (1994: 530–1) that the 'neo-television' which began around 1980—the expression, coined by Umberto Eco (1983), refers to the new multi-channel television with a high entertainment content—has contributed to the declining popularity of *fotoromanzi* like *Grand Hotel*, whose circulation fell from nearly 900,000 in 1976 to 400, 000 in 1992, because their functions have been taken over by romantic television fictions, such as the US soap operas and the *telenovelas* imported from Latin America.

Trends since the Late 1970s

In establishing its predominance as the cultural form to which Italians on average devote most of their time—2.8 hours a day in 1987–8 (ISTAT 1993b: 223)—television has contributed to a trend towards *home-based leisure*, a trend which was detected in Italy as early as 1966 (SIAE 1967: 10) and which has been clearly visible in all the industrialized countries since the 1970s. A number of factors have been invoked to explain this and it is difficult to say which of them, if any, is preponderant: the cheapness of television compared with other forms of entertainment; the post-1973 'oil crisis' and recession which squeezed consumer spending and made people go out less (in Italy there were restrictions on the use of cars and selective closures of places of public entertainment to save energy costs); the increased supply of television programmes (in Italy this began with the end of the RAI's monopoly of the airwaves in 1976, which led to a rapid increase in the number of channels and in overall programme hours); the disappearance of a separate 'public sphere' (Habermas 1962; Elliott 1982), that is to say, the decline of forums of public debate and sites of social activity outside the home and at the same time the ever-increasing mediation of social processes by mass communications—a process which Baudrillard has called 'the implosion of the social in the media' (1985). In Italy, additionally, the wave of terrorism in the 1970s, the so-called 'leaden years', is widely regarded as having contributed towards home-based leisure in the cities by producing a curfew mentality. Even before Berlusconi's entry into politics at the beginning of 1994 it had become commonplace to talk of 'neo-television' as saturating social life in Italy and its ubiquitous presence had begun to be satirized in other media, from novels such as Nico Orengo's *Ribes* (1988) to films like Maurizio Nichetti's *Ladri di saponette* (1989) and Nanni Moretti's *Caro diario* (1994).

And yet it is difficult to make empirically verifiable claims about the effects of television on patterns of consumption or on social behaviour in Italy. From the early research which looked pessimistically at the medium's potentially harmful effects on children (e.g. Tarroni 1960) to recent optimistic scenarios in which 'postmodern' viewers construct their own individual narratives out of fragments of programmes with the remote control handset (Curti 1990: 324, 332–4), much writing about television consumption has rested on untested or untestable generalizations. This applies also to claims about the emergent 'rule of television' (*telecrazia* or *videocrazia*) which is supposed both to have ushered in and been reinforced by the electoral success of Forza Italia in March 1994. Berlusconi's rise to political power would doubtless have been impossible without his control of half the nation's television (see Lyttelton 1994: 26) and it rightly brought demands for an urgent revision of the law on media monopolies. But it does not prove that Italy is now ruled by and through television (for critical scrutiny of these claims, see Ortoleva 1994: 147–9).

One also needs to remember that, for all its importance in the emergence of new patterns of cultural consumption in Italy since around 1980, television has not acted alone. If 1980 can be said to have constituted, after the years of the economic miracle, a second watershed in the history of cultural consumption, it is because along with the emergence of 'neo-television' the 1980s also saw a boom in newspaper readership (see Lumley, 'Peculiarities of the Italian Newspaper', Chapter 11 above) and in home video use, as well as developments in information and communication technology, of which the most visible domestic applications to date have been the home VCR, home computer (including video games), teletext systems, 'smart' digital telephone systems, portable cellular telephones (3 million users by 1995), and fax machines. Some of these technologies interface with the television set, forcing it to take time out from the live transmission of programmes, and they have therefore produced a further set of modifications to the media system.

It is equally important to note, however, that the consumption of these technologies has been far from uniform. As in other countries where they have been taken up, new divisions have been created, and old divisions reinforced, between those who can afford them or who have the skills and confidence to use them and

Table 15.2. Average cultural and leisure expenditure by main geographical subdivisions, 1992 (lire)

	North	Centre	South
Education[a]	19,118	12,384	10,158
Books	24,400	25,406	16,447
Newspapers and magazines	33,942	28,715	20,459
Audiovisual hardware and software[b]	22,958	22,130	11,659
Radio and television licences	11,287	9,456	10,155
Cameras[c] and film	12,582	11,435	6,841
Sports and camping goods	2,878	2,766	1,061
Toys	12,921	15,450	15,713
Recreational services	44,457	41,987	19,155
Flowers and plants	18,781	19,041	11,385
TOTAL CULTURAL EXPENDITURE	203,324	188,770	123,033
TOTAL CONSUMER EXPENDITURE	3,031,988	3,093,814	2,465,156
Proportion cultural/total (%)	6.7	6.1	5.0

[a] Fees and other education expenses.
[b] Televisions, radios, hi-fi systems, tapes, discs, etc.
[c] Including movie cameras and camcorders.

Source: ISTAT 1993*a*: 50.

those who do not, between the 'information rich' and the 'information poor', older and younger people, women and men (see e.g. Webster and Robins 1986; Kramarae 1988; Salvaggio 1989; Frissen 1992; and for an Italian discussion of some of these themes, Wolf 1992: 186–9). Indeed, if there is one thread that runs continuously through the history of cultural consumption in Italy—but the same may be said for other societies—it is that its forms are highly unequal. Table 15.2 shows that still in 1992 both real amounts and proportions of average family budgets spent on cultural and leisure goods and services were lower in the South than in the North and Centre. There were big differences in the amounts spent on both books and media hardware. The only items on which expenditure was relatively uniform were radio and television subscriptions and children's toys.

Even the near-universal ownership of television sets should not be read as a sign that all Italians now 'share' at least one form of cultural consumption. Applying Certeau's remark about France quoted earlier and Bourdieu's point about the unequal social determinants of cultural 'dispositions' and tastes, one might point out that for a Milanese middle manager television is just one cultural consumption among many in a repertoire which is likely to include opera, cinema, meals in restaurants, and novel-reading; whereas for an unemployed worker, a busy housewife, or an African immigrant worker in Bari television is probably the only one of these 'free-time' activities on the social agenda. When these different people watch television they may be consuming the same cultural form but they are likely to consume it in different ways, to select different programmes, give them a different kind of attention, watch at different hours, and attach different meanings to what they see. The study of cultural consumption can only have value if it is able to understand these differences, to make sense of acts of consumption *both* in terms of the wider social and spatial inequalities by which they shaped *and* in terms of the meanings they have for the consumers themselves in concrete social situations.

Further Reading

For *theoretical and methodological* orientation in English in the area of cultural consumption the following are highly recommended: Pierre Bourdieu, *Distinction: A Social Critique of the Judgement of Taste*, trans. R. Nice (London, 1984); Michel de Certeau, *The Practice of Everyday Life*, trans. S. Rendall (Berkeley, 1984); Daniel Miller, *Material Culture and Mass Consumption* (Oxford, 1987); Roger Silverstone and Eric Hirsch (eds.), *Consuming Technologies: Media and Information in Domestic Spaces* (London, 1992); Mary Douglas and Baron Isherwood, *The World of Goods: Towards an Anthropology of Consumption* (New York, 1979); M. Csikszentmihalyi and E. Rochberg-Halton, *The Meaning of Things: Domestic Symbols and the Self* (Cambridge, 1981). The work of Jean Baudrillard (see his *Selected Writings*, ed. M. Poster, Cambridge, 1988) is controversial but still rich in insights.

Among the Italian work on media consumption, Mario Morcellini (ed.), *Lo spettacolo del consumo. Televisione e cultura di massa nella legittimazione sociale* (Milan, 1986) and the section 'Analisi del pubblico' in Marino Livolsi and Franco Rositi (eds.), *La ricerca sull'industria culturale. L'emittente, i messaggi, il pubblico* (Rome, 1988), are both recommended. Mauro Wolf's *Gli effetti sociali dei media* (Milan, 1992) provides an excellent introduction to different research methodologies on media effects. For general *historical* accounts of consumption in Italy, see C. D'Apice, *L'arcipelago dei consumi. Consumi e redditi delle famiglie italiane dal dopoguerra a oggi* (Bari, 1981) and M. Ragone, *Consumi e stili di vita in Italia* (Naples, 1985). There are some interesting leads, drawing partly on this material, in Silvio Lanaro's *Storia dell'Italia repubblicana* (Venice, 1992). Long-term consumption trends are also discussed in D. Forgacs, *Italian Culture in the Industrial Era, 1880–1980: Cultural Industries, Politics and the Public* (Manchester, 1990).

On *television* consumption see L. De Rita, *I contadini e la televisione* (Bologna, 1963), S. Acquaviva and G. Eisner, *La montagna del sole* (Turin, 1984), and the already-cited work edited by Morcellini. On *radio* see Gianni Isola, *Abbassa la tua radio, per favore... Storia dell'ascolto radiofonico nell'Italia fascista* (Florence, 1990), Anna Lucia Natale, *Gli anni della radio (1924–1954). Contributo ad una storia sociale dei media in Italia* (Naples, 1990), and two stimulating essays by Peppino Ortoleva: 'La radio e il suo pubblico. Verso una storia degli ascoltatori', in F. Monteleone and P. Ortoleva (eds.), *La radio. Storia di sessant'anni* (Turin, 1984), and 'Il tempo della radio. Piccola storia del segnale orario', *Movimento Operaio e Socialista*, 11/2 (1986): 315–20.

On *reading* see S. Piccone Stella and A. Rossi, *La fatica di leggere* (Rome, 1964); G. Battistini, *Cosa leggono gli italiani. Contributo ad una documentazione sui consumi editoriali* (Milan, 1973); M. Livolsi, 'Lettura e altri consumi culturali negli anni '20–'40', in *Editoria e cultura a Milano tra le due guerre (1920–1940). Atti del convegno, Milano 19–21 febbraio 1981* (Milan, 1983), 61–77; M. Livolsi (ed.), *Gli italiani che (non) leggono* (Florence, 1986); and G. Zanoli, *Libri, librai, lettori. Storia sociale del libro e funzione della libreria* (Florence, 1989).

On *film* consumption, see M. Livolsi, 'Chi va al cinema?' in M. Livolsi (ed.), *Schermi e ombre. Gli italiani e il cinema nel dopoguerra* (Florence, 1988); and G. P. Brunetta, *Buio in sala. Cent'anni di passioni dello spettatore cinematografico* (Venice, 1989).

The most comprehensive *statistical sources* for trends in cultural expenditure are *Lo spettacolo in Italia* published annually since the 1930s (but with gaps in some of the war years) by the Società Italiana degli Autori ed Editori (SIAE, Viale della Letteratura 30, EUR, 00100 Roma); and the *Statistiche culturali*, published annually by the Istituto Centrale di Statistica (ISTAT, Centro Diffusione, Via Cesare Balbo 11a, 00184 Roma), which incorporate summaries of most of the SIAE figures. The SIAE yearbooks give totals of various types of cultural expenditure in great detail geographically, and with these figures one can see the synchronic differences between provinces as well as between the provincial capital (*capoluogo*) and the rest of the province. One can therefore chart diachronic change both nationally and province by province. ISTAT also publishes annual family budgets (*Bilanci delle famiglie* or *Consumi delle famiglie*) which since the 1970s have indicated by region, family size, and socio-economic class of main breadwinner the proportions of expenditure on 'cultural goods'. Another useful source is ISTAT's *Indagine multiscopo sulle famiglie. Anni 1987–91*, in particular for this theme vol. vii, *Letture, mass media, linguaggio* (Rome, 1993).

For individual media, statistics for *book production* (numbers of *titles*, broken down by type, e.g. literature, science, not numbers of *copies* printed or sold) are collected and published annually by the Biblioteca Nazionale Centrale di Firenze in the *Bollettino delle pubblicazioni italiane ricevute per diritto di stampa*. *Newspaper and magazine* circulation figures are published monthly in the magazine *Prima comunicazione*. *Radio* subscriptions have been collected since 1924 and *television* subscriptions (licences) since 1954 by the RAI (until 1944, EIAR). Detailed figures for the previous year, province by province, are published annually by the RAI in *Gli abbonamenti alla televisione*, each issue of which contains a historical summary of figures since regular broadcasts began. National totals of these figures are also included in the SIAE and ISTAT yearbooks. However, since a large number of people evade the licence fee, these figures need to be adjusted upwards to give actual numbers of viewing households. In 1993 the audience research agency AGB Auditel s.r.l. (Via Larga 13, 20122 Milano) estimated that 99.5 per cent of all Italian households owned and used at least one television set—20 per cent more than the proportion of paid-up subscribers (Auditel 1993: 1). Auditel uses electronic 'peoplemeters' to monitor which programmes are logged in, and out of at what times, by individual members of a large sample of households across the country. A daily table of these figures is provided on-line to subscribers, including the RAI and Fininvest. Auditel also publishes mean audience figures for each month and year. For a discussion of the techniques of audience metering see R. Kent (ed.), *Measuring Media Audiences* (London, 1994). For a critical discussion of the limitations of these types of audience survey, see David Morley, 'Behind the Ratings: The Politics of Audience Research', in J. Willis and T. Wollen (eds.), *The Neglected Audience* (London, 1990), 5–14, and Ien Ang, *Desperately Seeking the Audience* (London, 1991). Both Morley and Ang offer alternative approaches to audience research, as does James Lull, *Inside Family Viewing: Ethnographic Research on Television's Audiences* (London, 1990).

There are in addition many informal and indirect sources on cultural consumption, including numerous memoirs, collections of letters, autobiographies, oral histories, novels, and films, some of which are mentioned in this chapter, and which are often extremely valuable both for factual information and for the qualitative dimension. An interesting photographic sourcebook is C. Colombo (ed.), *Tra sogno e bisogno. 306 fotografie sull'evoluzione dei consumi in Italia 1940–1986* (Milan, 1986).

References

ABRUZZESE, A. (1989), 'Fotoromanzo', in *Letteratura italiana. Storia e geografia*, iii. *L'età contemporanea* (Turin), 1269–87.

ANFOSSI, A. (1968), *Socialità e organizzazione in Sardegna. Studio sulla zona di Oristano-Bosa-Macomer* (Milan).

—— TALAMO, M., and INDOVINA, F. (1959), *Ragusa. Comunità in transizione. Saggio sociologico* (Turin).

APPADURAI, A. (1986) (ed.), *The Social Life of Things: Commodities in a Cultural Perspective* (Cambridge).

Asor Rosa, A. (1981), 'Il giornalista: appunti sulla fisiologia di un mestiere difficile', in C. Vivanti (ed.), *Storia d'Italia. Annali*, iv. *Intellettuali e potere* (Turin), 1225–57.

Auditel (1993), *Audience televisive in Italia. Ricerca di base continuativa 1993. Il parco televisivo in Italia: possesso, utilizzo e caratteristiche del TV set* (Milan).

Austin, B. A. (1990), 'Home Video: The Second-Run "Theater" of the 1990s', in T. Balio (ed.), *Hollywood in the Age of Television* (London).

Baranski, Z. G., and Lumley, R. (1990) (eds.), *Culture and Conflict in Postwar Italy* (Basingstoke and London).

Baudrillard, J. (1985), 'The Masses: The Implosion of the Social in the Media', trans. M. Maclean, *New Literary History*, 16/3: 577–89.

—— (1988), 'The System of Objects', trans. J. Mourrain, in *Selected Writings*, ed. M. Poster (Cambridge).

Beccaria, G. L. (1985), 'Campanile... c'era', in Fondazione G. Agnelli (1985), 147–51.

Bettetini, G. (1985), 'Un "fare" italiano nella televisione', in Fondazione G. Agnelli (1985), 11–21.

Bourdieu, P. (1979), *Distinction: A Social Critique of the Judgement of Taste*, trans. R. Nice (London, 1984).

Calamandrei, M. (1959), 'La città in campagna', *L'Espresso*, 25 Jan.: 12–13.

Camera dei Deputati (1953), *Atti della Commissione Parlamentare di inchiesta sulla miseria in Italia e sui mezzi per combatterla*, vii. *Indagini delle delegazioni parlamentari. La miseria in alcune zone depresse* (Rome).

Castronovo, V., and Tranfaglia, N. (1994), *La stampa italiana nell'età della TV, 1975–1994* (Rome and Bari).

Certeau, M. de (1980), *L'Invention du quotidien*, i. *Arts de faire* (Paris, 1990).

Curti, L. (1990), 'Imported Utopias', in Baranski and Lumley (1990), 320–36.

de Grazia, V. (1992), *How Fascism Ruled Women: Italy, 1922–1945* (Berkeley).

De Martino, E. (1955), 'Intorno a una polemica [Intellettuali e Mezzogiorno]' (originally published in *Nuovi Argomenti*, 12), in *Mondo popolare e magia in Lucania* (Rome and Matera, 1975).

De Mauro, T. (1979), *Storia linguistica dell'Italia unita* (Rome and Bari).

Eco, U. (1983), 'A Guide to the Neo-Television of the 1980s' (originally published in *L'Espresso*, 30 Jan.), trans. R. Lumley, in Baranski and Lumley (1990), 245–55.

Elliott, P. (1982), 'Intellectuals, the "Information Society" and the Disappearance of the Public Sphere', in R. Collins, J. Curran, N. Garnham, P. Scannell, P. Schlesinger, and C. Sparks (eds.), *Media, Culture and Society: A Critical Reader* (London, 1986), 105–15.

Ellwood, D. (1985), 'From "Re-Education" to the Selling of the Marshall Plan in Italy', in N. Pronay (ed.), *The Political Re-Education of Germany and her Allies* (London), 219–39.

Faeta, F. (1979), *Melissa. Folklore, lotta di classe e modificazioni culturali in una comunità contadina meridionale* (Florence).

Fenati, B. (1994), 'Stili di consumo radiofonico', in F. Monteleone (ed.), *La radio che non c'è. Settant'anni, un grande futuro* (Rome), 51–63.

Fondazione G. Agnelli (1985), *Televisione: la provvisoria identità italiana* (Turin).

Frissen, V. (1992), 'Trapped in Electronic Cages? Gender and New Information Technologies in the Public and Private Domain', *Media, Culture and Society*, 14: 31–49.

Gell, A. (1986), 'Newcomers to the World of Goods: Consumption among the Muria Gonds', in Appadurai (1986) 110–38.

Ginsborg, P. (1990), *A History of Contemporary Italy: Society and Politics 1943–1988* (Harmondsworth).

Gribaudi, M. (1987), *Mondo operaio e mito operaio. Spazi e percorsi sociali a Torino nel primo Novecento* (Turin).

Grimaldi, F. (1977) 'I mezzi di comunicazione di massa e i giovani del Borghetto Latino', in B. Barbalato (ed.), *Mass-media e processi di trasformazione culturale in alcune borgate romane* (Rome).

GUNDLE, S. (1986), 'L'americanizzazione del quotidiano: televisione e consumismo nell'Italia degli anni cinquanta', *Quaderni Storici*, 21/62: 561–94.

HABERMAS, J. (1962), *The Structural Transformation of the Public Sphere*, trans. T. Burger and F. Lawrence (Cambridge, 1989).

HARPER, J. L. (1986), *America and the Reconstruction of Italy, 1945–1948* (Cambridge).

ISTAT (1986): Istituto Centrale di Statistica, *Sommario di statistiche storiche, 1926–1985* (Rome).

—— (1993a), *I consumi delle famiglie. Anno 1992* (Collana d'informazione, no. 24) (Rome).

—— (1993b), *Indagine multiscopo sulle famiglie. Anni 1987–91*, vii. *Letture, mass media, linguaggio* (Rome).

—— (1994), *Statistiche culturali. Anno 1992* (Annuario, no. 34) (Rome).

KRAMARAE, C. (1988) (ed.), *Technology and Women's Voices: Keeping in Touch* (London).

LANARO, S. (1992), *Storia della Repubblica italiana. Dalla fine della guerra agli anni novanta* (Venice).

LIVOLSI, M. (1994), 'I lettori della stampa quotidiana e periodica (1972–1992)', in Castronovo and Tranfaglia (1994), 521–46.

LUMLEY, R. (1990), *States of Emergency: Cultures of Revolt in Italy from 1968 to 1978* (London).

LYTTELTON, A. (1994), 'Italy: The Triumph of TV', *New York Review of Books*, 11 August: 25–9.

MANCINI, P. (1987), 'Between Normative Research and Theory of Forms and Content: Italian Studies on Mass Communication', *Mass Communication Review Yearbook*, 6: 135–53.

MILLER, D. (1987), *Material Culture and Mass Consumption* (Oxford).

MONTELEONE, F. (1992), *Storia della radio e della televisione in Italia. Società, politica, strategie, programmi 1922–1992* (Venice).

—— (1994), 'Radio pubblica ed emittenti commerciali dal 1975 al 1993', in Castronovo and Tranfaglia (1994), 175–206.

ORTOLEVA, P. (1986), 'Il tempo della radio. Piccola storia del segnale orario', *Movimento Operaio e Socialista*, 9/2: 315–20.

—— (1994), 'La televisione tra due crisi, 1975–1993', in Castronovo and Tranfaglia (1994), 85–149.

PASOLINI, P. P. (1975), *Scritti corsari* (Milan).

PICCONE STELLA, S. (1994), '"Rebels without a Cause": Male Youth in Italy around 1960', *History Workshop Journal*, 38 (autumn): 157–78.

RAI (1957): Radiotelevisione italiana, 'Ascolto delle trasmissioni e interesse per i vari generi nella provincia di Napoli', in *La televisione e il suo pubblico* (Turin).

SALVAGGIO, J. L. (1989) (ed.), *The Information Society: Economic, Social and Structural Issues* (Hillsdale, NJ).

SIAE (1960): Società Italiana degli Autori ed Editori, *Impiego del tempo libero in Calabria. Indagine statistica campionaria* (Rome).

—— (1967), *Lo spettacolo in Italia. Statistiche 1966* (Rome).

SPINAZZOLA, V. (1985), 'Da "Grand Hotel" a"Diabolik"', in V. Spinazzola (ed.), *Il successo letterario* (Milan).

TARRONI, E. (1960), *Ragazzi, radio e televisione* (Bologna).

WEBSTER, F., and ROBINS, K. (1986), *Information Technology: A Luddite Analysis* (Norwood, NJ).

WOLF, M. (1992), *Gli effetti sociali dei media* (Milan).

Cultural Policy

FRANCO
BIANCHINI,
MASSIMO
TORRIGIANI,
AND
RINELLA CERE

Introduction

ITALIAN cultural policy, especially at national level, has been decidedly oriented towards a narrow definition of 'culture', one which encompasses mainly three elements: the arts, heritage, and the media. Since other chapters in this volume deal with literature and the media, we have chosen to focus on policy-making related to the visual and performing arts and to the heritage, covering archaeology, architecture, and art, including galleries and museums.

Given the complexity of the cultural field and of any kind of policy aimed at intervening in it, the chapter does not pretend to be an exhaustive discussion of the topic. Our intention is rather to chart a map and open a discussion. In Italy, especially compared to other European countries like France, the debate about cultural policy has been for insiders, and is found usually only in specialized journals or reports produced by governmental bodies. One of our aims is to begin to open up this issue to a wider audience. A further problem in the literature is the dearth of critical analysis, historical contextualization, and interpretation which relates cultural policies to party political priorities and strategies, to intellectual debates, and to changes in patterns of cultural consumption. However, our impression is that the theoretical poverty and analytical deficiencies which characterize available works on national government cultural policies in Italy may simply reflect the policies themselves. The latter were often developed in response to pressures from particular lobbies and interest groups, and the primary objective of expenditure decisions was in many cases simply to reward political clienteles and exercise patronage.

The collapse after 1992 of the system of power controlled since 1963 by Christian Democrats and Socialists may have produced, perhaps for the first time in the history of the Italian Republic, the conditions for the development of cultural policies more firmly based on intellectual debates, and on the findings of empirical research into trends in cultural production, distribution, and consumption.

Cultural Policy-Making 1943–1994

The Institutional Framework

In cultural policy terms, the transition from the Fascist regime to the Republic was marked by two distinct trends. First, the Republic's politicians showed a will to break with the direct and explicit subordination of culture to centrally decided political and ideological directives, which had been typical of Fascism. This was clearly enshrined in the Constitution of the Republic of 1948, which stated that 'art and science are free, as is their teaching' (Article 33, paragraph 1). One commentator has rightly observed that the Constitution's authors, the Constituent Assembly, wanted to make explicit the 'negation of the ideological-cultural monism inherent in the totalitarian Fascist State' (Merusi, quoted in Palma and Clemente di San Luca 1987: 70). Secondly, and in contradiction with the first trend, policymakers maintained a sense of continuity with the past by administratively linking education policy with cultural policy, defined as a series of measures for the protection of cultural heritage and the provision of support for 'high' cultural forms such as ballet, classical music, opera, theatre, and the visual arts.

The first trend was a reaction to the role played under Fascism by the Ministero della Cultura Popolare (shortened to Minculpop). From its foundation in 1937, Fascist governments used this ministry to attempt to create, through the establishment of a new 'national culture', a broad popular consensus around the political aims of the regime, and to counteract potential opposition among the intellectuals. The Minculpop was in charge of all aspects of policy, including censorship and propaganda, in the fields of film, the performing arts, publishing, and radio.

The second trend had already been established under Fascism by the Ministero dell'Educazione Nazionale, which was in charge not only of education, but also of the conservation of the 'national heritage'. It can be seen as rooted in the Italian tradition of emphasizing the importance of high culture and the heritage in the formation of national consciousness and citizenship. This tradition had begun with Humanism in the fifteenth century, and developed into a programme for political action during the Risorgimento, some of whose ideas inspired the first governments of the Italian Republic.

After the establishment of the Republic in 1946, the division between the responsibilities of the former Minculpop and of the Ministero dell'Educazione Nazionale was maintained. This institutional feature characterized Italian cultural policy-making until the 1990s. The responsibilities of the Minculpop passed after the fall of the Fascist regime to the Presidenza del Consiglio dei Ministri and then in 1959 to the newly established Ministero del Turismo e dello Spettacolo, which absorbed the responsibility for tourism policy previously entrusted to the Commissariat for Tourism. Following a referendum in 1993, the Ministero del Turismo e dello Spettacolo was abolished, and its responsibilities returned to the Presidenza del Consiglio dei Ministri.

The remit of the Ministero della Pubblica Istruzione (Ministry of Education), which inherited the responsibilities of the Fascist Ministry of National Education, included the running of the Direzione delle Antichità e Belle Arti (Directorate for Antiquities and Fine Arts). This Directorate formed the core for the establishment in 1975 of the Ministero dei Beni Culturali e Ambientali (Ministry for Cultural and Environmental Assets). The latter is currently the only department exclusively devoted to cultural matters at central government level. Its responsibilities include artistic and architectural heritage, museums, galleries, the fine arts, archaeological sites, monuments, books and libraries, archives, and publishing. Although it performs this range of complex functions, this ministry has less than 0.5 per cent of the total state budget.

The other government departments in charge of aspects of cultural policy are the Ministero della Pubblica Istruzione, which is responsible for arts teaching and training at all levels; the Ministero degli Affari Esteri (Ministry of Foreign Affairs), responsible for international cultural relations, for running Italian Cultural Institutes in about eighty countries, and promoting Italian culture abroad through events, exhibitions, and other activities; the Ministero delle Poste e Telecomunicazioni, which promotes investment, research, and training in the communications field, regulates the broadcasting system, and supervises the RAI, the state broadcasting corporation; the Ministero dei Lavori Pubblici (Ministry of Public Works), in charge of restoration projects for buildings, monuments, and sites of historic interest, which are carried out under the supervision of the Ministero dei Beni Culturali.

The DC and Aspects of National Cultural Policy-Making from 1945 to the *Centrosinistra*

Central government cultural policy-making in Italy from the early post-war years was characterized by its extreme fragmentation, with responsibilities scattered across different ministries and administrative levels. Italy, unlike France, has never had a unified cultural ministry. This is in part because of continuing unease among post-war politicians and intellectuals with the use of the terms 'culture' and 'popular culture' in a cultural policy context. For instance, most Italian intellectuals have used the term 'mass culture' in preference to 'popular culture'. Such feelings were in part a consequence of the use and abuse of the term in cultural policy-making by the Minculpop. Another feature of state cultural policy-making, already in the late 1940s, was the total absence of strategic development programmes with clear objectives, articulated in properly timed and costed action plans. The Christian Democrats, however, through their control of government decision-making and their pervasive presence in key posts within different cultural institutions, were able to influence the production of culture in Italy through censorship and the curtailment of activities against their interests. This was particularly evident in the case of film policy under the strategic leadership of Giulio Andreotti, who was Under-Secretary for Entertainment in DC-led governments from May 1947 to August 1953 (see Forgacs 1990: 121–2). During this period, members of the Centro Cattolico Cinematografico sat in on meetings of the state board of censors, bringing about an interlocking of state and private Catholic interests.

The DC's hegemony over central government cultural policy-making was furthered in the 1960s and 1970s through their alliance with the Socialists (PSI), to whom in 1963 they handed over the Ministero del Turismo e dello Spettacolo, which had been established four years previously. The Socialists' idea of cultural policy-making had initially been based on a recognition of the need for more systematic and strategic state intervention. Socialist intellectuals also paid greater attention than Catholic and Communist intellectuals to popular culture, understood as the self-generated cultural traditions of the subordinate classes.

In spite of their reforming intentions, the Socialists failed to use their control of the Ministero del Turismo e dello Spettacolo to widen the definition of culture on which policy was based, so as to encompass more popular and contemporary cultural forms, and to demonstrate how it would be possible to implement policies with longer-term social, educational, economic, cultural, and technological development goals. The PSI gradually bowed to the conceptions and practices pursued by the DC. Valerio Strinati describes such a process of 'adaptation' thus:

In reality, the PSI, although flying the flag of public intervention and planning, never coherently pursued this policy. On the contrary, it accepted the limits and constraints imposed by the DC on every innovative reform and attempted to pursue its own objectives only through a strategy of gradualism and compromise. This allowed the DC to discourage the more progressive projects by co-opting Socialists into existing cultural institutions, thus ensuring its own primacy within the cultural policy-making field. This was the beginning of practices centred on the *lottizzazione* [sharing out] of political powers which has constituted one of the most serious factors in the downfall of the PSI in the eyes of the Italian public. (1980: 282)

The Emergence and Development of Regional and Urban Cultural Policies

Although the establishment of a system of regional government was explicitly mentioned in the Constitution of 1948, until 1970 only five Regions existed with special powers (*Regioni a statuto speciale*) in areas with specific linguistic, ethnic, and cultural identities: Friuli-Venezia Giulia, Trentino-Alto Adige, Val d'Aosta, Sardinia, and Sicily. The 1970 reform instituted fifteen other Regions with 'ordinary powers' (*Regioni a statuto ordinario*) in the rest of the country. As a result, a new institutional layer responsible for cultural policy-making emerged between local and central government. The Regions 'immediately understood the strong potential of cultural policy in enhancing their political identity' (Bodo 1990: 9). Regional councils sought to extend their initial responsibilities for the administration of museums and libraries to a wider field, ranging from the protection of the heritage to the promotion of diverse cultural activities. However, imbalances in cultural provision and expenditure persisted, with the regions of the mainland South lagging behind the rest of the country. By contrast, Sicily and Sardinia, like the other three regions with special powers, enjoyed levels of regional cultural expenditure which were among the highest in the country (Bodo and Parisi 1992).

The Regions engaged in a political struggle with central government, which was reluctant to relinquish its powers. Central government failed to match the decentralization of administrative functions with the decentralization of funding. The development of regional cultural policies was indeed progressively slowed down from the late 1970s by a reduction in central government transfer of funds. It was urban local authorities—the *comuni*—rather than the Regions, which developed high-profile cultural policies in response to interrelated processes of social, political, and cultural change. Urban municipalities understood much more clearly than central government the need to respond to the growing, more differentiated, and sophisticated demand for cultural provision. This was the product of a growth in leisure time and disposable income, both of which were in part a result of advances made by the trade unions in the aftermath of the 'Hot Autumn' of 1969.

The emergence of new urban cultural policies was related in two respects to the rise of post-1968 urban social movements—feminism, youth revolts, gay activism, community action—whose activities had a clear cultural dimension. First, the new movements saw cultural and political action as inextricably linked. Secondly, these urban movements were often associated with 'alternative' cultural production and distribution circuits comprising free festivals, recording studios, independent record labels, rock bands, independent film makers and cinemas, free radio stations, small publishing houses, radical bookshops, newspapers and magazines, visual arts exhibitions in non-traditional venues, and 'underground' theatre groups, as well as associations and co-operatives acting as promoters and managers of cultural events of different types. ARCI, a nation-wide cultural and recreational association linked to the PCI and the PSI, was instrumental in mediating between the two main parties of the left and the urban movement's cultural groups. This cultural universe, in its philosophy and practice, challenged traditional distinctions between 'high' and 'low' cultural forms and adopted a broad definition of culture, combining in imaginative ways old and new, highbrow and lowbrow, arts and media.

Many of the Communist and Socialist politicians who introduced the most radical urban cultural policies in Italy in the late 1970s and early 1980s had absorbed the social movements' definition of culture and recognized that culture formed an integral part of the agenda of urban policy and politics. The PCI and the PSI formed municipal administrations together in most of the larger Italian cities after the local elections of 1975, and established Assessorati alla cultura (cultural policy departments) and special cultural budgets.

Cultural policies were used by this new breed of politicians and policy-makers to achieve a variety of strategic objectives. In an attempt to counteract trends towards social atomization and home-based cultural consumption, one of the aims of cultural policies was to reassert the function of the city centre as a catalyst for civic identity and public sociability. Open-air festivals were organized to consolidate opportunities for participation in public life for people of different ages, sexes, social classes, and lifestyles. These strategies were often a response to public desires to 'reclaim' spaces within the city for community use, particularly at night, which had been expressed by the symbolic occupations of city centres organized by the youth protest movement (*movimento*) of 1977 and the feminist 'Reclaim the night' demonstrations of the late 1970s.

The *comuni* were much more successful than central government in demonstrating the potential of cultural policy-making. Urban cultural policies were more in touch with grass-roots movements and with economic and social change. They achieved greater media and political visibility, were more open to public discussion, and had a substantial political, social, and in some cases even economic impact.

Some of these initiatives were called *effimere* (ephemeral) by critics, who emphasized by contrast the need for expenditure on 'permanent' cultural infrastructures such as libraries, museums, art schools, and multi-purpose arts centres. The controversy over the *effimero* was, in part, also a conflict between the different cultural policy orientations of the state on the one hand and the left-controlled *comuni* on the other. In Rome, for example, there was a public wrangle between the *comune* and the officers of the Soprintendenza, the area-based agency of the Ministero dei Beni Culturali. The *comune* had initiated a programme of open-air cultural events in archaeological sites, mixing heritage settings with popular culture. For example, science fiction movies were shown inside the Coliseum and at the Circus Maximus. Opposition to such use of historic monuments split the City Council alliance between the PCI and the PSI, with the Socialists taking the side of the Soprintendenza. This split contributed to the defeat of the left-wing administration at the 1985 local elections.

The heated debate over the *effimero* in the late 1970s and early 1980s was a clear illustration of how much the political and media status of urban cultural policy had grown. The *effimero*, however, meant different things in different cities. If one takes, for example, the cases of Bologna and Rome, one is struck by the specificity of municipal cultural strategies in spite of an underlying similarity

□ la Repubblica
martedì 16 luglio 1991 **corte dei conti**

La Corte dei conti, con un durissimo rendiconto, boccia la gestione del patrimonio pubblico nel 1990. Il debito alle stelle

Così marciscono i tesori d'Italia

Stato, pessimo gestore di musei abbandonati e caserme "appaltate"

di MASSIMO GIANNINI

Nella foto, il famoso «Davide» di Michelangelo

Inestimabili opere d'arte valgono solo 1.424 miliardi. Esplode l'abusivismo nel demanio marittimo. Alti ufficiali ristrutturano, col denaro pubblico, gli alloggi di servizio. Lo scandalo dei campionati Mondiali di calcio

ROMA – Lo Stato non è un condominio. Eppure, chi ne gestisce l'immenso patrimonio, non sembra più degno e capace di un qualsiasi azzeccagarbugli che amministra i beni di un popoloso stabile di periferia metropolitana. Palazzi, terreni e arenili dati in affitto a privati per un piatto di lenticchie; caserme prestate ad alti ufficiali, che ne fanno fastose residenze a spese dell'Erario; migliaia di «auto blu», ad uso e consumo dell'ultimo dei portaborse, interamente sovvenzionate dall'Amministrazione; pinacoteche e musei che ammuffiscono nell'incuria, saccheggiate per sovrammercato da orde di ladri.

L'elenco di «crimini e misfatti», perpetrati a vario titolo sull'immensa e inestimabile proprietà pubblica, è lunghissimo. E a riper correrlo tutto – nelle cinquantano cartelle del rendiconto generale del patrimonio dello Stato per il 1990, presentato ieri dal procuratore generale della Corte dei conti Emidio Di Giambattista – c'è n'è d'avanzo per esprimere rabbia e rammarico per l'enorme sperpero di risorse, che una sana gestione potrebbe invece finalizzare al parziale riequilibrio del deficit dei conti, già lanciato verso i 160 mila miliardi per il 1991.

La situazione generale – «Per quanto attiene ai risultati della gestione – ha osservato Di Giambattista – nel 1990 si è avuto un peggioramento patrimoniale di 116.477 miliardi, leggermente inferiore a quello esposto nel 1989 (116.552 miliardi)». Insomma,

Quanto si ricava con i beni demaniali

Categoria di demanio	Ricavo 1990 (in migliaia di lire)	Utilizzatori
Marittimo	73.564.208	31.188
Idrico	111.005.410	112.341
Militare	3.725.611	1.775
Aeronautico	5.726.804	597

Nella tabella, la "scomposizione" dei soggetti che utilizzano i beni patrimoniali e il demanio artistico dello Stato

Chi beneficia delle 'regalie' pubbliche

	Numero	Utilizzatori privati, regione, ecc. Ricavo (in migliaia di lire)	Utilizzat. Numero	Utilizzat. Statali	IACP
Beni Patrimoniali	28.480	41.064.572	19.621	5.727	11.262
Demanio artistico-storico	2.307	6.200.062	1.493	780	—

Nella tabella, i ricavi ottenuti dallo Stato con i beni demaniali, e il numero di soggetti «beneficiari» dei cespiti

effettivo delle quotazioni di molte opere d'arte, anche perché ha talvolta sborsato fior di quattrini per venirne in possesso («valga per tutti – ha ricordato Di Giambattista – il caso del quadro di Raffaello rappresentante Santa Caterina che, già appartenente alla Collezione Contini Bonacossi, è stata acquistata in un'asta di Christie's per 2 miliardi di lire; un caso sul quale sta indagando la Procura della stessa Corte dei conti»).

Abusivi demaniali – Un altro fronte sul quale la magistratura contabile reclama più stringenti azioni ispettive è quello del demanio marittimo. Qui proliferano come funghi «le occupazioni abusive», anche da parte di mafia e camorra, come ha denunciato l'Alto commissario Domenico Sica: «Occorre un piano per la difesa delle coste – ha rilevato il Pg – e rimossa l'arrogante permanenza di abusi su aree demaniali».

Caserme «in appalto» – Dalle spiagge alle caserme. La Corte dei conti denuncia per l'ennesima volta le concessioni un po' «allegrotte» di alloggi di servizio, specialmente militari, «sovente attribuiti a dipendenti per i quali l'assegnazione non è normativamente prevista». Non solo: ma una volta ottenuto l'alloggio, i graduati se lo ristrutturano a piacere, con i soldi pubblici: «Si è rilevato – si legge infatti nella memoria del Pg – che le rotazioni nell'assegnazione di alloggi di servizio ad alti ufficiali delle Forze Armate comportano spese di manutenzione che costituiscono vere e proprie ri...

Fig. 28 According to UNESCO, 30 per cent of the world's artistic treasures are in Italy. Readers of Italian newspapers are frequently reminded of this, but the finger is usually pointed at the national failure to protect and utilize this heritage. Treasures languish in the vaults, thefts from churches multiply, museums are indefinitely closed for 'restauro', state property is exploited for private ends—the catalogue of woes is made into a potent metaphor for the degeneration of the idea of the 'public good'.

in political contexts: the coming to power of left administrations and of new Communist *assessori alla cultura*, Sandra Soster in Bologna and Renato Nicolini in Rome.

The Bologna experiment was in part a response to the needs of unemployed and underemployed youth. The 'Progetto giovani' (Youth programme), initiated by Bologna City Council in 1981, was an attempt to build on the 'autonomy' reclaimed by young people in the field of cultural production. The *comune* forged a new relationship with young independent cultural producers and encouraged self-managed forms of training built on informal skills and bridging the gap between amateurism and professionalism (Bloomfield 1993: 100).

The Rome experiment, for its part, was an attempt by the council to establish a dialogue with both traditional cultural institutions and the grass-roots cultural politics of the *movimento*, which was made up of disparate groups: from Rome's feminist collectives to the 'Metropolitan Indians' and the marginalized youth of the slum suburbs known as *borgate* (Bianchini 1989). Renato Nicolini, the architect of the cultural 'revolution' in Rome, was an unorthodox Communist who felt closer to the cultural aspirations of the *movimento* than to the bureaucracy of the PCI. He established Rome's first ever Assessorato alla cultura and set about transforming the Roman cultural landscape through projects like the *Estate romana* (Roman summer), an annual summer programme of cultural events. This is how an enthusiastic reporter described the *Estate romana* of 1979:

At midnight thousands of people wander about the beautiful parks, which it is unusual to see open and illuminated, and through the Renaissance streets around Via Giulia, decorated with torches . . . They walk, dance, eat, watch films, ballet, and plays, listen to music of all kinds, meet, talk, form transient relationships . . . People meet at Villa Ada to have a go at studiously old-fashioned dance styles; ladies in their fifties, in sequinned dresses, mix with youths in Fiorucci outfits . . . later a good half of them will move to a completely different part of town to watch a couple of horror movies. (Petrone 1979)

The experiences of Rome and Bologna are significant also because of their electoral impact. Local politicians began to realize that there were votes in cultural policy. For example, the popularity of the *Estate romana* certainly contributed to the rise of Nicolini's personal preference vote at the local elections from 4,000 in 1976 to 33,000 in 1981.

A growing number of local authorities endowed themselves with cultural policy departments, budgets, and specialized personnel. For example, between 1980 and 1982 expenditure on item 409 of municipal budgets—from which the organization of programmes of cultural events is funded—grew in real terms by 69 per cent in the 'red belt' (the regions where the PCI was predominant—Emilia-Romagna, Tuscany, Umbria, and the Marches) and by 30 per cent and 36 per cent respectively even in the DC-dominated regions: the 'white belt' (Trentino Alto-Adige, Friuli-Venezia Giulia, Veneto) and the *Mezzogiorno* (Latium, the mainland Southern regions, Sicily, and Sardinia) (Felicori 1984: 174).

The Years of the *Pentapartito* Governments (1982–1992)

During the 1980s national government cultural policy was, at least according to official pronouncements, primarily directed towards exploiting the economic development and job creation potential of cultural heritage, as is evidenced by the fact that the major initiatives in this field were taken by economic ministries. In fact these initiatives on the heritage were often simply instruments for patronage and for rewarding the clienteles of the parties in power, whether in industry, the media, or at the helm of prestigious cultural institutions. This was particularly evident from 1983 to 1987 under the *pentapartito* (five-party coalition) government headed by PSI leader Bettino Craxi, comprising Christian Democrats (the largest and controlling partner), Socialists, Liberals, Republicans, and Social Democrats.

A first sign of the shift to a more economic orientation had been the establishment in 1982, under an earlier *pentapartito* led by Republican Giovanni Spadolini, of the FIO—Fondo Investimenti e Occupazione (Investments and Employment Fund), established by the Ministero del Bilancio (Budget Ministry). The official aim of the Fund was to promote the use of cultural heritage for wealth and job creation purposes. The Fund was criticized by policy-makers within the Ministero dei Beni Culturali because it reduced the role of the state merely to that of financing projects identified and developed by private enterprise.

The next important policy initiative was the establishment of the *giacimenti culturali* (cultural deposits) through a law passed in 1986 on the initiative of the Ministero del Lavoro (Ministry of Employment). This stipulated that funds should be made available to finance inventory, training, and employment projects in the cultural heritage field—including archives and archaeological areas, monuments, and museums—specifically related to the application of technological innovations. The *giacimenti culturali* experiment was heavily criticized and subsequently abandoned partly because, as Leon and Causi have noted (1990: 3), like the FIO, it gave the private sector the responsibility of identifying the heritage assets to be developed, confining the role of the state to that of mere provider of funds for private enterprise. It failed to develop an effective employment strategy, with the result that the jobs created were only temporary. An even more serious criticism of the *giacimenti culturali* initiative is that, like the FIO, it channelled funds to a wide range of enterprises—from computer manufacturing and software production firms to providers of training and other services. These enterprises carried out projects often without clear prioritizing, guidance, monitoring, and evaluation by the experts in the Ministero dei Beni Culturali. The relevance, as well as the cultural and employment benefits, of such projects in many cases were difficult to demonstrate.

The Years of Tangentopoli: The Ronchey Act and the Abolition of the Ministero del Turismo e Spettacolo (1992–1994)

The next wave of legislative reforms came in early 1993 under the new Government led by Giuliano Amato, a close associate of PSI leader Bettino Craxi. This

Government took a series of innovative initiatives, although it could not see all of them through because—like its successor under the leadership of an independent, the former Bank of Italy Governor Carlo Azeglio Ciampi—it was essentially in charge of managing a period of political transition between the general election of April 1992 and that of March 1994. The Ministero dei Beni Culturali in both the Amato and Ciampi Governments was headed by Alberto Ronchey, a well-known journalist. In January 1993 the Italian Parliament approved a bill proposed by him which came to be known as the Ronchey Act. It started from the principle that Italian museums should become as financially self-sufficient as possible, with a more effective use of their premises, personnel, and collections.

According to UNESCO, 50 per cent of the world's artistic heritage sites are located in Italy (Wright 1991: 25). Italian legislation makes no distinction between state archaeological sites, galleries, historic monuments, and museums: they are all defined as 'cultural assets', and all come under the responsibility of the Ministero dei Beni Culturali and the Soprintendenze (Bobbio 1991: 12). According to Ministry estimates, in 1990 there were in Italy 710 state museums, galleries, historic monuments, and archaeological sites (Bobbio 1991: 14), and about 2,300 museums owned by municipalities, foundations, the Church, and private individuals (*Il Sole–24 Ore*, 29 Nov. 1993). This number is larger than in other European countries, although the number of visitors is smaller. No Italian state museum, for example, has annual attendances of 2 million and over, such as are attained by the National Gallery and the Tate in London, the Prado in Madrid, the Louvre and the Orsay Museum in Paris, and the Vatican Museums in the Vatican City (Bobbio 1991: 15).

Italian museums are beset by seemingly intractable problems. Owing to a number of factors—including the inefficient distribution and relatively low skills profile of museum wardens, absenteeism, and protracted restoration work—many museums are closed, and the opening hours of those which are not are often severely limited. Only 5 per cent of the entire Italian artistic heritage is catalogued (Leon 1993), including large parts of the collections of many museums. Many works of art are held in storage and never shown to the public—for instance, half of the 4,000 or so paintings owned by the Uffizi Gallery in Florence are permanently in storage. Theft of artworks is widespread because of serious deficiencies in museum security systems and the difficulties in controlling the myriad archaeological sites and historic buildings scattered across the country. The training of the managers of the Soprintendenze and of museum directors emphasizes curatorial aspects with little attention paid to the use of museums within wider cultural, social, and economic development strategies. The management and public accessibility of museums tends to be seen as less important than the preservation of the artefacts.

Many Italian museums are based on collections which for centuries have been housed in relatively small, historic, architecturally and artistically significant buildings, belonging to the Church or the aristocracy. These museums were born as private collections, long before the emergence in the late eighteenth century of the modern idea of the large, purpose-built, 'encyclopaedic', educational state museum, found in countries like Britain and France. Some commentators and policy-makers argue that Italian museums should become more polyfunctional, following the models of the Beaubourg, the British Museum, the Louvre, or the Museum of Modern Art in New York. However, in many of the historic museum buildings in Italy it is either very difficult or impossible to locate educational, information, recreation, and mass tourism functions without fundamentally and irreversibly changing these buildings' nature and structure. It may be more appropriate to build on and celebrate the existing organic relationship between museums and the urban fabric in which they are situated. Andrea Emiliani, superintendent for artistic and historic heritage for the four eastern provinces of Emilia-Romagna, recently made some stimulating suggestions:

The visitor, by looking around, even within the confines of the neighbourhood, will be able to see links between the museum and an exciting continuum of churches, mansions, convents . . . The museum, in other words, breaks out of its institutional walls . . . It is in the city that the museum finds the opportunities which are denied to it by space constraints within its own building: the lecture hall, the workshop, the bar. (1991: 9)

What Emiliani advocates is a form of planning which integrates museums into the rest of the city socially, physically, economically, culturally, and symbolically.

The Ronchey Act tried to address the problems and grasp the opportunities of Italian museums. It authorized the use of closed-circuit television for surveillance purposes, and encouraged transfers of personnel from one province or region to another, in order to improve accessibility to museums, especially in the most visited towns and cities. It also extended opening hours by drawing on volunteers, and enabled private companies to bid for licences to run cloakrooms, cafés, guided tours, restaurants, and shops, as well as external relations and marketing services. The private sector will also be able to bid for the production of catalogues, guide-books, postcards, souvenirs, gadgets, and audio-visual materials. The law specified that private-sector bidders are more likely to succeed if they submit a package of proposals for investment encompassing both prestigious and established institutions and lesser-known, relatively minor museums or archaeological sites. Half of the income derived from licences will go to the Ministero dei Beni Culturali, and the remaining half to the Soprintendenza in whose territory the archaeological site, gallery, or museum is located.

It is too early to assess the impact of the Ronchey Act, which is still in the process of being implemented. However, one can already glimpse the beneficial effects of measures like the transfer of wardens from overstaffed, less popular museums to others which attract large numbers of visitors but are inadequately staffed.

Under the Ciampi Government, the most important reform in the field of cultural policy followed a referendum in April 1993 which abolished the Ministero del Turismo e dello Spettacolo. The Ministry had been severely criticized for its funding policy, the main beneficiaries of which had been the *teatri stabili* (repertory theatres) and the *enti lirici* (opera houses). Funds were often distributed to reward electoral clienteles, rather than according to criteria of artistic merit or to fill real gaps in cultural provision. A second important strand of criticism concerned the remit of the Ministry. It was felt that it would be more appropriate to transfer the responsibilities of the Ministry in the performing arts field to the Ministero dei Beni Culturali, and to establish separate, more specialized bodies in charge of policies on sports and tourism.

A decree issued by the government in October 1993 ruled that the Presidenza del Consiglio dei Ministri, headed by the Prime Minister, should inherit the functions previously performed by the Ministero del Turismo e dello Spettacolo. The Presidenza thus became the second important department concerned with central government cultural policy. Its remit includes the co-ordination at national level of policies on the press and copyright, film, the performing arts (both subsidized and commercial), sports (chiefly through CONI, the Italian National Olympic Committee), and tourism, for the formulation and implementation of which the Regions are now responsible. The decree stated that the funding of activities in all these areas should be transferred from the Presidency to the Regions on 1 January 1995, although there have been delays in effecting this transfer of powers.

Critical Assessment

The cultural policies of national governments in Italy between the fall of Fascism in 1943 and the early 1990s were fragmentary and non-directive. The two most important departments in charge of cultural affairs and of the other smaller half-dozen offices in charge of cultural policies were never either in the thick of the political battle or at the centre of important public debates. The ministers responsible for cultural matters were generally second-rate politicians. The definition of culture adopted was narrow and traditional; budgets were small; public visibility and discussion virtually nil; involvement of intellectuals and artists in policy-making sporadic and haphazard. Large portions of the available funds remained unspent; bureaucracies were oversized, sluggish, and often relatively incompetent; cultural institutions such as museums and public libraries suffered from overstaffing, administrative rigidities, and inadequate skilling; the application of new technologies was infrequent and unplanned. Co-operation between or even within ministries was insufficient; policy programmes and objectives were unclear or non-existent; the overall philosophy of intervention narrowly curatorial rather than developmental—in other words, it was aimed almost exclusively at preserving existing cultural assets rather than at using them as resources within wider social, environmental, economic, or cultural development strategies.

Cultural policies—where they existed—were designed and implemented for individual cultural forms—theatre, film, circus, and so on. They were almost never targetted at specific geographical areas or particular 'communities of interest' or social groups. Little attention was paid to distribution systems and to research, or to careful financial planning and to the monitoring and evaluation of policy impact. Many able and dedicated professionals working in state cultural institutions were well aware of all these problems. But inflexible administrative hierarchies failed to give them the autonomy and powers necessary to effect reforms. Reformers were not able to organize a strong movement of public opinion denouncing— for example—the serious neglect of the country's cultural heritage and encouraging a more responsible attitude to it. The relative weakness of heritage conservation pressure groups like Italia Nostra indicates limited public awareness of these issues. This was particularly problematic in relation to the conservation and maintenance of archaeological areas, individual historic monuments, museums, and natural landscapes. There was greater public awareness and—perhaps in part as a consequence—a much more effective legislative framework to protect the integrity of historic town and city centres as whole units. In fact, it could be argued that this is one of the few areas of state cultural policy-making in which Italy is at the leading edge of theory and practice in the world.

On the whole, cultural policies were explicitly linked neither to the official rhetoric of reconstruction of the country in the early post-war years nor to the project of modernization which was central to the initial pronouncements of the centre-left governments, under the influence of the Socialists. They were often simply instruments for the exercise of political patronage and even the misappropriation of public funds. They were largely shaped by pressures from particular lobbies and clienteles, including the major subsidized cultural institutions.

For all these reasons, it is much more difficult to identify a coherent and consistent approach to national cultural policy-making in Italy than it is in France, from de Gaulle's Culture Minister André Malraux to the current minister Jacques Toubon, through Jack Lang (minister 1981–6 and 1988–93), not to mention Britain, from the establishment of the Arts Council in 1946 to the present. This is not to say that there were no specific political-strategic designs behind the DC-dominated cultural policies. It can be argued that one of the objectives of the Christian Democrats was to make sure that intellectuals and artists were not too closely involved in the process of public policy-making. Their involvement in the formulation of organic, dynamic, development-oriented cultural policies would have exposed the lack of substance and backwardness of policy-making in other areas. Moreover, it was important for the DC to neutralize some of the radical potential of anti-Fascist and oppositional intellectuals and artistic movements, by having direct, and basically exclusive, access to the means through which censorship could be exercised.

The policy initiatives taken by the Regions from the 1970s largely failed to establish regional networks of production and distribution infrastructures in the cultural industries, with fruitful links between regional capitals and their hinterlands. As a result, the dominance of the Rome–Milan duopoly over the Italian cultural economy was not seriously challenged. Many city authorities, however, did manage to achieve significant results—particularly in the late 1970s and early 1980s in municipalities controlled by the left—with comparatively low levels of expenditure. They made a very innovative use of programmes of cultural events in public spaces. They also took a wider, more holistic view of culture than that adopted by national governments, encompassing in some cases not only the arts and the heritage, but also the built environment, food, leisure, local history, and the media. They often stimulated genuine public debate on policy directions and priorities, and were able to respond to emerging public demands and trends in a rapid, flexible, and informal way, perhaps because they were not encumbered by the previous adoption of formalized policy statements.

These urban cultural policies were often very imaginative in providing new opportunities for cultural consumption. However, they failed—with a few exceptions, like that of Bologna—to support local production and to organize distribution systems for local products. They also largely failed to modernize municipal libraries and open new museums and multi-purpose arts and media centres. Resources tended to be concentrated too heavily on city centres, while the culturally deprived outer housing estates and suburban areas were all too often left behind.

There were undoubtedly—especially in the 1980s—many examples of involvement by private enterprise in cultural projects whose *raison d'être* was more to take money from state coffers than to address real needs and problems. However, there were in the same decade important and prestigious projects which would never have been implemented without substantial private-sector initiative and investment. For example, Fiat—in co-operation with public-sector partners—restored and refurbished the Castello di Rivoli near Turin, with the provision of spaces for art exhibitions and a contemporary art museum. Another example is the Centro per l'Arte Contemporanea Pecci in Prato (Tuscany), an innovative complex—comprising a museum, a library, a theatre, and a documentation centre—which emerged as a joint initiative of the municipality of Prato and private-sector partners.

Lastly, it is important to highlight the role of the savings banks—the *Casse di Risparmio* and the *Banche del Monte*—as a strength of the Italian cultural policy system. These institutions have the statutory duty to devote part of their profits to charitable activities and have made important financial contributions to many cultural projects, individually or in co-operation with the public sector.

Current Trends and New Directions

Following the victory of a right-wing coalition at the 1994 general election, the new Prime Minister Silvio Berlusconi appointed Domenico Fisichella, a political scientist and Alleanza Nazionale parliamentary deputy, to head the Ministero dei Beni Culturali. Fisichella did not have sufficient time to formulate and implement a cultural policy programme because the Berlusconi Government lasted only until December 1994. However, he gave some indications about his cultural policy objectives in a series of interviews in May and June 1994. He recognized the strategic importance of culture in what he called 'the post-materialistic society' which had emerged from 'the third industrial revolution—the revolution of information technology and leisure' (1994c). More specifically, Fisichella expressed his agreement with the Ronchey Act, and commitment to its implementation. He argued that the remit of the Ministero dei Beni Culturali should encompass activities and events of *national* importance in the fields of classical music, film, opera, and theatre, currently under the responsibility of the Presidenza del Consiglio dei Ministri, although he fell short of advocating the establishment of a new Ministry for Cultural, Artistic, Sports, and Leisure Activities, as proposed in June 1993 in a bill submitted to Parliament by his fellow Alleanza Nazionale MP, Maurizio Gasparri (Fisichella 1994a).

Fisichella also emphasized the need to expand the budget of the Ministry, especially if its responsibilities were widened (1994c), and the role of 'national culture' as a unitary force: 'we have to deepen the knowledge of our heritage in a unitary vision of our national culture . . . We have to create a stronger image of Italy on the international scene' (1994a). He is clearly a firm believer in the values of traditional 'high culture': hence his emphasis on what he considers 'the best in our tradition . . . opera and classical music' (1994a). He asserted that:

We must identify within the performing arts those elements which have artistic, or aesthetic, worth, if I can use this expression without being looked upon as an aristocrat. And if people think I am an aristocrat, I don't mind, because it is true, I am an aristocrat, not by birth, but in spirit. I am a member of the bourgeoisie. (1994c)

It is possible to identify other themes and issues characterizing the cultural policies of the right-wing coalition government formed in May 1994. Forza Italia's programme for the March 1994 elections argued that private enterprise should be encouraged to invest in the development potential of cultural heritage. Forza Italia, however, laid itself open to criticism because of its close identification with Fininvest, which may benefit from cultural policy reforms introduced by the new government. For example, the March 1994 issue of *Fininvest News*, the 'house organ' of Fininvest, advocated the role of the group as promoter of a new, entrepreneurial approach to arts patronage, 'through the design and organization of events, jointly with public and private sector partners, for making the most out of the monumental and cultural heritage, and of the traditions of our cities and regions' (Rampello 1994: 5). It is disturbing that a member of the board of Fininvest, Gianni Letta, was appointed by Berlusconi as Under-Secretary to the Presidenza del Consiglio dei Ministri, with responsibility for policies on the performing arts, sports, and tourism.

The importance of cultural policy in the agenda of national government in Italy is likely to increase. The first pronouncements by Fisichella and Berlusconi, as well as the electoral programme of Forza Italia, suggested that cultural resources will be exploited in a more systematic and integrated way than in the past, especially to promote the image of the country abroad and develop tourism.

There is indeed a consensus across the political spectrum that culture is becoming an increasingly important resource for the country's economic development in times of economic restructuring, with the crisis of traditional forms of manufacturing industry and services. There is also a near consensus on the need for more integrated policies—especially at national government level, where there are moves towards the establishment of something resembling a ministry for cultural affairs—and on the formation of public–private-sector partnerships, which are in part a response to cuts in public expenditure.

Some aspects of cultural policy, however, are more controversial. These include: the provision of support for radical, independent cultural producers, particularly in youth and popular contemporary cultural forms; the democratization of access to traditional cultural activities such as theatre, opera, classical music, and ballet; and the development of policies aimed at Italy's growing ethnic and racial minority communities.

Another area of uncertainty and potential controversy concerns the future of relations between central and local government. The left administrations which emerged in some large Italian cities from the local elections of November and December 1993 appeared to be ready to introduce cultural policy innovations. By March 1994 the impact of the work of the left administration in Naples led by PDS Mayor Antonio Bassolino—to take just one example—was already evident. In a speech in Strasbourg, Bassolino stated that 'Naples is experiencing a great renewal. There is a new city that is freeing itself from the legacy of years marked by the nefarious connection between politics and business. There is a new Naples, for which culture is the most precious resource' (*La Repubblica*, 10 Mar. 1994). Naples City Council opened new parks throughout the city; it cleaned up and made accessible to the public monuments in the historic centre which it had not been possible to visit for many years; it closed the seafront in the city centre to traffic on Sundays, and enlivened it with street performers and stalls, attracting large numbers of people of all ages.

It is unclear, however, whether municipalities controlled by the left will be able to implement more ambitious and costly projects involving the restoration of historic buildings and districts, the provision of new public spaces, the modernization of public libraries, the provision of improved cultural facilities in deprived outer housing estates, and the development of new infrastructures for local cultural industries. Such schemes would require substantial transfers of funds from the state which left-controlled local authorities may find hard to obtain under the right-wing government.

There are signs—especially in pronouncements by Forza Italia and Alleanza Nazionale—of a new-found emphasis on expressing and celebrating national pride, history, and traditions through prestigious cultural initiatives. New orientations in government policy-making could accentuate a certain chauvinism and/or cultural provincialism. Moreover, 'strong' national government policies for the development of cultural tourism and 'flagship' initiatives focused on high culture and heritage could restrict access to cultural facilities, and accelerate processes of 'colonization' of public spaces by tourists, of commodification of culture, and of gentrification— for example, through increases in rental, land, and property values in 'culturally regenerated' urban districts.

Further Reading

There are few relevant books in either English or Italian dealing specifically with cultural policy-making in Italy. In English, some of the chapters included in *Formations of Nation and People* (London, 1984) and in Z. G. Baranski and R. Lumley (eds.), *Culture and Conflict in Postwar Italy* (Basingstoke and London, 1990) give useful insights into issues concerning the cultural industries, including film and the media, as well as on debates on Italian 'cultures' and definitions of 'culture'. David Forgacs's *Italian Culture in the Industrial Era, 1880–1980: Cultural Industries, Politics and the Public* (Manchester, 1990) carefully analyses political attitudes towards the cultural industries. Very useful for an understanding of the cultural policies implemented in cities governed by the left in the late 1970s and early 1980s are Franco Bianchini, 'Cultural Policy and Urban Social Movements: The Response of the "New Left" in Rome (1976–85) and London (1981–86)', in P. Bramham *et al.* (eds.), *Leisure and Urban Processes* (London, 1989), and Jude Bloomfield, 'Bologna: A Laboratory for Cultural Enterprise', in F. Bianchini and M. Parkinson (eds.), *Cultural Policy and Urban Regeneration* (Manchester, 1993).

In Italian a good overview of the history, institutional framework, and debates characterizing Italian arts and heritage policies is provided by the following: U. Eco *et al.*, *Le isole del tesoro. Proposte per la riscoperta e la gestione delle risorse culturali* (Milan, 1988); F. Isman, *Pietra su pietra. Dieci anni di restauri in Italia* (Bari, 1991); La Biennale di Venezia—Sezione Progetti Speciali (ed.), *Il consumo culturale. Una storia degli italiani dal 1945 ai giorni nostri* (Venice, 1991); G. Brosio and W. Santagata, *Economia delle arti e dello spettacolo in Italia* (Turin, 1992); L. Bobbio, 'La politica dei beni culturali in Italia', in L. Bobbio (ed.), *Le politiche dei beni culturali in Europa* (Bologna, 1992); Associazione Mecenate 90 (ed.), *Lessico dei beni culturali* (Turin, 1994).

References

BIANCHINI, F. (1989), 'Cultural Policy and Urban Social Movements: The Response of the "New Left" in Rome (1976–85) and London (1981–86)', in P. Bramham *et al.* (eds.), *Leisure and Urban Processes* (London), 18–46.

—— and PARKINSON, M. (1993) (eds.), *Cultural Policy and Urban Regeneration: The West European Experience* (Manchester).

BLOOMFIELD, J. (1993), 'Bologna: A Laboratory for Cultural Enterprise', in Bianchini and Parkinson (1993), 90–113.

BOBBIO, L. (1991), 'La gestione dei musei: verso il superamento dell'anomalia italiana?', *Economia della cultura*, 2: 12–23.

BODO, C. (1990), 'Italian National Report', paper presented at the International Conference on Cultural Policies, Tokyo, 22–4 Feb. 1990.

—— and PARISI, G. (1992), *La spesa regionale per la cultura: 1985–88* (Milan).

EMILIANI, A. (1991), 'Il museo italiano: limiti e potenzialità', *Economia della cultura*, 2: 6–11.

FELICORI, M. (1984), 'Feste d'estate: indagine sulla politica culturale dei comuni italiani', in A. Parisi (ed.), *Luoghi e misure della politica. Quattro esercizi di misurazione sulla politica locale* (Bologna), 143–92.

FISICHELLA, D. (1994a), 'Raddoppierò i miei Beni', interview with P. Vagheggi, *La Repubblica*, 20 May.

FISICHELLA, D. (1994*b*), 'Il ministro della Penna d'Oro', interview with L. Conte, *Il Giornale dell'Arte*, June.

—— (1994*c*), 'La nuova società postmaterialista', interview with A. Detheridge, *Il Sole—24 Ore*, 19 June.

FORGACS, D. (1990), *Italian Culture in the Industrial Era, 1880–1980: Cultural Industries, Politics and the Public* (Manchester).

LEON, P. (1993), interview with M. Torrigiani, Rome, Nov.

—— and CAUSI, M. (1990), 'La politica economica dei beni culturali', *Note di ricerca Cles: Centro di ricerche e studi sui problemi del lavoro, dell'economia e dello sviluppo*, 3: 3–8.

PALMA, G., and CLEMENTE DI SAN LUCA, G. (1987), 'State Intervention in the Arts in Italy from 1945 to 1982', in M. C. Cummings, Jr., and R. S. Katz (eds.), *The Patron State* (Oxford).

PETRONE, F. M. (1979), 'Tutta la città ne parla', *Rinascita*, 27.

RAMPELLO, D. (1994), 'Nel segno della continuità la presidenza Confalonieri', *Fininvest News*, 4.

STRINATI, V. (1980), *Politica e cultura nel Partito Socialista Italiano (1945–1978)* (Naples).

WRIGHT, P. (1991), 'Inside Italy', *Museums Journal*, June: 25–33.

17

Fame, Fashion, and Style:
The Italian Star System

STEPHEN GUNDLE

THERE is a sequence of scenes in Federico Fellini's 1959 film *La dolce vita* which encapsulates the idea of stardom. Crowds of reporters and photographers at an airport rush across the tarmac to catch a glimpse of American star Sylvia Rank (Anita Ekberg) as she emerges from a plane to set foot in Italy for the first time. From the moment the door opens and she appears, the viewer is treated to a performance of familiar rituals and gestures: the friendly wave and euphoric, Hollywood smile of Rank/Ekberg, the return inside the plane and fresh reappearance at the request of the photographers, the capricious refusal to repeat the gesture for a third time, the admiring comments drawn by her opulent figure, the promotional 'aside' as the star is invited to taste a pizza brought up to the steps for the occasion, the concern of her producer to restore distance and whisk her away. There then follows a hotel press conference conducted in a babel of languages in which meaningless questions are given standard answers (at one point Rank turns to her secretary and says 'Edna, what is the answer to that question?') and the viewer is given a flavour of the larger-than-life, exuberant, childlike nature of the blonde star whose irrepressible presence dominates the first half of the film.

La dolce vita is an unusual film in that it is equally famous for having incorporated in a collage a series of real events and practices (albeit superficially disguised for the purposes of a feature film) and real people, and for having itself given rise to new stars and gestures and a new style. Ekberg, a moderately famous actress in the USA, achieved lasting stardom as a result of the film, while the male lead, Marcello Mastroianni, became the new symbol of Italian masculinity abroad. Ekberg's costumes were copies of outfits designed by the Fontana sisters for Ava Gardner, while Mastroianni's sharp, unfussed dress style raised international interest in Italian menswear. The film gave a name to unauthorized celebrity photographers who became known the world over as *paparazzi*. Most significantly, the film communicated an idea of Rome as a centre of glamour, hedonism, leisure, cosmopolitanism, and free expression—symbolized by Ekberg's legendary dip in the Trevi fountain—that continues to fuel the city's tourist and fashion industries.

This dual nature of Fellini's film bears witness to the fact that, while Italy has been primarily an importer of stars, particularly American stars who brought with them a rhetoric and techniques that largely defined the dominant idea of stardom, it has also been a producing ground of stars—sometimes for international consumption—and a site for widening the lexicon of star phenomena. The aim of this chapter is to explore the production and consumption of stars in Italy and to examine the functions performed by foreign and domestic celebrities. As part of the discussion, the interrelationships between different types of star and between these and the public will be analysed. Attention will also be paid to the role of stars in the economic system and their contribution to perceptions of Italianness (*italianità*).

Stardom and Italian Society

According to Edgar Morin and Francesco Alberoni, authors in 1959 and 1963 respectively of books which opened the way to the serious study of star phenomena, stars only arise in societies that are democratic, capitalist, predominantly urban, and at least moderately prosperous, possessing an extensive network of mass communications. Only in such societies, they argued, do the necessary preconditions exist in terms of political and economic development, social differentiation, and capacity for individual expression. In fact what they were describing, and in Alberoni's case attempting to theorize, were the necessary conditions for the existence of an American-style star *system* understood as a specific product of monopoly capitalism. The creation and serial production of star personalities for presentation and consumption as merchandise is clearly a feature of a social system whose economy is geared to mass production. However, stars need not be generated in this way. Although the relationship with the mass media is unavoidable, they may emerge spontaneously, as a result more of public favour and the symbolic meaning that they acquire than of the alchemy of producers and studios. They may also arise in less developed societies or be imported.

Because of the ubiquity of American mass culture and the models it proposes, there has been a tendency to assume that it encapsulates the whole experience of stardom in contemporary societies. In fact this is not true. American stars are omnipresent owing to the immensely powerful commercial machines which generate and diffuse them and universal, idealized qualities which render them attractive and useful in a wide variety of contexts. But, outside of the USA, American stars often take on connotations and acquire meanings that were absent in the country of origin or which were unforeseen by the cultural industries that gave rise to them. In a real sense they become different. Moreover, the mass cultural context of other countries may have evolved in ways different from the USA such that the forms of stardom as well as the types and functions of stars will be different.

In the case of Italy there are a number of features of society which need to be taken into account before the specificity of the star system can be grasped. Not only did these features condition the historical development of stars but they continue, to varying degrees, to shape the presentation, appearance, and role of stars even today.

First, in the film industry there has never been a studio system of the American type which has selected, groomed, presented, and managed stars. Although Cinecittà briefly performed a function of this type during the war and RAI-TV has acted as a powerful source of television stars and stardom, no comparable degree of rationalization ever occurred. Even Titanus, the company which at the height of the Italian film industry's success in the 1950s became a sort of 'quasi-major on the Tiber' (Barzoletti *et al.* 1986: 27), produced only ten films per year and employed existing stars rather than grooming its own. Another leading company, Lux Film, never produced directly or owned its own studios. Exclusive contracts with actors were not unknown, but they were a rarity. This means that production has always been more casual, that stars have become such by various means, and that their maintenance of a star position has depended on their personal skills in maintaining a relationship with the public.

Secondly, the Catholic influence in society, exceptionally strong in the 1940s and 1950s and declining but still significant from the 1960s, ensured that for many years transgression and gossip about stars' private lives were all but absent. Despite Alberoni's insistence on the importance of transgression (stars live out the secret aspirations of their audiences), moral misdemeanours that became public in Italy (such as Sophia Loren's Mexican proxy marriage to Carlo Ponti in 1957 or the unmarried singer Mina's pregnancy by the married actor Corrado Pani a few years later) gave rise to outcries that divided public opinion and briefly threatened the popularity of the stars concerned. Even now most stars, especially women, place great store by the maintenance of a respectable public image. Motherhood and family are routinely stressed. Moreover, the central position occupied by the family in social relations and the persistence of a provincial dimension in Italian life has meant that even in youth culture no real rebel figures have ever been produced (see Baldazzi 1989: 154–9). The exception that proves the rule in this case is provided by the singer Vasco Rossi, whose lyrics are littered with references to excitement, danger, and such outcast icons as James Dean and Steve McQueen.

Thirdly, because for much of the twentieth century Italy has been a politically divided and unstable society which has experienced dictatorship and in which normal alternation between parties in government has never occurred, it cannot be said to have reached the stage theorized by Alberoni in which a clear separation obtains between the holders of institutional power and stars (1973: 30–3). Stars have on a variety of occasions taken on political meanings or been drawn into political conflict, and politicians have even more frequently presented themselves or been perceived as stars. Not only Mussolini but Stalin, Togliatti, and in more recent times Sandro Pertini, Bettino Craxi, and Silvio Berlusconi have all been the objects of continuous public interest and adulation.

Fourthly, the cult of virility, of exaggerated masculinity, which permeated much public and even political discourse before 1945 (and which, in degenerate form, persisted long after) contributed to a situation in which there was a high degree of gender differentiation in star personas. In particular conservative/traditional ideas about masculinity exercised a very long-lasting influence.

Fifthly, the low level of national integration has meant that, in place of formal institutions and official traditions, sport and entertainment have often been the principal source of a shared set of national cultural symbols; thus stars within fields such as popular music, cycling, and football have been called upon to perform a function in terms of national mobilization. Such functions have also on occasion been performed by film and television stars. One way in which this is reflected is in the fact that stars have not only generally been of lower-class origins—as is the case everywhere—but that they have also been predominantly Southern, in keeping with a conventionally 'backward' national imagery (Bollati 1983: 93–123). It should also be noted that many stars, despite being nationally well known, are admired intensely only in their own regions of origin.

Finally, Mediterranean criteria of beauty have played a significant role, although always in relation to strong and usually dominant criteria of an American/North European derivation. This has meant a preference for dark hair and eyes, for more rounded forms and a slightly plumper physique in the case of women, and for natural, spontaneous beauty rather than excessive artificiality.

Foreign and Domestic Film Stars

For most of the twentieth century Italy has been a net importer of cultural goods, mostly from the USA, and consequently foreign celebrities have always circulated (Forgacs 1990: 25–9). For Italians as for non-Americans generally, Hollywood stars fulfilled an ideal. They represented the extraordinary, the fantastic, and the desirable. Throughout the golden age of cinema, from the 1930s to the 1960s, they constituted an incomparable pole of attraction. In film fan magazines such as

GENTE

7 FEBBRAIO 1994 · N. 5 · ANNO XXXVIII · SETTIMANALE DI POLITICA, ATTUALITÀ E CULTURA · ABB. POSTALE GR. II/70 · RUSCONI EDITORE L. 2.700

Con la dieta "trifasica"

IL TAGLIANDO DA SPEDIRE PER SAPERE DI QUANTE CALORIE AVETE BISOGNO

ECCO IL "PANCIONE" DI STEFANIA

A "BUCCE DI BANANA" ESPLODE LA RIVALITA' TRA LE DUE "VAMP"

Ma è vero che gli uomini preferiscono le bionde come ai tempi di Marilyn Monroe e Jane Russell?

Fig. 29 The continuing role of the Hollywood golden age in providing reference points for the contemporary television star system is shown by this cover of the illustrated weekly *Gente* (7 February 1994). It depicts two 'showgirls', one blonde (Valeria Marini) and one brunette (Gabriella Labate), both of whom featured in the 1994 Saturday evening variety show *Bucce di banana* (*Banana skins*) on RAI 1. Their alleged rivalry is compared to that of Marilyn Monroe and Jane Russell in the 1953 film *Gentlemen Prefer Blondes*. In this way, extra allure is added and the historical memory of the audience is mobilized to generate interest in the show.

Cinema illustrazione, Stelle, and *Hollywood* they displayed their vitality and beauty, their material wealth, and their carefree lifestyle. Innumerable articles littered with superlatives bore witness to the exciting and surprising features of their lives while photographs highlighted their immaculate apparel, luxurious homes, private swimming pools, and dream cars. Although in many ways they were out of reach, young men and women none the less wanted to be like them and to join the Hollywood olympus. These dreams of possible communion between American stars and Italian fans stretched across classes and regions and for many years were reinforced by the memory of the tremendous success achieved in the mecca of cinema by a young migrant from the backwaters of Puglia, Rodolfo (Rudolph) Valentino. Attacked by Italian Fascists for his 'effeminate' qualities (de Grazia 1992: 209) and also for exchanging his Italian passport for an American one, Valentino remained a symbol for those who believed they could conquer a place for themselves in Hollywood. Such illusions were fuelled by promotional contests like that held in Italy in 1926 by Twentieth Century Fox to find a replacement for Valentino after his sudden death. The competition was won by Alberto Rabagliati, whose nascent Hollywood career was cut short by the arrival of the talkies but who later became a successful singer of the crooner type back in Italy. The 'Valentino myth' is also referred to by Sophia Loren in her English-language autobiography (Hotchner 1979: 13–14).

It is probably true to say that the biggest stars in Italy, those who have enjoyed the most extensive following and who have united more people of diverse origins in admiration of them, have always been Americans. This can be explained not just by reference to the universality and abstract nature of American stars and the power of the industries that furnished and promoted them but in relation to the particular place of the USA in Italian popular culture and to its role in defining processes of modernization (see D'Attorre 1991; Ellwood and Brunetta 1991). In the North, in the cities and among more modern sectors of the population, those whose leisure activities were predominantly commodified, it was always the Americans (and sometimes the British too, lumped together with the former in the category of *anglosassoni*) who aroused most general enthusiasm. By contrast, Italian actors and actresses were nearly always seen, especially by the urbanized, modern, and well-informed, as mere copies, or second-rate equivalents of more glamorous American originals. In the 1930s and 1940s the vigorously masculine Amedeo Nazzari and the exotic dark lady Doris Duranti were known in Italy as the 'Italian Errol Flynn' and the 'Italian Dorothy Lamour', while the comic Erminio Macario was equated with Eddie Cantor and the variety actress Gemma Bolognesi was even termed the 'Italian Mae West'. This practice was not limited to the autarkic Fascist period. The new female stars who emerged in Italy from the late 1940s as the film industry recovered and expanded were also seen, particularly at the outset of their careers, as local versions of the more full-bodied, Latin-looking stars that were produced by Hollywood in place of the blonde, northern European-looking women of the 1930s. With pictures of Rita Hayworth, Jane Russell, and

Ava Gardner filling magazines and occupying billboards with their poster images, several of the young women who entered beauty contests like the Miss Italia pageant were singled out as *bellezze cinematografiche* or *bellezze americane* on account of their shapely figures, vivacious personalities, and ambition to get on. Silvana Mangano, star of *Riso amaro* (*Bitter Rice*) was dubbed a 'Rita Hayworth of the Italian periphery' by the director who launched her, Giuseppe De Santis (Faldini and Fofi 1979: 154). The practice was still going on years later with the blonde Virna Lisi being compared to Marilyn Monroe, the Tuscan comic Roberto Benigni being equated with Woody Allen (purely on the basis of a tenuous physical resemblance), the singer Zucchero to Joe Cocker, and so forth. In some cases such comments were intended as flattery, in others as dismissal of the second-rate, in yet others merely as the location of new individuals in relation to an existing star universe.

It is undeniable that some stars were modelled or modelled themselves on Americans or arose out of Americanizing processes within cultural industries. The ubiquity of American images of stardom made this virtually inevitable. For example, Isa Miranda, a former typist who following her success in Max Ophuls's *La signora di tutti* (*Everybody's Lady*) in 1932, became one of the leading stars of the 1930s, was from the start 'a sort of Italian reply to Hollywood, something half-way between the declaredly sexual provocation of Marlene Dietrich and the declaredly spiritual depth of Greta Garbo, the epochal legs of Marlene and the disquieting eyes of Greta'. She was launched as an actress within 'an idea of stardom that, despite its "autarkic" desire (or perhaps because of this), was wholly geared towards American models, preferred and pursued because they were far-off and unattainable' (Caldiron and Hochkofler 1978: 12). Much the same point can be made about Nazzari, frequently described as the Italian Errol Flynn, 'a Clark Gable for backward regions' (Castello 1959: 408) or 'a sort of home-grown Gary Cooper' (Pruzzo and Lancia 1983: 10).

However, it would be misleading to accept these descriptions at face value. Even those film stars who were closer to American models had characteristics of their own that derived from their origins and education, mode of formation, and relation to their audiences. In the case of Nazzari, the American associations derived principally from the fact that he was 'the only home-grown presence capable of filling the screen in the style of the greats of American cinema' (Pruzzo and Lancia 1983: 10). The brusque manner, taciturnity, unflinching virility, absolute dependability, and keen sense of honour of his screen character marked him out as a personality with connotations that audiences recognized as specifically Italian (Spinazzola 1974: 79).

The same point can be made about the shapely starlets (dubbed *maggiorate fisiche* in Italian) of the 1940s and 1950s, since they exhibited some of the same characteristics, albeit adapted to the post-war period. Silvana Pampanini, Gina Lollobrigida, and Sophia Loren emerged in a context defined by certain US stars, in which the emphasis shifted from the face to the body, and in which female representations were freeing themselves of the coy, submissive typologies of the Fascist period (see Gundle 1995). In some ways at least, they were closer to international standards of stars than their pre-war predecessors, as *Time* magazine observed in 1954 when it labelled Gina Lollobrigida the first star of an American type to emerge in Italy (Anon. 1954: 34). Thanks to the favourable conjuncture, they took part in international productions and were temporarily assimilated within the Hollywood star system—although only Loren achieved lasting success and for this reason became the symbol of Italianness for foreigners. Yet the *maggiorate* were significantly different from those they were equated with. They were younger, more spontaneous and natural in behaviour and appearance, and were identifiably Italian and lower-class in their tastes and aspirations. On screen at least, their eroticism was an earthy and rural one that contrasted with the urban polish peddled by Hollywood. Within the Italian context moreover they took on particular meanings because 'the female body, intact and uncontaminated by the look of Fascist ideology, a creature of the earth, rich with joyous sensuality, generous in its proportions, warm and familiar [was] a body landscape, along whose outline you could read the future of a nation that had to start again from scratch' (Grignaffini 1988: 123). The barefoot Mangano, her feet firmly rooted in a specific territory and landscape, set the pattern for a whole series of actresses chosen by male directors and producers. Many, including Loren (*La donna del fiume*) and Elsa Martinelli (*La risaia*) were launched in films with rural lower-class settings. These differences were quickly perceived by Hollywood and for this reason Italian beauties enjoyed a high novelty and commodity value there throughout the 1950s and 1960s.

These considerations suggest that American typologies were sometimes imitated but perhaps more frequently they were re-elaborated or taken as a point of departure. This point is reinforced by the fact that there were also many stars who bore no relation at all to American models, who could only be understood in the context of Italian society, and who in no sense formed vehicles of dreams and fantasy, whether imported or home-grown. These personalities acted as sources of collective rather than individual identification. Typically such stars were of lower-class origin, or at least were embraced largely by lower-class audiences who saw them as being of their own, although on occasions the reference was more specifically regional. The best example of this type of star is Anna Magnani, the passionate, raven-haired variety actress who established a unique screen personality with her portrayal of the pregnant bride-to-be Pina in *Roma città aperta*, which she then reinforced in a series of similar roles in films such as *L'onorevole Angelina* and *Bellissima*. Instinctive, maternal, strong, and independent, neither young nor beautiful, with a bad figure, but warm and authentic, she became a national symbol and laid down a set of reference points in terms of naturalness, authenticity, and a Mediterranean idea of femininity that was very influential and created a paradigm that no later Italian actress could completely escape. Magnani was increasingly marginalized by an Italian cinema that moved away from neorealism but until her death in 1973 she retained a special place in people's hearts; 'an

actress for intellectuals, she was a star for the audiences of third-run cinemas'
(Carrano 1988: 231). Although she was unmistakably Roman, Magnani transcended
the strongly regional characterization of many of the stars whose fame was largely
confined to Italy. As the socio-economic and cultural profile of the country changed,
she was not eclipsed like another maternal idol of the lower classes, the sensual,
full-figured actress of Greek origin, Yvonne Sanson; rather she remained the symbol of popular endurance and national rebirth.

Many Italian stars remained essentially local idols even if their fame extended
more widely. For example, most male comic actors were from the South and
enjoyed their greatest popularity there. This applied even to Totò (Antonio De
Curtis), the Neapolitan comic who in dozens of films made between 1948 and
1967 represented the Italian version of the downtrodden small man constantly
seeking to make do in adverse circumstances. Popular singers and sports heroes
also aroused passions that were usually of a local or sectoral nature.

What role did these domestic stars play? In essence, they interpreted in a practical way the feelings, experiences, frustrations, hardships, and hopes especially of
lower-class people living in less developed areas. They appealed not because they
were distant but because they were close to their audiences. They also provided
symbols of continuity with the past combined with varying elements of change
during a period of immense, disorienting social and economic development. This
contrasted with and complemented the overwhelmingly optimistic outlook of
American stars and some of their Italian equivalents (see Gundle 1990: 211–17).

As Italy became a predominantly industrial society in the 1950s, the upbeat,
fantasy-oriented, consumer-related notion of stardom that had first been communicated powerfully in the 1920s gained at the expense of alternative notions.
Through Hollywood on the Tiber, which was precisely the phenomenon satirized
in La dolce vita, American movie companies and actors brought with them a taste
for publicity, hedonism, luxury, and fashion that profoundly influenced Italian
models for decades to come. Yet the specificity of Italian society was never eliminated. The success of the comic actor Alberto Sordi, whose career prospered as
that of Totò went into decline, was based on a unique attraction–repulsion that
derived from his representation of all the typical negative traits of the Italian
character—mammismo (the man's excessive attachment to his mother), wily individualism, servility, cowardice, distrust, distaste for rules and procedures. Although
he was not a star in any conventional sense (Carrano 1988: 242), he revealed, in
innumerable films satirizing old ways and new totems, the peculiarly Italian features
of a process of modernization that observers tended to see in terms of 'homogenization' and 'Americanization' (for example Bocca 1963: 7; Rossellini 1956).

Idols of the Small Screen

Television stars (or 'personalities' as they are more commonly called in English)
were rather different in nature from the larger-than-life dream stars who were

associated above all with American cinema. In Italy, as elsewhere, television stars had, because of the size of the screen, the nature of the audience, and the mode of consumption, to be 'familiar' and 'normal', not extravagant but domesticated. As they appeared regularly and entered people's homes, they were not fantasy personalities but respectable neighbours and friends (Goffredo 1968: 56–8; see also McLuhan 1974: 331). In part for this reason, they were more standardized and middle-class, in keeping with the social model of the Catholic political élite. Yet this did not mean that domestic traits were absent. Indeed, 'in a country that had made television the central vehicle of cultural socialisation, star phenomena took on a very particular and "home-made" physiognomy' (Monteleone 1992: 348).

One of the first such personalities was the Italian-American Mike Bongiorno, whose 1955 quiz show *Lascia o raddoppia?* (a local variant of the American *The $64,000 Question*) contributed decisively to the runaway success of television in Italy. A bland Mr Average who dressed like a shop dummy and spoke with a curious American-Piedmontese accent, Bongiorno became enormously popular and sowed the seeds of a career that lasts to this day. His extreme mediocrity (witheringly analysed in Eco 1992) did not limit his appeal but rather enhanced it. He appeared in photo-romances, in films (*Ragazze d'oggi*, *Totò lascia e raddoppia*, etc.) and was seen as the 'ideal fiancé' by young women. Even a puppet of him was put on sale.

Some other male presenters who began their careers between the mid-1950s and the mid-1960s achieved similar levels of success. What men like Bongiorno, the ironic Enzo Tortora, the detached Corrado (Corrado Mantoni), and the punctilious Pippo Baudo had in common was a cordial manner, a middle-class background, an above average level of education (not Bongiorno, but he was forgiven because he was American), a certain old-fashioned courtesy, and a touch of gallantry. They stood as examples of the possibility of a unified and standardized Italian person, the premisses for which were laid in the transformations associated with the economic miracle. As products of the pedagogical and predominantly conformist model of broadcasting favoured by RAI-TV, they aimed to address a homogeneous national whole regardless of differences of age, intellectual level, and economic status.

Before the 1980s women were generally confined to subordinate and often silent roles. On the one hand there were the exotic personalities plucked from beauty contests or variety theatre who, decked in jewels and ostentatious evening wear, acted as assistants or dancers. On the other hand, and much more importantly, not least because they lasted much longer and won the enduring affection of their audience, were the announcers (*signorine buonasera*). These modest, demure, respectable, middle-class young women, who conjured up the idea of a fiancée rather than a lover and exhibited 'housewifely inexpressiveness' (Monteleone 1992: 303; Eco 1992: 157), were very popular with young girls, who admired their elegance and polish (in fact very modest) and for whom they also constituted a model of economic independence. They were inundated with letters, offers of marriage, requests for advice and autographs (Del Buono and Tornabuoni 1981: 34).

The domestic, familiar quality was underscored by the fact that, with television, for the first time, ordinary people could achieve fame as contestants in quiz shows, which fuelled tremendous curiosity and facilitated identification with the medium. This was enhanced by the fact that *Lascia o raddoppia?* contestants were often eccentrics: the dandy Mariannini, the busty tobacconist Garoppo, the female football expert Bolognini, and so on (see Delli Colli 1983: 24–30). There were dozens of press articles about them, they appeared on magazine covers, they received gifts of scooters, money, clothes from manufacturers; and on occasion they endorsed products in advertisements before slipping back into anonymity (Di Dario 1992: 48).

Many of the male stars have lasted down to the present (although on Tortora, see Lumley 1986 and 1988). Moreover, even after it lost its monopoly, the RAI remained the main producer of 'generalist' or 'national-popular' television stars. This was an especially valuable position to occupy because of the ever more central role assumed by television in both star production and social relations in the 1980s. Theatre, popular music, cinema, and sport all experienced crises as forms of entertainment and as industries independent of television and were to some extent gradually absorbed by it. This occurred over a period of years but was especially marked from the late 1970s. It was increasingly difficult to be a star without appearing on television, and television stars tended to overshadow all other domestic stars—as is apparent in the content of the popular magazine press which, as Alberoni noted, has always been the main medium of the cultivation of star cults (1973: 61). Almost from the moment television first appeared there was a reorientation in magazines geared to popular music and cinema (e.g. *Sorrisi e canzoni* added the term TV to its name). Something similar occurred in family magazines like *Oggi* and *Gente*.

In the mid-1980s RAI-TV heavily promoted its stars in an attempt to head off the challenge of the private networks that, by 1984, had fallen under the control of Silvio Berlusconi's Fininvest company. However, the attacks that Berlusconi's allies the Socialists made on RAI and its costly personalities alienated celebrities like Pippo Baudo and the showgirl and presenter Raffaella Carrà from the state broadcasting company (Di Dario 1992: 308–68; Martini 1985: 9–114). It was relatively easy in this context for Berlusconi to step in and tempt them to switch to Fininvest with the promise of fabulous contracts. In 1982 Bongiorno had been the first to cross over and revive his flagging career, followed by Corrado. Berlusconi also cleverly recruited widely from the ranks of the minor stars of the flagging low-budget cinema and among the aging has-beens of Italian popular song to give his channels a 'national-popular' feel, after having carved out an audience for them largely using imported US material (Rizza 1990: 536).

The expansion of commercial broadcasting coincided with the passage from what Umberto Eco termed the phase of paleo-television, in which the pedagogical criteria of public service broadcasting dominated, to the phase of neo-television, in which the medium became omnipresent, self-referential, and predominantly entertainment-oriented (Eco 1990: 245–6). This transition had consequences for the pattern of television stardom. The massive expansion of television and the daily rather than weekly rhythms that came to characterize scheduling following Fininvest's importation of American methods produced a more rapid circulation of personalities and a further 'normalization' of celebrities to the extent that the only thing that really makes them distinctive is the fact that they appear regularly on television (Vaime 1992). With few exceptions, they are not idols or symbols but mere presences. As magazine feature articles show, their standard of living in many cases is no better than that of many lower middle-class families. It is also worth noting that a marked sectorization has occurred. In itself this is not new, as from the 1940s the stars of photo-romances were only ever known to their readers; but it is new to television. Youth programmes, soaps, local programmes, and even shopping channels produce personalities that attract intense interest and admiration among subsections of the population and are unknown to everyone else.

The 'scaling down' of star figures to the level of everyday life produced attempts to enliven an increasingly bland television star system. In a context marked by permanent Christian Democratic domination of government, in which controversy of any sort was on the whole avoided, some stars opted to boost their allure by endowing themselves with the aura of the great stars of the golden age of Hollywood. For example, the showgirl Milly Carlucci presents herself in various versions of a 1950s type of stardom in hairstyle and dress, while the sexy soubrette Valeria Marini offers herself as a home-grown Marilyn Monroe and another soubrette, Pamela Prati, cultivates her image as 'television's Sophia Loren'. Given much coverage in magazine articles and picture features, this widespread practice of partial retrospective impersonation has two longer-range effects. First, it perpetuates the old perception of Italian stars as pale copies of American greats. Secondly, it reinforces foreign norms of physical appearance in terms of hair colour (blonde), ideal body weight (slim), and height (tall). Only in cinema is there space for the few deemed to represent typical examples of Italian female beauty, such as Ornella Muti and Monica Bellucci, who fill the places occupied in the past by Gina Lollobrigida and Claudia Cardinale.

Ultimately the attempt to restore allure to television stars cannot work, for the familiarity of television—exacerbated by distracted viewing and channel-hopping—would seem inescapably to give rise to a measure of contempt. Gossip magazines like *Novella 2000* and *Eva Express*, whose readerships reach astronomical levels each summer, accelerate the trend towards 'normalization' of television and music stars by publishing nude beach or bathing shots of them, with or without their complicity. In this way the public is given opportunities to admire the beautiful bodies of stars but also, in other instances, merely to express disgust or superior satisfaction at their mediocrity or ugliness. The desire to see stars exposed as vain and foolish or subjected to humiliation is confirmed by the success of television shows like *Blob*, a compilation of gaffes and examples of bad taste from all channels that is broadcast nightly on RAI3, and *Scherzi a parte*, a sort of *Candid Camera* in which the unwitting victims are celebrities.

Stars and the Economic System

Stars have always had economic functions for cultural industries. Precisely because audiences are interested in them, eager to see them and hear them perform, they constitute a powerful marketing tool for films, records, and magazines. In periods of economic growth and especially since the development of a consumer market of mass dimensions this function has widened, and entertainment stars have been involved in an ever greater range of tie-ins and promotions. In Italy this practice was much slower to develop than in the USA and was never as complete. In the past only some, not all, domestic stars took on this sort of role and even those that did, did not do so exactly along American lines.

The consumer role of Italian stars expanded from the late 1950s as a result of *Carosello*, the programme of advertisements shown nightly on RAI-TV from 1957. *Carosello* created a sub-star system of its own that was actually much more systematic than any operative in other fields, because stars were linked by contracts to advertising agencies. Sports champions, soubrettes, actors, and comedians all rounded out their earnings by promoting food, drink, and household goods. Even Eduardo De Filippo sang the praises of Illy coffee, while Dario Fo linked his name to numerous products including Gillette razors and a brand of motor oil (Ferri 1988: 8–9, 25–6). In addition to using known names, some up and coming, others well-loved but in decline, *Carosello* created some stars of its own, including the cartoon black chick Calimero, who became a great favourite with children.

For many years there were always some stars, including Sordi and Mastroianni, who refused to take part in advertising. These were generally film stars who saw the cinema as art, and therefore preferred to remain aloof from commerce. However, by the 1980s the numbers of those refusing advertising had dwindled to virtually nothing. Even Sophia Loren, perhaps to maintain a public profile no longer sustained through regular film or television work, advertised American Express, Parmacotto ham, and Annabella fur coats. For stars of the small screen, advertising became routine. For example, Raffaella Carrà lent her name to Scavolini kitchens, while Pippo Baudo stuck appropriately with institutional advertising, for example for Yellow Pages. This enhanced commercial role was facilitated by the massive expansion of advertising that occurred with the development of commercial television and the effects it had on RAI-TV, which itself became more commercialized, introducing sponsorship of programmes and turning presenters in part into salespersons. No star, however, was as completely identified with consumption as Mike Bongiorno. This was appropriate, for he had always represented the 'American dream' of prosperity for Italians, who associated him with *Lascia o raddoppia?* and its products and sums of money prizes. With his American background, Mike very easily converted to, and indeed relished, the sales and promotions that were associated with his quiz shows.

The commercial role of stars needs to be considered as part of the broader trend whereby Italy became a fully-fledged consumer society and stars became the leaders and illustrators of cultural trends, offering advice on all manner of topics, including beauty, diet, home furnishings, wedding rituals, and voting choices. In a context in which the main purpose of the creation of a star is to sell something, they have no autonomy from the logic of consumption (Sartori 1983: p. xvi). It also needs to be borne in mind that in the 1980s the whole notion of stardom was widened to incorporate areas and spheres that in the past did not produce stars, including business, journalism, academia, and fashion. The spectacularization of a range of figures was a mechanism for arousing interest, winning approval, acquiring leverage, and generating business. In a media-dominated society, no one or no enterprise could claim to be important without visibility. However, this does not mean that an entertainment mode spread to all spheres. Public personalities only had in common the fact that they were well known and admired. Their ways of relating to the public, to the media, and public perception of them were all differentiated. Idols of production celebrated in business magazines like *Capital* and *Class* stressed achievement, not leisure values (Morelli 1989).

This phenomenon, described as *neo-divismo* (neo-stardom) (Morelli 1989) and considered in relation to *post-divismo* (Reggiani 1985) was born of the interaction of the mass media with economic forces and the increasingly central role of the media in social and economic organization. Stardom, it has been argued, became a phenomenon not just of show business but of all business—it became a technostructure that was related to the interaction of books, films, merchandising, music, videos, computers, etc. (Sartori 1983: 251).

This multiplication of star phenomena was related to social fragmentation and to the eclipse of universal models. It was also the result of a demand for simplification through personalization in complex societies. The key position is still occupied, however, by entertainment stars—really it is they who have come to occupy a strategic role in the industrial system of the country, because entertainment feeds into a vast number of businesses and is able to add elements of dream and desire. They are cultural leaders who suggest fashions and lifestyles to consumers, and consequently have a catalytic role in relation to spending and consciousness. Some stars realized the potential for entrepreneurship that this accorded them and launched out into a range of activities; one such was Edvige Fenech, television presenter, actress, film producer, and clothes designer.

The link with fashion is particularly important because it became Italy's most successful industry in the 1980s (Balloni 1994: 398–9). Historically, Italian couturiers, especially in Rome, enjoyed a close relationship with foreign stars, although for most purposes they used young Italian women of aristocratic background to model their clothes. The Fontana sisters' wedding dress for Linda Christian's marriage to Tyrone Power in Rome in 1949 and the regular work they did for Ava Gardner was a great help in creating a market in the US for an Italian look (Steele 1994; Bianchino and Quintavalle 1989: 35–43). Very little interest, however, was taken in the Italian stars of the 1940s and 1950s. They were not seen at all as setters of taste or fashion. *Estetica*, a magazine for hairstylists and cosmeticians, featured exclusively American and British stars such as Grace Kelly, Deborah Kerr, Elizabeth Taylor, and Audrey Hepburn. Of the Italians only Isa Miranda was considered an icon of elegance. The others were tolerated only in so far as they accepted and conformed to established upper-class standards of dress. But even then they were often deemed to be plebeian and vulgar, in both behaviour and shape. Only the 'Italian Christian Dior' Emilio Schuberth cultivated a show-business clientele that included Lollobrigida and Loren. Other designers preferred slim, tall, poised, well-bred actresses like the former model Elsa Martinelli, who came to the fore in the late 1950s. The *Dolce vita* style paradoxically had nothing to do with mainstream Italian life; in fashion terms, it was a re-creation of various unlinked dress styles and behaviour models (very few of which had their origin in Italy) that the Italian public associated with foreign stars and with a newly visible international set.

The diffidence in fashion circles towards domestic stars persists to this day, whereas well-known designers such as Armani, Valentino, and Versace court Hollywood stars and compete to dress them on occasions such as Oscar night. The latter two, moreover, contributed decisively to the promotion of the supermodels who have been alone in the 1980s and 1990s in providing icons of glamour that film stars, who typically prefer to be seen as serious artists, no longer wish to and television celebrities are unable to provide. With the sole exception of Carla Bruni, the supermodels are not Italian or even vaguely Latin in appearance; instead the regal bearing and unattainable aloofness of a Linda Evangelista or a Nadja Auermann quite explicitly recall the great Hollywood stars of the past (for Versace's views on this, see Falck 1995: 85). It is the dream of perfection they provide that unleashes unlimited material desires.

In the 1980s the designers themselves became international stars and within Italy they also assumed something of the status of gurus on social and economic matters as well as questions of style and fashion. However, they were obliged also to make use of domestic stars in order to exploit fully the domestic market for their products. On the one hand, the association of fashion goods with supermodels, American film stars, and beautiful domestic celebrities triggered aspirational impulses to emulation (if I wear designer label X then maybe I will acquire some of the allure and exclusivity of star Y). On the other hand, magazine feature articles and television appearances of ordinary or even rather vulgar singers and soubrettes wearing designer items provoked more reassuring sensations of accessibility (if even personality Z can look stylish and polished wearing designer label X, then surely I can too). This diversified marketing strategy was important in extending the reach of Italian fashion to the sort of women who, in the past, admired singers and starlets and sought to produce at home copies of their outfits.

The emphasis on appearance and presentation, combined with the wider importance of the media in social and economic relations, inevitably conditioned politics. Politicians began to appear on screen from 1962, the year *Tribuna politica* (the equivalent of party political broadcasts) was introduced, but from the 1980s they began to appear as guests in entertainment programmes, particularly those hosted by Baudo, Carrà, and others which had mass audiences. There was also a tendency for politicians to present themselves as stars to some degree, by paying attention to image and dress, and putting family and aspects of their personal lives on display. Leading political figures had always enjoyed a special star status on account of the unusually deep political divisions in the country, but this was a new phenomenon that was related to the decline of the conventional mass party, the central role of television in electioneering and social communications more generally, as well as the widening of the concept of stardom. It concerned politicians at all levels (for analyses of these trends, see Pasquino 1985 and Gundle 1992) .

This change in the nature of political mobilization was no less important than the collapse of the traditional parties in the corruption scandals of 1992–3 in paving the way for Berlusconi's extraordinary operation in political marketing in 1994, for it shifted power away from organized voluntary activity towards cultural industries and in particular towards Fininvest, which acquired a unique capacity to condition social, cultural, and economic relations in a wide variety of spheres. In the context in which it occurred, the extension of the company's operations into the political sphere was almost inevitable, and a natural corollary was the use by Berlusconi of a star strategy to conquer the state. If in 1983 the judgement of one specialist in mass communications that 'the élite of the new-style stardom has truly taken power' seemed far-fetched (Sartori 1983: 320), by 1994 it had acquired the aura of incontrovertible truth.

Further Reading

General insights into the phenomenon of stardom may be gained from R. Dyer, *Stars* (London, 1982), C. Gledhill (ed.), *Stardom: Industry of Desire* (London, 1992) and J. Stacey, *Star Gazing: Hollywood Cinema and Female Spectatorship* (London, 1994). The literature on Italian stars is poor, however. Only C. Sartori, *La fabbrica delle stelle. Divismo, mercato e mass media negli anni 80* (Milan, 1983), has attempted to develop and evaluate F. Alberoni's pioneering work, *L'elite senza potere. Ricerca sociologica sul divismo* (Bologna, 1963), by studying changes in patterns of star phenomena in Italy, while no one has followed G. C. Castello, *Il divismo. Mitologia del cinema* (Turin, 1959), in seeking to write a history of stardom. Furthermore serious biographies even of film stars are rare. Books on television, sport, and popular music generally have little to say on this theme, although there are some suggestive comments in V. Di Dario's *Pippo, Mike e Raffaella. La televisione italiana dagli esordi ai nostri giorni* (Milan, 1992), Franco Monteleone's *Storia della radio e della televisione in Italia* (Venice, 1992), and G. Baldazzi's, *La canzone italiana del Novecento* (Rome, 1989). P. Carrano's useful essay 'Divismo', in M. Livolsi (ed.), *Schermi e ombre. Gli italiani e il cinema nel dopoguerra* (Florence, 1988), is concerned only with domestic film stars in the period between 1945 and the early 1980s. The most useful source material is provided by the volumes published by Gremese dedicated to single stars (Isa Miranda, Amedeo Nazzari, Marcello Mastroianni, Sophia Loren, Gina Lollobrigida, Totò, etc.), two of which (Loren, Lollobrigida) have been published in English by Citadel Press. These contain full accounts of the stars' careers, extracts from contemporary reviews of their films, and numerous illustrations. For further information, it is necessary to turn to autobiographies, memoirs, the popular press, and personal testimonies.

References

ALBERONI, F. (1973), *L'elite senza potere. Ricerca sociologica sul divismo* (Bologna; first published 1963).

ANON. (1954), 'Hollywood on the Tiber', *Time*, 16 Aug.: 32–6.

BALDAZZI, G. (1989), *La canzone italiana del Novecento* (Rome).

BALLONI, V. (1994), 'L'industria della moda', in P. Ginsborg (ed.), *Stato dell'Italia* (Milan).

BARANSKI, Z. G., and LUMLEY, R. (1990) (eds.), *Culture and Conflict in Postwar Italy* (Basingstoke and London).

BARZOLETTI, G., *et al.* (1986), *Modi di produzione del cinema italiano. La Titanus* (Ancona).

BIANCHINO, G., and QUINTAVALLE, A. C. (1989), *Moda dalla fiaba al design: Italia 1951–1989* (Novara).

BOCCA, G. (1963), *La scoperta dell'Italia* (Bari).

BOLLATI, G. (1983), *L'italiano. Il carattere nazionale come storia e come invenzione* (Turin).

CALDIRON, O., and HOCKHOFLER, M. (1978), *Isa Miranda* (Rome).

CARRANO, P. (1988), 'Divismo' in M. Livolsi (ed.), *Schermi e ombre. Gli italiani e il cinema nel dopoguerra* (Florence).

CASTELLO, G. C. (1959), *Il divismo. Mitologia del cinema* (Turin).

D'ATTORRE, P. P. (1991) (ed.), *Nemici per la pelle. Sogno americano e mito sovietico nell'Italia contemporanea* (Milan).

DE GRAZIA, V. (1992), *How Fascism Ruled Women: Italy 1922–1945* (Berkeley).

DEL BUONO, O., and TORNABUONI, L. (1981), *Album di famiglia della TV. 30 anni di televisione italiana* (Milan).

DELLI COLLI, L. (1984), *Dadaumpa. Storie, immagini, curiosità e personaggi di televisione in Italia* (Rome).

DI DARIO, V. (1992), *Pippo, Mike e Raffaella. La televisione italiana dagli esordi ai nostri giorni* (Milan).

ECO, U. (1990), 'A Guide to the Neo-Television of the 1980s', in Baranski and Lumley (1990), 245–55.

—— (1992), 'The Phenomenology of Mike Bongiorno', in *Misreadings* (London) (first published 1961).

ELLWOOD, D. W., and BRUNETTA, G. P. (1991) (eds.), *Hollywood in Europa. Industria, politica, pubblico del cinema 1945–1960* (Florence).

FALCK, J. (1995) 'Finché c'è top c'è speranza', *L'Espresso*, 10 Feb., 80–85.

FALDINI, F., and FOFI, G. (1979), *L'avventurosa storia del cinema italiano raccontata dai suoi protagonisti, 1935–1959* (Milan).

FERRI, K. (1988), *Spot Babilonia* (Milan).

FORGACS, D. (1990), *Italian Culture in the Industrial Era, 1880–1980: Cultural Industries, Politics and the Public* (Manchester).

GOFFREDO, D. (1968), *Psicologia del divismo televisivo* (Rome).

GRIGNAFFINI, G. (1988), 'Female Identity and Italian Cinema of the 1950s', in G. Bruno and M. Nadotti (eds.), *Off-Screen: Women and Film in Italy* (London).

GUNDLE, S. (1990), 'From Neorealism to *Luci rosse*: Cinema, Politics, Society 1945–1985', in Baranski and Lumley (1990), 195–224.

Gundle, S. (1992), 'Italy', in D. Butler and A. Ranney (eds.), *Electioneering* (Oxford).

—— (1995), 'Sophia Loren, Italian Icon', *Historical Journal of Film, Radio and Television*, 15/3: 367–85.

Hotchner, A. E. (1979), *Sophia Living and Loving: Her Own Story* (London).

Lumley, R. (1986), 'The Tortora Case: The Scandal of the Television Presenter as Media Event', *Italianist*, 6: 157–70.

—— (1988), 'The Tortora Case: A Very Public Death', *Italianist*, 8: 110–14.

McLuhan, M. (1974), *Understanding Media: The Extensions of Man* (London).

Martini, P. (1985), *TV sorrisi e milioni. L'avventurosa storia dei divi e della televisione italiana* (Milan).

Monteleone, F. (1992), *Storia della radio e della televisione in Italia. Società, politica, strategie, programmi 1922–1992* (Venice).

Morelli, A. (1989), 'I nuovi eroi della produzione: il divismo nei periodici di economia e finanza', *Problemi dell'informazione*, 14/4: 553–65.

Morin, E. (1959), *Les Stars* (Paris).

Pasquino, G. (1985), 'I mass media e la comunicazione politica', in Pasquino (ed.), *La complessità della politica* (Bari).

Pruzzo, P., and Lancia, E. (1983), *Amedeo Nazzari* (Rome).

Reggiani, S. (1985), *Dizionario del postdivismo. 101 attori italiani del cinema e della TV* (Turin).

Rizza, N. (1990), 'Il palinsesto come fattore di produzione', *Problemi dell'informazione*, 15/4: 529–40.

Rossellini, R. (1956), Preface to B. Rondi, *Il neorealismo italiano* (Parma).

Sartori, C. (1983), *La fabbrica delle stelle. Divismo, mercato e mass media negli anni 80* (Milan).

Spinazzola, V. (1974), *Cinema e pubblico. Lo spettacolo filmico in Italia 1945–1965* (Milan).

Steele, V. (1994), 'Italian Fashion and America', in G. Celant (ed.), *The Italian Metamorphosis, 1943–1968* (New York).

Vaime, E. (1992), 'I teledivi della porta accanto', *L'Unità*, 24 Sept.

18

Popular Song and
Musical Cultures

MARCELLA
FILIPPA

SONGS offer a unique vantage point for the study both of social behaviour and of a culture's repertoire of images. Viewed historically, they are a valuable source for anyone who wants to examine the conflicts and changes between generations in the society which produced them and the evolution of taste, in the sense used by Bourdieu (1979) of a marker of 'distinction' or social differentiation which enables people to recognize themselves as belonging to a group or class and to express their differences from others. My analyses and examples in this chapter are limited mainly to popular music, including the so-called *canzonetta* (popular or light song), the *canzone d'autore* (written by a known singer-songwriter), the political song, light music, and certain forms of experimentation; I shall also refer to folk music and jazz. In all cases the emphasis is on the relations between society and musical production, with music being used as a way into social history.

In a study of workers' protest songs, Alessandro Portelli remarked (1983: 224) that there are certain songs which do not reproduce reality but represent it. To some degree this holds good for other musical genres too. The more a song is heard, sung, reproduced, and sold, the more it may be used as a source for the study of mentalities and the imaginative repertoire of a society. The historian who wants to reconstruct this kind of history, in particular through well-known popular songs, those which most closely reflect the behavioural world of a given society, has available a source which in Italy is still very little used. And yet it is a source which allows him or her to interpret the historical process, to 'slip inside' it, to paraphrase Siegfried Kracauer, for whom the historian's task is that of

penetrating its outward appearances, so that he may learn to understand that world from within . . . He must venture on the diverse routes suggested to him by his intercourse with the evidence, let himself drift along, and take in, with all his senses strained, the various messages that happen to reach him. Thus he will more likely than not hit upon unexpected facts and context some of which perhaps turn out to be incompatible with his original assumptions. (Kracauer 1969: 84–5)

Song indeed does not reproduce reality but represents it. It reworks it, reformulates certain aspects of it, those which most closely reflect widespread states of mind and perceptions, or which avoid others. In the Second World War, for instance, which more than any previous war involved the civilian population and in which hunger, death, and fear were ever-present, love songs and escapist songs were widely popular. A passion for life, a desire to forget the horrors of war, however briefly, came to the fore in many people's tastes. According to Paquito Del Bosco, one of the most sensitive observers of the music of this period, of over 2,500 songs published between 1940 and 1943 as sheet music, scores, or in magazines, only a hundred or so contained any reference to the war, whether precise or vague (Del Bosco 1989: 211–12). In fact the proportion of songs with military or heroic subjects was exactly the same as it had been in the peacetime years of the Fascist regime. The titles are indicative of the kind of song that was popular: 'Mille lire al mese', 'Porta un bacione a Firenze', 'Com'è bello far l'amore quanno è sera', 'Ma l'amore no', 'Luna marinara'.

Many critics have viewed these songs as 'escapist' or childish and have referred to them disparagingly as *canzonette* (literally 'little songs'), treating them as products of a mass market geared to the lowering of consciousness. This position was theorized by Adorno, who at the height of the vogue for swing and jazz was a musical consultant for the Radio Research Project at Princeton and in 1938 described the new popular audience for this music in these terms:

They listen atomistically and dissociate what they hear, but precisely in this dissociation they develop certain capacities which accord less well with the concepts of traditional aesthetics than with those of football and motoring. They are not childlike, as might be expected on the basis of an interpretation of the new type of listener in terms of the introduction to musical life of groups previously unacquainted with music. But they are childish; their primitiveness is not that of the underdeveloped, but of the forcibly retarded. (Adorno 1938: 41)

Similar views were expressed in Italy in the 1960s and 1970s, during the wave of students' and workers' protests, when so-called escapist songs began to be severely criticized. Specialists and musicologists such as Michele Straniero, Sergio Liberovici, and Emilio Jona, themselves among the protagonists of the workers' campaigning songs that had their centres in Turin, Milan, and Rome, claimed that this type of song was not born of any need for communication, 'but of the cold pursuit of a precise aim: that of being sold, and broadcast on the radio, and on record, in dance halls and, more recently, on television and juke boxes' (Straniero *et al.* 1964: p. li). They regarded these songs as the equivalent of a digestive pill, as lacking spontaneity, mirroring the alienated and neurotic modern condition. The consumer of this music was seen as controlled and submissive, as against a listener to a kind of music which was a form of resistance to power.

In contrast with such views, there are approaches (for instance that of Certeau 1984) which concede more complex forms of identity to listeners, who are seen not as an audience crushed by a consumer-oriented industry but as people who make choices, who make use of so-called mass consumerism by elaborating strategies, if sometimes unconsciously, and forms of microexistence. Adorno's brand of determinism, according to which consumption is always the consequence of a controlling strategy on the part of the culture industry, is also contested by other writers (for instance Frith 1978) who suggest a correlation and an interchange between the world of consumption and that of production, rather than an irremediable and unalterable subordination of the consumer to producer.

Indeed in the 1960s and 1970s, as in earlier decades, a number of protest songs were based on the tunes of hit songs, or so-called popular songs. This is surely a clear sign of contamination, of the persistence of musical styles which were also popular with working-class audiences, who overlaid them with political lyrics, but which were borrowed from older oral traditions. According to the musicologist Roberto Leydi (1973) a variety of components came together in the proletarian repertoire, even if elements borrowed from bourgeois culture often predominated.

Let us look at some examples, chosen over time. The anarchist Pietro Gori—possibly best known as the writer of 'Addio a Lugano'—wrote 'Vieni o maggio, t'aspettan le genti' ('Come, o May, the people await you') to be sung to the tune of 'Va' pensiero' from Verdi's *Nabucco*. After the murder of the Socialist parliamentary deputy Giacomo Matteotti in June 1924, Milanese anti-Fascists made up alternative verses to the tune of 'Il foxtrot della nostalgia' by Bixio and Cherubini. In the 1958 election campaign the Christian Democrats made use of the tune of 'Nel blu dipinto di blu', the song by Domenico Modugno better known as 'Volare' which had won the San Remo Festival of the same year. Minimal sleight of hand produced the watchword 'Votare DC' (Vote Christian Democrat). In Turin at the end of the 1960s, women workers at the Alpina, one of the largest Italian factories making stockings and knitted goods, used a song by the Milanese *cantautore* (singer-songwriter) Enzo Jannacci, 'Vengo anch'io, no tu no' as a basis for the 'Alpineide', a campaigning song exposing managerial high-handedness and exploitation. During those same years political or trade union messages were often propagated to popular tunes.

With these sorts of changes, superimpositions, and persistences, the exact dating of a song becomes a problem. As Portelli puts it (1983: 224): 'A song cannot be carbon-dated, because once born it goes on living and growing, and its very genesis contains within it the cultural layering of the community which has produced it.' For example, it has been established by Leydi (1973) that the tune of the popular Resistance song 'Bella ciao' was borrowed from a children's clapping song, 'La me nona l'è vecchierella', which in its turn derived from a widely sung and well-known ballad, 'La bevanda sonnifera', while its words were adapted from another ballad known as 'Fiore di tomba', which Leydi classifies as a narrative song. It is the story of a young woman who asks to die rather than leave her lover, and to be buried deep in the ground with the man she loves and with her parents, predicting that a beautiful flower will grow on her tomb, to remind all passers-by that she died for love. The corresponding words in the partisan version are

> E se io muoio da partigiano, tu mi devi seppellir.
> Seppellire lassù in montagna sotto l'ombra d'un bel fior.
> E le genti che passeranno e' diranno o che bel fior.
> E' questo il fiore del partigiano morto per la libertà.

And if I should die as a partisan, you must bury me. | Bury me up in the mountains under the shade of a lovely flower. | And the people who pass by will say oh what a lovely flower. | This is the flower of the partisan who died for freedom.

The historical quality of a popular song may thus lie not so much in the information it contains as in the changes that take place in its form, in its words and music.

In addition to the songs themselves, there are other sources which allow us to reconstruct the context in which a song was produced and consumed. Oral sources are particularly valuable, in the form of the testimonies of people who lived through the period, whether as songwriters and performers, fans and buffs, or merely as listeners, careful or otherwise. These accounts can provide valuable information about messages transmitted, codes of behaviour, the imaginative repertoire of the period, and the tastes of a whole generation. There is always something of a two-way relationship, cultural, social, and political, between the language of the lyrics of a song and the society in which it is produced. In the 1930s, for example, the image of the woman which emerges from 'consumer' songs is that of the woman as eternal child, simple, genuine, and down-to-earth: an ideal woman, portrayed as a stereotyped, bucolic image, who lives in the country, far from the deafening and corrupt world of the city. She is a *bambina*, *piccina*, *bambola*, *monella*, or *birichina*, blonde with blue eyes and turned-up nose. Her body is asexual, very rarely mentioned; just about the only exception is the song 'Ma le gambe', a 1938 hit by the Trio Lescano which includes the words:

> Saran belli gli occhi neri
> saran belli gli occhi blu,
> ma le gambe, ma le gambe
> a me piacciono di più.

Black eyes may be lovely | blue eyes may be lovely, | but legs, but legs | are what I like the most.

In fact, these were the leitmotifs of Fascist propaganda: marriage, procreation, the woman as mother and 'angel of the hearth'. The women in these songs are pink, plump peasants. Songs such as 'Reginella campagnola' ('Little queen of the fields'), 'La strada del bosco', 'Rosabella del Molise', 'Abruzzo tutto or' ('Abruzzo the golden'—in reality an arid, poor, and mountainous region) chimed well with the autarkic propaganda of Fascism, the demographic campaign, and the battle for wheat, the revival of popular traditions, of the so-called 'threshing-floor' parties and peasant festivals. This ruralism exerted an influence on the vocal style, which drew on peasant dance rhythms, and on fashion: floral dress patterns and a hair-style with plaits wound round the head, both of them typical peasant styles, were introduced.

The ideal interpreter of this musical genre was Carlo Buti from Florence (1902–63). The first singer to owe his career to the radio, he was popular both with rural audiences and with those on the outskirts of the cities. As well as the hit 'Faccetta nera' ('Little black face'), the song that epitomized the Fascist war in Ethiopia, Buti sang 'Chitarra romana', 'Portami tante rose', 'Violino tzigano', and a famous paean to the countryside, 'Se vuoi godere la vita':

> Se vuoi godere la vita vieni quaggiù in campagna
> è tutta un'altra cosa vedi il mondo color di rosa,
> quest'aria deliziosa non è l'aria della città

If you want to enjoy life come out to the country; | it's another world, everything looks rosy, | the air's like wine, forget the city air.

The remainder of this chapter develops these theoretical and methodological considerations with reference to three examples, taken respectively from the late 1930s and early 1940s, the 1950s, and the late 1980s and early 1990s. Each example illustrates the way Italian musicians have reworked musical genres borrowed from elsewhere and deals with the meanings of their music for audiences, the cultures of listening.

Jazz, the Devil's Music

A number of musical styles were present together in the Italy of the 1930s: not perhaps as mass phenomena, but with an important role in forming new musical tastes that were shared by a mainly youth public. Of these, jazz has proved to be the most interesting and complex phenomenon. It was vilified and officially pro-scribed from the mid-1930s by the Fascist regime as it laboured to revive the 'true values' of the home-grown song; but, as so often with forbidden fruit, jazz became immensely popular with the young generations, because of both the innovative potential of the music and the originality of the words. Contrary to what has been maintained, its listeners were not exclusively middle-class or intellectuals; jazz also appealed to many young working-class people living in the big cities, as well as in the provincial towns. They bought records, heard them at friends' houses, and continued to listen even when this was expressly forbidden by specific legislation, 'as though we were listening to Radio Londra' (the BBC Italian Service), according to the oral testimony of one Turin worker who subsequently became active in the Communist Party after the Second World War.

At the very moment when jazz was becoming an accepted part of the Italian musical world—even the big orchestras of the EIAR were to some degree taken by it—there was a tendency to pigeon-hole it as a phenomenon typical of societies defined as primitive and barbaric, liable to pollute Italy's robust and healthy youth. On 9 July 1942 the following statement appeared in the Fascist daily newspaper *Il Giornale d'Italia*:

Swing is the music of the Negroes of Harlem, a frenetic dance lacking all harmony and grace, a mental form of decadence, entailing a ridiculous mode of speech and dress; it is a manifestation of solidarity with the Anglo-Saxon and is therefore anti-European; it is a form of hysteria typical of degenerates, it is snobbery, one of the embodiments of the snobbery of defeat. It is a music favoured by wogs. . . . I saw something like it in the heart of Africa, in music played by a tribe which enjoyed a reputation for total barbarism. But the rhythm those Negroes danced to was almost sedate by comparison.

From 1939 onwards laws were issued censoring lyrics and prohibiting the sale of American records; in order to complete the process of so-called Italianization, Jews were now excluded from show business. On several occasions jazz was defined as 'Afro-demo-pluto-Judaic-Masonic-epileptoid music'. The racial campaign promoted by the Fascist regime had begun in 1938, and since there have always been Jewish composers and performers, from Mendelssohn, Offenbach, and Gershwin down to Rubinstein, Horowitz, and the Menuhins, a very large number of musicians were affected by the proscriptions. Indeed, the measures adopted in this moral crusade were of unprecedented stringency, and they intensified after the USA joined the war in December 1941. The music of Walt Disney's films was banned; recent recordings which had never appeared in catalogues were suppressed, along with all names and words which did not have a thoroughly Italian ring to them. Louis Armstrong became Luigi Braccioforte, his 'Saint Louis Blues' became 'Le tristezze di San Luigi' (literally, 'the sorrows of St Louis'); Benny Goodman became Beniamino Buonuomo and his 'Stompin' at the Savoy,' somewhat less vividly, became 'I Savoiardi'.

But the attitude of the regime was sometimes ambivalent. The music of Gershwin, though explicitly banned, was transmitted during those same years at the Littoriali—annual competitions held by young Fascist university students: many leading Fascists were jazz enthusiasts, for instance Achille Starace, Galeazzo Ciano, and even Mussolini's fourth son, Romano, born in 1921, who became well known in Italy as a jazz musician after the war.

Fig. 30 Popular music became a site of fierce ideological conflicts in the last years of the Fascist regime. In 1937 *La Stampa* claimed that the EIAR broadcast more hours of jazz than any other radio service in Europe. Soon afterwards the mounting anti-Semitic campaign (from 1938) and the entry into the Second World War (June 1940) led to measures to restrict these broadcasts and promote Italian dance music and songs instead. *Il Canzoniere della Radio* was a monthly magazine carrying the words and music of hit songs. This 1940 cover by Gino Boccasile projects an image of youth and middle-class elegance—including the thin woman whom Fascist ideologues had a decade earlier associated with decadent modernity and lack of fecundity—which could at the same time feasibly pass for Italian.

One of the most thorough students of jazz in Italy, Adriano Mazzoletti, has pointed out that a copy of the work by Ezio Levi and Giancarlo Testoni, *Introduzione alla vera musica di jazz*, published in Milan in 1938, was presented by its authors to Vittorio Mussolini, the Duce's second son, with the dedication: 'With gratitude to one of the first people in Italy to understand and appreciate real jazz in Italy' (Mazzoletti 1983). One year later Ezio Levi, who was Jewish, was forced to leave the country because of the racial laws, and to emigrate to the USA. At least until the end of 1939, music catalogues continued to include mention of foreign records by Louis Armstrong, Count Basie, and Bing Crosby, to name but a few. Furthermore the EIAR continued to broadcast songs which were in fact Italian translations of American originals. Cinico Angelini, Pippo Barzizza, Natalino Otto, and Kramer Gorni continued to write and sing swing, no longer defined as such, but strongly rhythmical and syncopated. Otto (1912–69) was one of many Italian singers of the period who became known for a new singing style, inspired by transatlantic models and freer, anti-conformist canons. Whole generations sang his hits, from 'Maestro Paganini', 'Polvere di stella', 'Op op trotta cavallino', 'La canzone del boscaiolo', 'Il ritmo d'amore' to 'Ho un sassolino nella scarpa', which he sang in pure Dixieland style. Beppe Fenoglio's novel *Il partigiano Johnny*, about the Resistance in Piedmont, contains an episode where the protagonist surprises two girls playing Otto's 'Lungo il viale' on the gramophone. A few years later, with the end of the war and the arrival of the Anglo-American troops, jazz became synonymous with the restoration of freedom. As the music critic Gianfranco Baldazzi puts it:

It was to be the jazz of the white big bands, specializing in sophisticated and irresistible dance music, which acted as background music to the disembarkation of US troops on Italian soil. For ordinary war-weary people, this music, broadcast over the radio and on what were known as V-records (or Victory records) was part of the 'liberators'' gift-pack, along with bars of chocolate and cartons of Lucky Strike. This was no longer the black jazz of New Orleans, made up of a series of chaotic improvisations, and with all the thrill of a high-class brothel, but music which was wonderful to dance to, played by famous clarinettists or trombonists who had become conductors of big bands. Historic names such as Benny Goodman, Glenn Miller, and Artie Shaw had already been the idols of vast American audiences for a decade. (Baldazzi 1989: 67)

Fred Buscaglione, a 1950s Myth

'He had jazz in his blood', was how the Turin-born jazz veteran Renato Germonio described Fred Buscaglione, who died in 1960. Back in May 1941, Germonio had written an article in defence of jazz in *Il lambello*, a fortnightly review produced by the Fascist university students of Piedmont, containing the following passage:

Do not imagine that the present article was written by some lone champion of this art form—yes, art form. The time has come to take the jazz phenomenon seriously, not to give a damn about being dubbed a crank or a fanatic. . . . Have you never felt an inner thrill, an agreeable rush of rhythm and well-being when listening to a good performance by our own Kramer, the greatest Italian hot-artist?

Germonio recalls that at the height of Fascism they had had the nerve to shoot a film of amateurs playing jazz in a city park, their faces blackened with soot. This was an evident gesture of provocation and transgression: the first of many such gestures which would lead to Fred Buscaglione becoming a model for so many young people of the time.

Buscaglione was born in Turin in 1921 and spent much of his life there, heir to a tradition of his district of origin to live off marginal types of work on the fringes of legality and, in his case, a certain disinclination, not shared by his peers, to work in the great Fiat car factory, the symbol of Turin. He preferred music to a steady job, and that passion ran through his whole existence. By the end of the 1940s he was one of Europe's most promising jazz violinists. A composer and arranger, his works contain elements of swing and bebop, but also of the *avanspettacolo* (live variety acts before a cinema show) and the *café chantant*, combined with Afro-Cuban and Brazilian rhythms.

According to the lyricist Leo Chiosso, who wrote most of Buscaglione's words, his songs during those years contain 'no scenes of domestic banality, no bars on the outskirts of town; his world always verges on the chic. The mood of the time was to lift the underdog, the poor, the car-factory worker and agricultural labourer out of the greyness of their lives, to steep them in a world where every woman would say to them: "Grazie dei fior"' (quoted in Castellucci and Mollica 1981: 26; 'Grazie dei fior' was a tear-jearker which won the first San Remo Festival in 1951). Buscaglione countered these stereotyped scenes with ironic, cynical send-ups, debunking the legendary America of the time and bringing ordinary people into his songs, the sort of people who populated the limited urban world into which he had been born. His particular gift was to smile at the limitations and more pathetic aspects of life, to wax ironic over the new values emerging from an aggressively consumerist society. His songs rebelled against mothers at prayer in tremulous expectation, weeping wives, and pale, sick children—that whole world of sentimental tragedy which pervaded the light music of the time, symbolized most eloquently by the San Remo Festival.

Another of Buscaglione's hallmarks was the close parallel between the songs he sang and his own lifestyle, making him an anomaly in the show business world of the time. He built up an image of himself which he projected in both public and private, dressing in the American style imported through gangster films and the stories of Damon Runyon and Mickey Spillane, with a brilliantined quiff and Clark Gable moustache. He lived dangerously, like the people he sang about, and his myth was further boosted by his all too apposite and tragic death, which was also like that of the characters he sang about. In Rome on 3 February 1960 he drove his brand new salmon-pink Ford Thunderbird (which had cost the astronomical sum of 6 million lire) slap into a lorry loaded with blocks of tufa. His early death was later to be compared to those of James Dean and Marilyn Monroe. This was the time of Fellini's *La dolce vita*, and Buscaglione's violent end endowed him with something of the aura of one of its characters. According to the newspapers he had a rendezvous with Anita Ekberg, one of the stars of Fellini's film, a few hours before he died. No one will ever know if this was true.

After his death the press concocted an assortment of varying and contradictory images around him. Orio Vergani, one of the main personalities in Italian journalism at the time, dismissed him as follows in the *Corriere della Sera*: 'Poor Buscaglione. He could not have foreseen that death, which stood awaiting him at a crossroads, after some desolate night on the tiles, to crush him as one swats a fly.'

The papers of the left, *L'Unità* and *Avanti!*, on the other hand, heaped praise upon him for his interest in and responsiveness to characters from the working-class world into which he had been born. The Communist daily reported that he had played at the Festa de *l'Unità* at Rimini the year before without asking for a fee, and that he had never ceased to move among 'the simplest people, the working classes who reminded him of the hard years of his youth, and among whom he always made his closest friends'.

At his funeral in Turin, police cordons were broken at several points; dozens of people were hurt, and many fainted. This passionate reaction was a completely new phenomenon on the Italian scene at the time, comparable with the emotions aroused by the funeral of the racing cyclist Fausto Coppi, who had died a month earlier, or by the death of the entire Turin football team when their aeroplane crashed into a hill at Superga near the city in 1949. Over a hundred thousand fans attended his funeral: young girls, shop assistants and workers who, for the first time, now dared to ask their employers for a few hours off. The coffin was followed by 'a crowd of youngsters with school books under their arm', as the dailies wrote. This was the first full-blown funeral of a show business star, and his myth would live on for years.

Some time ago a poster appeared on the walls of Turin signed 'El Paso'—a youth club which had occupied a public building and transformed it into a centre for alternative cultural activities—in solidarity with two imprisoned anarchists. This poster reproduced an image of Fred Buscaglione, all moustaches and ironic smile, dressed to kill, with a black shirt and white tie, and holding a sub-machine-gun, accompanied by the words in comic strip form: 'Depressed? Money problems? Try your local bank.' Over thirty years after his death, the myth of Fred Buscaglione was being given a new political and ideological twist. It is a myth which summons up a stereotyped image, as interpreted by Buscaglione in his songs, and which looks back to the American *film noir* of the 1940s.

Posse and Rap

In Italy the last decade has produced musical genres and styles drawing upon earlier traditions, including the campaigning songs of the 1970s; it has reinterpreted,

El Paso: Solidarietà con gli anarchici in galera Alfredo Bonanno e Pippo Stasi, (particolare), 1989.

Fig. 31

recycled, or built up new myths on earlier models, often without any real understanding of their historical meaning; and it has reintroduced dialect forms and
music originally belonging to other, strongly antagonistic social realities.

This is the case with posse. It first emerged as a musical style at the end of the
1980s, as a result of the occupation of universities and the student movement
known as *la Pantera* (the Panther), and linked to the occupation of social centres
by young people. It is an Italian version of the politicized rap which originally
came from the USA, and it combines the slogans of political demonstrations with
the campaigning songs of earlier decades to create a kind of equivalence between
Afro-American radicalism and the Italian university occupations: a fragmentary,
violent style, a patchwork of sounds and voices, its subject-matter is the landscape
of the Italian city and its outskirts. It is the music favoured by the young groups
of Via dei Volsci, in the old working-class district of San Lorenzo in Rome, with
strongly 'antagonistic' traditions and self-images. The music is played in premises
taken over from the so-called *movimento*—the youth protest movement—full of
graffiti and signs written in red, posters of the symbolic figures who are its ideal
mouthpieces, such as Malcolm X or Che Guevara. Among the groups that have
emerged in this district is Assalti Frontali, who recorded a new version of 'Liberare
tutti' ('Free everybody'), a campaigning song about prisons. The original version
was released in 1972 by the far left organization Lotta Continua on the 45 r.p.m.
protest record *12 dicembre* (the title commemorates the date in 1969 when sixteen
people were killed by a bomb planted by the right in a bank in Piazza Fontana,
Milan). Assalti Frontali also set to music an interview with Sante Notarnicola,
'Omaggio a Sante' (in *Batti il tuo tempo*, Radio Onda Posse, June 1990). Notarnicola
was a young man from Puglia who emigrated to Turin in the 1950s. The newspapers of the early 1960s called him 'the bandit who killed with a smile'; he was
sentenced to life imprisonment for murder and bank robbery, together with
Cavallero, Lopez, and Crepaldi, the so-called Cavallero gang. Today Notarnicola
lives in semi-liberty in Bologna. In prison, he went over to the Red Brigades, and
for some time he has been making common cause with the young groups which
have come into being in Bologna, Rome, Milan, and Turin. He has been collabor-
ating with the musicians of the posses and the rappers of the so-called 'antagonistic movement' for some years; from being a 'bandit', he has become a new myth
for modern youth, a sort of latter-day Robin Hood, an ideal link-up between
terrorism, gang violence, and youthful anger, in a phenomenon which has no
sense of distance or critical detachment, and is marked by total involvement, both
emotional and ideological.

During these same years, the South has seen the birth of various independent
and self-producing circuits, groups making original reworkings of the dialect tradition and a part of the ethno-folk heritage of the previous decades. They included
the Almamegretta from Naples and I Nuovi Briganti (the New Brigands) from
Messina in Sicily, who have written protest songs against vivisection:

Terribile inganno perpetrato da scienziati senza cuore. Scienziati sì ma senza cuore
Scienziati sì ma dell'orrore
. . . Apri la mente, dai, non fare il finto tonto

A hideous trick played by heartless scientists | scientists, yes, but horror scientists | . . . Come on, wise up, don't act dumb.

They also include the Sud Sound System from Salento, in Puglia, who have sung 'Mafia business controlla lu Salentu, | Mafia business controlla la miseria' ('Mafia business runs Salento | Mafia business runs poverty'), and the 99 Posse, whose songs were used for the soundtrack of Gabriele Salvatores's film *Sud* (1994).

In some cases these groups have been inspired by narrative traditions such as those of the African *griots*, who tell stories they have heard from their fathers, but have fused this use of oral tradition with the influence of the latest commercial mass production. Sometimes we find reworkings of the rhythms of the so-called *tarantolati*, of the 'tarantola che m'pizzicatu' ('tarantula which bit me'), with its liberating rites and dances, and which Italian and foreign anthropologists observed until fairly recently; and of new versions of the tarantella sung until the 1970s by workers' groups (for instance the one from Pomigliano d'Arco in Campania) interwoven with the culture of the trance and of possession typical of Jamaican tradition, forging a new musical style known as *tarantamuffin*—tarantella plus ragamuffin.

The Sardinian group Sa Razza Posse uses its songs to express the attitude of many young Italians towards the South: an ambivalent feeling compounded of both love and hate, of anger at work denied and yet of pride in having been born there, part of an unbroken tradition, as for instance in Sardinia, of deep attachment to the land, of pride and dignity. One of their songs goes:

> Non ho un lavoro non ho tanti soldi
> Solo il tanto giusto quanto basta per campare
> E l'alternativa è una: immigrare in continente
> Perché ormai la fabbrica è chiusa e la miniera non esiste più
> Ma la mia terra non la voglio abbandonare. . . .
> Ci sono nato ci sto vivendo è come casa mia
> Ma io non voglio morire morire nella strada.

I've got no work, not much money | Only just enough to get by | The only alternative is to emigrate to the mainland | Because now the factory has closed and the mine's been shut down. | But I don't want to leave my own land. | I was born here, I live here, it's my home | But I don't want to die on the street.

The Mau Mau, from Turin, sing in the Piedmontese dialect; they have a black percussionist and their songs are about a mixed-race city, about immigration, anger, and madness. In 1991, in their first record, the Bolognese group Isola Posse sang in protest against the Gulf War with a song called 'Stop al panico':

Niente pace, niente giustizia. Ne ho sentite anche troppe di cazzate e vomita sentenze e di una bocca che scrive parole di fuoco su un gioco con un buono ed un cattivo, un Occidente indignato (è l'ONU che lo ha dichiarato) e accanto un pacifismo violento. Attento: non confondo Saddam con Che Guevara ma a Panama è la Casa Bianca che spara.

No peace, no justice. I've heard enough crap and pompous orators and a mouth writing fiery words about a game with one good guy and one bad guy, an outraged West (so the UN has declared) and, alongside, a violent pacifism. And watch it: I'm not confusing Saddam with Che Guevara, but in Panama it's the White House which is doing the shooting.

The history of these various groups has yet to be written. No serious study has yet been made of them and it is difficult to assess their importance or to establish how representative they actually are, partly because they often produce their own work, which is then withheld from the record market at the authors' express request. Such information as they do give in their songs, their words, their music, and the accounts of themselves that emerge in short interviews to the press or private radio stations reveal them to be outsiders who wish to remain so, ideally linked to other political and musical figures and groups who have preceded them. Their imaginative repertoire emerges as a veritable battlefield where different and in some cases mutually contradictory traditions meet and clash. They represent, or at least would like to think of themselves as representing, continuity with the political generation of the 1970s and the more recent experience of the student anti-establishment activity linked to the *Pantera* movement. But at the same time there is an observable sense of change by comparison with the generations of young people who preceded them, in particular that of the 1960s, which we cannot go into here but which would undoubtedly repay further study, since it relates also to the international musical scene, particularly the rock scene.

Whereas in the 1960s little attention was paid to Italian popular music—which indeed often seemed to be less an indigenous form of youth culture than an imported foreign product—and musical taste had turned mainly to British and American rock (Frith 1978; Carrera 1980, 43–8), now, however arbitrarily, there has been a return to producing songs in the Italian language, to the reclaiming of an identity more closely linked to Italy's cultural traditions, including the re-appropriation of Southern traditions, as we have seen in a number of groups.

For these groups, music is not their only vehicle for the transmission and reception of cultural messages. They also make frequent contacts with prisoners, drug rehabilitation centres, and counsellors. There is a national centre for liaison with the various social centres, a network which co-ordinates the self-managed centres in all Italian cities and puts them in touch with one another. But music undoubtedly continues as the chief theatre of action and the main vehicle of protest favoured by these groups, a form of ritualized resistance—this notion has been mediated in Italy by the sociologist Rita Caccamo De Luca (1980) in her discussion of the work produced in Birmingham in the 1970s (see Hall and Jefferson 1976).

Thus we see a general reappearance of myths, slogans, and symbolic figures, to be alternately glorified or vilified, often presented in a somewhat confused manner, with various overlapping layers of interpretation and splinters of historical memory, sometimes wrenched clumsily from the context which had originally produced them. Che Guevara and the keffiyeh worn to concerts and on stage, the Cavallero gang (a musical group from Turin bears its name) and the Southern tarantella, attacks on Berlusconi—'the viper [*biscione*, symbol of Berlusconi's Fininvest corporation] of profit slithers slowly and slimily', as the Mau Mau shriek— and the Mafia. The South is represented as a mythic place, but also, to recall the title of one of Ernesto De Martino's books (1959), as a land of remorse; of nostalgia and fascination but also of anger.

Meanwhile, however partially, the record industry is appropriating these languages and this musical style, reworking them for a wider and perhaps less conflict-ridden young public. The highly polarized and widely sold rap records of the singer Jovanotti are one example of this. One rap group even took part in the 1994 San Remo Festival, which is still one of the most widely followed events in Italy, and which represents the musical tendencies of the moment, often emptying them of content so as to offer them to a wider public, and grafting them onto commercial circuits on a national and international scale. The representatives of the so-called *canzone d'autore*—*cantautori* and performers of committed songs who have turned alternately to French, British, or American models—rarely take part in the San Remo Festival, though there have been sensational exceptions such as that of the *cantautore* Luigi Tenco. In January 1967 he entered with 'Ciao amore ciao', a song which in its final version addressed the problems of internal migration, but which had originally been an anti-war song. Tenco shot himself in the head that same night, leaving a note explaining the reasons for his desperate gesture: namely, exclusion from the finals and his disappointment at having failed to be understood by the Italian public.

In 1992, to keep his memory alive, the Tenco Club was set up in San Remo. Every year it organizes a sort of anti-festival in which the foremost Italian and foreign *cantautori* take part. In 1994 it was won by an Italian posse, a reflection of the culture and concerns of the youth of recent years.

Discography

A. Historical collections

Il dizionario della canzone italiana (Castaldo, G.), Curcio, 1990, with 36 cassettes and/or CDs.
Il fonografo italiano (Del Bosco, P.; Gregoretti, U.), 50 parts and 50 LPs.
La canzone italiana. Gruppo Editoriale Fabbri, 1978, 50 parts with 50 EPs. Second rev. edn., 1982, 50 CDs and/or cassettes.
Le canzoni dei ricordi. Cetra, 31 LPs from the 1930s to the 1950s.
Fred Buscaglione, Fonit-Cetra, 2 LPs.
Criminalmente Fred, Polygram, 1992, CD and/or cassette.

B. Posse and rap

The following list represents some of the work produced by Italian groups in recent years. It should be remembered that many groups refuse to become part of commercial circuits on principle; many songs therefore have a network exclusively linked to independent production, and are often known only in their own towns or provinces.

Articolo 31, *Messa di Vespiri*, Crime Squad, 1994.
Assalti Frontali, *Terra di Nessuno*, Cordata, 1992.
Comitato, *La casa è un diritto*, Just For Fun, 1992.
Dj Gruff, *Rapa Dopa*, Century Vox, 1993.
Frankie HI—NGR MC, *Verba manent*, BMG, 1993.
Il Generale, *Guarda la luce e non il dito*, Wide, 1993.
Isola Posse All Stars, *Stop al panico*, Century Vox, 1991.
99 Posse, *Curre Curre Guagliò*, Esodo/Flying, 1993.
Nuovi Briganti, *Nuovi Briganti*, X Records, 1992.
Onda Rossa Possa, *Batti il tuo tempo*, Assalti Frontali, 1990.
OTR, *Quel sapore particolare*, Century Vox, 1994.
Salento Posse, *Salento Showcase*, Ritmo Vitale, 1994.
Sangue Misto, *8 × M*, Crime Squad, 1994.
Various artists, *Baghdad 1.9.9.1.*, cassette, 1991 (independent production).
Various artists, *Fondamentale*, Century Vox, 1993.
Various artists, *Italian Posses*, vol. 1, Flying, 1992.
Various artists, *Sud*, soundtrack of the film by Gabriele Salvatores, Sony, 1994.

References

ADORNO, T. W. (1938), 'On the Fetish Character in Music and the Regression of Listening', in *The Culture Industry: Selected Essays on Mass Culture*, ed. J. M. Bernstein (London 1991), 26–52.
BALDAZZI, G. (1989), *La canzone italiana del Novecento* (Rome).
BORGNA, G., (1991), 'Inseguendo qualcosa nella notte...', in D'Attorre (1991).
—— (1980), *La grande evasione* (Milan).
BOURDIEU, P. (1979), *Distinction: A Social Critique of the Judgement of Taste*, trans. R. Nice (London, 1984).
CACCAMO DE LUCA, R. (1980), *Rituali di resistenza. Una ricerca sulla questione giovanile inglese* (Turin).
CARPITELLA, D., CASTALDO, G., PINTOR, G., PORTELLI, A., and STRANIERO, M. (1978), *La musica in Italia* (Rome).
CARRERA, A. (1980), *Musica e pubblico giovanile. L'evoluzione del gusto musicale dagli anni Sessanta ad oggi* (Milan).
CASTALDO, G. (1990) (ed.), *Il dizionario della canzone italiana* (Rome).
CASTELLUCCI, C., and MOLLICA, V. (1981), *Fred Buscaglione forever* (Florence).
CAVALLO, P., IACCIO, P. (1981), *Vincere! Vincere! Vincere! Fascismo e società italiana nelle canzoni e nelle riviste di variet, 1935–1943* (Rome).
—— DEL BOSCO, P., IACCIO, P., and MESSINA, R. (1989), *La guerra immaginata. Teatro, canzone e fotografia (1940–1943)* (Naples).
CERTEAU, M. DE (1984), *The Practice of Everyday Life*, trans. S. Rendall (Berkeley, 1992).
CRISTANTE, S., DI CERBO, A., and SPINUCCI, G. (1983), *La rivolta dello stile. Tendenze e segnali dalle subculture del pianeta terra* (Milan).
D'ATTORRE, P. P. (1991) (ed.), *Nemici per la pelle. Sogno americano e mito sovietico nell'Italia contemporanea* (Milan).
DEL BOSCO, P. (1989), 'Una guerra senza motivo', in Cavallo *et al.* (1989), 209–29.
DE MARTINO, E. (1959), *La terra del rimorso* (Milan).

FENOGLIO, B. (1968), *Il partigiano Johnny* (Turin).

FILIPPA, M. (1990), 'Fred Buscaglione, un mito degli anni Cinquanta', in *Piemonte vivo*, 2: 44–51.

—— (1992) 'L'attimo catturato: immagini per un storia sociale', in A. Accornero *et al.*, *1944–1956. Le relazioni industriali alla Fiat. Saggi e note critiche* (Milan), 330–43.

—— (1994), 'Orchestra e café chantant: dal maestro Angelini a Fred Buscaglione', in V. Castronovo (ed.), *Storia illustrata di Torino* (Milan).

FRITH, S. (1978), *The Sociology of Rock* (London).

GILLIS, J. (1974), *Youth and History* (New York).

GUNDLE, S. (1994), 'Musica leggera: non solo rime scontate e infatuazioni del rock', in P. Ginsborg (ed.), *Stato dell'Italia* (Milan), 606–9.

HALL, S., and JEFFERSON, T. (1976) (eds.), *Resistance through Rituals: Youth Subcultures in Post-War Britain* (London).

HEBDIGE, D. (1979), *Subculture: The Meaning of Style* (London).

KRACAUER, S. (1969), *History: The Last Things before the Last* (New York).

LEYDI, R. (1973), *I canti sociali italiani* (Milan).

LUZZATO FEGIZ, M. (1976), *Morte di un cantautore. Biografia di Luigi Tenco* (Milan).

MAZZOLETTI, A. (1983), *Il jazz in Italia, dalle origini al dopoguerra* (Bari).

PASSERINI, L. (1994), 'La giovinezza metafora del cambiamento sociale. Due dibattiti sui giovani nell'Italia fascista e negli Stati Uniti degli anni Cinquanta', in L. Levi and J. C. Schmitt (eds.), *Storia dei giovani. L'età contemporanea* (Rome and Bari).

PICCININI, A. (1994), *Fratellini d'Italia. Mappe, stili, parole dell'ultima generazione* (Rome).

PICCONE STELLA, S. (1993), *La prima generazione. Ragazze e ragazzi nel miracolo economico italiano* (Milan).

PORTELLI, A. (1983), 'Tipologia della canzone operaia', in *Movimento operaio e socialista*, 2: 207–24.

Radio Sherwood (1993) (ed.), *Camminare sotto il cielo di notte* (Padua).

SAVONA, V., and STRANIERO, M. (1979), *Canti dell'Italia fascista (1915–1945)* (Milan).

SOLARO, A. (1993), *Posses italiane* (Florence).

STRANIERO, M., LIBEROVICI, S., DE MARIA, G., and JONA, E. (1964), *Le canzoni della cattiva coscienza* (Milan).

TOOP, D. (1991), *Rap. Storia di una musica nera* (Turin).

ZWERIN, M. (1985), *La Tristesse de St Louis: Swing under the Nazis* (London).

Paninari

DAVID FORGACS

THE *paninari* were a short-lived trend in youth culture in the mid-1980s, but they remain of historical interest for a number of reasons and they provide a good illustration both of how cultural consumption works and of how it had evolved in Italy by that time.

First, the very fact of their existence demonstrated that by the 1980s there were parts of Italy (the *paninari* were concentrated in Milan and a few other cities of the North and Centre) where certain teenagers had enough money, spare time, and independence from their families to establish a youth trend based on public socialization and fashion dressing. In other words they showed how fast things had moved since the 1950s, when such a trend would have been impossible.

Secondly, they bear out the notions of cultural consumption as 'distinction' (Bourdieu) and 'appropriation' (Certeau and others) discussed in Chapter 15 above. The choice of a burger with fries and a Coke in the Burghy restaurant in Piazza San Babila is not one which most of the *paninari*'s parents would have made. It would not have been 'sensible eating'. But they made it for precisely this reason, as a gesture of distinction or social differentiation and as a fashion statement. At the same time, it is evident that the *paninari* were not just succumbing passively to a set of advertised American and French icons (fast food, Ray-Bans, Levis, Lacoste shirts, Moncler anoraks, etc.) but were creatively appropriating and reworking them into a distinctive mix of styles, adding their own elements, such as an invented hybrid language which drew on Spanish and Latin as well as Italian and the Northern dialects (*cucador* for a boy who 'pulls girls', *gallo* for boy; *sfitinzia* for girl/girlfriend; *sapiens* for parents, etc.) and the Italian scooter or small-cyclinder German motorcycle.

Fig. 32

Thirdly, *paninaro* culture was one of partial integration into middle-class culture and not simply one of protest, of alternative and oppositional lifestyle, as the youth cultures of the late 1960s and early 1970s had been. The latter had been typically 'proletarianized', rejecting middle-class conformity and commercialism in dress, language, and politics, creating or appropriating alternative spaces of socialization, marking out their boundaries in the city with sprayed slogans, and turning their social marginality into a badge of identity, whereas the *paninari* were middle-class rich kids (it cost around a million lire to kit oneself out in the regulation wear) whose gesture of protest or self-differentiation was one of generation and personal outlook rather than of class or politics, who were proud of their stylish clothes, who met and ate in shiny bars, and whose alternative language was the private code of an exclusive in-group, like that of the 'droogs' in Anthony Burgess's novel *A Clockwork Orange* (1962), rather than one which turned outwards to desecrate bourgeois norms with deliberate vulgarity.

Fourthly, if the media and consumer society made *paninaro* culture possible in the first place, the media also served to spread public awareness of it, again in a way that would not have been possible half a generation earlier. It generated its own cult magazines, like the one whose cover is reproduced in Figure 32, consisting of idealized cartoon-strip stories of everyday *paninaro* life, film, and fashion tips. But the most important vehicle for making people aware of it and its distinctive language was a television show aimed at a mainly youth audience, *Drive In*, written by Antonio Ricci, which featured a comic *paninaro* character.

In retrospect the *paninari* can be seen as having marked a turning-point in youth culture and values, the beginning of a shift, which was not limited just to the middle class, away from the counter-cultural leftism of the generation born around 1950 towards a more consumption-based and style-conscious ethos.

Two Ideas of Stardom

STEPHEN GUNDLE

These photographs depict Gina Lollobrigida and Sophia Loren, the two most popular Italian female film stars of the 1950s and 1960s. Both were ordinary young women of humble backgrounds who first got into films through beauty contests and whose popularity rested to a large degree on their shapely figures and vivacious personalities. To this day they are often referred to as examples of a typically Italian female beauty.

The photographs are not reproduced here in order to contrast the two women, although the publicity-driven rivalry between them in the 1950s led to the formation of partisan camps of opinion which attributed different political, moral, and aesthetic values to them. Rather the purpose is to compare two ideas of stardom which in the post-war years existed side by side in magazines and publicity material.

Figure 33 shows Gina *circa* 1952. Some identifiable star features are present in the photograph and would have been recognized as such by contemporaries: in particular, the low-cut gown and the partial display of Gina's bosom. But, apart from these, what is striking is the down-to-earth accessibility of the subject. The naturalness and absence of polish, evident especially in the imperfectly groomed hair, are quite disarming. Also significant are the demure, closed-mouth smile and the modesty implicit in the slightly lowered position of the head. The legacy of neorealism and Anna Magnani is present here but so too is a rather older idea of femininity not as strength but as coyness. These 'home-grown' qualities are all reinforced by the studio-bound portrait photograph which by a—probably not deliberate—use of shadow brings the subject down to a commonplace level. Apart from her well-proportioned features and beauty, Gina exhibits here no special allure or glamour.

Fig. 33

Fig. 34

If Figure 33 reflects a European, and in some ways specifically Italian, idea of stardom as down-to-earthness and accessibility, Figure 34, by contrast, shows Sophia Loren in typical Hollywood mode. Taken in the USA in the mid-1960s, the photograph situates the subject in a sun-drenched outdoor setting and identifies her with sport and leisure. The aspirational qualities of the image are underscored by Sophia's well-groomed yet casual appearance, her suntan and make-up and her euphoric smile exposing a flawless set of white teeth. What the viewer is offered is an image of ease, perfection, and fulfilment that, as early as the 1920s, Hollywood made into a trademark. This sort of image does not invite feelings of quasi-egalitarian identification; rather it fuels a 'field of tension' in which the star acts as a focus for dreams of physical improvement, material wealth, and personal happiness.

The Hollywood photograph is also different in that it is more explicitly sexual. By staring straight into the camera, as was the norm with American pin-ups, Sophia is offering male viewers a message of availability. This is underscored by the rather obvious sexual symbolism of the croquet balls and mallet. The image of Gina, by contrast, does not offer the male viewer a message of unambiguous availability. Rather, what is offered is an image of sensuousness that has emerged from many social and cultural filters. However, precisely because its nature was encoded, this sort of gender imagery exercised a great appeal for the educated American men who frequented art houses in the 1950s and 1960s.

The difference between the two photographs is not just one of models of stardom but of period. Ultimately, the optimistic, upbeat idea of stardom associated with Hollywood proved to be the more powerful and durable. Yet stars like Gina and Sophia who had made their debuts in the Italian cinema of the early 1950s were never fully and definitively absorbed into it. They were always marked by a degree of authenticity that not even the image-makers of Hollywood could cancel in their aim for typicality over individuality. In this sense the European/Italian idea of stardom persisted in strong individuals who left an indelible mark on the collective imaginary of the film-going public everywhere.

Chronology

Politics

1900
King Umberto I assassinated by anarchist Gaetano Bresci (July).

1903
Giovanni Giolitti heads first of three governments up to 1914; the period is marked by his opening to the Socialists (PSI) and the Catholics, but also by his control of elections through prefects.

1905
Catholic trade unions formed.

1909
Gaetano Salvemini denounces Giolitti's 'government of thieves' for political corruption in the South (Mar.).

1910
Associazione Nazionale Italiana founded.

1911–12
Libyan War: Italy defeats Turkey and colonizes Tripolitania and Cyreniaca.

1913
First general election in which all males over 25 are entitled to vote (Oct.).

Culture

1901
Death of Giuseppe Verdi (27 Jan.); *Italiani del Nord e Italiani del Sud*, by Alfredo Niceforo.

1902
Estetica, by Benedetto Croce; International Decorative Arts Exhibition in Turin.

1906
Una donna, by Sibilla Aleramo.

1909
First Futurist manifesto published in *Le Figaro*, Paris (20 Feb.).

1914
'La settimana rossa' ('Red week'): strikes
and protests across central Italy (June).

1915
Pro-war demonstrations organized by
interventionists. Italy enters First World War
(May) in alliance with Britain, France, and
Russia against Germany and Austria-
Hungary.

1917
Defeat and mutiny of Caporetto (Oct.) after
Italian army is routed by Austrians.

1918
Italian troops defeat Austrians at Vittorio
Veneto.

1919
Foundation of Catholic Partito Popolare
Italiano (PPI) (Jan.) and of Fasci di
Combattimento (subsequently Fascist Party)
in Milan (23 Mar.). In the peace agreements,
Italy gains the Trentino and South Tyrol
(Alto Adige) from Austria but not Trieste
and Dalmatia, which are ceded to the new
state of Yugoslavia. Protests by nationalists
against 'la vittoria mutilata'. D'Annunzio
and his legionnaires occupy the port of
Fiume (now Rijeka) in Dalmatia and
proclaim it part of Italy (Sept.). First general
election with proportional representation
(16 Nov.): PSI becomes biggest party with
32.4% of vote and 156 seats. PPI second
party with 20.6% and 100 seats. Fascists get
no seats.

1920
Lock-out in engineering industry (Aug.),
followed by occupation of factories in
northern cities (Sept.).

1921
Foundation of the Communist Party of Italy
(PCd'I) (Jan.); general election: 35 Fascists
elected (May).

1922
March on Rome (28 Oct.): Benito Mussolini
becomes prime minister.

1924
Socialist member of Parliament Giacomo
Matteotti murdered by Fascists (June): the

1914
Cabiria, film by Giovanni Pastrone.

1919
L'allegria, poems by Giuseppe Ungaretti;
headquarters of the Socialist paper *Avanti!*
burnt down by Fascists (15 Apr.); *Ordine
Nuovo*, left Socialist weekly, founded by
Antonio Gramsci, Palmiro Togliatti, and
others in Turin (1 May).

1921
Sei personaggi in cerca d'autore, by Luigi
Pirandello.

1923
Publication of several Socialist papers
suspended (12 Dec.); Education Act
introduced by Giovanni Gentile.

1924
First regular radio broadcasts; *La coscienza di
Zeno*, novel by Italo Svevo; death of

event sparks off a crisis for the Fascist government, with opposition parties withdrawing from Parliament.

1925
Mussolini speech in Parliament (3 Jan.) marks beginning of totalitarian regime.

1926
All opposition parties declared illegal (Nov.); arrest of leading Communists, including Antonio Gramsci.

1929
Conciliation (Lateran Pacts) between Italian State and Catholic Church (Feb.), including treaty, concordat, and financial settlement.

1935–6
War in Abyssinia, ending with declaration of Italian Empire in East Africa.

1937
Gramsci dies aged 46 after ten years' detention (27 Apr.).

1938
Laws for the Defence of the Race: first restrictive legislation under Fascism against Italian Jews, to be followed by further legislation up to 1945.

1940
Italy enters Second World War on side of Germany and Japan (10 June).

Giacomo Puccini (his last opera *Turandot* is first performed in Milan in 1926).

1925
Ossi di seppia, poems by Eugenio Montale; Croce writes and obtains signatures for anti-Fascist counter-manifesto (published 1 May) to Gentile's *Manifesto degli intellettuali fascisti*.

1929
Gli indifferenti, novel by Alberto Moravia.

1932
Mostra della Rivoluzione Fascista opened in Rome to celebrate tenth anniversary of the March on Rome; *Fontamara*, anti-Fascist novel written in Switzerland in 1930 by ex-Communist Ignazio Silone, appears in German translation, and subsequently in many other languages; Trotsky writes in 1933: 'The book deserves a circulation of millions of copies.'

1936
First issue of the review *Cinema*, edited by Vittorio Mussolini.

1937
Ministry of Popular Culture founded; Cinecittà inaugurated.

1938
Manifesto degli scienziati razzisti (14 July); physicist Enrico Fermi collects Nobel Prize in Sweden and emigrates with his Jewish wife to USA (Dec.). 'Monopoly Law' leads to drastic reduction in US films imported. Work under way on construction of EUR suburb (Esposizione Universale Roma) and arterial link roads to Rome for E42 exposition, planned for the Fascist twentieth anniversary celebrations of 1942.

1939
'Legge Alfieri' gives commercial boost to domestic film production.

1941
Paesi tuoi, novel by Cesare Pavese.

1943

Allied landings in Sicily (9 July). Rome bombed (19 July). Mussolini forced out of office (25–6 July); Marshal Badoglio (Head of Armed Forces) becomes prime minister. Armistice with Allies announced (8 Sept.); Italian army disbands, Badoglio and the King retreat from Rome to Brindisi. German troops overrun Northern and Central Italy; armed Resistance begins. Mussolini, rescued from imprisonment by Germans, sets up Republic of Salò in the North (23 Sept.). SS, assisted by Fascists, round up over 1,000 Jews in Rome for deportation to death camps (16 Oct.).

1944

Palmiro Togliatti, general secretary of Communist Party (now renamed PCI), returns from Moscow and introduces party line of alliance with other anti-Fascist parties and support for Badoglio government and monarchy (Mar.).

1945

Liberation (25 Apr.); Mussolini executed by partisans (28 Apr.); Alcide De Gasperi (DC) heads coalition of anti-Fascist parties, including PCI (Dec.); he will remain prime minister until 1953.

1946

Elections to Constituent Assembly and referendum on form of the state (2 June). Women vote for the first time. A majority in the referendum chooses republic (54.2%) over monarchy (45.8%).

1947

De Gasperi flies to Washington (Jan.); formalization of US support for DC; approval of Article 7 inserting the 1929 Concordat into the Constitution (25 Mar.); PCI and PSI ministers excluded from government (May).

1948

Constitution of the Republic comes into force (1 Jan.). General election (18 Apr.): DC wins large majority (48.5% in Chamber of Deputies), defeating PCI–PSI alliance (31%). Attempted assassination of Togliatti (14 July) provokes mass protests and militant actions in many areas.

1949

Parliament votes to join NATO (11 Mar.); papal excommunication of adherents of Communism (12 July).

1943

Ossessione, film by Luchino Visconti.

1945

Roma città aperta, film by Roberto Rossellini; *Cristo si è fermato a Eboli*, by Carlo Levi; *Uomini e no*, Resistance novel by Elio Vittorini; first issue of *Il Politecnico* (29 Sept.) edited by Vittorini.

1946

Paisà, film by Rossellini; *Sciuscià*, film by Vittorio De Sica; Gino Bartali wins Tour de France; first Miss Italia beauty contest; Vespa scooter launched by Piaggio; launch of magazines *Grand Hotel* and *Bolero Film*.

1947

Gramsci's prison letters (*Lettere dal carcere*), published by Einaudi; *Se questo è un uomo*, memoir of Auschwitz by Primo Levi; *Artemisia*, historical novel by Anna Banti; Fausto Coppi wins Tour de France; Lambretta scooter launched by Innocenti.

1948

Ladri di biciclette, film by De Sica; *Riso amaro*, film by Giuseppe De Santis; *Menzogna e sortilegio*, novel by Elsa Morante.

1949

Catene, film by Raffaello Matarazzo, sets trend for tear-jerkers (*strappalacrime*).

1950
Peasant land occupations in S. Italy (Mar.); foundation of Catholic trade union confederation (1 May); establishment of the Cassa per il Mezzogiorno, the Development Fund for the South (10 Aug.).

1950
Launch of illustrated weekly *Epoca*, published by Mondadori.

1951
First Festival of San Remo organized by the RAI (29–31 Jan.).

1952
Death of Croce (20 Nov.); first national fashion show organized in Florence for American buyers.

1953
General election: DC wins 40% in Chamber of Deputies (June).

1954
Notorious electoral reform law (nicknamed *'legge truffa'*—'swindle law'), designed to boost the majority of the largest party, is defeated in Parliament. Trieste, whose nationality had been disputed with Yugoslavia since 1945, is returned to Italy (Oct.).

1954
RAI begins regular television service (Jan.); Giovanni Guareschi, editor of satirical review *Candido* and author of the Don Camillo stories, imprisoned for libelling De Gasperi (Apr.); *La strada*, film by Federico Fellini.

1955
Italy admitted to United Nations (Dec.).

1955
Launch of Fiat 600 car (Mar.); weekly magazine *L'Espresso* begins publication (Oct.); Giangiacomo Feltrinelli sets up publishing firm in Milan; first transmission of popular television quiz *Lascia o raddoppia?* (19 Nov.).

1956
Togliatti reiterates Khrushchev's criticisms of 'personality cult' and Stalin's legacy (13 June); in Oct. the PCI condemns Hungarian workers' uprising and supports Soviet intervention; PSI attacks Soviet actions.

1956
First issue of newspaper *Il Giorno* (21 Apr.).

1957
Treaty of Rome establishing European Economic Community (Mar.).

1957
In the PCI 101 intellectuals criticize party support for Soviet intervention in Hungary; launch of Fiat 500 (July); Feltrinelli is first publisher in the world to bring out Boris Pasternak's novel *Dr Zhivago*.

1958
General election: DC (42%) and PCI (23%) are largest parties; Amintore Fanfani (DC) forms new government (July); Law introduced (20 Sept.) by Lina Merlin (PSI) closes state-licensed brothels (*case di tolleranza*); death of Pius XII; Angelo Roncalli becomes Pope John XXIII (Oct.).

1958
Danilo Dolci charged with slandering Italian government for comments to foreign press on poverty and illiteracy; Torre Velasca built in Milan by architects BBPR; the song 'Nel blu dipinto di blu' ('Volare') by Domenico Modugno wins the Festival of San Remo and tops the charts for over twenty weeks.

1959

John XXIII's first encyclical affirms aspiration to unity of Christendom and world peace (June).

1960

Mass protest against congress of neo-fascist party, the MSI, in Genoa, followed by general strike; DC prime minister Tambroni resigns amid crisis provoked by his attempt to bring MSI into government (July).

1961

Constitutional Court upholds Article 589 of Penal Code allowing punishment of wife and not husband in adultery cases.

1962

Fanfani forms government with PSI support (Feb.); nationalization of the electricity industry (Nov.); reform of secondary schooling includes raising of leaving age to 14. Second Vatican Council opens in Rome (Oct.); it will introduce reforms in Catholic Church and its relations with society.

1963

Engineering workers' contract signed after long dispute (Feb.); general elections (Apr.): DC loses 4% of votes but remains largest party (Apr.); death of Pope John XXIII (3 June); PSI enters government (Dec.), marking the beginning of centre–left (*centrosinistra*) coalitions.

1964

Attempted *coup d'état* by Gen. De Lorenzo (14 July); over 1 million attend Togliatti's funeral (25 Aug.).

1966

Third centre–left government formed (Feb.); student killed by neo-fascists at Rome University (Apr.).

1959

La dolce vita, by Fellini. *Il Gattopardo* (*The Leopard*), by Giuseppe Tomasi di Lampedusa (published by Feltrinelli 1958), wins the Strega prize and becomes an international success.

1960

Rocco e i suoi fratelli, by Visconti. *L'avventura*, by Michelangelo Antonioni, wins Special Jury Prize at Cannes Film Festival.

1961

La notte by Antonioni. Second RAI channel begins transmission (Nov.); *Accattone*, film by Pier Paolo Pasolini; *Il giorno della civetta*, novel by Leonardo Sciascia.

1962

Dario Fo and Franca Rame leave the television show *Canzonissima* because of censorship (Nov.); *Il giardino dei Finzi-Contini*, novel by Giorgio Bassani; *Opera aperta*, by Umberto Eco; first issue of comic strip *Diabolik*.

1963

Mani sulla città, film by Francesco Rosi about building speculation in Naples; *Marcovaldo, ovvero le stagioni in città*, by Italo Calvino; formation of Gruppo 63, group of neo-avant-garde writers. *Lessico famigliare*, by Natalia Ginzburg, wins Premio Strega.

1964

Pasolini launches debate on debasement of language in Italy (26 Dec.); *Matrimonio all'italiana*, film by De Sica; *Apocalittici e integrati*, by Eco; Sergio Leone's film *A Fistful of Dollars* (*Per un pugno di dollari*) launches the spaghetti western.

1965

Mondadori launches its Oscar paperbacks, published weekly and cheaply; *Le cosmicomiche*, by Calvino.

1966

Thousands of historic works of art and books destroyed in Florence flood (4 Nov.); *La battaglia di Algeri*, film by Gillo Pontecorvo. *Blow-up*, by Antonioni.

1967
First occupations against government university reform (Feb.); anti-Vietnam war demonstrations across Italy (May); state of siege in Rome due to protest at US President Johnson's visit (Dec.).

1968
Violent confrontation between student protesters and police in Rome (1 Mar.); general elections: decline in PSI vote (May); general strike in protest at killing of two farmworkers by police in Avola in S. Italy (2 Dec.).

1969
General strike over pensions (5 Feb.). *Autunno caldo* ('hot autumn'): engineering, chemical and building workers in dispute over contracts. Divorce law passed (1 Dec.). Bomb kills sixteen people in bank in Piazza Fontana, Milan (12 Dec.): anarchists are accused by police and media and one of them, Giuseppe Pinelli, is found dead after police interrogation.

1970
Statuto del Lavoro (Labour Charter) approved by Parliament (14 May); first regional elections across Italy (7 June); riots in Reggio Calabria sparked off by decision to site regional capital in rival city of Cosenza (July); mass protest at visit by US President Nixon (27 Sept.).

1971
Constitutional Court recognizes legality of distributing and advertising contraceptives (17 Mar.); general strike over housing (7 Apr.); MSI gains in local elections in S. Italy (13 June).

1972
Beginning of trials of Pietro Valpreda and others accused of Piazza Fontana bombing (Feb.); general elections: MSI gains; assassination of Police Commissioner Luigi Calabresi, held responsible on left for death of Pinelli (17 May); US submarine base built in Sardinia.

1967
Lettera a una professoressa, by the School of Barbiana; *Edipo re*, by Pasolini; death of comic actor Totò.

1968
Pasolini poem criticizes students as 'figli di papà' (Apr.); Venice Biennale disrupted by protests from artists and students (18 June); *Il mondo salvato dai ragazzini*, by Morante; *Canzonissima '68* watched by an audience of 21.2 million. Pope Paul VI issues encyclical *Humanae vitae* against artificial contraception (July); Pasolini's film *Teorema* seized in Rome on obscenity charges (Sept.); the law making a woman's adultery a punishable offence is declared unconstitutional (Dec.).

1969
Zabriskie Point, by Antonioni; *Fellini Satyricon*; *Mistero buffo*, by Dario Fo; *Donna clitoridea donna vaginale*, by Carla Lonzi.

1970
Strategia del ragno and *Il conformista* by Bernardo Bertolucci; *Indagine su un cittadino al di sopra di ogni sospetto*, film by Elio Petri; *La strage di Stato*, book by a group of left journalists, denounces state's 'strategy of tension' behind Piazza Fontana bomb and other acts; *Morte accidentale di un anarchico*, Fo's satirical play based on the interrogation and death of Pinelli, performed by his company La Comune.

1971
Il manifesto published as daily paper (28 Apr.).

1972
Ultimo tango a Parigi, by Bertolucci, seized on obscenity charges; *Le città invisibili*, by Calvino; *Memorie di una ladra*, by Dacia Maraini.

1973

Engineering workers' strikes (Feb.); Enrico Berlinguer proposes 'historic compromise' between PCI and DC (Oct.); government austerity programme (Dec.).

1974

Law providing for public financing of political parties (Apr.). Divorce referendum: 59.1% of population vote to keep divorce law (12 May); six killed by bomb at left-wing demonstration in Brescia (29 May); bomb on Rome–Munich train Italicus kills twelve people (4 Aug.); general strike over cost of living and unemployment (4 Dec.).

1975

Voting age lowered to 18 (6 Mar.); Communists and Socialists elected as mayors of Turin, Milan, and Naples (July); 557,677 signatures collected for referendum on abortion (Dec.).

1976

Renato Curcio, leader of the Red Brigades (*Brigate Rosse*), is arrested (19 Jan.). Lockheed scandal involves government ministers (Mar.). Friuli earthquake (6 May); state prosecutor assassinated by Red Brigades (8 Jun.). General election (20 June): largest ever PCI share of vote (34.4%), but still falls short of DC (38.7%).

1977

Students block speech by Luciano Lama, leader of the CGIL, at Rome University; beginning of protests in major cities (Feb.); editor of *La Stampa* attacked and wounded by Red Brigades (16 Nov.).

1978

Trial of Red Brigades leaders. Abduction and killing of Aldo Moro, leader of DC and former prime minister, by Red Brigades (16 Mar.–9 May). Abortion law approved (22 May); President Giovanni Leone (DC) resigns after being implicated in Lockheed scandal (June) and Sandro Pertini (PSI) is

1973

Il Corriere della Sera no longer in exclusive ownership of Crespi family (28 May); death of actress Anna Magnani (26 Sept.); Pasolini opens debate in *Il Corriere della Sera* on effects of television (9 Dec.); *Amarcord*, by Fellini; birth of comic strip character Lupo Alberto.

1974

Death of De Sica (13 Nov.); *The Night Porter*, by Liliana Cavani.

1975

Law reforming the RAI: control passes from government to a parliamentary commission; first regular colour television transmissions. Growth of 'free radio' stations. First Giorgio Armani women's wear collection. Visit to Pope by 20,000 members of Catholic youth movement Comunione e Liberazione. Pasolini killed in Ostia (2 Nov.); Montale receives Nobel Prize for Literature (10 Dec.).

1976

Pasolini's *Salò, o le 120 giornate di Sodoma* seized on obscenity charges. Constitutional Court ruling declares RAI's monopoly of broadcasting unconstitutional at local level, opening the way for private radio and television (July); *Novecento* (*1900*), by Bertolucci.

1977

Radio Alice closed down by police in Bologna (12 Mar.); *Mistero buffo*, by Fo is broadcast by RAI 2 despite Vatican objections; *Le due società*, by Alberto Asor Rosa, provokes debate on generational and political divisions; *Padre padrone*, film by Paolo and Vittorio Taviani.

1978

'Legge 180', law inspired by work of radical psychiatrist Franco Basaglia, closes long-stay mental institutions and introduces community care (May); *L'affaire Moro*, by Sciascia; *Ecce bombo*, film by Nanni Moretti.

elected President (July); election of Pope John Paul II (Karol Wojtyla) (16 Oct.).

1979

At Fiat in Turin sixty-one workers dismissed but solidarity strike fails (Oct.); approval for installation of US Pershing missiles on Italian territory (Dec.).

1980

Establishment of Italian National Health Service (May); bomb in Bologna railway station kills eighty-five (2 Aug.); 14,000 workers made redundant by Fiat (11 Sept.); earthquakes in S. Italy (23 Nov.).

1981

Referendum retains 1978 abortion law (18 May); P2 Masonic lodge scandal implicates leading figures in government and public life (20 May); Comiso in Sicily chosen as site for US Cruise missiles (Aug.).

1982

Mafia assassination of Gen. Carlo Alberto Dalla Chiesa and his wife in Palermo (3 Sept.).

1983

PCI Congress formalizes break with Moscow (2 Mar.); general election: major setback for the DC, whose share of vote falls to 32.9% (26 June); PSI leader Bettino Craxi forms government (4 Aug.).

1984

Death of PCI secretary Enrico Berlinguer (11 Jun.); PCI just pips DC as largest Italian party in elections to European Parliament (17 Apr.).

1985

Regional elections: gains by PSI, losses by PCI (12 May); Francesco Cossiga elected President (24 June).

1986

Mafia maxi-trial opens in Palermo (Feb.).

1987

General election (June); DC (34.3%) improves position, PCI (26.6%) loses ground. Referendum confirms hostility to nuclear power (8 Nov.); Gianfranco Fini becomes general secretary of MSI.

1979

Third RAI television channel begins transmission (15 Dec.); *Prova d'orchestra*, by Fellini; *Se una notte d'inverno un viaggiatore*, by Calvino.

1980

Il nome della rosa, by Eco; by 1995 10 million copies had been sold world-wide.

1981

Death of Montale. First Emporio Armani opens in Milan. Silvio Berlusconi's private network Canale 5 begins transmissions of *Dallas*.

1982

Italy soccer team wins World Cup (11 July); 'Paninari' trend begins in Milan.

1984

Berlusconi's Fininvest group, which already owns Canale 5 and Italia 1, takes over Retequattro from Mondadori. The three networks are blacked out in Rome, Turin, and Pescara on the orders of the prefects (16 Oct.); Craxi government drafts decree (nicknamed 'Decreto Berlusconi') to enable transmission in absence of regulatory laws. *La Piovra* (Octopus—The Power of the Mafia) with Michele Placido starts on RAI 1.

1985

Death of Calvino (19 Sept.); *Quelli della notte*, cult comedy show with Renzo Arbore, begins on RAI 2.

1988
Death of Giorgio Almirante, founder of MSI (22 May); union demonstration of 300,000 for fair taxation (12 Nov.); 'golden sheet' scandal concerning contracts for couchette bed-linen leads to resignation of board of the state railways (25 Nov.).

1989
PCI Central Committee votes for assembly to reform the party (Nov.).

1990
Martelli Law on immigration (Feb.); 600,000 signatures collected for Segni referendum on electoral reform (Aug.).

1991
Leoluca Orlando founds La Rete ('Network') (24 Jan.); the Lega Nord is formed under the leadership of Umberto Bossi, uniting the separate regional Leagues of Lombardy and the Veneto (10 Feb.); referendum produces massive majority for abolition of preferential voting (9 June); PCI renamed PDS (Partito Democratico della Sinistra); hardliners leave to form Rifondazione Comunista.

1992
Arrest of Mario Chiesa in Milan, accused of taking kickbacks for the PSI, marks beginning of Tangentopoli scandals (Feb.). General election: Lega Nord vote rises to 8.7% (5 Apr.).

1993
Referendum majority for electoral reform (18 Apr.). Local and mayoral elections: Lega Nord wins Milan with 40% vote; electoral reform law passed, introducing uninominal (first-past-the-post) system (4 Aug.); left alliance mayors elected to Naples, Genoa, Rome, Venice, and Trieste (Nov.–Dec.).

1994
Silvio Berlusconi launches Forza Italia (Jan.); formation of Alleanza Progressista (including PDS and Rete) and Polo (Right) of Forza Italia, Lega Nord and Alleanza Nazionale (Feb.); general election: the Polo wins 366 seats to the Progressives' 213 (27 Mar.); Berlusconi becomes prime minister but resigns after eight months (Dec.).

1988
The Last Emperor, by Bertolucci, wins nine Academy Awards, including Best Picture and Best Director (12 Apr.).

1990
Broadcasting Act ('Legge Mammì') gives legal ratification to 'mixed system' of public and private networks. Despite introducing some mild anti-monopoly restrictions, it largely 'photographs' the existing RAI and Fininvest duopoly. *Nuovo Cinema Paradiso*, by Giuseppe Tornatore, wins Academy Award for Best Foreign Picture.

1991
Posse and rap concert in Parco Lambro, Milan, with Sud Sound System, Onda Posse, and Isola Posse. Death of Natalia Ginzburg. Pope John Paul II instructs bishops to take a firm line against abortion. Sophia Loren wins Academy Award for acting career.

1993
'Legge Ronchey': reform of Italian museums, including encouragement of private-sector funding.

1995

'Technical' government headed by Lamberto Dini. Pension reforms.

1995

Referendum on media (11 June): a majority is in favour of retaining existing arrangements, opposing anti-trust restrictions and radical reductions in television advertising proposed by left.

Index